Mountain Justice

Justice

**Homegrown Resistance
to Mountaintop Removal,
for the Future of Us All**

EDINBURGH · OAKLAND · BALTIMORE

For Bill

"You cannot save the land apart from the people or the people apart from the land. To save either, you must save both."

—Wendell Berry

Contents

Flyover

If you look at Appalachia's Cumberland Plateau from a satellite's point of view, high above the Earth's surface, it looks like it has a skin disease, its surface spotted with scabby places. Come in closer, as high as an airplane, flying low from southwestern Virginia north into southern West Virginia. At first you'll see long ridgelines and wide valleys, then the typical ruffly jumble of Cumberland Plateau mountains.

In far southern West Virginia these mountains look pristine, draped in a lush, thickly textured, living, breathing blanket of forest, in early summer colored with more shades of green than you can imagine, the greens of hundreds of kinds of trees and shrubs. This is the mother forest for all of eastern North America, from which life has flowed to places stripped of it by glaciers and other catastrophes. Its gorgeous intricacy has evolved continuously since long before any humans were here to see it, on old, old mountains worn down to a multitude of soft, rounded hills and steep little hollows. Together forest and mountain, sweet air, and plentiful streams make this an intimate, homey landscape that's easy to love. People who live here believe that this is what heaven must look like.

The trees here today are not old growth. Here, as throughout central and southern Appalachia, virtually all of the forest was cut early in the twentieth century. But lumbering technology was primitive then, just men with saws and horses. During and after that logging, little of the land was plowed up, and much of the soil remained intact. The forest that grew back in that soil was and is diminished, but still fabulously rich and diverse.

If you look carefully from your airplane view, here and there you'll also see the remains of older strip mines, small enough in scale that they mar, but don't destroy, the overall pattern of hills and hollows. The forest has closed in around them. As with old-style logging, old-style coal mining for the most part left intact enough of the natural fabric of life for the mother forest to regenerate.

But on the horizon, just to the north, you'll see a dozen or more enormous gaps in the natural landscape visible from dozens of miles away—visible, in fact, from space. What looks from a satellite view like scabs are really open wounds, some of them miles across, all caused by mountaintop removal and similar modern, large-scale methods of strip mining for coal.

Mountaintop removal (MTR) does exactly what it says. At each MTR site, a mountaintop is stripped of trees, blown to bits with vast amounts of explosives, then pushed aside by giant equipment—all to expose a layer of coal. (A large dragline, the ultimate MTR machine, can move a hundred or more cubic yards in a single bite.) After that coal is mined out, still more trees are stripped and still more mountain is blown up and pushed aside to expose a lower layer of coal. MTR mining commonly lops hundreds of feet off the top of a mountain. Hundreds of thousands of acres of ancient forested Appalachian mountains have been "removed" this way and will never again support the glorious mosaic of biologically rich and diverse forest-and-stream communities that evolved there over millions of years.

Strip mining on such a very large scale began in Appalachia in the 1980s and has expanded dramatically since 2000, spreading from West Virginia and eastern Kentucky into southwestern Virginia and then eastern Tennessee and Alabama. From your airplane view you can read the coal companies' plans for further expansion in the ongoing clear-cutting of many more thousands of acres of forest. Often the cut trees are not even harvested but simply bulldozed together and burned, the flames shooting as high as the wasted poplar, oak, maple, and beech trees once stood, so urgently voracious is the coal companies' demand for more and more and more.

Come closer still, and stand on a hill overlooking a mountaintop removal site. (You'll have to make an effort to find such a place, because most large-scale strip mines are hidden from public view, as though the people responsible for them are ashamed of what they're doing.) There you'll see how the open wounds of strip mining ooze poison down into the hillsides and hollows and waters below. Rubble and knocked-over trees and flyrock tumble offsite into adjacent forest. Runoff silt clogs thousands of miles of mountain streams—and hundreds of miles of streams are now completely buried under debris. Aquifers are cracked by blasting, wells dried up or poisoned. Flash floods run off the stripped mountaintops. Landslides slip from unstable slopes. Heavy metals and other toxins leach out of slurry ponds and valley fills. Blackwater spills kill or impair everything living downstream. Coal dust and chemicals used in coal processing sicken schoolchildren. Overloaded coal trucks destroy roads and kill people in collisions.

Strip mining devastates the communities down in the hollows between the mountains, where homes, schools, and churches are clustered. The wealth extracted from these mountains through logging and mining has long flowed out of the region rather than to the people who live here, and the current strip-mining boom has destroyed much of what previously remained of the region's wealth of sustainable natural resources. Communities have shriveled to remnants of their former selves, as people have fled the direct physical effects of the mining or been forced to leave home to seek work. (MTR employs lots of big equipment but few workers.) The people still living here have stayed not because they're doing well but because this is their home, because living here is an essential part of who they are.

Although most people here believe that King Coal's destruction of the mountains and their people is wrong, few are willing to stick their necks out to say so—and for good reason. People who stick their necks out often get whacked in the head, particularly in Appalachia's coalfields, where power has long been maintained by violence in many forms, all of them ugly. And besides, why bother? Why take care of your home if your only hope for a decent life is to leave it? Why take care of the mountains if they too will soon be gone? Those who do speak out against mountaintop removal have done so regardless of the odds against stopping it. Standing up for what's right is part of who they are, and doing so—whatever the cost—makes them more fully themselves, more fully human and free.

Likewise, across the country Americans know that the way we live has gone wrong. We sense that our use-it-up-and-move-on way of life is in its endgame. If we think about it at all, and are honest with ourselves, we know that in a finite world fueled by a finite amount of sunlight, we can't forever have unlimited amounts of whatever we want to consume. If we haven't yet reached a point where our consumption and waste are beyond the limits of nature's capacity to support them, surely we're headed in that direction and accelerating toward it. And if, in the endgame of our current way of life, we use up or render unusable everything we can get our hands on, without much regard for the future, then somewhere very much like the deathscape of an MTR site is where we'll all be living in the future.

Most people don't stand up and speak out about this either, let alone try to do anything about it. Why bother? Why stick your neck out? Those who do, like their compatriots in Appalachia, do so because working to make change for the better makes their lives more meaningful and worthwhile. They know that our future, like it or not, will unfold in a world in which we're aware that we do live within natural limits. Life in that future can be better than what we have now—more honest, satisfying, just, graceful, and beautiful. These goods need have no limits.

In the past few years, hundreds of such people from all over the country have joined local Appalachians to stand up against strip mining and open the door to better ways of living for Appalachians and all Americans. Their work is for our future, for all of us. This is their story.

Mountain People

In early January 2005, I received an email about a new campaign against strip mining from Bo Webb, a coalfield resident fighting mountaintop removal mining in southern West Virginia. I had first met Bo the previous summer, when I was trying to write about MTR and couldn't quite wrap my head around it. I grew up in western Pennsylvania, where the hills and valleys of the coalfield landscape are similar in scale to those near the Coal River, where Bo lives, and I knew about the smaller-scale strip mining of decades past: My great-grandfather's farm had been stripped half a century ago. When I read about MTR, I couldn't make sense of how such huge mining operations could take place in such an intimate jumble of small and swervy mountains. I needed to see it for myself, and when I sought guidance from Coal River Mountain Watch (CRMW), a group of local people seeking to end MTR and sustain their community, Bo volunteered to show me around.

Bo was born in West Virginia, he later told me, as we sat by the river at his house, "in a coal camp house, near Whitesville, about eleven miles from here. My dad worked at a coal mine, and he got paid in scrip, and we used that scrip at the company store and paid grossly inflated prices for all the products." When coal's boom-and-bust cycle went bust in the mid-1950s, Bo's dad went to work in Cleveland, but the rest of the family stayed in West Virginia. As soon as his father could come back and work at another coal mine, "he jumped on that, because he loved the mountains." During another bust, in 1960, he went back to Cleveland and started working for General Motors. "So we moved to Cleveland. I was twelve years old." After graduating from high school there, Bo joined the Marines, was sent to war in Vietnam in January 1968, and came back to Cleveland the following year. "I got an apprenticeship as a tool and die maker," he says. "I had to have a career, and I didn't want to be a coal miner.

"The whole time I was in Cleveland we always came 'back home' [to West Virginia] on the weekend and holidays. And I continued to do that after I came back from the Marines. I brought my wife right here, to this property—this was my grandmother's property—and she sat on this rock right over here [by the river], and she fell in love with this place." After his grandmother died, Bo bought the land. He put a mobile home on it, for vacations, in the mid-1980s.

Meanwhile, he and his wife, Joanne, had a son and a daughter. In 1981 he'd started his own machining business, still in Cleveland. After a fire in his shop in 1998, Bo decided, "Let's move back to West Virginia and relax. I just want to fish and hunt, and I'm young enough to enjoy it. I'm not going to have any elaborate type of lifestyle, but we'll be OK. We'll be fine." So they moved here in February 2001.

"That first summer, boy I enjoyed this place. Had a big garden. I kept hearing this thing about mountaintop removal, and every now and then I'd hear these little rumbles in the mountains. I started doing some research on the internet about it, and lo and behold I found out they were blowing my mountains away, and they were moving closer. And I heard about Coal River Mountain Watch." Bo began helping them out from time to time.

Bo called the state Department of Environmental Protection (DEP) after a flood in 2001, asking for a water test at the river in front of his house, "because I was getting a funny smell, and all the smallmouth bass in this river—they're gone. I used to be able to catch three-, four-pound smallmouth." A few miles up the river, there'd been a blowout from an old underground mine, and all the mud and whatnot from that blowout came downriver to Bo. (Blasting for MTR often cracks previously stable abandoned underground mines and hillsides so that water that's collected in the old mines comes gushing out.) Bo complained for three weeks before someone from the DEP came out. "That's the response we get," Bo says, "because we don't count." According to the guy from the DEP, the stream's pH was a little low, "but he never explained anything," Bo says, and of course three weeks earlier the reading might have been a lot different. "The bass are not back yet. Last year [2004] I saw a few fingerling. It killed the fish." This got Bo riled up and ready to fight.

It never occurred to Bo *not* to fight MTR's effects on his home place. "I think that's because I got out of here," he says. He moved to Cleveland when he was still young, "and shed the oppression, the atmosphere here. I guess the worst type of oppression is when you don't know you're oppressed, so you just follow along. I've heard it many times: 'Well, that's the way it's always been, that's the way it always will be. The coal company's gonna get the coal and there's nothing you can do about it.' I don't come from that school—especially [after] being in the service and being in Vietnam, and thinking I was doing something for the country. And I come back and it looks to me like the country's turned its back on its citizens, and it made me angry. I saw a lot of violations of human rights in Vietnam, and I started looking at this, and it reminded me of that. So I wanted to do something about it."

When I met up with Bo in the summer of 2004, our first stop was Marsh Fork Elementary School, a short drive downriver from Bo's home. There we saw a coal silo looming over the school, close to the edge of the schoolyard, part of a coal processing operation run by a subsidiary of Massey Energy. Coal dust and the toxic chemicals used in this facility's method for processing coal settle on the playground and seep in through the school's ventilation system. Several children and teachers have contracted unusual cancers, Bo tells me, and headaches, respiratory problems, and other illness are far too common among the schoolchildren there. All this is hard enough to believe. What were the government officials who allowed this to happen thinking? What were the coal company executives and their lawyers thinking? But worse still, right behind the processing plant, just a few hundred yards from the school, a 385-foot-high earthen dam holds more than a billion gallons of slurry, a black, chemical-laden liquid waste from coal processing. (Julia Bonds, founder of CRMW, calls this "waste holding back waste," as the dam itself is made from MTR rubble.) If the dam were to fail—and Bo tells me local workers who helped build the dam say its construction is faulty—the wall of escaping slurry would roar downstream right over the school.

Bad as all of this is, at first look it seems like a limited and manageable problem: Relocate the processing plant, drain the slurry, remove the dam, and the school and the valley below should be safe. A stranger driving through the valley might think that the school problem is the worst of MTR effects here. You can still see mostly forested mountainsides on either side of the road that runs along the river. Coal facilities and little towns that look rather down-at-the-heels appear at intervals along the way—but this is southern West Virginia, deep in Appalachia, and you might well expect to see evidence of both coal mining and poverty here.

But veer off from the valley a few miles downstream from the school and head up into the hills to Kayford Mountain, and there you'll see the true enormity of MTR's effect on this landscape and its natural and human communities. Kayford is the lone hilltop in its neighborhood that's not controlled by mining companies. All around Kayford, as far as the eye can see, the giant machinery of MTR is dismantling the mountains. In their place, wherever the coal is gone and the machines have moved on, heaps of rubble support either no life at all or thin monocultures of exotic grass, with patches of scrub here and there. The view from Kayford shows that the forested mountainsides along the Coal River are no more than a narrow beauty strip. The river itself has lost most of its headwater streams and is choked with sediment. Miners have been replaced by machinery. The hollows that feed into the valley have been emptied of families who've lived there for generations and stripped of the abundant animal and plant life that coevolved there for millennia. The mountains themselves have been blown up and are forever lost.

The Coal River valley is by no means the only place where this is happening, nor is it the only place where local activists are trying to fight it. The email Bo sends me in January has a link to a call for action against MTR throughout Appalachia's coalfields—in eastern Kentucky and Tennessee and southwestern Virginia as well as southern West Virginia. "Mountain Justice Summer [MJS]," Bo writes, "is going to be the campaign that ends the destruction of Appalachia!"

Over the next few weeks, Bo fills me in: "We realize that we are not going to stop MTR in West Virginia without outside help. We envision MJS as a movement that will bring in a broad spectrum of people from all walks of life. We are committed to nonviolent direct action." However, he adds, "I also know for a fact that when we do a direct action here in the coalfields, we will be met with violence. It is the history of the coalfields and I see no reason why it will be any different this time.

"As long as we stay focused, and on message, we will be OK. Let's all hope and pray that America listens and demands an ending to this insanity."

Neither Bo nor his fellow activists see "this insanity" as being limited to MTR. Now that the easiest and best sources of coal and other essentials have been depleted, here and elsewhere, across America and around the world, and returns on efforts to extract them are diminishing, it's increasingly urgent that we stop blindly squandering resources needed to create and sustain the new ways of life we can now see we'll need in the not-so-distant future. "I am hoping that our movement will bring attention to the big picture," Bo writes. "I know that a world with a growing population of over 6 billion people is headed for chaos when it continues to rely on finite fossil fuels. When we resort to blowing up a mountain to extract a ten-inch seam of coal, we definitely have a glaring problem.

"I think Martin Luther King summed it up pretty well when he said, 'This hour in history needs a dedicated circle of transformed nonconformists. The saving of our world from pending doom will come, not through the complacent adjustment of the conforming majority, but through the creative maladjustment of a nonconforming minority.'

"I don't know if MJS will be successful or not. I don't know what results we will get. I just know that it needs to be done. Time is short, and I think the time is right."

Resistance to strip mining in Appalachia did not, of course, begin with MJS in 2005. It's been going on for decades. For most of that time, Jack Spadaro's been involved. "I came out of a little mining community in southern West Virginia, near Beckley," Jack says. "My father worked for a mining company for about twenty years. My grandfather worked in the coal mines for forty-five years. I have an uncle who worked in the mines for thirty-some years. I got a degree in mining engineering thinking that I wanted to go into the industry and make a lot of money. But what happened was, I saw what was going on and I couldn't be part of it.

"In 1972 I was teaching in the engineering program at West Virginia University, and I got sent for the spring and summer down to a place called Buffalo Creek, in Logan County, where a coal waste dam failed and killed 125 people and left 4,000 people without homes and wiped out 17 communities. From that point forward—I wasn't born an environmentalist, but I certainly became one." Jack joined forces with others who were fighting the ill effects of strip mining, including Ken Hechler, then a congressman and now, more than three decades later—in his nineties—still fighting.

According to CRMW's Julia Bonds, part of what enabled the 1970s movement against strip mining to arise in Appalachia was that prior to that, in the 1960s, volunteers with such federal "war on poverty" programs as VISTA and other outsiders came to Appalachia to do social service work. "When they did," she says, "they brought their cameras and tape recorders with them. And they sat down and they talked to these people, and listened to these people who lived up in these hollers. And then these people didn't feel so alone and so oppressed." Together, the locals and the outsiders began to organize to address problems in Appalachia. When the government "figured out what was going on and who was coming in (they called them 'outside agitators') and helping people organize, they pulled the funding" from the programs that had brought the outsiders here. "But the movement had already started." Today, she adds, "we're not dependent" on Washington for funding that start-up wave of organizers. "We're doing it ourselves.

"Back in the '60s and '70s the women led the charge [against strip mining]. They're the ones that lay down in front of the bulldozers and stood up in front of the coal trucks." Women, especially older women, are generally perceived as less threatening than men, who in tense coalfield confrontations are apt to get into fights. "It's less violent with women in the front line. But it seems as though women are more apt to get things rolling, too.

"Of course·we didn't accomplish what we were setting out to do, or we wouldn't be" fighting MTR today. They did manage to persuade Congress to pass the Surface Mining Control and Reclamation Act (SMCRA), in 1977. But just before the final version of SMCRA was passed, fatal flaws were added to the bill.

Jack says that he and Ken Hechler "agreed, in 1977, when [SMCRA] was signed into law, that it was probably a mistake. In the first versions of the law [MTR] wasn't allowed, but then Congressman [Nick] Rahall from West Virginia, who had replaced Hechler, and Senator Wendell Ford from Kentucky got language put into the act to allow mountaintop removal. They at that time sold it as something that would only happen occasionally, it would only be for something special like building a school or some other use that would be of benefit to the community." But no restriction to that effect was actually written into the law. "To get the variance on [the requirement that reclaimed land be returned to its] 'approximate original contour' and allow mountaintop removal you had to demonstrate that you had the plans to use it for something other than just a mine. The states, then, when they were given authority under the act to be the regulatory authorities, they always granted the permits no matter what the intended use.

"That's been part of the problem all along. The way the law was written, the states could get authority to enforce the federal law. And nearly every mining state did that." Tennessee is the lone exception in southern Appalachia. It still has direct federal enforcement of SMCRA.

"So we went back to the same old system and the same old people who'd been failing to regulate for the twenty-some years before. Since 1981 there hasn't been any true enforcement in the field, on the ground, at mine sites. All the [MTR] mining operations in West Virginia are illegal. They're operating contrary to the federal law. Not one is legal."

SMCRA "was supposed to be a solution," Jack adds, "but instead it became the vehicle for the industry to legitimize what it was doing. And they've done now, on a massive scale, what the law was intended to prevent, the dumping of spoil onto mountainsides in steep-slope areas."

Under SMCRA, valley fills were supposed to be small and of limited use. "The justification [for allowing them at all] was they needed a place, for their first few cuts onto the mountainside, to put the overburden material. That's [all] the valley fill was supposed to be, and everything else would be returned to 'approximate original contour.'

"When they got into mountaintop mining where they took off the top 400 or 500 feet of the mountain, they [decided that they] needed larger valley fills. So they created a rule allowing something called a durable-rock fill. And they got a prostitute engineer named Arthur Casagrande (he was from Harvard, a geotechnical engineer) to write the justification for durable-rock fills. Unfortunately, some people in the Carter administration fell for it.

"So they wrote into the rules [by which SMCRA is administered] something that allowed them to do it. All through the Reagan-Bush years the MTR operations proliferated. Rules became weaker and weaker. All through the '80s the sizes of the [valley] fills grew, the sizes of the operations grew, and no one checked them. Nobody had the courage or the will or the knowledge, really, to check them. Even through the Clinton administration, in the '90s, the fills and mountaintop removal operations proliferated.

"The valley fills in this region are the largest earth structures in the country now," Jack says. "They are sometimes 500 or 600 million cubic yards of material—in one fill. Some are as long as six miles long—one fill."

By the mid-1990s, "citizens had just had enough. They were literally being run off their land by these operations. At Blair Mountain, the site of the famous labor struggle, a man named James Weekley was going to have his hollow filled in by a huge operation operated by Arch [coal company]. And Mr. Weekley came to Charleston [West Virginia] and hired a lawyer named Joe Lovett." In August 1997 Joe Lovett, just starting out as a lawyer, met Jim Weekley, who gave Lovett his first tour of MTR and persuaded him to try to stop the permitting of a huge MTR operation slated for the hollow where Jim and his family had lived for more than two centuries. Joe started to research mining law and discovered a whole host of ways in which MTR violates provisions of federal laws still enforced by federal agencies. (Lovett was aiming to bring this case to federal court, not West Virginia state court, where he knew he was likely to lose.) Presiding over these violations is the Army Corps of Engineers, which, under the Clean Water Act (1972), has responsibility for determining how much environmental damage will be caused by activities that fill in streams, and granting or denying permits for such activities accordingly.

For example, Section 404 of that act specifies that "fill material" placed in waterways must be chosen to avoid "adverse effect" and achieve some desirable purpose, such as making it possible to build on or farm a patch of wetland. Calling coal waste "fill" doesn't make it fit Section 404's definition, nor is simply finding somewhere convenient to put that waste a permissible purpose. Nonetheless, the Corps has routinely issued permits allowing the filling in of streams with waste from MTR operations, contrary to both the letter and the spirit of the Clean Water Act—and contrary to the way land users other than coal companies are treated. (Farmers and construction companies, for example, are not allowed to fill in streams just because they need somewhere convenient to put waste material.)

In addition, the National Environmental Policy Act, which passed in 1969, requires that federal agencies study a project's likely effects thoroughly and compile an environmental impact statement (EIS) based on that study before approving any project that could significantly harm waterways or their environment. The Corps had never required an EIS during the permitting process for any MTR operation.

Furthermore, the Corps had routinely been violating several provisions of SMCRA for which it, rather than individual states, retained responsibility. SMCRA requires MTR sites to be restored after mining to "approximate original contour"—that is, a mining company that blows up a mountain is supposed to pile the rubble back up into something approximating that mountain's original size and shape. SMCRA also bans mining within 100 feet of a stream (known in legalese as the "stream buffer zone") without careful study verifying that that stream would not be harmed by the proposed mining activity. The Corps routinely granted variances that let mining companies off the hook for these provisions.

In short, Joe Lovett discovered plenty of grounds for suing the Corps for failing to enforce laws governing mountaintop removal. He lined up several more plaintiffs to join Jim Weekley, secured the legal and financial help of the Washington, D.C.-based organization Trial Lawyers for Public Justice, and in early 1998 filed a letter of intent to sue both the Army Corps of Engineers and the West Virginia Department of Environmental Protection. The resulting case, *Bragg v. Robertson*, led to a settlement in December 1998 that compelled the federal government to complete a two-year study leading to an EIS on the cumulative effects of MTR on the entire multistate coalfield region of Appalachia. Meanwhile, the settlement also forbid the Corps to grant any "Nationwide 21" permits for new strip mines that would have valley fills covering more than 250 acres. (Under the Nationwide 21 process, the Corps grants permits for valley fills without public notice and with no EIS on the presumption that they will cause "minimal adverse" impact.)

The settlement deal did not, however, block the proposed MTR operation threatening Jim Weekley's hollow. In January 1999, Joe Lovett filed for a restraining order with federal Judge Charles H. Haden II, who put the mining on hold until Lovett and Weekley could bring the case to trial. Settlement deals and other legal maneuvering before the scheduled trial date led to a block on moving forward with the proposed mining as well as an agreement that the Corps and the DEP would tighten up most aspects of enforcement of mining regulations, specifically including the "approximate original contour" requirement. (You who are reading this should not at this point become hopeful. Settlement notwithstanding, enforcement remained just about nonexistent.)

One issue that was not resolved by the settlement was enforcement of the stream-buffer-zone rule. Coal-industry lawyers refused to compromise on this, so Joe Lovett asked Judge Haden to compel the DEP to enforce it. On Oct. 20, 1999, Haden ruled not only that the buffer-zone rule must be enforced—but also that MTR valley fills were *all*, by definition, violations of that rule. The judge forbid the DEP to allow *any* mine permits that would result in mine waste being dumped in permanent or seasonal streams anywhere in West Virginia.

For those opposed to MTR this was a terrifically hopeful ruling. That hope didn't last long, though. Judge Haden soon agreed to suspend his ruling while state and coal-industry lawyers appealed it to the federal 4th Circuit Court of Appeals. On April 24, 2001, that court overturned Haden's ruling on the grounds that the state DEP must be sued in a state court, not the federal court system. Pursuing this in West Virginia's state court system, where judges must regularly stand for reelection and are highly vulnerable to coal-industry pressure, would likely meet with failure. Joe Lovett instead worked around the jurisdictional problem by filing suit against the Corps, a federal agency, in Judge Haden's federal court, for the Corps' own failure to enforce the stream-buffer-zone rule. On May 8, 2002, Judge Haden ruled in Lovett's favor. In December 2002, the 4th Circuit struck down Haden's ruling as "overbroad."

Meanwhile, following George W. Bush's inauguration as president in early 2001, when he replaced Democrat Bill Clinton, incoming Republican appointees set about tailoring mining rules and regulation, and their enforcement (or lack thereof) to better suit the coal industry.

For example, Jack Spadaro recalls, "there was a requirement [in the 1998 settlement of *Bragg v. Robertson*] for an environmental impact statement on the overall effects of this type of mining. And the draft statement, under Clinton, said yes indeed this is a severe problem and we have to curtail this mining, we have to get control of it. But it was just a draft statement. When the Bush administration came in, the guts of the statement remained the same—they couldn't change the science. But the conclusion under the Bush administration was that the solution to the problem would be to streamline the permitting process and make it go faster. The conclusion of course didn't match the science. And that's where it stands now [in 2005], pretty much. The Bush administration is allowing, in their oversight role over the states, the permitting process to accelerate. No holds."

As a result of this, Jack says, "what we're seeing now is, more than ever before, a true grassroots movement in the coalfields. In West Virginia a poll done by a conservative newspaper showed that about 70 percent of the people in West Virginia would be in favor of abolishing mountaintop removal." Jack agrees that most of that 70 percent wouldn't stick their necks out and advocate this in public, but he thinks they'd vote for it if they were given the chance.

"People are fed up. There is now a real populist movement, the people from mining communities joining environmentalists, and labor in some instances, and forming coalitions that can do some good. The problem is now, on a national level, we have a conservative government and a corrupt government, the most corrupt in the history of the country perhaps."

Jack confronted that problem directly in connection with an enormous coal slurry spill in Inez, Kentucky, where on one night in October 2000 more than 300 million gallons of sludge burst from an enormous "pond" similar to the one that looms over Marsh Fork Elementary School. Most of the sludge went into two streams that overflowed and flooded nearby homes. The Exxon Valdez oil spill in Alaska released 10.8 million gallons; the Inez spill was 30 times as big. Nonetheless, it received almost no media attention until the spill reached the Ohio River, days later.

People living in Appalachia's coalfields sometimes wonder how it is that environmentalists across America can be so passionate about Alaska but apparently indifferent to the ongoing environmental catastrophe wrought by strip mining in Appalachia. Perhaps it's because Appalachia, though spectacularly biodiverse and wildly productive of flora, fauna, and fresh water, isn't pristine wilderness. Perhaps also it's because Appalachia is inhabited by "hillbillies," denigrated for generations by American popular culture.

In their response to the Inez disaster, government authorities apparently relied on both the national media's lack of interest and the reputed ignorance of Appalachian locals. When local people went to public meetings after the big sludge spill, they expected at least *some* action from the environmental agencies, Inez resident Nina McCoy recalls. Instead, "the EPA, when they had one of their first meetings with the people [whose water supply and land were poisoned], they told the people that there was nothing harmful in the sludge, that it was *fine* because everything in it was on the periodical table of the elements. And then they went on to say: 'You can ask your biology or your chemistry teacher.'" As it happens that's Nina, who teaches at the local high school. And her students did ask her what that meant. They'd just studied the periodic table, and of course what the EPA was saying made no sense.

"So then what happens," she says, "is [that most local people] just kind of give up. They're not drinking the water—they know better—but they just don't know how to fight it. So many times I think that is what we really need to focus on, not necessarily shooting everybody who runs the coal companies [she's joking here—a joke with a bitter edge], but actually getting back our [government] agencies, to make the people feel empowered.

"We have corporations that think there should be no rules, and the people just think: 'Well, uh, OK, no rules'—I guess. They're afraid that the company will leave if [it has] to follow the rules." At the same time, miners and their wives are telling their neighbors "that EPA was shoving them around: Do this! Get out of here!," even though at public meetings, "we saw an EPA lawyer and coal company lawyer patting each other on the back."

At the time of the Inez spill, Jack Spadaro was still director of the National Mine Health and Safety Academy, which trains the nation's mine inspectors and is run under the federal Mine Safety and Health Administration (MSHA). "Because I had years of experience regulating coal-waste dams—that had been my specialty for a long time—I was asked to be part of a [federally appointed] team to go to Inez and investigate the coal slurry spill. I was put in charge of the engineering aspects, the geotechnical investigation to determine the cause. And we were doing well. We went down in October, November, and December of 2000 and began investigating, doing a drilling program at the site of the spill to find out what had happened, interviewing people."

They found that "a reservoir of slurry about 100 feet deep and about 70 acres failed by breaking into [abandoned] underground mine workings beneath the reservoir and spilling out into Coldwater Creek and another watershed, Wolf Creek. If it had all gone down Coldwater Creek, people would have drowned.

"In January 2001 when the Bush administration came in—honestly, on Inauguration Day of 2001 our investigation was halted. We were told to wrap it up in a few days and begin writing our report. Well, we had thirty-five, forty more people we wanted to interview. And we had a whole lot of evidence that the company, which was a subsidiary of Massey Energy, had submitted documents to the government six years before, when there had been another [slurry pond] breakthrough—those documents were essentially lies about what was underneath that impoundment." The breakthrough six years before had been "the same sort of failure. Into Wolf Creek. So they submitted a plan to rectify the situation in 1994. But the plan showed that there was fifty feet of cover between the [underground] mine workings and the bottom of the reservoir, and a hundred-foot coal barrier. In reality we found, through this drilling program, about fifteen or eighteen feet of coal barrier and less than fifteen feet of cover over top of the mine workings. We discovered in the investigation, in interviews, that people at the mine knew that there was only fifteen feet of cover. But they submitted a document showing a fifty and a hundred-foot barrier. So they lied in their submittals to the government.

"I felt that the company should then have been cited for that, and for knowing and willful negligence at least, if not outright fraud for what they'd submitted to the government. But the Bush administration didn't want to do that. So they had people tampering with the writing of the report." Jack's team would send drafts in "and they would be rewritten. The head of [MSHA], appointed by Bush, a guy named Dave Lauriski, started poking his fingers into this investigation, and I felt that was inappropriate. So I withdrew, I resigned publicly from the investigation and stated my reasons.

"It came time to do a public release of the report, and Lauriski called me several days before the release and essentially ordered me to sign the report. And I refused to do it. Twice. The report was issued without my name on the report.

"I fought with the Bush administration for the next two years about this. It was mainly about the government aiding and abetting a company that had violated the law and put people at risk. Because when that thing failed, it killed 1.6 million fish, wiped out water supplies to seventeen towns, killed everything for a hundred miles, all the way to the Ohio River." In June 2001, federal officials changed the locks on Jack's office and placed him on administrative leave, accusing him of abusing his authority as director of the mine inspectors' academy. After that trumped-up charge failed to stick, Jack was ordered transferred to Pittsburgh, far from his family and home in West Virginia. He opted to negotiate an early retirement and has continued to fight against abusive mining practices ever since. (His nemesis Dave Lauriski himself resigned as head of MSHA in November 2004, shortly after a government report questioned the propriety of contracts he'd awarded to corporate cronies.)

Jack believes that "there's still a lot that could be done [against MTR] in litigation. I think we can revisit some of those same issues that were brought up in the late '90s in federal court on a state level. And then also go back in federal court and hammer away at the same issues, since nothing was really ever resolved on things like approximate original contour, the illegality of mountaintop removal and the valley fills, the Clean Water Act—none of it's been really resolved." The absence of such clear judicial resolution enabled the Bush administration to continue to use regulatory directives and redefinitions allowing mining companies to violate the laws' apparent intent on these issues. For example, in May 2002, the Bush administration redefined "fill" for the purposes of the Clean Water Act as *anything* that would have the effect of filling in a streambed, thus gutting the act's requirements that fill placed in waterways must be chosen both to avoid "adverse effect" and to achieve some desirable purpose.

Supporting litigation is currently the main focus of Jack's current efforts against strip mining. "I'm in for the long haul. I think we can win this. Because I think what is happening is not only illegal, it's just plain wrong."

As of 2005, Jack says, MTR in West Virginia has "removed close to 400,000 acres; 320-some thousand in Kentucky; 150,000 total strip mining in Ohio; about 90 to 100 thousand acres in southwestern Virginia. It's up to close to a million acres that have been completely wiped out." (Reliable data on the extent of strip mining is hard to come by. These figures are from research Jack did in the early 2000s, through government contacts. Since then, the acreage affected has grown considerably.)

"About fourteen people have died in flash floods in the last three years," Jack adds to the reasons why MTR is "plain wrong." Hundreds of homes have been flooded "from rapid runoff from mountaintop removal operations.

"When I first started in the mining industry, in the 1960s, there were hundreds of thousands of miners working. We've produced more coal in the last few years in West Virginia than we ever have in history—with the fewest number of miners, because of mountaintop removal. It's put people out of work. A handful of people are making a profit from this. There's a handful of people controlling the corporation who are really making the money. And the rest of us are suffering for it."

I catch up with Bo again in West Virginia in mid-February, where he introduces me to his daughter Sarah and son-in-law Vernon Haltom, and Patty Sebok, a fellow CRMW activist who's married to a disabled underground coal miner. Together we drive down to Blacksburg, a pretty little college town in western Virginia, for a meeting of about three dozen people aiming to organize MJS. One person has traveled here from Atlanta, the rest from around the region—West Virginia, western Virginia, western North Carolina, eastern Tennessee, and eastern Kentucky.

In addition to the crew from Coal River, West Virginians at the meeting include Larry Gibson, the one person still living up on Kayford Mountain. Larry rode down to Blacksburg with Abraham Mwaura, an organizer with Ohio Valley Environmental Coalition (OVEC) in Huntington, West Virginia.

From Tennessee come Amanda Womac and john johnson, a big bearish fellow in plaid flannel shirt and camouflage pants, with a long ponytail and long brown beard. (john says he doesn't believe in capitalism.) Both are affiliated with Katuah Earth First! in Knoxville. So are Paloma Galindo and her husband Chris Irwin, a law student, who is intense, fast-talking, impatient, and very much attached to his laptop computer, on which he makes many notes during the meeting. Chris and Paloma have apparently done a large share of the work of organizing MJS to date. Chris speaks probably more than anyone else at the meeting, john and Paloma nearly as much as him. When Bo introduces me to Chris, as a writer working on a book, my impression is that Chris is wary, bristly, thinking that I'll waste his time if he lets me. (Months later, when I tell Paloma this, her reaction is: "No! Not Chris!" Later, still thinking surely I was mistaken, she asks Chris who, after a long pause, admits it was true.) Like john, Chris and Paloma are in their mid-thirties.

Several people, in their twenties and thirties, affiliated with western North Carolina's faction of Katuah Earth First! have driven up for the meeting. Although North Carolina is outside the coalfields, a core group of half a dozen or so Asheville-area anarchist eco-activists, with the support of a larger network there, is strongly committed to MJS. One of those here today is Sage Russo, in his mid-twenties, short and slight for a man and much-tattooed, with dark curly hair and a tidy beard, an improbable mix of Brooklyn (where his father's family lives) and North Carolina mountains (where his mother's from). Sage is a dedicated Christian, highly unusual among anarchists.

Prominent among the local Blacksburg folks organizing the meeting is Chris Dodson, in his twenties, also small and slender, with blond dreadlocks, homemade-looking patchwork long shorts, hiking boots, a mellow demeanor, vegan but not evangelical about it. (When individuals during the meeting volunteer to solicit food donations for summer, he says he'll ask a man he knows who raises rabbits to donate meat for those who "eat bunnies.")

Dave Cooper has traveled here all the way from Lexington, Kentucky—but he's well accustomed to travel. Since a year ago last fall, Dave's logged many thousands of miles to scores of places throughout the region and beyond, presenting a slideshow and talk on MTR, hoping to make a wider public aware of and outraged about it. Sitting next to Dave is Bill McCabe, a coalfield native now living in eastern Tennessee and working on staff with Sierra Club's Environmental Justice Program. He describes himself as "not a tree-hugger" although, he adds, "my church is in the woods." While he personally supports MJS, he says Sierra Club won't officially endorse it. (All of the nonprofits opposing MTR are keenly aware that direct support for civil disobedience would threaten their tax-exempt status.)

For a day and a half, the organizers report back on what's been going on, region by region. They discuss issues of concern to the whole campaign. They talk about what needs to be accomplished in the next month, from courting media to tweaking the MJS website, and individuals volunteer to "bottom line" making specific things happen. By prior agreement, no one is "in charge" of MJS, and decisions are made by consensus rather than majority vote; proposals are discussed and modified, concerns voiced and addressed, until all present reach agreement.

The group also discusses an emerging problem with the term "mountaintop removal." Officials and mining companies in Tennessee say there is no MTR there—they call it "cross-ridge mining" and claim it doesn't destroy whole mountains. Bo notes that coal companies generally are redefining "mountaintop removal" very restrictively, so they can say they're not doing it. He suggests using the term "steep slope strip mining" to get around this subterfuge.

At lunch on Saturday, passing mention is made of "taking over a mountaintop" near the end of summer, either an active MTR site or a place proposed for MTR. CRMW folks don't know anything about this but laugh and say they know plenty of mountains they could suggest.

After lunch, Bo tells the meeting that CRMW's top priority this summer is to stop Massey's operations next to Marsh Fork Elementary School—stop the coal-loading and coal-prep operations, fix the dam, stop blasting at the MTR site above the school. School ends for the summer on June 8. Might MJS do a direct action to shut the coal plant down in mid- or late May? Bo emphasizes that permanently shutting this site down is doable, as the school was there long before the coal plant, which should never have been permitted, making this a potential early success story for MJS, one that would provide encouragement and build campaign momentum.

After some discussion about needing an overall public statement of goals for MJS, john proposes that the group write an MJS mission statement to broadcast to potential allies and the world at large. After much discussion, here's what they come up with:

Mountain Justice Summer (MJS) seeks to add to the growing anti-MTR citizens movement. Specifically MJS demands an abolition of MTR, steep slope strip mining and all other forms of surface mining for coal. We want to protect the cultural and natural heritage of the Appalachia coalfields. We want to contribute with grassroots organizing, public education, nonviolent civil disobedience and other forms of citizen action. Historically coal companies have engaged in violence and property destruction when faced with citizen opposition to their activities. MJS is committed to nonviolence and will not be engaged in property destruction.

Posted on the MJS website and reproduced again and again in MJS literature, this would serve as both a definition of and a guideline for MJS throughout the summer and beyond.

Shortly after the meeting in Blacksburg, Bo does a radio interview for a station in Asheville with Julia Bonds. (Bonds's friends call her Judy, and that's what I'll call her here from this point on). Judy's family lived in the same hollow, near Whitesville, for nine generations. Then, in 1994, Massey moved in. Neighbors moved out. Judy's home was covered with coal dust and rattled by blasting. Fish died in the streams her family had always relied on.

"My grandson lay in bed one night when it was raining," Judy recalls, "and we knew other dams had failed. He was eight years old at the time, and he tried to reassure me, because he knew I was worried. He said, 'Mawmaw don't worry. If that dam [above our house] breaks, I've got a path that we can just climb the mountain, and a cave that we can hide in.' I didn't have the heart to tell my grandson that we'd never make it.

"My grandson developed asthma, and things became worse and worse." Finally they moved, the last people in their hollow to leave. Judy would have stayed, but she feared for her daughter and grandson.

"Most Americans simply do not understand where their so-called cheap electricity comes from," she says. "There's nothing cheap about it. And Americans need to understand that coal from cradle to grave is dirty. There's no such thing as 'clean coal.' And they need to understand that [with] our materialistic lifestyle, the use of excessive electricity that you don't need, we're destroying our children's future. We're selling our children's [future] necessities for our luxuries."

Bo notes that their local allies against MTR are few—there's a lot of apathy and intimidation in the coalfields, he says. Massey, the coal company that dominates Coal River valley and mines extensively elsewhere in the region, hires most of its employees from out of state, Bo says, because coal companies would prefer to rid the coalfields of natives who might someday be in their way or complain about what they're doing. (West Virginia's population in 1950 was more than 2 million, and had grown each decade for the past century and a half; by 2005 its population had shrunk to 1.8 million. While West Virginia's population was shrinking, the overall population of the United States nearly doubled between 1950 and 2005. West Virginia's anomalous population loss is overwhelmingly concentrated in the coalfields in the southern part of the state.)

Bo explains to the radio listeners that a mix of toxic chemicals (and in winter, antifreeze) is sprayed on coal at the plant next to Marsh Fork Elementary School—and that three teachers there have died of cancer in the past few years; a former principal, just retired, now has bone cancer; two girls who went to school there have had ovarian cancer, highly unusual in very young women—one of them has died. Other kids at the school have asthma and blood disorders.

"We're inviting everyone in," he says. "There's a place in this [campaign] for everyone. This is not just an Appalachian problem, it's a national problem. It's a worldwide problem, when you come right down to it. America's cheap electricity does come at the expense of coalfield residents. Why should someone in West Virginia lose their home for the profit of a coal company? That's not right. That's not American."

Around the time of this radio interview, I begin corresponding with john johnson, intrigued by how things he said at the meeting in Blacksburg, coming from an anarchist, eco-centric perspective, so closely connect with Judy and Bo's sense that MTR exemplifies a rush toward bankruptcy in America's current way of life. "I agree totally," john says. "MTR is totally an example of the utter insanity of modern industrial capitalism. I don't think it's just America. It's the whole modern world. The flip side is that America and other cultures also have a lot of ingenuity and creativity when it comes to doing things differently."

john's a "damn Yankee," as he puts it. (Yankees live up north. Damn Yankees come south and don't go back.) He grew up in the Northeast, then his family moved to Tennessee when he was fifteen. In college, at the University of Tennessee at Chattanooga, he found himself becoming more open to "alternative ways of viewing the world. I'll be straight with you—part of it was from doing drugs, smoking pot and dropping acid. And part of it was from listening to punk rock music and heavy metal, which has a very rebellious, challenge-authority thing going on. And I started meeting people who were acting on their beliefs." He began attending protests and meetings of activist groups, and became involved in environmental/racial justice campaigns in Chattanooga. Among the environmental activists he met were people working on forest issues, who eventually connected him with Earth First! "In the early 1990s, I got exposed to EF!, I got exposed to the anarchist movement—I got exposed to the most radical wing of the anarchist movement, the anti-civilization bunch. Those ideas have had a profound influence on the way I view things." He's matured enough that he no longer thinks he has The Right Answer for the way the world should run, but "I do know there are slivers of the truth, there are things that I know could and should work, but not the totality."

In 1993, john and several others decided to reconstitute a southern Appalachian bioregional chapter of the radical environmental movement Earth First!, which they named Katuah, the Cherokee word for the region. Before then, in 1991, he'd decided to drop out of college and become a "full-time revolutionary activist, and to dedicate my life to overthrowing the government, and the corporations, and the whole social order, which I perceive as very wrong." At the same time, in the early 1990s, he was protesting against the first Gulf War and against police brutality.

By 1994, "I really liked the Earth First! take on things, the ideology of Deep Ecology and biocentrism."(Deep Ecology holds that humans are first and foremost part of nature, and that living ecosystems have the same sort of value and right to well-being as humankind, regardless of their usefulness to humans.) So john made a conscious decision to focus on environmental issues. Besides, "Earth Firsters are a lot of fun. Even the non-Earth First! [environmentalists], the mainstream conservationists, are great people.

"By 1996, 1997 my environmentalism had transformed from an intellectual thing to a totally heartfelt, passionate—I tell people that not only am I in love with my fiancée, Amanda, but I am hotly in love with the landscape of southern Appalachia." Before then, "I couldn't talk to you about the particulars of nature. I could just tell you why we needed to protect it," as our life-support system. "Now that I have this interest in it, and this love affair with it, I'm trying to learn it. Because I want to talk to people about the particulars, about salamanders, and freshwater mollusks, and the different kinds of trees."

While I'm enjoying seeing individuals as different as Bo, Judy, and john on the same page, other people are worried that MJS is becoming too radical-fringy.

One of those people is Dave Cooper. Born in Cincinnati, Dave grew up Republican, conservative, middle-class. When he was still in high school, during the Carter administration, the first Arab oil embargo and ensuing "energy crisis" hit home: "It was crystal clear that we needed to do energy conservation then," he says. "And then we just forgot about it." Dave went to Vanderbilt University, in Nashville, then worked at a General Motors plant in Ohio for seven years as a quality control engineer. When that plant closed down, he went to work for a defense contractor for three years.

During this time, in 1986, he joined the Sierra Club, mostly because he'd gone camping and hiking when he was a kid and missed it. He went on his first national Sierra Club outing that year, and "got exposed to some other Sierra Club people—and they're all talking about lobbying and writing letters to Congress. I thought they were a bunch of kooks." Two decades later, he's a full-time activist. In the past year and a half, he's done nearly 180 roadshow audiovisual presentations and other talks on MTR in 13 states, many of them at colleges and universities, some for radio and TV, others for churches, civic groups, environmental clubs, and even a corporation or two.

"I'm a little concerned," he writes in late February, "about the tilt of our MJS group and membership towards the EF! side. It needs to be more mainstream and we have to talk—and listen—to regular folks if we want to get our message across and be heard. I'm speaking to all these Rotary Clubs, and you really have to tone down the eco-blabber or they will tune you out immediately. I think this may be a problem this summer if we don't get the more mainstream groups like KFTC [Kentuckians for the Commonwealth] on board."

MJS at this point already includes very different sorts of people—and clearly understands the need to include people with a much greater range of differences if they're to have any success with building a mass movement against MTR.

One set of differences among MJSers concerns perspectives on nature: Some are more inclined to see nature in terms of the usefulness of its various elements to humans, while others see nature primarily as something that has value in and of itself. The first point of view is sometimes labelled "anthropocentric," the second "biocentric." In practice they're not so much two separate camps as they are two directions that encompass a whole range of attitudes toward nature. Extremists in either direction are unlikely to be interested in MJS: neither anthropocentrist extremists who see no value in nature at all beyond its utility to humans, nor biocentric extremists of the anti-civilization camp, who believe that the development of human society past the hunter-gatherer way of life has been a mistake. In between those extremes, most of the range of anthropo-to-biocentric opinion is present among MJSers from the start, with common ground found in the idea of nature as our life-support system; people who are working to protect that system primarily for its value to themselves can work side-by-side with others working to protect it for its own sake. The mutual respect needed for meeting on that common ground is relatively easy in this case, as MJS participants generally share a sense that humans are part of a larger natural community to which they have responsibilities, and a sense that it's wrong to plunder nature and leave it a wasteland.

Another set of differences concerns how activists see—or don't see—the fight against MTR as part of broader efforts toward more extensive, even revolutionary change in society. Several factors make it relatively easy for MJSers to live with differences among themselves on this issue. Foremost is the campaign's agreement to welcome and encourage all efforts to end MTR, and to welcome in everyone who wants to help, as long as all participants eschew both violence and property damage. Also helpful are a cluster of attitudes among the self-identified radicals in MJS, many of whom call themselves anarchists as well as Earth Firsters. Unlike libertarians, who envision a world of cussed individualists, every one for oneself, anarchists tend to favor self-organizing *communities* of cussed individualists. Solidarity and mutual aid matter—out of them, community is built. Self-defense matters, too, which EF!-affiliated anarchists involved with MJS construe as including defense of one's ecological life-support system. Thus, for this movement's anarchists, working together with non-anarchist coalfield activists defending themselves, their communities, and the land from MTR is a good ideological fit. It's helpful, also, that some of those coalfield activists see MTR as part of broader, systemic problems in America—helpful, but not necessary. There's no requirement for ideological unity in this campaign.

There's also no requirement for philosophical unity about nonviolence. MJS requires its participants to adopt nonviolence and avoidance of property damage as a tactic for this campaign, not as a way of life. Nonviolence and avoidance of property damage have often, perhaps more often than not, been linked in campaigns that adopt civil disobedience, for both practical and philosophical reasons. However, Earth Firsters have long been of several minds about this. EF! has consistently (or as consistently as such a loosely organized movement can manage) eschewed violence and taken care to avoid risks of physical harm to anyone in its actions. Although most individuals and campaigns have usually eschewed property damage as well, some have chosen to damage or destroy machinery that is used to harm living ecosystems. EFers have also differed about what exactly constitutes property destruction. (Does making a mess count? Pulling up survey stakes? Spiking trees?) In addition, most of the people involved in MJS (EFers as well as others) personally believe that they have a right to use violence in self-defense: If someone attacks them, they have a right to fight back. Others in the campaign, though, are personally committed to avoiding violence in all situations. MJS's nonviolent, no-property-damage position has been adopted both to enable such diverse people to work together and because there's general agreement that, as a practical matter, it's what's tactically best for this campaign.

MJSers encompass a wide range of differences about religion as well. Some are fiercely secular, actively hostile to organized religion. Others perceive themselves as spiritually engaged, but not necessarily in a church-going way. The movement also includes Christians whose anti-MTR activism is motivated by their religion. Most MJSers who have any sense of spirituality at all perceive it as connected with or activated by contact with nature. Most are at least somewhat familiar and comfortable with the precepts of Deep Ecology. A few of MJS's religious Deep Ecology believers see themselves as worshipping Gaia, or pursuing forms of paganism; most incorporate Deep Ecology into Christian or other religious beliefs and practices. By and large, MJS does pretty well with avoiding religious disagreements. The fact that religious MJSers typically have a sense that God speaks many languages, and that there are many paths to God, defuses much of the hostility to religion that "godless" MJS activists might ordinarily feel or express. It also means that differences about religion tend to be perceived as lifestyle differences, rather than heresy.

However, lifestyle differences turn out to be the source of some of the most dysfunctional divisions within MJS. Appalachians living in the coalfields have a range of rural lifestyles that have little in common with the urban-punk sensibility of many other MJSers. In addition, MJS's coalfield-based activists are mostly middle-aged; MJSers based outside the coalfields are mostly younger. Lifestyle differences among MJSers don't line up neatly along local/outsider or older/younger lines. Across those lines are endless permutations and combinations of hippie, hillbilly hippie, crusty punk, vegan, omnivore, "ninja," "pirate," and other preferences in clothing, food, music, and other matters. Still, for a host of reasons having to do with differences in life experience, coalfield locals and "outsider" activists often experience moments of mutual incomprehension, opportunities for giving or taking offense without real intention. With MJS's recruiting efforts focused primarily on college-aged urban activists, such moments look likely to multiply in the months ahead.

Tension across these various differences is inevitable. MJS's hope is that focusing on a clear common goal—ending MTR, combined with persistent efforts at mutual respect, and at finding strength rather than weakness in the sum of everyone's differences, will be enough to make those tensions manageable.

MJS activists are busy on many fronts this February and March. A donation wish list for MJS is now circulating. An activist in southwestern Virginia is working up a list of threatened and endangered fish and mollusks in the area, for use in challenging MTR there. Judy Bonds, Dave Cooper, and others are working on outreach to religious groups, from nuns in Ohio to Baptists in West Virginia, connecting support in the fight against MTR with religious responsibility to care for God's creation. OVEC and CRMW, with outside funding promised, have begun seeking "coalfield organizers" to hire for the summer. Folks in Tennessee are researching coal companies and permits there, mobilizing activists to attend or submit comments to hearings on mine permits for sites north of Knoxville up near the Kentucky border. They're also moving toward appealing a court ruling against a challenge to the federal Office of Surface Mining's failure to study and consider environmental impacts before permitting the MTR site at Zeb Mountain, recently bought by National Coal Corporation (NCC). (Zeb and NCC are prime targets for MJS action in Tennessee.)

In early March, Chris Irwin bounces his truck back into the woods to photograph a twenty-five-acre landslide a few ridges southwest of Zeb Mountain, on a former strip mine officially deemed "reclaimed" in accordance with government regulations. "It was as if the 'reclamation' was a cancer that had finally burst from the skin of the earth," Chris reports. "What caused [the] megaslide is evident—you can hear it, water. At least four different sources of water were cutting through the shale and coal-blended soil. An unstable substrate combined with water and really steep slopes creates landslides. Ridgetops may be cheap for coal companies to blast—it's impossible to repair."

"We see slides fairly frequently, but rarely one this size," an official with the Tennessee Department of Environment and Conservation (TDEC) observes. And, in fact, on his way to the big slide, Chris saw several other, smaller landslides that he'd not heard about. That such slides could happen on "reclaimed" land at all, let alone "frequently," calls into question the adequacy of reclamation protocols—and presents an opportunity, as Chris and others in Tennessee see it.

"Normally Katuah Earth First! regards politicians as scum who are not to be trusted on any level," Chris writes in another email to the MJS listserv. "But tactically at this juncture in our campaign here in Tennessee all the arrows are pointing to our state agencies. TDEC regulates water permits for Tennessee. Mountaintop removal aka cross-ridge mining by its very nature destroys highland watersheds. TDEC has been wavering lately on the wisdom of being a rubber stamp for the final solution for our watersheds." MJS is aiming to compel them to instead protect streams by protecting their mountains.

In mid-March, MJS organizers from around the region once again gather for a weekend meeting, this time in Asheville, at Warren Wilson College just east of town. Close to four dozen people attend, at least a dozen or so newcomers since the meeting in Blacksburg.

Bo tells the meeting that there's been heavy blasting behind Marsh Fork Elementary School in the past month. In Kentucky, activists affiliated with KFTC (a few of whom attend part of this weekend's meeting) are looking to see what their role in MJS might be. Erin from Blacksburg reports on plans for a "Listening Project" in and around the town of Appalachia, Virginia, going door-to-door to hear people's concerns about mining in their neighborhoods. (Last August there, a three-year-old boy, Jeremy Davidson, asleep in his bed, was crushed to death by a boulder off an MTR site above his home.) Listening Projects have also been done or are soon to begin near Zeb Mountain in Tennessee and in Coal River valley. College students from several states are expected soon to visit Larry Gibson's place at Kayford Mountain, to see MTR firsthand, in the hope of drawing them in to MJS for the summer. Paloma reports that the MJS internet listserv now has 267 members, and that 2 or 3 people are signing up at the website each day, volunteering to help this summer.

"Looks like we'll have more people than we know what to do with," john johnson says.

Chris Irwin responds, "We'll know what to do with them."

Much of the weekend is devoted to working out a rough-draft calendar for the summer, and to meetings of and report-backs from working groups focused on Listening Projects, training camps to be held early in the summer, finances, art, intake process for volunteers, media and outreach, logistics of housing and feeding and transporting volunteers, music, and scouting for possible actions sites and to learn what's happening with mining in various places. Informally, in conversations during breaks in the meeting, activists are still considering a mountaintop occupation sometime during the summer, with possible locations to be scouted in the next few weeks and discussed at the next monthly meeting, in April.

Kayford Mountain in West Virginia is five hours of fast driving from Asheville, mostly on highways. There's a network of wide, well-built highways throughout this region (thank you Sen. Robert Byrd), but when you get off these roads you're often quite quickly on narrow, light-duty roads with no shoulders and steep drop-offs, not built to withstand heavy truck traffic but subjected to it nonetheless to suit the convenience of mine operations. Coal trucks pound the hell out of roads running within a few yards of people's homes, and come tearing around blind curves too fast for anyone who happens to be in the wrong place at the wrong moment to get out of their way. Dozens of people on foot and in cars have been killed this way. Sharing the road with coal trucks is scary, and people who live in the coalfields live with that fear every day.

When I visit Kayford one afternoon in late March, I meet Larry at the Stanley family cemetery, near the top of the mountain, amid a constant din of working equipment from the surrounding mine sites. Trees around the cemetery are still winter-dormant. On the back of a white-painted rock marking the entrance to the cemetery Larry has painted a Bible verse, Psalms 95:4: "In his hand are the deep places of the earth. The strength of the hills is his also." Larry's family has been burying relatives here since the early 1800s.

Members of the Stanley family have lived here for 220 years, Larry tells me. (Larry's grandmother was a Stanley.) They lost most of their land a century ago, in 1906, as so many other southern Appalachian families did when land companies greedy for timber and mineral rights moved in. "We had 566 acres. We now have fifty. A crooked land company and a crooked notary cheated my family out of [the rest] because they couldn't read," he says.

Gesturing to the trees at one side of the cemetery, Larry says: "Before they started this, in '86, you could come in here and above the trees there you could see a pasture, with cattle and horses in it. *Above* the trees." Now there's nothing but sky there. The mountainside where the pasture was located has, like all the mountains for miles around now, had its top blown off and been reduced in height by hundreds of feet, with the rubble pushed aside into valley fills. "This here [Kayford] was the lowest point. Everything around me was higher, about 300 feet higher than this."

The strip mining that surrounds Kayford stretches for seventeen miles. Larry's little fifty-acre island in the middle is the only place that isn't controlled by mining companies. "Thirteen permits, 7,538 acres, several different companies," Larry says.

As we're walking up the private access road to the cemetery, we stop to look at tire tracks from a big mining truck that's been using the road without Larry's permission, presumably to dump something beyond the edge of the cemetery. Similarly, mining trucks tear up the private dirt road that goes through Larry's property past several cabins maintained by relatives, because it's a shortcut to property a mining company controls and has been logging just beyond the cabins. Flyrock from blasting has landed in the cemetery and its parking area from as far as 1,500 yards away. In fact, Larry's picked up flyrock all over his property—on the road, in his yard, plenty of places where he or someone else could easily have been standing when it fell. "We've had rocks coming on our property as heavy as five tons," Larry tells me. Later he'll show me photographs, and tell me to look for flyrock boulders along the road I'll take down the mountain. Some are as big as easy chairs.

For all the land that's being torn up by mining here, there are very few mining jobs. "When I was a boy, in 1960," Larry says, "they had 25,000 men. Now 500 men take out five times as much coal as the 25,000 did." The coal companies hire just a few locals "so they can tell people: Well, we're hiring. But you go sit at the mine site and watch the cars when they're coming out—Pennsylvania, Ohio, Tennessee, Missouri [license plates]."

Just a few hundred people live in the hollow below Kayford now, all clustered along the road by the creek, none up in the hills. There used to be a high school here for 1,500 students, but it closed. "We have one elementary school in the hollow, and they're talking about closing it down. [Since 1960,] we lost sixteen schools that I remember."

I ask why people around here aren't angry about all this. "They feel powerless," Larry says, adding that the mining companies have succeeded in dividing and conquering. "They're very good at keeping them fighting amongst themselves. The people that they hire intimidate the people that they don't hire. Fear is so thick you can cut it with a knife." There's good reason for that fear. Since Larry began speaking out against MTR and the destruction of his home place, he's been keeping a list of attacks against himself and his property. It's now a very long list. He's been run off the road. His cabin was burned down in 2002, after a threat the day before. His dogs have been killed. People have shot up his house. People have come here and shot at headstones in the cemetery—he shows me the marks from bullets hitting a relatively new stone. His camper, parked up here, was shot up so badly he had to put a new door on it. "They ripped the windows out of it, they shot it up, turned it over." The cap on his truck has been busted up. Mining companies also exercise control through "the flow of money" among locals: "If they ain't making any money, they wait for crumbs." They don't want to rock the boat lest if a job opens up the company won't hire them. Or, if they don't wait for "crumbs," they leave.

We take Larry's truck up past his home, then continue on along the dirt road past his relatives' cabins. He thinks there's likely to be blasting off that side of his property right about now, and he'd like me to see it.

We drive past a sign warning about blasting, and I ask Larry how that can be, are they allowed to turn his property into a blast site just by posting a sign? "What sign? I don't see no sign," he says, grinning. "You gotta know, us hillbillies, if there's not a picture, we cain't read." In fact, the sign marks the edge of his property, and we trespass a short ways onto land the mining company has been logging, to see what's happening. (Seems a fair exchange, since miners' trucks have been trespassing across the private road through Larry's property as a shortcut to get here.)

When we get out of Larry's truck, the land we're standing on, which Larry says they're going to drop by several hundred feet, is peppered with flyrock. Some pieces I see are big as bricks—and they came from a blast site 500 yards away, Larry says. Certainly, looking down into the enormous mine site several hundred feet below us, the active mining looks that far away. They're currently blowing off another 150 to 180 feet of rock to get at an 8-foot seam of coal.

Several times Larry asks: "Do you hear a whistle?" expecting a warning whistle—although they don't *always* whistle a warning before blasting. "If there's a tree still standing and you hear a blast, get behind it. Actually, I think you'd be hard-pressed to find a tree now." After the recent logging, only scattered spindly little trees remain, too thin to offer cover.

We'll never know whether my being there stopped the blasting that day; mining companies don't like to publicize their MTR operations. "They don't know who you are," Larry tells me. "They know I've been at the cemetery with you." Several mining company pickup trucks have driven past while I've been here, their drivers waving at me and Larry. Larry knows they keep track of his comings and goings because they talk about it on public communications radio channels, which he sometimes monitors.

"I want to emphasize to you how dangerous this area is," Larry says, "not just for strangers but for the people—they have no responsibility toward the people that live here." Larry is fifty-nine years old. He looks older.

Dave Cooper and others continue to be concerned that MJS isn't doing well enough at including mainstream environmental groups; the KFTC members Dave invited to the Asheville meeting left early and remain wary.

Others are concerned that MJS is inadequately rooted in local communities, and thus risks doing more harm than good. One organizer, thinking of leaving the campaign, writes in a letter to friends that:

This campaign holds the terrifying possibility of eroding away what foundation for change has been created. [MJS should not be] inciting people from outside of Appalachia to come to our region, while spending a very limited energy towards asking the coalfield residents and organizers what vision they themselves hold.

Direct action in Appalachia this summer, being chiefly organized, or being perceived to be organized, by EF! activists from Knoxville and Asheville will not stop or slow MTR. It will gain attention to the issue, but it will alienate locals and make them less [trusting] of groups like OVEC, Appalachian Voices, CRMW, and the array of others who have spent years planting and cultivating seeds of change. If MJS comes into West Virginia, Virginia, Kentucky, and Tennessee this summer and attempts to plant, by relative force, grown trees of this needed change, and then disperses, the trees will die. Those residing in the areas where the proverbial trees are planted will not understand the intricacies of sustaining them, but there will be more than a few who are ready and willing to cut them down and use their branches to beat the hell out of OVEC, KFTC, and the rest, and ultimately all our visions of a better world.

Concerns about MJS's inclusiveness and "outsider" problems come to a head with publication of an article in West Virginia's Charleston *Gazette* in May, a few days before MJS's planned kickoff rally in Charleston, at the state capitol. The article begins: "Environmental activists from around the country are being urged to descend on Appalachia this summer for a series of protests.... sponsored and promoted by a Tennessee-based affiliate of the controversial group Earth First!" MJS organizers are most upset by one particular quote in the article: "'Frankly, OVEC is wary, as we don't know all the groups and individuals involved,' said Vivian Stockman, project coordinator for the Ohio Valley Environmental Coalition. 'We are very relieved to see this note on the [MJS] website: "MJS is committed to nonviolence and will not be engaged in property destruction."'" The best that can be said of this is that Abe Mwaura, OVEC's representative at recent MJS meetings, hasn't adequately conveyed to Vivian what MJS is up to. Many MJS organizers, Bo Webb among them, see Vivian's statement as a betrayal.

The *Gazette* article's most insidious quality, though, is its treatment of violence. It notes the potential for "confrontation" at MJS's rally on Thursday, asserts that Earth First! is "linked" to "violent 'eco-terrorism'" with specific reference to tree-spiking and the planting of a pipe bomb by opponents of EF! in an EF! organizer's car in California in 1990, and notes that in West Virginia, in 1999, "a mob attacked [West Virginia] Secretary of State Ken Hechler and other anti-mountaintop removal activists who were re-enacting the march that union miners made in 1921 during the Battle of Blair Mountain." (Larry Gibson and Judy Bonds also were among those who were attacked.) The article's overall implication is that MJS will be a magnet for violence, and that sensible people might be wise to stay away.

Thursday's rally turns out to be thoroughly civil. MJSers pass out fact sheets about coal and MTR at the Friends of Coal rally being held right next to and just prior to the MJS event. Several hundred people attend the FOC event, many of them miners given the day off from work and a bus ride to do so. A few FOCs (or FOCers, pronounced "fuckers" by some MTR opponents) stay to watch the MJS rally. There are no confrontations, and a few courteous conversations.

After the rally, coal-industry supporters in the region's media begin to refine what through the rest of the summer will become a persistent labeling of MJS as a bunch of weird outsiders who are somehow both dangerous and frivolous. "We learned this week," the *State Journal's* political editor writes, "that West Virginia will be treated to a visit by the traveling eco-circus…. Until August, West Virginia will be thick with Birkenstocks and patchouli oil. These are the kind of environmentalists who say they won't use violence but are dangerous enough to have to make that clear. We can expect padlocked gates, people chained to equipment, human shields in front of pine trees, and maybe even a sit-in. Throw in some dried fruit and a glass of soy milk, and you've got yourself a party."

Shortly after the rally, out of the blue, Bo Webb receives an email from Peabody Coal saying they don't do MTR and shouldn't be an MJS

target. I tell Bo that I've been seeking interviews with representatives
from several coal companies, and none has been willing to talk with me.
(After a few months of this, I give up and rely instead on the companies'
press releases and statements made by their employees at public events.)
Bo's reaction: "It doesn't surprise me that they won't meet with you. Now
that MJS is out, they have to strategize and work on certain buzz words
so they can all tell the same lies."

Heading toward Knoxville for the next MJS organizers' meeting, in
April, I stop for a walk in the woods on a mountain near Caryville, a few
miles south of Zeb Mountain.

The leaves are just beginning to come out on trees along the trail
here. Maples are leafing out, but the mast trees—oaks, hickories, other
nuts—are barely showing leaves. Shadbush is blooming up here; down
in valley, where the season's further advanced, dogwood's already in full
bloom. I hear a Carolina wren calling "teakettle, teakettle, teakettle, tea."
Migrating birds are now coming through—on this sunny day I hear quite
a bit of warbler noise, even as late as mid-morning. Blooming along the
trail are pure white trillium, violets (white, light purple, red purple, dark
purple, white with purple streaks), jack-in-the-pulpit, toadshade trillium
not yet turned its mature red, white star chickweed, wild strawberry, several yellow buttercuppy things. The last of the various ferns' fiddleheads
are unfurling. The flowers of bloodroot have already gone by; May apple
and columbine are up and leafy but not flowering yet. Ramps ought to
be up and ready for digging, and morels up and ready for picking too,
though I don't see any myself.

In the woods today, I meet Jim Massengill, an older fellow who
grew up on the mountainside facing Caryville here and still camps
up here on the mountain. Jim's family has lived here for long enough
that one of the mountains nearby was named after them. He at first
thinks I'm here to poach morels, and he starts his conversation with
me with warnings about snakes and game wardens. We chat warily for
a while, and then he says, speaking of himself and his neighbors: "We

love these mountains. We *love* these mountains." I ask him what he thinks of coal companies' plans to blow up the tops of many of these mountains. Without hesitation he says: "We're gonna stop that." No longer wary, we talk about strip mining and the horrific clear-cutting that's preceding it on thousands of acres of beautiful mountainside like the one where we're standing.

Jim's family arrived here in the 1830s or 1840s, migrating south from Kentucky. At one time, they owned 11,000 acres. Like Larry Gibson's family, they lost most of it a century ago. In the late 1800s, "a land company came in here and they had what they call gun thugs," Jim explains. "And they run all the people out of these mountains and took the land. That's what I was told." Timber was taken out first, followed by coal.

When Jim was a child, in the late 1940s, the only road over this mountain was one dirt lane. That road was first paved only a few years ago, and this summer it's to be fixed up and widened—a convenience for logging and mining trucks, I guess. Federal funding is involved, ostensibly to make the road safe for school buses.

Jim remembers huge old hemlocks being taken out of the woods near here, some years back. "They left them alone [when the land was first logged] because the people that owned the land would not let them cut them. There was eleven of them. Monster hemlocks," as big as nine feet across at the base. "I cried when I seen them cut. I'd seen them since I was a kid."

Jim's father owned and worked a scattering of little "dog-hole" coal mines in the area, where he scraped out enough coal to make a modest living. His father's working life extended into the first wave of strip mining in the 1950s and 1960s, but he wouldn't have anything to do with that. "He didn't believe in strip mining. He was a deep miner. He wouldn't work in strip mines. They destroyed the timber, they destroyed the land."

About ten years ago, up on this mountain not far from here, Jim tells me, "I was on a four-wheeler, and I seen a bunch of wild turkeys, and I just eased up on them." They were at a place on a hillside where miners had drilled augur holes sideways into the mountain to take out small deposits of coal left behind by previous mining. "Snakes [copperheads] were coming up out of the augur holes, and [the turkeys] were pecking them and eating them. I sat there and watched them for probably thirty minutes. I never seen nothing like that." The turkeys were so focused on what they were doing that they didn't run from Jim, who was quite close. "Usually, a wild turkey—you get close to it, and it's gone. But they were really eating those snakes up. They'd peck 'em in the head, reach and get 'em, throw 'em up, and swallow 'em down." From the number and variety of snake stories Jim has to tell, I wonder if he isn't some sort of snake magnet. He tells me he once stumbled into a den of maybe fifty copperheads out in the woods near his old home place. "Man, they scared me to death." I'm sure they did. I tell him I think maybe I won't want to go hiking off-trail with him.

I promise to put Jim in touch with some of the folks in Knoxville working on the MJS campaign. He later sends me an email: "It would take days to really show you the damaged mountain and wood lands in this area. I would be honored to talk to you or anyone that can help us (the people of this area) stop all this nonsense. I alone don't have the knowledge to get it done, but with your help we can get a lot done."

The April MJS meeting is held in a classroom at the University of Tennessee in Knoxville, less than an hour down the road from Caryville. In response to the growing concern about inclusiveness, and particularly in response to the controversy stirred up by how OVEC's Vivian Stockman was quoted in the Charleston *Gazette*, the meeting starts with a long discussion about equality and solidarity—how to allow diverse voices to be heard and to enable various groups and individuals to participate in MJS.

Diane Bady, OVEC's co-director, here instead of Abe today representing OVEC, says that OVEC does want to be involved with and supportive of MJS. She mentions "an enormous amount of anger directed at Vivian" over the newspaper article she was quoted in, and says Vivian has found that anger painful to deal with. Diane says that in the past OVEC has worked on campaigns in which well-intentioned outsiders have come in to help and have done things that cause problems that OVEC later has had to clean up; they've made OVEC's work more difficult rather than bolstered their energy and resources, and then left. OVEC does want MJS to succeed, Diane emphasizes.

Larry tells the group that there are folks in West Virginia who do not feel invited. For the past century and more local voices haven't been heard, they've not been taken seriously or valued—so failing to invite people opens old wounds. Bill McCabe affirms that MJS needs to respect and listen to folks in the mountains who've been working against MTR (and other strip mining before it) for years, long before MJS was dreamed of.

Chris Dodson notes, at this point, that there are different groups working to the same end, and we don't all have to do things the same way. If we disagree, we should do it with respect.

Patty Draus, Dave Cooper's partner, observes that people at MJS planning meetings are well voiced, but people who are not yet at the table aren't. Another woman from Kentucky says that there at least, people don't have a clear idea of MJS. They think that civil disobedience is all there is to it. There's little awareness, for example, of ongoing and planned work like the Listening Projects.

A while back, john johnson says, MJS organizers made an effort to come up with a comprehensive survey of existing local organizations working against MTR. Obviously we've missed people, he says. The group brainstorms for a while about who's not at the table today and should be contacted.

The inclusiveness problem is not just about getting strangers to the table, but also affects group dynamics among those who are already here. In that connection, john says that he's an anarchist, not a leader, and notes that there's no hierarchy in MJS. He acknowledges that the big mouths (himself included) need to make more space for others to speak up—but at the same time everyone else needs to be more aggressive about checking them. We made a mistake over the past few months, he adds, creating the impression that everyone has to completely agree with MJS to work with it. Nonprofit organizations aren't going to endorse civil disobedience—but even if they don't sign on officially, many of their members will want to help and should be encouraged to do so.

john adds that he's uncomfortable with a strict policy of following the lead of coalfield locals, because by itself that won't necessarily result in straight-up confrontation with coal companies and their profits. He has a responsibility to act on his own principles, he says. He believes he *has* to act on behalf of his life-support system, the ecology of his home bioregion. But he also believes that we should listen to local voices in sorting out how.

Bo sees the inclusiveness issue as related to the ugly rhetoric about MJS "outsiders" poised to invade the coalfields—and he's angry about it. Coal companies have used this sort of rhetoric about "outsiders" for a hundred years, he says. "There are no outsiders in America."

After lunch on Saturday, regional report-backs are full of specific plans for the months ahead. In West Virginia, CRMW has learned that Massey is requesting a permit from the state DEP to build a *second* coal silo right next to the existing silo beside Marsh Fork Elementary School. CRMW and others are requesting a public hearing on the application; MJS's schedule for its time in West Virginia this summer should stay loose until they know when that hearing will be scheduled. A Listening Project has begun in the neighborhoods near Marsh Fork Elementary, and letters about the school have been published in Charleston and other West Virginia newspapers. Speaking events with Judy Bonds and other coalfield activists are scheduled not just around the region but around the country. Abe Mwaura's been busy organizing in Logan County, ordinarily a place very hostile to any efforts to hold coal companies accountable. And OVEC and CRMW are setting up a house in Coal River valley for half a dozen grant-supported summer interns as well as additional traveling MJS activists.

In Tennessee, plans are being made for MJS time in Nashville, in the

Knoxville area, and in the coalfields north of Knoxville, near Caryville and Zeb Mountain, including a "variety of ideas" for direct action. In the past month, they've been working to get hearings on MTR-related permits, and working on fundraising. Lawyers are being contacted for legal support this summer.

After the meeting is over, I sit down for what becomes a long talk with john johnson about the state of the campaign against MTR and how he came to be so involved in it. He tells me he first heard about MTR in the late 1990s, but at that time he was already stretched pretty thin as an activist and didn't think he could take on another issue.

"But then we found out about this project on Zeb Mountain" and he thought: "Holy shit, it's in my backyard now." Here in Tennessee, john reminds me, "technically it's 'cross-ridge' mining, because they're going to put the mountain back together, supposedly. If you go to the Office of Surface Mining, [they say] 'There's no mountaintop removal in Tennessee.' But it's still massive strip mining, and really disgusting."

Unlike southern West Virginia and eastern Kentucky, which have seen so much MTR that most of the landscape is now affected by it, in Tennessee so far there are only a few islands of MTR (such as the Zeb Mountain site), with the natural fabric of most of the landscape still sufficiently intact to support normal forest regeneration. MJS's goal in Tennessee is to keep it that way, to prevent MTR's spread.

After he found out about Zeb Mountain, john helped arrange to bring Dave Cooper and Judy Bonds to Tennessee for anti-MTR road-show presentations in Knoxville, Chattanooga, and Crossville, alongside himself and other Tennesseans talking about how MTR was moving into Tennessee. More Tennesseans got involved, and they met more people fighting MTR elsewhere in the region.

In 2003, john and two other activists affiliated with Katuah Earth First! blockaded a road at the Zeb Mountain site by locking them-selves to large metal drums filled with concrete. (Unfortunately, they'd decided to mix the concrete on site, to avoid having to move large drums full of it. When police arrived, the concrete hadn't yet set, so disassembling the blockade was ridiculously easy for them. Next time, they'll know better.)

Then, in August 2004, Jeremy Davidson was killed by MTR operations in Virginia. KEF! "had already been working with some people in that area on [trying to prevent] a timber sale in the Jefferson National Forest." So when people in Virginia suggested the idea of organizing a protest in response to the boy's death, KEFers came up and joined in. "The Jeremy Davidson murder was really a big catalyst for [MJS]: Omigod, a three-year-old kid, killed in his sleep by a boulder from a strip mine."

Around this time, Chris Irwin and others were talking with Sue Daniels, a biologist at Virginia Tech, about the idea of a "Mountain Justice Summer," a campaign to address MTR the way Mississippi Freedom Summer and Redwood Summer had used nonviolent direct action and civil disobedience to address racial injustice and forest destruction. Chris started talking up this idea among KEF! people in Tennessee. Judy and Dave and other folks in West Virginia and Kentucky thought it was a good idea, too. (Sue Daniels provided much of the initial energy and vision for MJS. It was a great shock when, toward the end of 2004, she was killed in a murder-suicide committed by a man who had apparently become personally obsessed with her.)

"If I had my druthers," john says, noting that Chris Irwin would disagree with him about this, "we'd wait until next year to do MJS, because it would give us more time to organize for it." Better still, "instead of saying 'wait until 2006,' I wish that we'd started thinking about it in 2003," to be better prepared for doing it now. "It's a super-pressing issue. But if we had another year, we would be avoiding some of the issues that have come up, about people not feeling good about being invited, and about us not putting enough energy into grassroots organizing." More time would have made it possible "to build more relationships with more people." Still, john believes that MJS has now, at this point, got enough of this done to be on track for pulling off a successful summer.

john would like to see more people who have concerns about MJS raise them out in the open, in meetings. And he notes, about "some of the people I've been a little worried about," worried that they're creating an unhealthy power dynamic within the group, "I've heard them acknowledge that we need a bigger tent, and I've heard them acknowledge—a little bit, not as much as I'd hoped—that we have to address the power dynamics, and that we have to keep reminding people that we want them to be full participants. And that we want a community of equals, not a community of leaders and followers." I don't know this at the time, but later learn that there have been ongoing problems of this sort within KEF!, mostly involving Chris and Paloma.

I note that in this month's meeting, he and Chris were a lot quieter than in previous meetings. "Yeah. That was totally intentional," john says. "It's hard, because we care so much. And it's not like we have bad ideas. But there does come a time when we have to recognize that we are talking too much, to not just pay lip service to making space for other people but to really make the space. If we have this thing where Paloma says something, Chris says something, I say something, then everyone else says OK, I feel uneasy about it.

"Regardless of all that, I think things are really moving in a good direction. I think we did open up some space this weekend, and I hope that that continues."

This summer, john says, "I want people to come here and fall in love, and maybe decide to stay. I want to see people [who grew up here and left] come home and fall in love. I want to see people who live here, both in the coalfields and adjacent to the coalfields, become empowered to really challenge King Coal. So I want to see several high-profile, pretty intense, nonviolent direct actions throughout the summer. I want to see a lot of people helping out with grassroots organizing and listening." And he wants to be able to say at the end of the summer something that can't honestly be said today: that "mountaintop removal is an internationally recognized environmental issue—and if not quite internationally then a nationally recognized environmental issue," so that Americans everywhere recognize that "there is a conflict in the coalfields, because the way coal is mined fucks up the land and fucks up people's lives."

john believes that the direct action component of MJS is poised to do this "the same way Earth First! created more tension around the logging of the old growth forests in the Pacific Northwest—a lot of people know about that because people blocked roads and sat in trees and occupied offices and raised hell."

But given the nature of MTR, the total nature of its destruction, way more is at stake, john says, than in the western forests, where forest of some ecological value does grow back even on most clear-cuts. "The mountains are not going to come back. [MTR] is the Final Solution for the forests, and the mountains themselves."

Meanwhile, at Zeb Mountain, mining is still continuing as fast as NCC wants to do it. "You know," john says, "we're probably not going to be able to save that mountain." But they might make it cost so much to mine it that nobody wants to take other mountains. "We want to send a clear message to the industry that they just can't get away with this stuff.

"I want to see mass outrage, and public discussion about how electricity is produced and used in this country. MTR is the poster child for everything that is wrong with industrial civilization. And there's this collective denial in our culture: The president says global warming's not an issue, so global warming's not an issue. Global warming *needs* to be an issue, and all the other environmental issues need to be issues. [Otherwise], at some point, everyone is gonna wake up and say: Oh shit, the ecosystems have collapsed and we're all gonna die."

After the meeting in Knoxville, I drive north and catch up with Bo back home in West Virginia. I've been thinking about MJS's potential to encourage a virtuous circle, starting with a few locals like Bo and Judy standing up against MTR, others from elsewhere in the region and outside it joining them and encouraging more locals to stand up, and so on. "That's what we're hoping to do," Bo says. "We've been working on trying to get locals organized for a couple years, and it's like pulling teeth. A lot of the local people are against [MTR]. They just are afraid to speak out." Bo hopes that getting national news coverage will help a great deal with this. Outside the region, you tell people about Marsh Fork Elementary School and their jaws drop. It's so egregious. If people here start seeing national coverage of the issue, Bo hopes that will "empower" more of his neighbors to say "You can't do that!"

He thinks the school is "the right issue" to mobilize anti-MTR sentiment into action. For the next three weeks he and his friend Ed Wiley, who lives a few miles upriver and has a granddaughter attending the school, will be "going door to door, listening to people and talking about the school, to see how they feel about it—and what do they *know* about it, what do they actually know about the sludge dam above it, what do they actually know about the prep plant, what a prep plant does, and the coal silo, and adding another silo, and the chemicals used, and how much [blasting nearby] can that dam take, the dangers of it." They'll hand out free pH testing kits so folks can test the streams by their homes for acid mine runoff. And they'll ask people if they'd be willing to go door to door and talk about this themselves, or hold a sign up at the school: "Will you stand next to me, and stand up for your child and other children on this river? Because it's their future. And if we allow it to continue—shame on us, because it's our responsibility as adults to protect our kids, whether the government's doing it or not.

"If the government's turned its back on us, and they're not going to protect us, we have to protect ourselves. They're forcing us to be revolutionaries. I hate using words like that. But they are not protecting us. We don't get the same protections other citizens do.

"We're all Americans. Look at how many Americans from West Virginia have volunteered in times of crisis and died—per capita, more folks from West Virginia have died in wars than any other state. There's no such thing as an outsider in America. We're all in this together. And we'd better start standing up together, because the corporations are taking our country over."

The "outsider" propaganda directed against MJS this year plays to a deep-rooted and well-founded suspicion of outsiders here, where there's such a long and pervasive history of outsiders coming in and taking over land and coal and timber rights. Bo points out the obvious counter to that: "If you want to talk about outsiders, let's talk about the coal companies," most of whose executives and stockholders live far from the coalfields. "They're all outsiders. Look at the big four-wheel-drive trucks going up and down the road here along the Coal River—they're from Virginia, from Kentucky, more and more from Ohio. They're bringing in outsiders to displace our workers. Because our workers don't like this" kind of mining, the destruction it entails. The coal companies manage to turn the "outsider" label to their advantage only because "they work on this twenty-four hours a day, three shifts. They have many people, we have few, and we're going in a lot of different directions.

"The organizations fighting MTR have been doing a protest here, and then six months later 'Hey, let's go over there and protest,' and let's write this, let's fight this permit and that permit. I think we need to focus as one whole group of people that comes together, that sees an injustice and says 'We're gonna concentrate on this and nothing else, and we're gonna get a victory here.'" Bo believes that their best shot at such a victory is at Marsh Fork Elementary School "because it's so atrocious. And I think it's winnable—and if we can't win that one, we're not gonna win any of them.

"I would like to see an awakening in America that there's something wrong not just in West Virginia but there's something wrong in Kentucky and Tennessee and Virginia—and Pennsylvania and Ohio. As a matter of fact, there's something wrong everywhere. When it comes to mineral extraction, humans that are in the way are being screwed.

"We need a thought revolution," Bo says. "A military revolution's not going to do it. We can't defeat the government. We have to change people's minds."

Bo recently did a presentation on MTR with Julian Martin of the Highlands Conservancy, one of the mainstream groups that MJS hasn't quite got inside its tent. "Julian said it real well: If you've got to blow up a mountain, that's not acceptable. If you gotta get the coal, do it underground, responsibly. But this is not acceptable, this has to stop, and if we have to turn off the lights to stop doing that, then that's what we're gonna have to do." Actually, MTR provides a small enough percentage of coal used that conservation measures could easily make up for it: We don't have to turn *all* the lights off, only the ones we don't really need anyway.

"MTR is for profit," Bo adds. "End story. There's no other reason for it. And if coal companies had to pay for the environmental impact and all the cleanup, of course it wouldn't be profitable. If corporations have the same rights as citizens, let's make sure they have the same responsibilities as citizens.

"I do believe that in the end the truth will win. I believe that if you can explain the truth, and get it out there, in the end it will win. And if I thought it wouldn't win, I'd go start shooting the bastards. Tomorrow.

"You've gotta be optimistic to do what we're doing [with MJS]. We haven't got anywhere doing it the same way. We've got to make a bold change in direction. I don't know what else to do. I don't know what direction to take other than this [civil disobedience campaign]. And I'm trusting that the American people, when they see this, are gonna go: 'This isn't right.' And maybe they will even start understanding that they're living in slave cities. They're slaves to the man, too. Maybe we'll create an uprising all over."

May passes in a blur of activity mostly aimed at getting ready for and recruiting people to come to the MJS training camp at the end of the month, and at getting the campaign up and running with actions in West Virginia. Dozens of intake forms for people seeking to attend camp are processed; one sent by a West Virginia state trooper apparently seeking to infiltrate the camp is screened out. Fundraisers are held, volunteer lawyers are lined up, logistics for the rest of the summer begin to be sorted out, state water testing protocols are researched, and plans for the campaign's time in each state take shape. Farther afield, Project Censored begins following MTR among its "news stories of social significance that have been overlooked, under-reported or self-censored by the country's major national news media." In mid-May, hits on the MJS website pass the 10,000 mark.

During this time, I talk with Chris Irwin about how he became an activist, and how he sees the summer ahead.

"My family's from east Tennessee," he tells me. "We've been here in Knoxville for six generations." When Chris was 13, he and his immediate family moved for a few years to West Virginia. Where they lived, near Charleston, "was such a weird combination of massive pollution [from chemicals emitted by industry along the river] and natural beauty. I hated it. The river caught on fire" while he was living there. One time when it rained, the rain ate the paint off their car. Every family he knew had someone with cancer. "And then when cancer started eating my stepfather, inside and out" he found it "unbearable" to be at home, "so I just grabbed my books and I was outdoors constantly," in the forest near his home. "Then they clear-cut all that forest. And I realized everything was really messed up."

After Chris's stepfather died, he and his mother moved back to Tennessee. He started reading about environmental groups and issues. ("Every high school had the guy who wore an Army jacket, lived in the library, and played chess, the quiet geek reader," and Chris was one of those.) He read more and more through college. He started going to environmental protests and was arrested twice in antinuclear protests at Oak Ridge, Tennessee. He joined the Peace Corps and went to West Africa. In the late 1990s, he hopped trains to the Pacific Northwest, where he met Paloma in 1998, when they were both in jail after a forest action. By then he was involved with Earth First!

"[Paloma]" swore she'd never leave the Northwest. I told her I would stay. She saw me mourning my bioregion after a while and gave in, said: Alright, I'll try the South out for a while."

A few years ago, in what had become Chris's practice of monitoring Tennessee Department of Environmental Conservation permits (he'd been involved in fighting certain state road-building projects, which require permits from TDEC), "I started getting these cross-ridge mining permits for Zeb Mountain," saw that "they were turning these streams into industrial drainage ditches," and wondered why. "I hadn't heard about mountaintop removal at that point.

"Then I went to this action camp," in Kentucky in 2002. Larry Gibson spoke there about Kayford, and afterward Chris told Larry about the permits at Zeb. Larry said "he'd seen that before, and here's what's going to happen next" in the sequence of destruction that plays out on MTR sites.

So Chris "read everything I could get my hands on, on what was going on in West Virginia." MTR, Chris saw, was "coming south, following the coalfields."

By then, Chris, john johnson, and KEF! generally were involved in fighting timber sales on exceptionally biodiverse National Forest land in far southwestern Virginia, at the edge of the same coalfields through which MTR was progressing toward Tennessee. In August 2004, Chris asked a guy he knew there to help him scout and understand MTR in Virginia—and a few days before they were to do this, Jeremy Davidson was killed there.

Chris drove by the Davidsons' house with his friend, "and we talked about it the whole weekend." Chris's friend set up a community meeting, "and they said 'let's have a march'" through the town of Appalachia. Chris, back in Knoxville, publicized the march through KEF! and other channels. Dozens of KEFers came from Tennessee and North Carolina, and so did Judy Bonds and other anti-MTR activists from West Virginia and Kentucky. At least 200 people showed up, Chris says. "Coal miners showed up. They led the march." Chris has focused on fighting MTR, and on organizing the Mountain Justice Summer campaign, ever since.

"I think what will happen [as a result of MJS] is one of these states— I think Tennessee is most likely, because we're not owned by the coal industry—will pass something that will kill [large-scale strip mining]." Chris believes this will happen through pressure being put on the governor and legislators. "We want [MJS] to appear large and scary to the governor, to the general assembly, and to National Coal." He thinks chances for banning MTR in Tennessee are good "especially if we can form coalitions with hunters and four-wheelers and fishermen. The environmental community's not going to do it [alone]. If it ends up being just a bunch of tree-huggers, then we're going to lose." If Tennessee does pass such a measure, "I think maybe Kentucky will follow suit.

"So many people through miseducation have been pacified into thinking they can't fight back. Sometimes all it takes is an example of a few people who successfully do fight back and show that that's not true. Thoreau said that 'most men lead lives of quiet desperation.' I think everyone is living that right now. Everyone knows things are really messed up, but we've all been pacified into thinking that resistance is impossible—especially people in the coalfields. Not only can we fight back, but we outnumber the bastards ninety to ten, which is one of the secrets they don't want us to know. And fighting back is a lot of fun. And it's healthy. Edward Abbey said that the antidote to despair is direct action. It's not psychologically healthy for us to just internalize things and not fight back.

"A lot of people think that we're all conservative in these hills. I get that impression from these [activist] groups that are—I hate to say it but often from the North. It's a form of classism. I don't know how many times I've been told, basically: 'These dumb hillbillies don't understand direct action. They'll just freak out, and they're super-conservative.' But when you talk to them, you find out that they were using their pickup trucks to blockade [against mining companies during the strip mining boom of the 1970s]. They think that petitions and stuff are bullshit, but they recognize when you are using your body to lock yourself to the equipment and shut down mines. Too many people, especially college-educated people, have this Beverly Hillbillies crap in their mind." And the coal companies will use this, telling local people that these "outsiders" coming in "want to destroy your community."

Before leaving Tennessee, I revisit the woods near Caryville. It looks like early summer down in the valley by the highway now, but up here it's still spring. Maples are leafed out, oaks showing only reddish leaves. Blackberries are just coming into bloom. The night after I was last here, in April, an ice storm came through and froze the early growth off the trees up on top of the mountain but not down in the valley. The trees and shrubs up here have had to start over with leafing and haven't yet caught up.

I hear lots of birdsong this morning. The warbler migration has already come through—what I hear today are summer residents wrapping up their mating season and beginning to raise their young. A swarm of tadpoles is swimming in a puddle in the middle of the trail. I see elk prints (similar to whitetail deer but quite a bit larger) in the mud here, but no elk.

Under the thickening forest canopy, the spring ephemeral wildflower show is mostly over now: I see two fading yellow trilliums, some yellow buttercuppy flowers, patches of purple violets, purple geranium. May apple is now blooming, and a few white anemone. A glorious diversity of herbs has emerged from the forest floor since my last visit, many leaf sizes and shapes and plant habits. And now that the trees have leafed out, I can more fully appreciate their diversity too: buckeyes, maples, oaks, cherry trees, shagbark hickories, tulip poplars, pines. Trees of various ages tell me this forest hasn't been clear-cut in many decades, if ever, although stumps here and there and the lack of any really old trees affirm that it has been selectively logged.

Elk, tadpoles, wildflowers, birds, and diverse hardwoods tell me that even though this area has been logged repeatedly, and patches of it have been strip mined, the logging was selective enough to leave much of the soil intact and the mining was small-scale and patchy. Enough of the fabric of life here has remained intact for this rich, resilient ecosystem to heal itself and support most of the species that lived here before humans began altering this landscape.

Jim Massengill has told me that for generations local families owned and hung onto and managed much of the forest around here for timber so that it would continue to be an intact forest that could be selectively harvested in the future. He's deeply offended by the wave of careless logging going on in the region now. My first thought about this logging was that it must be the leading edge of mountaintop removal coming in. In fact, heedless clear-cutting began here in the late 1980s and accelerated in the 1990s as chip mills moved into the region, spreading north and inland from the coastal pinelands much as MTR is now spreading south from southern West Virginia and eastern Kentucky. Where the two creeping catastrophes meet, an ugly synergy is created: If there's little point in saving trees for their potential gain in value, when the only market you foresee is a chip mill, there's even less point in saving any when the land is about to be blown up under them. Prices for the low-grade wood fit only for chip mills are low right now, though—low enough that, as I've seen, sometimes timber clear-cut off MTR sites is simply burned or bulldozed aside. This makes a lot of people who love these forested mountains sick—and mad as hell.

A few days later, back in West Virginia, in Naoma, near where Bo lives, I stop by the house that's just been rented for the summer internship program. There I talk with Hillary Hosta, who'll be living there and managing things this summer. Plans for the program are focused along the Coal River and up the still-inhabited hollows branching up from the river. The hope is that once people elsewhere in West Virginia's coalfields see what's happening here, CRMW and OVEC and other activists will start hearing from them about what they want to do in their own areas and how the developing network of activists can help.

Hillary was born in Los Angeles and moved to Canada with her family when she was twelve. In the mid-1990s, when Hillary was still in college, she attended the first Ruckus camp, an activist gathering arranged by a founding Earth Firster, Mike Roselle. Five weeks later, Hillary hung her first banner, off a bridge in Seattle, and has continued as an activist ever since.

She moved to Appalachia this spring, and she's falling in love. "The landscape I am definitely loving," she says. "It's growing on me, very much. But it's the people who really, in a way, have broken my heart. Because you fall in love with them, and then your heart is broken because of what they're dealing with daily."

Hillary thinks change will begin to happen "when people here are aware that this relationship [between local Appalachians and coal companies] is inequitable and unnecessary. Many people here really feel like there are only two options: They live with this abuse and receive very, very little in return. Or they don't live with this abuse, they receive nothing, and they will have to leave their homes because they will have nothing. And then the coal companies can just come back in after they're gone, and strip it all. And they really don't believe that there's another option, and that's what so sad."

Coal River valley is "simmering" right now, Hillary says. "Maybe it's been simmering for some time, and I just got here and am noticing the undercurrents. Maybe people have been bubbling for a long time and just haven't had the spark, the event hasn't happened that's really made it bubble up over the top.

"Marsh Fork Elementary could be that [spark]. I think that's asking a lot from Marsh Fork as a campaign tool. I think that Marsh Fork will help us gain momentum, grow in size, grow the ranks of coalfield residents who have had enough. I think Marsh Fork is [also] a tool that can be used effectively to reach out to other people in the nation and the world. What makes it a beautiful campaign tool is how horrible, how terrible, what an atrocity it really is.

"One of our challenges is going to be when people from the outside world [who've learned about Marsh Fork] come in here and go: Why are you standing for this? Why are you taking this? Why is this happening? People [here] will want to defend their position—just like a wife will defend her [abusive] husband." What Bo calls the slave mentality, Hillary sees as the mentality of a battered woman defeated by her circumstances.

Recently Hillary watched *Matewan*, the John Sayles movie about coal miners' struggle for a decent life in Appalachia early in the twentieth century. She was struck by how "the power dynamics in the relationship between coal and these communities has not changed at all," and how then as now coal companies used much the same rhetoric about "outsiders" (then, mostly exploiting ethnic differences) to divide people who might otherwise be allies. "They're using that tactic today, using already-existing cultural prejudices and differences and fear about one another. Fear: the all-powerful tool of oppression. They're using fear of loss of economic stability, fear of loss of [jobs] to divide the community so that they don't unite and rise up as one to resist the oppression. Because they would win. Because the possibility of the power dynamic shifting [would] exist then."

Using fear this way also deflects anger at the coal companies toward other targets—toward those outsiders. "They're using the same tools because they still work. They're putting out propaganda saying: Oooh, be afraid of the ecoterrorists. These beautiful people who've given of themselves to do public service, some for ten years or more. Beautiful, harmless people who care about community and the world they live in. And they are putting the label 'terrorist' on them. It's really outrageous. And then they're hitting on the really cheap points where they know that there are social hang-ups that people have with one another," such as with hairstyle and clothing. "They're saying you need to be afraid about these differences, so you should be afraid of these people. They're using stereotypes that are easy homeruns for them because they're already there. The Birkenstock-wearing, patchouli-smelling hippies that don't pay taxes—those are some pretty strong stereotypes. It's not difficult for them to reinforce."

Hillary doesn't intend to remain an "outsider" here—she hopes she can stay for a while. Since she was eighteen, she's never stayed in any one place for more than ten months. But funding for the Naoma house and intern project runs out in September, and she says, "I need to be able to sustain myself. I own nothing. I don't own a TV. I don't own a bed. I would like to stay here beyond September, because I have so many campaign ideas. So many. They go beyond what I can accomplish in three months. And I do care about this place. I'd like to be here maybe for a few years working."

Judy Bonds recently attended a formative meeting for a new organization, Christians for the Mountains. "We talked about the need to have [churches] and religious leaders play a part in the care of the Creation," she tells me. "The care of the Creation is on the back burner [for most churches in America], and I've noticed a move on the religious right side [toward playing] a part in this. And I'm just thrilled. I believe that that is the salvation of the religious right. The religious right now is absolutely going against Jesus's teachings. And it breaks my heart. Not only that, it makes me ashamed. They actually are turning people away from Christianity instead of bringing people into the fold. A lot of activists have lost their faith because of the religious right. I've tried to tell people in the religious community: There's a lot of people out there who think we're hypocrites. [Where] the teachings of Jesus of love and understanding, caring for the sick and the elderly, caring for the people that are in prison, people that are lost [are concerned], it's as though the religious right has been hijacked by Satan.

"I honestly think that God cares a lot about that Creation—not just man, but everything He created. Everything in the Bible tells me so," Judy says. The Bible says that after God created everything else but not yet humankind, he looked around and saw that it was good. "Genesis 9:12 is one of my favorite scriptures," she says. "God said this is a covenant made between you and me and every living thing on Earth for perpetual generations—not just between myself and man, for now. I don't just care about man. I care about every living creature on this Earth. I think man has ignored that because of his own greed."

Judy was raised Free-Will Baptist. "Of course as I got older I went on my way and forgot about the church. I always believed in God, I always was a Christian, but it was something that didn't cut into my everyday life. This journey [fighting MTR] has taken me right back into my spirituality and to my Christianity. I truly believe that for any type of movement, particularly environmental movement, to gain momentum and to present its case effectively to the people of America, Christianity and the religious aspect [have] to be a part of it. I truly think there has to be a movement within the religious community to join in for this to work and for us to save this Earth, our children's future, God's Creation, and our souls. I truly believe that."

Judy believes that Americans today are "a generation that's addicted to comfort, to instant gratification, addicted to technology, addicted to everything that makes their life really easy," all of which creates a barrier, a buffer between the comfort-seeking individual and the natural world. "And I do think it's designed to be that way," she says, "particularly with the TV dumbing people down, particularly our children. All the games and technology that children have is to take their minds off nature and get back to what's 'really important,' and it keeps them in the house.

"I would like to bring Earth First! and the religious community closer together. Earth First! are doing God's work, they just don't realize it and they won't acknowledge it. I know a lot of people think this is funny." Judy doesn't. She respects the spirituality of john johnson, for example, and wants some of the legitimacy associated with conventional religion to rub off on Earth First!, which she thinks gets an unfairly bad rap. Judy believes that the pagan Earth Firsters doing God's work are going to have a much easier time of it with God in the next world than, say, the operator in Tennessee who hangs a giant "Jesus is Lord" sign on his coal silo.

"I've seen the look on some Earth Firsters' faces when you talk about God. But no matter where I go, I'm going to talk about the care of the Creation, because that's who I am. And when you quote Genesis [about the covenant between God and humankind and all the other creatures on Earth], you can see something in their eyes go: 'What? What? It says that in the Bible? That's pretty radical stuff.'"

In the 1990s, Judy and other anti-MTR activists could plausibly believe that momentum on this issue was going their way. Joe Lovett's lawsuits were resulting in settlements and rulings that, it seemed, would start to rein in MTR. Even in West Virginia's notoriously pro-coal state government, in spring 2001 a fellow named Matt Crum took charge of the DEP's enforcement of environmental regulations violated by coal companies in West Virginia. Crum actually enforced the law—for example, by encouraging inspectors to shut down mining operations responsible for blackwater spills (spills of chemical-laden liquid waste from processing coal) until they fixed the problem causing the spill. In the past, inspectors had felt pressured to turn a blind eye to such violations.

Around this time, Judy recalls, "We [anti-MTR activists] had decided: Now is the time for civil disobedience, and people of faith need to be the first people to do this. We all agreed on that, and we were in the process of picking a place, and the perfect site, and the perfect circumstance for this to happen—because you don't just pull something out of your hat." And then terrorists took down the World Trade Center, on September 11, 2001. "It set everything back. It seemed like that was all everyone could think about. The newspapers, the media paid no attention to anything but 9/11."

Still, she was anxious to move forward with their plans. MTR was continuing, accelerating, and delay meant more and more destruction. "I was impatient, and everyone said no, now's not the time to do this, let's just wait a while. So we got back into our comfort zone—fighting permits, going to permit hearings, a lawsuit."

By 2003, Judy and other anti-MTR activists knew that testifying at hearings was getting them nowhere, and that anti-MTR lawsuit results were apt to be overturned on appeal. By then, it was also increasingly obvious that the Bush administration was failing to live up to previous settlements and apparently hellbent on weakening the mining regulations that they already were systematically failing to enforce. At the state level, things looked no better: In August 2003, incoming DEP head Stephanie Timmermeyer fired Matt Crum and restored cozier relations between the DEP and coal companies.

Matters did not improve in 2004. Apparently not content with failing to enforce the stream-buffer-zone rule, in January 2004 the Bush administration proposed changing the rule to grant mining companies variances that would let them off the hook if they *tried* not to mine closer than 100 feet from streams "to the extent possible, using the best technology currently available." The best technology *imaginable* can't make it practical to stay a hundred feet from a stream if a valley fill is planned, so in effect what the Bush administration was proposing was to exempt mountaintop removal operations from the buffer rule.

The pattern of anti-MTR legal rulings heading for slapdown on appeal continued through 2004 as well. Back in October 2003, Joe Lovett had filed suit in federal court seeking to bar the Army Corps of Engineers from issuing any more of its Nationwide 21 permits for any proposed MTR operations, regardless of the size of the proposed valley fill. (Both CRMW and OVEC were parties to this suit.) In July 2004, Judge Joseph R. Goodwin ruled that such permits violate the Clean Water Act and could no longer be used anywhere in his district, the Southern District of West Virginia. In September, the Bush administration announced that it would appeal Judge Goodwin's ruling to the 4th Circuit Court of Appeals. Meanwhile, the Corps was failing to obey Judge Goodwin's ruling, and the judge refused Joe Lovett's motions to compel them to do so.

In November 2004, President George W. Bush won re-election. The coal industry could count on four more years of proven friends in power in Washington. Judy and others fighting MTR couldn't afford to wait those four years out. MTR was destroying their home places. They needed to act now. And so the Mountain Justice Summer campaign began.

The coming summer is filled with unknowns, and Judy is reluctant to predict how it might turn out. "The biggest vision I have is bringing it to a national level, working the religious component, working with Mountain Justice Summer and all the [volunteers from] different states coming in," while she and Bo and Dave Cooper and others continue to work the roadshow outside the coalfields. "I see all these components working together. I'm not placing my hopes on one thing. You have to make them all happen, and they have to fit together."

Judy would like to see MJS in West Virginia drop banners and stealthily put signs in strategic places—"because, believe me, people in the coalfields appreciate humor, and appreciate a little bit of an outlaw, people who dare to stand up." This shouldn't really be seen as "outlaw" behavior, but instead as free people being free to express themselves openly. In the coalfields that makes you somewhat an outlaw. "A lot of people, particularly if they're not from Appalachia, have not figured out that central Appalachia's a banana republic, plain and simple. It is not like being in America. The same rules do not apply." That's why the effort to bring national attention to mountaintop removal and all its ill effects is so important. If Americans outside the region understand that this is happening *in America*, Judy and other coalfield activists hope and believe that good people everywhere will find that unacceptable and won't allow it to continue.

Judy has believed for years that civil disobedience is a key for bringing this to national attention. "We know we're taking a chance," she says, "but what else do you do? If you continue to do what you have done," plug along in your activist comfort zone of writing letters and going to permit hearings, "and you come up against a stone wall, and every option that you have is blocked, you've got to go to the next step. We've run out of options. And so it's come to MJS."

I ask Judy how is it that she, unlike most of her neighbors, is willing to stick her neck out and fight MTR? "It was the protection of my family, my grandson and daughter, that got me involved in this. And my home place. And the outrage and the anger. The outrage turned to anger then back to outrage then to frustration and anger again. Then it led to understanding, and education. Every morning I'd wake up with coal dirt on my car. And then I got to looking in my house and the coal dirt was everywhere. It permeated everything. And then I got to thinking: Does everybody live like this? And then I educated myself and I became even more outraged.

"My mother was a very strong Appalachian woman, very outspoken." Both of her grandmothers "were also very strong, very outspoken." She attributes this partly to Cherokee culture, as her Scotch-Irish ancestor who first came to this region, before most Native Americans were forced out, married a Cherokee woman "and Cherokee women had a lot of autonomy. When she married into the Scotch-Irish family, she lost that public autonomy, that public respect, that public place of leadership." But not necessarily in private. Judy thinks that Cherokee background is what drives a lot of the Appalachian women involved in the fight against MTR, as many of them count Cherokee women among their ancestors. "I'd always heard there's an old saying in Cherokee, and it's Appalachian [too], that while the men sat around the campfire and talked about what to do, the women got out and done it."

On the other hand, she says she blames "a lot of this materialistic culture on women. The men like the power and the profit. But for a man to keep that trophy wife, he has to provide that trophy with all the beautiful trimmings. And she craves that. I've noticed a lot of the women of the coal miners [want] tanning beds and diamond rings and fancy cars and fancy shoes, plenty of clothes. I know that, because I was there once. There's never enough—always more, more, more, more."

Judy knows her Cherokee ancestors and her anger at how her home and family have been affected are good reasons why she should fight against MTR, but they don't fully explain why she has devoted her life to this. What sent her down this path remains, ultimately, a mystery. "I don't know. I just feel compelled to do it. I try to touch it, but it's something I can't touch. It escapes my grasp, every time I try to touch it. Now I can't ever go back. Because I know the truth now.

"You're not going to get every coalfield person, just like you're not going to get every American." In a way, though, Judy and her colleagues have already "got" most of their coalfield neighbors—most people know that MTR is not a good thing. The hard part is "getting them active, motivated to do something."

I ask Judy whether she thinks that maybe everyone involved in MJS or any kind of activist work that seeks to change the world is a misfit in some way. We're not comfortable with things the way they are, and that makes us more prone to act than our neighbors, who for whatever reason are better able to go along with the status quo.

"I think *they're* the misfits," she says. "I think we're the normal people. They've caught a disease, and they're not even aware of that. They're addicted to comfort." Looking at the big picture, Judy's right—only for a few decades out of all of human history has even the minority of humans in the fully industrialized world been able to view such a level of consumption as "normal," and this won't last. Their grandchildren won't live like they do. "We're trying to change that [mindset] before they get a rude awakening," she says. Changing that mindset and lifestyle before the resources needed to make that change are desperately depleted "is a lot easier than doing it [like] Mad Max.

"We're reaching out to college students, and trying to get the college students to reach out to the high school students because they're the ones going to be faced with this awful future of no resources and a mess to clean up." Judy's also trying to reach parents. "We're selling our children's feet to buy ourselves fancy shoes."

It's ironic that people seen by much of the rest of the world as ignorant hillbillies are so far ahead of most Americans in understanding this. Judy points this out when she's doing roadshows. After explaining to the audience why it's important to pass the Clean Water Protection Act (which would affirm that the law against burying streams applies to mining), she'll say: 'I think it's awful ironic that us ignorant hillbillies have to teach America about the Clean Water Act and the importance of having clean water.' Some people find it funny. Some people *don't* find it funny. And some people—it goes over their head."

Appalachia, because it's been passed by and in many ways left behind by mainstream modern culture, retains remnants of older culture useful for making a transition to ways of living well that don't depend on far-reaching consumption and destruction. Part of this is local lore about subsistence, about hunting and gardening and the wealth of edible and medicinal plants and other renewable resources in the woods here. But part also is habits of mind and living that don't depend on spending money. For example, entertainment is traditionally seen here as something you do for yourself and the people you know, not something you buy. This was the way it was "for eons, until the industrialized world came," Judy says. "People did entertain themselves. Setting on a porch, in a swing, or just setting there listening to the birds. Looking at the wildlife. Going for a walk. Walking up the road and saying 'Hi, how're you doing, neighbor?' Talking to your neighbor and looking out for your neighbor's children. It doesn't exist anymore except in a very few places in the country, particularly here. Here you can still see people setting on porches and talking." That it still exists here is because corporate America didn't deem Appalachia important enough to fully commercialize life here as it has elsewhere. There are no shopping malls or multiplexes along Coal River. That there's anything of the older way of life here, that it hasn't been displaced as it has elsewhere in the country, is an accident of neglect. "Lucky us." Judy isn't being ironic. She really means it.

A New Movement

There's been a school at the site of Marsh Fork Elementary since the 1940s. When Judy Bonds was a student there, in the mid-1960s, it was a middle school. She remembers that the school was rebuilt after being partly destroyed by fire in the 1950s, then rebuilt and expanded after another fire in the late 1960s or early 1970s. It became an elementary school in the 1990s.

The school is the lone survivor in the Coal River valley of a series of school closings and consolidations that began in the late 1960s, in tandem with depopulation of the valley after the mostly boom years in coal mining—from the 1940s to the early 1960s—ended. Depopulation accelerated in the 1980s as MTR began, as many families were forced from their homes by mining operations or lost their jobs to mechanization and out-of-state hiring. What population remains here now is concentrated along Rt. 3, as most of the hollows along the streams that feed, or formerly fed, the Coal River have been taken over by MTR operations.

When Judy was in middle school, the high school football team played on what is now Marsh Fork Elementary School's athletic field. On nights when games were played, you couldn't find a place to park within a mile of the school along Rt. 3. "Friday night football was really big," Judy remembers. "Not everybody went to the same church, but everybody went to the same school. The school was a real close tie, for our sense of community.

"When I went to school here, there was no mining around this school whatsoever. [At] football games, you could look up on the hill and see people with bonfires up there watching the football game from the top of the mountain. It was kind of comforting to look up there and see those people standing up there." Now that mountainside is off-limits to all but Massey employees working the enormous mountaintop removal site just over the ridge.

That MTR site feeds coal to the Goals Coal prep plant, a Massey subsidiary, where coal is washed with water and chemicals by the river right next to the school. Coal moving along the prep plant's conveyor belts and into and out of its coal silo sheds dust and chemicals into the air just 150 feet from the school grounds. The byproduct of the coal's washing, called slurry or sludge—black goo laden with toxins—gets pumped up into the 2.8 billion gallon slurry pond back behind the 385-foot earthen dam that looms over the plant and the school.

Construction on the dam began in 1985. "Of course I did not know that in '85," Judy says. "A lot of people did not know that dam existed—thought it was a few buildings up there, and they's loading coal up there. I didn't find out about that dam until 1997 or 1998, when I found out about the one [down the river] at Marfork [and] someone said: 'Well, don't you know there's a dam over the elementary school?'

"The coal companies really do not want anyone to see what they're doing, don't want anyone to know what's going on in Appalachia. It's as though we're the coal companies' private serfdom. And that's how they treat us: 'How dare you! Don't look at that.'"

If you did dare to look, if you hiked up through what was left of the mountains here in 2005 and picked your way through the mine sites, here's what you would have seen: A long tramp through woods gets you to a long drainage ditch that feeds into the sludge pond. (Yes, the pond collects rainwater runoff from the mine site as well as sludge from the prep plant. No, this is not a safe design.) Follow the ditch downhill, clamber over the Massey access road that circles the pond (watch out for trucks on patrol), and continue along the ditch to where it empties into the sludge pond. Seen from maybe a quarter mile back from the dam, the top of the dam's wall looks pretty high above where you're standing—exactly how high is hard to guess, though, since scale is hard to reckon on enormous MTR sites devoid of natural features. The pond—a lake, really—is irregularly shaped and too big for you to see all of it at once when you're standing at the edge. Where you're standing, trees line the edge of the pond. The top layer of liquid on the sludge pond is oily, black, opaque, ugly.

If there's blasting today anywhere nearby, you'll surely feel it here. Blasting at the MTR site behind Bo's house a while back shook Ed Wiley's house several *miles* up the river. Since that blasting took place about midway between Ed's house and this sludge pond, Ed worries that what rattled his house might also have damaged the dam. In addition, a great deal of other blasting has taken place much closer to the pond.

In some places, dead trees stick out of the pond near its edge, having been submerged as the pond filled. As the trees rot, they'll break off and could clog the overflow system intended to ease liquid out of the pond during times when runoff from rain is heavy. If that system gets clogged, the uncontrolled rush of water could overwhelm the dam. This and other potential dam-failure scenarios worry parents enough that some won't send their kids to school on days when heavy rain is forecast.

On your way to and from the sludge pond, you'll pass by active mine sites with miners at work. But not very many miners. This whole mining complex, including the sludge pond, the prep plant by the school, and all the 1,849 acres of surface mine sites feeding it, employs perhaps 60 to 80 workers. Maybe twenty to twenty-five more miners work in a nearby underground mine that also feeds the prep plant. Surprisingly, you don't see much coal being taken out of the strip sites. Most of the thick, easy-to-reach coal seams were mined out of Appalachia long ago. The seams you'll see exposed here now are thinner and seem hardly worth the effort of removing hundreds of feet of mountain to reach them. Still, they work these sites 24-7, using floodlights at night. (If you're leaving the sludge pond toward sunset, pause where you can look back down on it to see the reflected sunlight off the sludge, a spectacularly unnatural and oddly beautiful effect.) You ought to be well camouflaged and careful as you pass by the active sites, as security tends to be more vigilant there, where there's so much expensive equipment vulnerable, than at the sludge pond.

Back in the woods you'll see a great deal of dust, in the air and on the ground, with no evidence of either current or recent spraying of water to keep dust down as required by mining permits. The trees that you're walking among will probably be gone soon, likely burned rather than harvested for lumber or even firewood. Wasted forest, wasted mountains and hollows and streams. Only the memory remains of places that used to be here—Clay's Branch, Shumate Hollow—places where hundreds of local people, many now displaced from their former homes, grew up exploring and hunting.

At 11:30 AM on Tuesday, May 24, 2005, about two dozen people have gathered in front of Marsh Fork Elementary School, clustered under a big oak tree that looks like it's dying—perhaps poisoned by the particulates and chemicals emitted by the prep plant next door. It's raining when I arrive, but it soon stops.

Reporters have been invited here today, and Bo Webb tries out his talking-to-media spiel on me: "I'm here because for the past year and a half—gosh, longer than that—we've been trying to bring attention to the abuses of these kids at the school by this mine company. We've gone to the West Virginia Department of Health and Human Resources, the county health department, the West Virginia Department of Environmental Protection, the governor's office, the county school board, the state school board, and the federal EPA, various politicians— and they keep passing the buck.

"We filed [under the] Freedom of Information Act for the MSHA reports on the sludge dam. I've got some of them with me. The dam has various leaks. The toe of the dam is leaking, which is one of the most dangerous places. The downstream foundation of the dam is leaking. There's widespread leaks all over the dam, and we think it's time to stand up and get attention. Someone is not doing their job. They're either being paid off by the coal company, they're intimidated by the coal company, or they don't want to stop progress—or maybe they just do not want to admit that the school's here. But it's not just the schoolkids that are in danger [according to] these MSHA reports. It's everyone downstream. That dam's holding back 2.8 billion gallons, and there's a lot of lives that they're playing Russian roulette with here. So that's why I'm here today.

"I want a government that has the authority—and I believe the federal EPA has the authority—to shut down this mine site, shut down that dam, dry it out, cap it, and throw them [Massey] out of here. They should not be allowed to mine in this state. They have more violations, Massey Energy does, than all other coal companies combined in West Virginia. I think that they have lost the right to mine coal in this state, in my opinion. Anyone that abuses these kids like they have been doing should be shut down. If [another company] wants at some future date to mine coal underground up there, responsibly, we would not be opposed to that. But we want the kids moved out of that school, we want the school torn down because it is laden with chemicals and toxins, and we want another school built up the road, upstream."

Most of the people here today are longtime locals, like Bo, but some "outsiders" are here to support them, including Hillary and the interns now living just up the road in Naoma, as well as a carload from Tennessee—Chris and Paloma, Gena (one of Chris's fellow law students, very active in the fight against MTR in Tennessee), and john johnson, whose role today is to provide security for cars.

CRMW's Patty Sebok arrived here early today, she tells me, and soon afterward a car carrying two state troopers pulled up. (State police told CRMW the day before that they'd be there, to make sure the demonstrators were safe from traffic on the road, which typically travels quite fast.) "I showed them the pictures [aerial views of the sludge pond looming over the school] and I started telling them the story about what sits behind the school and what's going on.

"They said that they had heard rumors that there was a camp going on, an action camp," referring apparently to the weeklong MJS training camp that's to begin near Pipestem, West Virginia, this evening. "And they said that they were concerned because they heard it was the 'earth movement people.' And I said, 'Well, I don't know who the earth movement people are, and he said, 'Well, they blow up power lines and things like that.' And I said, 'Well, I'm not going to blow up the power line—I wouldn't have any power!' And he started laughing, and kind of got relaxed a little bit. And he said, 'You all are our people,' and I said 'That's right.'"

Debbie Jarrell, Ed Wiley's wife, tells me: "I've lived here all my life. Generations of my family have lived here. I have a ten-year-old granddaughter inside the [school] building right now. The reason we're here is not only the slurry pond, not only the prep plant, or the silo, or them wanting to put another silo right beside that. How much poison do our kids need? It's time for the community to put their foot down. And that's why I'm here."

Melissa Beckner moved here only about four years ago, she tells me. Her daughter goes to this school. "She had the little childhood sicknesses, but she never was really sick until she started kindergarten [here] last year, and she has been sick ever since. She has to take [medication] for allergies and asthma, she keeps a headache, she keeps a sore throat, a stomachache. And I didn't know, I thought it was just her," until Ed and Debbie told her about other kids at the school being sick. And not just the kids are sick. "I keep headaches," Melissa says, "just from being around here. I didn't keep headaches until I moved down here. And I keep sore throat, upset stomach. It's from being around here. I mean, I live down here. We just want to save our kids, and keep them safe."

CRMW—primarily Bo and Ed—went door to door recently to try to get a handle on how many kids at the school have health problems. "There *are* a lot of sick kids," Bo says. "Sore throats, coming home with headaches, coughs. Sometimes the next morning they're OK, and they'll come home from school and it'll be the same thing. Sometimes they'd be like that all week, and then the weekends they'd feel better, and then Monday when they went back to school they would start feeling worse." Of 125 homes surveyed, 60 had kids attending Marsh Fork Elementary. Of those sixty, fifty-three had children with health problems, mostly respiratory (asthma, chronic bronchitis) but also symptoms such as headache and nausea that get better when the child is away from school. In addition, several students, former students, and teachers have contracted unusual cancers in recent years. Some have died.

Larry Gibson's here today too, down from Kayford half an hour or so away. He's holding a sign that says: "Remember Buffalo Creek—125 dead." "My family lost sixty-six people to the Buffalo Creek disaster in 1972 because of coal," he tells me. Larry's father's family had been there for generations. "You got this over here," he says, pointing to the coal processing plant, "and you got the impoundment above the school. How safe do you think these kids are? It doesn't take a rocket scientist to figure out what they're doing here is wrong."

The comparison with the Buffalo Creek disaster isn't unduly alarmist. Here as there, the dam is flawed—different flaws, but potentially fatal just the same. And here as there, the coal company knows the dam is flawed. "I helped build [this] dam," says Jackie Browning, another local man attending the protest today. "I was the main dozer operator on that dam, from '94 to '99 till I got disabled from chemicals.

"A lot of [the dam] has got big mud pots in it. You have to compact a dam. Back when they used trucks to haul the refuse [the ungraded mine wastes used to build the dam] up there, you had to put the refuse down in two-foot lifts and it had to meet a strict compaction test. And that determines the strength of that dam. Well, when they put the belt line up there [in 1997, to transport the mine waste previously hauled by the trucks], the belt carried lots of water with the refuse." In rainy weather, "you'd start to push that slate across that dam" from where the belt brought it, maybe 150 feet in from one side, push it across the top of the dam, 960 feet wide, toward the other side. "You've already got water in that slate. You have to push from the belt head over 800 feet. You cannot, on these rainy days, push that far without hanging up—you can't get all the way across." But you have to keep hauling what the belt delivers, so the loads of slate-mud-water pile up maybe 200 feet from the far side of the dam. Mud oozes out of the pile into the resulting low spot between the growing pile and the far side, "and that thing just fills up with this soft mud, like jelly." When the weather improves, the belt starts delivering waste without so much water, "and you just start filling that [low spot] in," right over the mud. "There's no compaction there. Underneath there's a big deck of Jello." And Jello, of course, is not a good structural material. "How come when they used trucks they had to meet a compaction test? It was strict. Now they use dozers to push, they do not compact proper at all, and nobody worries about it." Inspectors don't come when it's raining, and when they do come, it looks fine and they're told everything *is* fine. "On paper, they'll say everything's passing. But it's not. I went down [about two months ago] and talked to them, and the engineer told me, 'We know we've got problems.'"

Jackie is also keenly aware of how toxic the chemicals used at the plant really are. He's badly disabled from his own exposure to them, and wonders what they're doing to the children attending school here. "I was down at the plant [working] on the coal pile for a little while," he says, just a short distance from the school, "and that's where I got the exposure. The last six weeks that I worked they increased the chemicals, about three or four times what they's supposed to, in order to get that real fine coal out. The more chemicals they use, the more coal they can recover. They increased so high that my system couldn't stand it. It's just like I drank acid, it just ate me up." Since then, Jackie has been plagued by multiple chemical sensitivity and a range of neurological and respiratory symptoms.

By just before noon, close to sixty people have gathered in front of the school. Four police cars are here. Several of the protesters, including

Bo's daughter, Sarah Haltom, are carrying cameras to document whatever happens. Local TV and radio reporters are here, too.

Chris Irwin, Judy Bonds, Hillary, and a couple of others are holding a large banner reading "Massey Energy Corporation Raping Our Homeland" as the demonstration prepares to move up the road from the school toward the driveway and gate of the coal facility. The demonstrators line up along the road in front of the school, holding up signs so people in passing cars can read them. Some drivers, a few dozen over the next hour or so, honk their support as they go by.

At noon the procession starts up the road, with Bo in the lead, alongside Jackie Browning, who looks a bit nervous. At the entrance to Goals Coal two police cars have stopped traffic in both directions. Another police car is parked in the plant's driveway, which is closed to deliveries right now. (They've also got a back entrance, so the demonstration may be inconvenient but isn't actually shutting the facility down.) Demonstrators and the big banner stretch across the driveway in front of the gate, but at the request of police, they refrain from blocking it completely.

When everyone has reached the plant entrance, and the police have allowed traffic to resume on the road, Bo speaks to the crowd, followed by Jackie and then Judy. "It is time to join together to halt this destructive mining practice that destroys our homes, communities, and Appalachian mountains and culture," Judy says. "From across Appalachia and the entire country, Americans are building a strong movement called Mountain Justice Summer. Who is Mountain Justice Summer?" The crowd shouts back: "We are!"

"We are the ones whose homes are being blasted," Judy continues, "whose homes are being dusted, whose children are being poisoned every day. We are everyday citizens who have been abused and denied our rights for over 130 years. It's a shame that we have to beg our government for our basic human rights, to live in our homes in peace and send our children to a clean school without fear of being poisoned or crushed to death by a dam. We welcome all of our brothers and sisters that will join us to fight for justice for mountain people this summer and beyond. Welcome, Mountain Justice Summer."

Next, Bo reminds the crowd that two days from now representatives from the state DEP will hold a hearing at the school. "Massey has applied to build another silo identical to that monstrosity over there, right next to it," he says. "Give our kids some more coal dust and chemicals, I guess. They haven't killed them with that one, they want to speed it up." Bo asks everyone here to come to the hearing. "We want them to do their jobs. We want that sludge dam shut down and dried out. Take their license away! They don't have the right to have a license in this state!"

Debbie Jarrell addresses the crowd briefly, describing the siting of the silos as "pure arrogance" and reading a list of demands, including: 1) that the coal processing plant beside the school be shut down; 2) that the school be cleaned up or a new, safe school be built nearby, in "*our* community," not a long drive away like the other schools that have replaced those closed in the valley; 3) that Massey withdraw its request to build a second silo; 4) that Massey stop blasting that affects local homes; and 5) that Massey shut down all of its surface (strip) mine sites.

It's now shortly after 12:30. The protesters move to line both sides of the driveway but, cooperating with the police, still refrain from blocking it. Bo and Judy walk across the bridge and up the driveway to deliver the list of demands to Massey.

"You know, that was so strange," Judy tells me later. "[At first,] no one stopped us, so we just kept going. And all of a sudden the police said: 'Whoa, whoa, wait a minute! Where are you going?' And then here came the two Massey employees [security guards], and they just completely ignored me. Here I was, a woman standing there—and I was invisible to them. All they wanted to see was the male. And I'm glad Bo was there and said what he said, but I just kept listening and watching because I thought: 'OK, I'm being peaceful, I'm gonna listen.' So I did.

"I could have just kept going. That really would have got their attention. But I never thought about that. There was a calmness and a peacefulness in me. I felt like I was doing the right thing."

Bo and Judy ask that someone in authority come out to receive and discuss the list of demands. Massey security people say no one will meet with them, and ask them to leave. By now, Judy says, one of the guards "was becoming a smart-aleck, and he was beginning to make Bo very angry. Bo controlled his anger pretty well though, until the man took his hands and fluttered them out like we were insects and said: 'Go on, go on, get off here. You're trespassing. If you don't leave, we're gonna arrest you.' And the policeman said: 'It's over.' And Bo said: 'No! Trespassing? You say *I'm* trespassing? If you think I'm trespassing, then I want you to keep your coal dust and your flyrock off my property, *Marty*,'" calling the security guard by name.

"And at that point I had to bite my tongue to keep from laughing," Judy recalls. The guard said: " 'Go away, go away, you!' And so Bo said, 'You know, I'm not going anywhere. What happens if I just stand here?' And the policeman said: 'Well, we'll just have to arrest you.' Bo said, 'I reckon you're gonna have to arrest me.' And then the policeman looked at me and said, 'What are you gonna do?' And I said: 'Well, I'm with him.' So they took Bo, got him by his arm and walked him away. No one even come near me," Judy continues. "No one put their hands on me. They acted like I wasn't even there." (Bo sees this a little differently: "I really believe it's because they did not want to arrest Judy Bonds," he later tells me. "They know she's a powerful force.") "So I looked at the policeman and I said: 'What do you want me to do?' He said: 'Oh! Just follow this way.'"

It feels sad to see them led away. When I tell Bo this later he says: "That's good. That's good that that was the effect."

On the way to the car, Judy continues, "I said a prayer thanking God for the safety of the people [at the demonstration] and asking Him to watch over everyone while we were gone, that they would do what they should be doing, stay calm, and not get in trouble." When Bo and Judy reached the police car, "they had no idea where they were gonna put me, so they finally cleared out the front seat. They were stunned,"

Judy thinks, about having to arrest them, "and they were really very respectful."

Meanwhile, the crowd is chanting: "Massey close the plant." The driveway re-opens for business, and a cement truck comes on through.

The police car holding Bo and Judy drives away, heading for the state police substation downriver near Whitesville. "I have to say the ride to Whitesville was scary," Judy says. "That was the scariest part of the day"—though not because she's just been arrested, but because of the driver's speed. "That guy flew!"

At the police station Bo and Judy are charged with trespassing and are released after the demonstration disperses. The police apologize for having had to arrest them.

Later that day, at 8:30 PM, not much more than an hour's drive away, sixty-eight people gather in the dining hall at the Appalachian Folklife Center near Pipestem, West Virginia, for the opening circle of Mountain Justice Summer's training camp. (Two more MJSers are stationed at a table near where the driveway enters the camp. They're being cautious about security. Already either law enforcement or coal company operatives are keeping an eye on the camp. As I drove into camp for the first time myself, I passed a black sedan with tinted windows with a man in the driver's seat talking on a cellphone, parked in a good position to note the license plates of cars heading to camp.) The group here tonight includes most of the faces I've been seeing at MJS meetings, plus quite a few new ones. It's a young crowd. While many of those who've been organizing MJS these past months are in their thirties, the majority of people here at camp are in their twenties; only a very few older people, in their forties and fifties, are here. There are more men than women, but not overwhelmingly so. Dress trends toward hippie or crusty punk or camouflage, with an overlay of hiking/camping gear.

One by one, going around the circle, the MJSers identify themselves and state what they hope the campaign will accomplish this summer. Larry Gibson says: "My people are an oppressed people," and it's hard to reach oppressed people who don't know they're oppressed. It's MJS's work to reach them. Nineteen years ago, when he first started fighting MTR, he says he "couldn't get two people together" to work with him. He's deeply touched, teary, to see so many people here today. Later he tells me: "Before, for so many years, I would look behind me and I wouldn't see anyone. When I first started talking about this, I couldn't even get my own family to listen to me."

Most of the other people in the circle simply state their names and give brief, one-sentence summaries of what they'd like to see this summer. Abigail Singer, an Earth First! activist who's lived in Knoxville off and on for several years and has been involved with MJS since its beginnings, wants to "inspire the rest of the country to transition to a sustainable lifestyle." One of the Asheville organizers says: "What I'd like to see is National Coal Company's stock prices drop like a rock." Hyena, from Kentucky, wants to work on developing "a real clear picture" of the way of life we want to have, not just what's wrong with what we do have.

john johnson's supposed to deliver a rabble-rousing rant after the go-around. Instead, he starts crying. Like Larry, he's touched to see so many people here—and he says *more* people are coming. He says he hopes that MJS will be the spark that begins the end of the "death machine that's gripping the entire planet." MTR, john says, represents everything that's wrong with the modern industrial commodity-market way of life. He says he doesn't have much of a "spiritual practice," but believes that "the mountains are asking for our help."

More campers arrive overnight, bringing the total at breakfast to about eighty. Workshops scheduled for today cover nonviolence and de-escalation training, MTR issue education, and mountain culture and cultural-sensitivity issues. All are mandatory for anyone here who wants to participate in the coming campaign.

Also relating to cultural sensitivity, a "potty mouth jar" has been set up in the camp's main meeting hall and dining room. Anyone who cusses (defined as using a word you would not use in talking to someone else's grandmother) owes 25 cents—and the fine is 50 cents for each "Jesus Christ!" or "Goddamn!" The idea behind this is to train MJSers from outside the region not to inadvertently offend religious, personally conservative locals. Because the language of many of the folks here is customarily pretty salty, this turns out to be a pretty good fundraiser as well as a cultural sensitivity tool.

At lunch, I catch up with Dave Cooper, who just arrived this morning. Dave gave a talk in Louisville last night, then stopped at home to get some sleep with the intention of driving here in the morning and arriving midday. "I woke up at 2:30 in the morning. I was so excited I couldn't get back to sleep, so I just got in the car at 3:00 and was driving all night." Finding more than eighty people here was "a dream come true," he says. "We worked really hard to get to this point, there's real good energy here, the weather's nice, it's a beautiful spot, everybody's in a good mood—so we're off to a really good start."

Chris Irwin, too, thinks MJS is off to a good start, his ambitious goal earlier this year of thirty or forty full-time MJS volunteers looking pretty realistic now. "I think maybe 30 percent of the people here will travel from place to place" for the whole summer, he says. "But then another 35 to 40 percent are going to [stay in one place]—like we're going straight back to Tennessee [after the camp concludes] to begin our organizing and preparing." The number of full-time MJSers (staff, in effect) "make us the largest nonprofit staffed organization fighting mountaintop removal in America. Ever." The turnout comes as a relief to Chris, "after all this hard work, months and months, and thinking: Good God, there's going to be 20 people that'll actually show up. And that was a real danger, because I think a lot of people still don't know what MTR is. If Americans were more aware, I think we'd have a thousand people here."

When I catch up with john outside the dining hall, he tells me: "I'm high as a kite. Not on—well, maybe a little bit of caffeine, but nothing else. There's a great crew of people here. I'm totally impressed with how engaged people are." In the past, john's seen forest-defense camps where a good many people seemed most interested in partying. Here, today, people are focused on the work at hand. "People are taking it real seriously," john says. "I'm totally pleased."

Chris Dodson, now one of the interns at the Naoma house, tells me: "Exactly what we're all going to be doing [at the house] is going to become more clear when we can all get together and plan it all out. Everybody's sort of coming from a different place. But my perception of it is that we're going to be assisting with logistical stuff for MJS when MJS is in the area. And beyond that, we're going to be doing similar things to what CRMW and OVEC have been doing, in organizing that community, Coal River valley, specifically with regards to Marsh Fork Elementary. There's probably going to be a lot of door-to-door, a lot of hearings and stuff. But then my vision, also, is to have MJS things being coordinated with the community, and hopefully from the community." And he hopes that the program at the Naoma house will not shy away from civil disobedience.

"I bet that we could really make change at Marsh Fork. I don't think they're going to build another silo. They're trying to, but we're kicking their ass. They're not going to. And I think it's possible for that whole facility to be done. Soon."

That afternoon, I sit in on Dave Cooper's MTR 101 workshop, adapted from his roadshow. Like the roadshow, today's workshop relies on slides, accompanied by Dave's narration of facts about MTR: MTR in West Virginia is concentrated south of Charleston, west of Beckley. MTR uses explosives made of ammonium nitrate (a common chemical fertilizer) and diesel fuel—the same powerful mix that was used to bomb the federal building at Oklahoma City. Most of the land, and by far most of the forested mountains in West Virginia, is controlled by out-of-state owners, typically coal or timber or land-holding companies. Appalachia's mixed mesophitic forest is the most biologically diverse hardwood forest in the world. MTR is profitable only because coal companies are allowed to externalize so many of its costs. Coal companies called the fatal 1972 Buffalo Creek sludge-dam disaster an "act of God." The slurry pond looming over Marsh Fork Elementary School overlies old underground mines—if it breaks through to the mines below, millions of gallons of sludge will gush through the old mines and blow out a huge flood God knows where. Lespedeza, the exotic grass typically planted on "reclaimed" MTR sites is, in addition to being ugly, inedible to livestock and wildlife. MTR brings poverty and depopulation not only because it employs so few people but also because the ill effects of MTR preclude other economic activities.

Dave Cooper generally tries to bring coalfield locals along to speak at his roadshows. Today he's joined by Larry Gibson and Pauline Canterbury, a seventy-five-year-old resident of Sylvester, the next town down the Coal River from Whitesville. Pauline's (and Sylvester's) main problem is coal dust. In 1997 Massey got permission to put a processing plant in Sylvester. The plant is built just upwind of the town, where a bluff used to shield the town from wind. In building the plant Massey blasted off the bluff, and as soon as the plant began to operate, airborne coal dust began to fall on Sylvester. *Lots* of coal dust. (Pauline's attic has so much coal dust in it that it's a fire hazard.) Pauline and her neighbor Mary Miller (who call themselves "the Dustbusters") collected dust samples daily for two years. They took their evidence to state officials and to the federal Office of Surface Mining. They took Massey to court and got an injunction. Massey built a multimillion dollar fabric dome over the plant—and still the dust rains down on Sylvester.

"We're being sacrificed for cheap energy for the rest of the world," Pauline tells the MJS group. "Our homes have lost 90 percent of their value because of MTR mining. Their goal is to get us out because flat land is hard to find in West Virginia," and Sylvester is a fairly wide, flat place in the valley, potentially useful for processing plants, storage depots, and other coal-related facilities. But coal dust is not their only problem. The Coal River now runs at just a trickle when it's not raining, because so much water is being taken out to wash coal—and then pumped up into giant slurry dams like the one by Marsh Fork Elementary and another up behind her home. There are no escape routes from the valley should any of these huge dams break. Locals can't even go to visit their ancestors' graves without a coal company escort, as old graveyards were mostly sited high up and many are now surrounded by strip mining.

"It does my heart so good to see all you young people here," she says. "This is your world. I'm just sorry that I'm leaving it like we are."

Pauline is followed by Larry. "When we go into this" summer, he says, "above all we've got to be right," to do the right thing so that the people remaining in the coalfields after the summer's over will be better off, better able to speak for themselves, to protect themselves, and to end MTR. Larry is keenly aware of the potential dangers MJS poses for coalfield locals, as the bad things that have happened to him have often followed times when he's had outside supporters up at Kayford.

The high point of the day comes early in the evening, when Bo and Judy arrive at camp and are greeted with enthusiastic applause and many hugs. On their way here, they tell us, they stopped to pay their fines in Beckley, at the Raleigh County magistrate's office. A police officer they passed in a hallway said to them: "I know who you are, and I know what you did yesterday. And I just want to say off the record that I respect what you did and I'm proud of you." They didn't know what their fine would be when they walked in. It could have been up to $100—but after they talked with the magistrate, he ordered a fine of just $5 each plus court costs.

Bo and Judy arrive at camp in time to represent West Virginia in a panel discussion on strategy for the summer, state by state. Just before this discussion, MJS's summer schedule is unveiled, showing the campaign moving from West Virginia to Kentucky, and then on to Virginia in June, back to West Virginia for most of July, then to Tennessee in August. There are eighty-five people in the room this evening. With more doing cleanup in the kitchen and security patrol outside, there are at least ninety people at camp now.

"I got chill bumps when I walked in this room today and saw all of you," Bo tells the crowd. This is the right issue, and the right time, he says, to change the way people are enslaved to corporations in cities all over America as well as here in Appalachia. West Virginia's new governor, Joe Manchin, who before his election had business with coal and timber interests, on his first day in office said: "West Virginia is open for business." Today, in reaction to yesterday's action at Marsh Fork, the governor's office called CRMW to set up a meeting with the governor to discuss the school. Bo hopes MJS will keep up the pressure on Massey (and the governor) about the school this summer, keep the moral high ground, and make this a national issue. More immediately, he hopes to see lots of people turn out for the state DEP hearing at the school tomorrow evening. "Without question, tomorrow night is going to be the largest opposition, ever, in West Virginia, to a mining permit," he says.

A young woman named Ali presents for Kentucky. "We don't have an awesome group like you all," she says, a little wistfully, gesturing toward Bo and Judy. The relatively low-key events planned for MJS in Kentucky are clustered in June: a backwoods camp, a "mountain witness" tour in Martin County, a film festival and rally in Lexington, and perhaps some visits to the homes and offices of coal company executives. (Earlier in the day, Dave Cooper told me that Kentucky isn't likely to see much in the way of civil disobedience this summer. "Mountain witness" tours run by KFTC are igniting a lot of interest in MTR in the state, but that interest hasn't yet coalesced into opposition with any momentum or clear direction. He hopes to see that change this summer, but he expects the fruits of this to be borne later.)

Speaking for organizers in Virginia, Erin tells the story of young Jeremy Davidson's death. Southwestern Virginia is "traumatized," she says, and no grassroots organization has arisen to fight MTR there. She suggests that people go to the area now to start Listening Projects and scouting in advance of the MJS camp slated for the area in late June. The other main event in Virginia this summer will be a demonstration at Massey headquarters in Richmond on July 8, coinciding with an international day of action against climate change. Planning for this is just beginning.

Speaking for Tennessee, Chris Irwin, manically caffeinated, delivers a grand rant on the history of mining and landscape in Tennessee. "We are really close to turning the tide in Tennessee, which is why we need your help," he says. MJS organizing there is focused on two coalfield areas, both near the Kentucky border: the New River watershed area (including Zeb Mountain) just west of I-75, and Eagan Mountain to the east of it. Chris notes that National Coal has bought up the land or coal rights to more than 100,000 acres, including the Zeb Mountain site. Eagan is being mined by Mountainside Coal, a Kentucky company. Paloma reports on the Listening Project in Elk Valley, in the shadow of Zeb Mountain; similar efforts are being planned around Eagan. "There is a place for everyone in this campaign," she says, from direct action, to legal monkeywrenching (filing requests for hearings and studies to slow the permit process down), to letting locals know what they can do about blasting and other problems. john johnson adds that the Tennessee Valley Authority (TVA), a huge producer of electricity, has signed contracts with Massey and Arch to buy MTR coal from West Virginia. TVA's headquarters in Knoxville will be another focus for MJS protest this summer.

Leaving camp late the next afternoon to drive to Marsh Fork Elementary School for the 6 PM hearing there, I pass a green minivan parked near the camp's driveway and angled to get a good look at cars leaving the camp. Two people, neither in uniform, sit in the front seats. They've apparently been there a while—the guy in the passenger seat has his feet propped up in the window. I wave as I pass, and a mile or so farther on as I approach the main road, the van pulls up alongside me and turns off in the other direction. (Later, I learn that a white Jeep Cherokee parked in the same place has followed a car leaving camp all the way to the hearing.)

When I arrive at the school, I stop under the big oak tree to chat with people from the camp, Chad and Gabrielle and their baby, Ukiah. A tall, big, middle-aged man approaches us and asks: "Are you for us or against us?" His tone is belligerent, his manner ambiguous. Feeling a bit protective of the very young little family, I step closer to the man and tell him I'm a writer. He hands me a paper to read, a quote from something published back in 1884 about a local land grab. He said his family's land had been taken from them by a 2 cent per acre tax: They couldn't afford to pay it, but a land company could and did. I thank him for the paper and head for the school gym, leaving him and Chad chatting.

More than 130 people assemble for the meeting, filling up the bleachers in the gym, facing a folding table and chairs at which several state DEP officials are seated. More than half of those attending are from MJS camp. Several state troopers stand near the doors of the gym.

As people arrive at the hearing, they're handed a list of rules, including one that says the only people who will be allowed to speak are those who've previously shown an interest in the permit under consideration this evening. Bo, standing with Judy, Sarah, and Vern, floats the idea of putting masking tape over the mouth of everyone who's not allowed to speak. Instead, he negotiates with DEP officials an agreement that everyone here who wants to speak should sign up to do so, but that the officials running the meeting reserve the right to schedule some of the speaking for another hearing, if this one runs too late. Each person who wants to speak will be allowed to do so for only two minutes.

Ukiah and her parents sit next to a thirty-something-year-old local woman, who's totally charmed by the baby. Other folks from MJS camp are looking noticeably more cleaned-up and conservatively dressed than usual. (Chris Dodson tells me, "I realized when I was coming here that I do not have any non-hippie pants. I'll have to work on that.") john johnson hands flyers about MTR to anyone who'll accept one. Local print and TV reporters work the room.

Outside, a stranger, not in uniform, is taking photos of license plates, walking from car to car, sometimes looking inside a car through its windows. Most likely he's either a coal company operative sending a message to locals that their presence here has been noticed, or plainclothes law enforcement keeping tabs on MJS. When two MJSers approach and ask him questions, he doesn't say a word and keeps "a completely blank look on his face," one of them later tells me. One of the two gets the idea of standing in front of the license plates, and for a while plays tag with the camera guy, dashing forward to where he's going, then veering off to another car when he does the same. Finally the guy with the camera cracks a smile and gives up.

The state official who opens the meeting looks nervous. The bleachers are now full to overflowing, with some people sitting on the floor.

First up among the speakers is a local man in a wheelchair, who has grandchildren at the school. He's followed by Larry Gibson, who displays a jar of coal sludge from the Inez disaster. Lined up front and center on the bleachers are Bo, Judy, Larry, and a cluster of other locals, including Pauline Canterbury and Mary Miller, the Sylvester Dustbusters, both wearing dust masks.

A state official in plain clothes—Dennis Stottlemeyer, assistant to state DEP head Stephanie Timmermeyer—runs the timekeeping with unseemly enthusiasm, ringing a bell with a flourish when a speaker's two minutes are up, and cutting power to the microphone if the speaker continues. Overall, though, he doesn't look happy. None of the officials at the table does. They look like they wish this would all go away. For most of the meeting their faces are stony, sober.

When it's Judy Bonds's turn to speak, she faces the crowd, turning her back on the DEP. (Later, she tells me why: "They never listen.") At the end of her speech against the proposed new coal silo, she turns around to face the state officials and says: "Shame on you." The crowd stands and cheers.

Bo Webb also turns to face the crowd. He talks about the leaks in the dam and invites everyone present this evening to invite their friends and neighbors to rally in front of the school on May 31, the following Tuesday afternoon, to demand that someone representing Massey come out and talk. He too ends by turning to the state officials. "You guys, your day is coming—especially *you*," he says, pointing at Stottlemeyer.

Pauline Canterbury, up next, speaks to the officials a bit then pauses and says sharply: "Are you gentlemen listening?" They had been talking among themselves. Pauline's Voice of Mom snaps them to at least a semblance of attention.

Dozens of people speak against the proposed silo, and against other effects and risks from the facility as well. Nowhere in the permitting process is there a chance for citizens to address the cumulative impact of coal operations on the school or on their community as a whole. The state officials here today are considering only whether to permit that second silo. All other comments and concerns are considered irrelevant—but not to the crowd, and not to john johnson. Speaking to the officials and gesturing toward the crowd, he says: "This is what a citizens' uprising looks like." Local people, as well as MJSers, smile and applaud.

The meeting breaks up shortly after 8 PM, after everyone who wishes to speak has done so, with the crowd in the bleachers in a good humor. Some people are singing, many chatting. The DEP officials keep busy at their table.

Outside, Bo and Judy thank the crowd for coming. "We already love you," Judy says, speaking to the MJS volunteers. "You are one of us. You are *Appalachians*. We will have justice this summer."

Debbie Jarrell, while real happy to see so many MJSers here, later tells me she feels "the hearing is a formality that they have to go through, it's not something that they really take into consideration. I don't feel like our opinions matter to them." Debbie is also disappointed that only a dozen or so locals attended the hearing. "There's 200-some kids go to that school," she says, and finds it very disappointing that more of their families and neighbors didn't come. She's hopeful more local people will show up on May 31.

In the crowd outside the school, I catch up with the man who before the meeting had wanted to know if MJS was "for us or against us." He tells me he'd worked in a coal prep plant and is sick from it. He's afraid to talk with me about it, won't even give me his name. But he says he'd sure like to show the woods near his home, not far from the school, to some of the MJS kids who came to the hearing. He knows some real nice places to go, he says. For now at least, he's apparently decided MJS is for him, not against him.

At breakfast the next morning, john johnson announces that the FBI has visited the local sheriff's office nearest the camp to talk about MJS, and that in response the sheriff's office has sent officers to visit people living nearby to tell them about the camp and ask them to report anything strange. It's not clear whether this has anything to do with the surveillance of cars going in and out of camp. At least four different unmarked vehicles (no obvious police cars) have been keeping an eye on the road leading to camp, very openly.

In addition, an incident at the camp's entrance has MJS security volunteers on heightened alert. One of the people involved tells me that last night several MJSers were down at the open tent set up as the camp's entry checkpoint, acting as security guards and greeters for any new volunteers coming in. "There's only one entrance to this camp," he emphasizes. Among the security volunteers that evening were several who "enjoy sneaking through the woods. One of [them] is famous for disappearing and then when you're walking in the woods all of a sudden he pops up out of nowhere. It's this person's favorite game," offered and usually accepted as a gesture of affection and friendship. This person had left the checkpoint for a while, leaving three of his friends there. "All of a sudden they heard something, somebody creeping around" in the woods across the driveway. They thought it was their friend, sneaking up on them as usual. So they conferred: "'Well, he's doing a pretty good job sneaking up. He's pretty quiet.' One of the people at the checkpoint was wearing a headlamp, and he went across the drive and kind of crept up on the person [in the woods] and turned on his headlamp. And all he can see is a vague outline and a pair of eyes. They stare at each other for several seconds." Then the guy with the headlamp asks his buddies: "Should I pursue?" He's joking at this point, still thinking the guy in the woods is their friend. And his buddies responded: "'YEAH!' So he pulls out his knife, a huge nine-inch-long knife, like a Marine Corps knife, a short sword—and then charges, still thinking it's one of them. The guy took off, ran like a bat out of hell. It's pretty funny. We're real sure it wasn't law enforcement. Law enforcement sneak teams, the feds or whatever, they operate in teams. It was just one person who ran away. I think it was probably a coal company person," perhaps seeking the camp's registration book, or wanting to eavesdrop near the security tent, or creeping down toward the main meeting building to hide someplace where he could monitor the next day's activities.

The camp takes all this in stride, without much fuss, and gets on with the day. Workshops today include Direct Action 101, led by Hillary and john, which covers the history and rationale behind nonviolent civil disobedience as well as the basics of planning and executing such protest actions—choosing targets and tactics, clarifying goals and messaging, assigning roles (arrestees, on-site supporters of arrestees, worker and police liaisons, media team, jail support, drivers, and so on), devising action scenarios and contingency plans, de-escalating potential violence, and so on. Another workshop focuses on camping skills, and Chris Irwin leads a legal workshop that boils down to three phrases, two of which you should repeat to yourself, one of which you should say to the police: Shut up. Cops lie. Talk to my attorney.

I spend most of the day talking with campers about how the campaign's going. One of those I catch up with is a security-minded, self-identified anarchist who'd refused to talk with me on tape earlier in the campaign but agrees now to talk about the idea of an "open revolution." I'd heard him mention this previously and wondered how he thought it connected with MJS.

"We want everybody involved" in fundamentally changing how the world runs, including "not just people that 'agree' with us [anarchists], but people who agree that the system as it stands right now is really not properly serving [people]. The United States of America is no longer a government of, by, and for the people. It is of, by, and for the corporations. A lot of people can see that who don't necessarily agree with many of our other points. We know that not everybody's going to agree with everything we say. We just want to make an open society where people are free to be different and to live the way that they want to as long as they don't bother other people. And we know that that's going to encompass a whole lot of different belief systems, a whole lot of different types of communities.

"In order to bring this about, we need to put pressure on various social forces and shine the light on various shady practices. And to do *that*, we need to do more than just pass out information. We're actually going to have to do action, and both interfere with business as usual and interfere with things that are contributing to erosion of democracy, erosion of autonomy, self-determination. People really love action. [And it shows] that resistance and change actually are possible. So many people think you can't change City Hall, this is the way it's always been, you just can't change nothing. Change *is* possible, if people just get up off their dead butts and do something."

Later I ask Sage, who also identifies himself as an anarchist, what he hopes to see happen this summer. "I really hope that everyone that came here from outside the area falls in love with it enough to not have it be a summer gig for them," he says. "Or if it is, that they're back here next year. I also hope that we maintain good relations with the people in every coalfield town that we go into. And I'm hoping that we're able to start to unify the [anti-MTR movement across the region's] states, so Kentucky's not just dealing with it as Kentucky, Tennessee not just as Tennessee. So that we feel more strength. And I'm hoping that everyone in the country, next time they see a 'clean coal' commercial, they're able to put the vision of what's going on this summer with it. And that the momentum just stays up."

For Sage, as for many southern Appalachians, living in this landscape is an ongoing conversation with God. "I think that's why religion has such a stronghold [here]," Sage says. "When talking about the land, religious stuff comes up all the time. You don't really hear that a lot of other places; they might love the land, have an ecological sense of what's going on, [that] a lot of history is there, but it's not a religious thing like 'I'm called by God to be here, I can't leave.'"

Many of the people, like Sage, who live in southern Appalachia and are active in MJS, have specific attachments to particular home places. But at the same time, they also identify with the entire region's landscape and culture, and recognize that it's necessary to protect the whole thing, not just your own home place. You're not going to be able to do it all by yourself in your neighborhood. You'll need—and want—to make connections with people in other parts of the region because they've got a lot in common with you, and you're not going to be effective unless you work together. Part of what's enabled the abusive power relationships between coal companies and local people is that communities have been small and isolated and not connected with each other, so that the large economic interests, which operate throughout the region, can control it.

I raise with Sage an idea Judy Bonds and I have talked about, that the religious connection to the land helps bridge the gap in MJS between the conservative Christian coalfield locals and the so-called "godless anarchist" outsiders, because so many of those "godless" ones have a deeply felt spiritual connection to the natural world, and to the southern Appalachian landscape particularly, and they recognize this in each other. "I'm the oddball Christian anarchist," Sage tells me, "and I constantly get crap for it." So he was surprised to hear, last night, in conversation among anarchist friends who ordinarily disdain religion, "they started talking religion. I was like: 'You've been here for a little bit, it resurged in you, and you couldn't leave it out of the conversation, could you?'"

Both the Christian coalfield locals and the anarchist revolutionaries are deeply uncomfortable with much of mainstream American culture, with how far astray this is from the way they believe the world ought to be. "It gets really simple," Sage says. "Maybe they [coalfield locals] sit down and start having a religious conversation with some folks that came for the camp. And they realize that they're not really matching up on religion. But they'll recognize that they are matching up what's in their hearts."

john agrees with Sage and Judy that the landscape-connected Christian spirituality of people in this region is akin to his own spirituality. "I've rejected my Christian upbringing," he tells me, "but I appreciate that there are Christians who have this spiritual connection and spiritual impetus to protect the land and to stand up for social justice." john says his criticism of Christianity can be "pretty vicious, but then I run into people who believe and who I really like and respect, who have what I consider a very good and very healthy interpretation of Christianity," one that leads them, as a religious calling, to work to change the world in ways john himself works toward. "I have a high tolerance for good Christians," he says. "I'll take my hat off and bow my head with them—at least be respectful. I have an extremely low tolerance" for the religious right, for people who identify themselves as Christian but have devoted themselves to furthering a repressive, uncritically capitalist agenda. "If people are going to believe in God, I want them to be motivated by a loving God who's going to encourage them to do good in the world—justice, not just charity."

One interesting and, john thinks, very good effect that's resulting from the mutual respect between Christian activists and anarchists in this campaign is that "there are some things that happen in the radical movement that have not happened here. There's a tendency among anarchist-militant types to pooh-pooh regular civil disobedience," where you simply offer yourself up for arrest, as Bo and Judy did at Goals Coal. "They view it as symbolic. To them it's not *direct* action," like shutting down a piece of mining machinery, for example, "and it's putting yourself at the mercy of this evil, violent system. And I've not heard that here."

Paloma tells me that one of the things she likes best about MJS is "that you have these different cultures coming together. You have this kind of counterculture of people that have spent a great deal of time examining their value system, and purposefully breaking some of the societal norms. And then once they break them, they're looking at them: How does that make me feel? Am I OK with that, am I not OK with that, do I want to continue this, or do I want to go back? And this is a

really healthy thing for people to do." But the people who do this often
"are in this bubble, [with] only people that are backing up that belief. So
they're breaking these rules, such as dressing or undressing in public,
or language, or how they behave," and, intentionally or not, perhaps
offending people outside their bubble, including some of the people
they're aiming to work with in this campaign. And people living inside
the bubble tend to become unaccustomed to others taking offense. "If
somebody who's part of this counterculture experiences something that
makes them uncomfortable, their response more often is going to be:
'Whoa! Why does that make me uncomfortable? Let's look at my own
beliefs, let's challenge my own beliefs.'"

This self-challenging habit can encourage self-improvement and
personal growth. However, together with the high value placed on
"autonomy" by this "counterculture," it also can license selfishness and
parasitism by individuals whose behavior, however outrageous, is likely
to go unchallenged by anyone inside their "bubble." Saying that a particular behavior is destructive, disrespectful, dishonest, wasteful, or just
plain wrong is generally considered uncool or oppressive in this subcul-
ture. This attitude is especially entrenched among some of its younger
members most disdainful of all things mainstream. None of this is much
of a problem at Pipestem. But it has potential, as the campaign continues,
for both sapping energy and resources from the campaign and sowing
division within it.

Still, not only is MJS trying to envision and bring about a better
future, in some ways the movement and the individuals who make it
up aim to embody that future. "I think MJS is unique," says Abigail. "It
brings together all different kinds of people: coalfield residents with
anarchists with everything in between. It also has a really realistic analy-
sis of power in our society. We're not putting all our faith in passing a
certain bill or getting certain politicians to endorse what we're doing. I
think that everyone here recognizes that while it's important to incorporate some legislative work into our organizing, that's not where the
real change is going to happen. The real change is gonna happen on

a local level, in people's communities. It's gonna happen on a cultural level. And we need to be working on all these different fronts, building our power collectively.

"I think this issue represents a whole big slew of issues that we all care about. There are so many different issues that we all could be devoting a lifetime to working on. It gets overwhelming. But MTR touches on so many things—human rights, environmental, cultural genocide essentially. And it's such a graphic example of all these things. I feel like it's a good example of what's wrong with our culture and why we need to change, a good one to start stimulating conversation on a national level. I'm hoping that this summer sparks a much larger uprising that looks not just at energy or protection of watersheds or cultural sensitivity, respect for different people—but an overall shift in consciousness, where people tie all these things together and examine their role."

Driving away from camp that night, about half an hour down the road, near the interstate, I come upon traffic backed up and several police cars flashing lights. A sign tells me this is a "sobriety checkpoint." It's about 10:30 PM on a Friday night, the beginning of the Memorial Day weekend. When I reach the checkpoint, a state trooper asks for my license and registration and shines a flashlight inside my car. As I'm taking out my license he says he sees coal dust on my car (not true, as far as I know) and asks if I've been driving around any coal tipples. I ask what this is all about. He says my car was at Marsh Fork Elementary School last night (an hour's drive away from where we are at that moment), they don't see many out-of-state plates around here, and what brings me there? I say I'm a writer. He asks do I write for a newspaper or magazine or what? I don't answer. He looks at my registration, shines his light through my car again, says "See you next Tuesday," May 31, and waves me on. At no point does he ask if I've had anything to drink that evening.

The next morning, Saturday, one of the campers helping with security announces that an intruder was heard during the night, walking around near one of the barns on the property, then near where campers' tents are clustered, apparently heading toward the road. Once again no, it wasn't our friend who likes to sneak up on people. And once again the best guess is that this isn't police, but is either a coal company operative or a curious local. My late-night experience with the police is also announced to the camp, with a warning: The police know who we are and are looking for us, so be sure to wear seat belts, don't carry contraband, and don't drive drunk.

There's a near-blizzard of optional workshops at camp today, on federal and state laws affecting coalfields, first aid, plant identification, Listening Projects, history of MTR, scouting, video activism, secure communications, water testing, and affinity groups (groups of like-minded people who come together to do an action, part of an action, or series of actions). At the same time, people are beginning to leave and to make plans to leave camp. Some have commitments back home after this Memorial Day weekend. Most will plug back into MJS later in the summer, when it moves to their area or they're free to travel to it elsewhere. Some will go back to their home places to continue working on MJS all summer, with now-and-then excursions to major MJS events throughout the region.

The main event of the day is the monthly MJS organizers' meeting, now including the new people at camp as well as the regulars. First focus is on the upcoming May 31 demonstration. This time, MJS is to join local activists, and the task at hand is how to integrate all these well-meaning "outsiders" into the effort against Massey at Marsh Fork Elementary.

Bo addresses the crowd. He's not asking anyone to get arrested on Tuesday. "You have your own free will," he says. "Whatever you decide to do is up to you." But he does ask that anyone who decides to do civil disobedience cooperate rather than resist arrest. The goal is to deliver the same list of demands to Massey, and to have a person in authority at the Goals Coal facility come out and talk with them. He asks that locals be allowed to try to deliver the demands before MJSers from outside the community do so.

john johnson reviews what happened to Bo and Judy on May 24—no handcuffs, taken away in a police car, ticketed and released. He notes that law enforcement might do things differently on Tuesday and adds: "I'm hoping that a bunch of us will stand in solidarity with them."

Hillary describes, hypothetically, a scenario in which successive waves of MJSers follow an initial wave of locals to present the demands. She asks what Bo and Judy think of this.

"I think it's perfect," Bo says.

Judy says it would "touch our hearts."

After a good bit more discussion, and with general agreement about what to do on Tuesday, the group moves on to other matters. The schedule for the weeks ahead gets tweaked a bit. The complexity of planning and executing multiple actions, some open but some covert, in multiple places is noted but not resolved.

The issue of nonviolence and property damage has been put on the agenda for discussion, as many people here think it's important to revisit this, given that many newcomers to the campaign here now weren't present for earlier discussions and consensus. To start with, Paloma sums up past MJS discussion. She notes that MJS's consensus against violence or property damage was adopted both to protect local activists from reprisals and because many people here wouldn't be involved with Mountain Justice Summer without that consensus. In addition, she notes, coal companies would surely use any violence or property damage this summer to discredit the campaign.

john adds that MJS wants to be able to accuse the coal companies of committing violence and property damage through mountaintop removal. For that accusation to be most effective, MJS itself must be nonviolent. He notes also that most coal miners are big guys, bigger than most of the people sitting in this room. As a practical matter, "we don't stand a chance" fighting back if physically attacked. If you're at an action, with MJS's own video cameras running, "take the lick," john urges—or allow him to step in and take it for you. If you're accosted someplace else, walk away from it if you can.

Chris Dodson notes that speech can be violent, too. MJSers should avoid making threats.

One of those who came to this campaign through Earth First! notes that "Earth Firsters have a long, proud tradition of making messes"—sometimes really messy messes. (An action a while back in which rancid lobster guts were spilled on the front lawn of the governor of Maine is cited as an example.) Does MJS forbid this sort of thing? Although no formal consensus is sought or reached on this point, there seems to be general agreement that if a mess isn't permanent and can be removed it might not count as property damage, but whether it's a good idea or not is another matter. Examples are suggested, some of which seem good to most people present, others not. Tactics like this will have to be sorted out action by action.

Hillary repeats a definition she's presented before: Nonviolence is resistance, not submission and not retaliation. If she thinks she's in a situation where she can't avoid retaliating rather than nonviolently standing her ground in resistance, she'd want to avoid or leave the situation. She seconds Chris's concern about violent speech—and also seconds john's offer to stand between anyone being attacked and the attacker. In this culture, and in that situation, she thinks, a man is less likely to hit a woman.

Some MJSers are committed personally to avoiding doing violence in any situation, but MJS doesn't require this commitment. Abigail emphasizes that MJS has made the decision to avoid violence and property damage for tactical reasons. Many participants in this campaign believe that in other circumstances violence in self-defense is justified. Some believe that violence or property damage, in at least some circumstances, can be acceptable tools for making change or responding to evil. Regardless of these philosophical differences, all who participate in MJS are expected to take care to avoid any violence or property damage in any actions connected with this campaign.

Parts of this discussion make some or many people in the room uncomfortable, as it exposes deeply felt differences. john notes that this issue is hard, that there ought to be ongoing discussion about it, and that we need to help each other out with it. There's general, relieved applause when this round of the discussion ends.

Late in the morning on May 31, driving up I-77 from camp toward Marsh Fork Elementary, I'm followed by a black sedan with tinted windows. The way the driver's following me is an obvious, in-your-face, send-a-message kind of tail: I slow down, he slows down. I pass another car, he passes too and pulls in right behind me. The driver is the car's only occupant. I don't get a close look at him but can see him talking into a cellphone or some other kind of communications device. He follows me off at the Beckley exit, where I decide to pull into a restaurant parking lot to see what happens. He follows me to the driveway then zooms past, as if to avoid allowing me a good look at him or his license plate. As I continue on toward the school, on twisty, windy Rt. 3 now, I look in my rearview mirror from time to time but don't see him again.

At 12:20 PM the Goals Coal entrance is open for business, no special security apparent, no police cars parked there yet. Eight or ten demonstrators' cars are parked near the school. Two TV stations have sent reporters. Judy Bonds is talking to them, not on camera, just chatting, filling in background. The protest is to begin at 1 PM.

Larry Gibson is here, too, along with Patty Sebok, Mary Miller, and about a dozen others. Patty tells me that G (federal) license plates have been seen on the road here today. She also tells me that children were outside in the schoolyard playing when she and a few others first arrived. School officials scooted everyone inside, as though the demonstrators were some kind of danger to the kids. She thinks this is ironic—as though the coal plant here isn't a danger.

By 12:45 about four dozen people have assembled. State police have arrived, three cars so far, and asked the crowd to stay off the road and walk along only one side of the road, for safety. Television reporters (three stations now) are doing stand-up interviews with locals. (One of the reporters later asks me: "Is this the Coal River valley?" I confirm that it is, and wonder what else she doesn't know about the coalfields she and her station are supposed to cover.) Parked cars stretch down the road farther than I can see, and a stream of people are walking from the cars toward the school.

At 1 PM, police cars head up the road to the plant to manage traffic, as marchers line up along the road in front of the school, single file, preparing to march to the plant. They're carrying lots of signs and banners, most made during this past week at camp. On the cliff face across the road, facing the coal plant, a bedsheet-sized banner is dropped proclaiming "Mountain Justice Summer."

It's a beautiful, warm, sunny day. About 130 people, mostly MJSers, make the short march from school to plant, where they find waiting for them half a dozen police cars. A line of eleven policemen stretches across the bridge to the coal plant, barring protesters from crossing. Bo directs everyone to gather in a double semicircle at the front of the driveway. Two of the interns from the house in Naoma, Benji and Chris, are tuning up guitars. Sage is playing his fiddle.

Allen Johnson, with Christians for the Mountains, offers a prayer. "It's gonna be a Christian prayer because that's where I am," he says, "that's where many of the people in this community are. That's not to try to at all discourage anybody who does not go along with this. That's fine. Wherever we are, we have to give everything we can.

"Your love, o Lord, reaches to the heavens. Your justice and mercy reach to the sky. Your righteousness is like the mighty mountains, your justice like a mighty stream. We thank you for this day, a beautiful day, that we can gather together to take action against the scourge of mountaintop removal and the blight that Massey and companies like that are perpetrating on our communities. We ask that your favor be upon us, and this be an effective message today that reaches out into the communities and touches the pens of the legislators, that touches the people in this community and in our state, this region, to take action to preserve your land. The earth is the Lord's, and the fullness thereof, and everything in it. This is not our land, it is your land you've given us to use properly and wisely and justly. God, we decry the obliteration of the streams, and we repent of that and desire that they be healed. God, we decry the murder of your mountains and ask that you give us the faithfulness to see them restored and healed. We decry the mercury emission [from burning coal] that poisons unborn babies. We decry the money [with which] companies like Massey corrupt our government, our churches, our communities. We name this as you, God, see it to be: sin, evil, iniquity. And we pledge ourselves anew to be instruments of healing and restoration of this land." "Amen," the crowd answers.

Bo speaks next. "You know, I don't go to church every Sunday but I am a spiritual person. And I want to tell you guys this past weekend I did have a spiritual moment that's still taking place inside of me right now. Last Friday, I drove over to where the MJS camp was at. I wanted to spend the night with everyone, and see what was taking place over there. I saw young people from all over America. They came from all parts of this country because something's wrong here, and they want to come and help." Bo notes that "everyone is sworn to nonviolence. It was a beautiful thing. I was really uplifted by it.

"And then when I got up Saturday morning, I looked and on the road that goes by the camp there were black SUVs with dark-colored windows going up and down, with tall antennas. And I found out a little bit later that the FBI had been out and talked to all the locals and told them these radical environmentalists were coming in there and they should be wary of them.

"I'm a Vietnam veteran. I'm a combat veteran. That really irritated me. And [now] I look over here [at the plant] and I realize something: All of those dark cars, whoever they were, they were at the wrong location. The terrorists are right across this bridge. They're terrorizing our community, and they're terrorizing our children in that school. And we want answers. I've got these MSHA reports I've kept carrying around with me for the past week. They won't talk about it. They won't even answer the news media when they call them. They're hiding behind the government, and having them do their dirty work for them. There

is no excuse that Massey can say for what they're doing to this school."
Waving the reports, Bo says: "We want justice!"

Three guitars and Sage's fiddle play "Amazing Grace" while the
crowd sings.

Vern Haltom addresses the crowd: "A lot of people don't know that
the person that wrote that song was repenting from the terrible, horrible
sins that he had been committing throughout his life. The man who
wrote that song had been a slave trader. In that man's day, slavery was
considered an economic necessity. But that man repented of his sins.
Massey Energy today stands in front of us and says that for economic
gain they must terrorize this school. Massey Energy says that for jobs
we must poison these children." (The crowd says: "Shame! Shame!")
"Massey Energy says that, as with the slaves of previous centuries, the
lives of these children are not worth [as much as] the economic gain of
those who profit from their lives. We are here today to say to [Massey
CEO] Don Blankenship and everyone of Massey Energy: Repent!
Repent and tear down this silo, close that sludge dam, release these children and this state from bondage!"

A couple of quick speeches by MJSers follow, then musicians tune
up and play "This Land Is Your Land," and the crowd sings. The police
wave the crowd aside to allow a large truck laden with cinderblocks and
other building materials to leave the facility. The driver gives a perfunc-
tory but polite wave of his hand as he drives off.

john johnson speaks: "Hi y'all. I actually wasn't going to say anything today, but my good friend Bo asked me to do something kind of
bad. He wants me to read this prayer. Bo, I thought we were buddies.
This thing is kind of rough." As requested, john recites the "Twilight
MTR Miner's Prayer," a poem printed in a pro-MTR publication thanking God for making coal mining possible and asking God to protect
miners' jobs. "Y'all that's pretty harsh," john says afterward. "We don't
want to make these men poor. We don't want these men unsafe. We
don't want their children starving. But we want them in jobs that don't
harm the mountains, that do not harm our communities, and that do

not poison our children. Many of us believe that trees, streams, rocks, and sky [cited in the poem]—all that stuff keeps us alive. Clean air, clean water, clean soil is our life-support system. And as it is obviously evident today, it is not godless men or godless women who are trying to stop the destruction."

john hands the megaphone over to Judy Bonds. "Never doubt that this is a battle between good and evil," she says. "Now is not a time to be silent. Now is a time to stand up and be counted. The earth is God's body. Psalm 24 says the earth is the Lord's, and the fullness thereof—and, amen, it belongs to God and it don't belong to Massey Energy. A man doesn't have a right to feed his family by poisoning my babies.

"We unite today, Lord, as your children. And we're called to reveal your will. We pray for your guidance, and we pray for a safe rally and for a safe summer. We pray that these little children—*all* God's little children—will be protected and safe from human greed and from violent coal companies. We beg that you help the people in the coalfields, and on Coal River, have more courage that they might stand up against the evil and the violence from Massey and from other terrorist coal companies that are blasting our homes and communities, poisoning and terrorizing our children, and destroying your creation, Lord. Have mercy on us, and forgive us our sins.

"The people of the coalfields, and of Coal River, and of Appalachia, and of America, and yea of the world will come together to beat this evil. The day that the shut-down orders arrive, I want to be one of the people that crosses that bridge and hand-delivers the shut-down orders to Massey Energy!" The crowd whoops its approval.

With the crowd singing "Which Side Are You On?," an old miners' union song, an elderly woman, Winnie Fox, supported by Debbie Jarrell and retired schoolteacher Janice Nease approach the bridge and are denied entry. They sit down in the driveway and are arrested. A conversation with the police ensues, with Janice attempting to present the demonstrators' demands, and Debbie holding Winnie's hand. After Debbie is handcuffed, she and Janice are led away. A police officer gently leads

Winnie off to one of the waiting police cars. She puts her arm around his waist to steady herself, and he puts his arm around her shoulder.

A group of three MJSers promptly takes the place of the three local women and are just as promptly arrested themselves. Four more MJSers follow, and so it goes until a total of sixteen are ultimately arrested. Four are local (Debbie, Winnie, Janice, and Larry Gibson), one is from elsewhere in West Virginia, and the remaining eleven are MJSers from out of state, john and Sage and Abigail among them. Unlike the previous protest, when the company shut down this driveway for the duration, trucks continue to move in and out of the facility all the while—no disruption of business as usual today. As the last of the arrestees are put in police cars, the crowd chants: "Kids Don't Need Massey Greed." The crowd lingers, chatting and singing and milling around, acting as though they and not Massey own the place.

As with Bo and Judy a week ago, today's arrestees are taken to the state police substation, charged with trespassing, and quickly released. john later tells me: "I'd kind of given up on that style of civil disobedience, what I call stuff-and-cuff, [where] you just kind of present yourself [to be handcuffed and stuffed into a police car]. But that action was powerful as hell—there's this line of cops, there's all these people, all the locals could see what was going on, the media could see it, the demands are made, we step forward, the cops are being cool—they don't even cuff the first, like, half of us because they don't know how many people are coming. It felt powerful." john says he heard that one of the cops paid Winnie's fine.

To celebrate, Bo invites everyone to come to his house for beer by the river. About forty people take him up on it. It's a hot afternoon, and a dozen or so MJSers take off their clothes and skinny-dip. Everyone looks happy and relaxed. It's especially sweet to see this right here, where Bo fell in love with this land and so in part MJS began.

A week after the second Marsh Fork demonstration, groups of MJSers converge on two urban demonstrations in cities tied to coal at the northern and southern ends of the coalfields.

In Pittsburgh, a small local group fighting longwall mining in Pennsylvania hosts a couple of dozen out-of-town MJSers for several days. (Longwall miners, underground, scoop out a seam of coal in a long line, then allow the void, where the coal once was, to collapse. The resulting subsidence affects the land above and near the mine like an earthquake.) MJS's visit to Pittsburgh culminates in a lunch-hour march through the downtown business district to a rally outside the city's convention center, where a coal-industry convention is being held. Bo Webb is here for CRMW, and Sierra Club is represented by Bill Price, their West Virginia-based Environmental Justice Program staffer. The sixty-some marchers include musicians with drums, horns, clarinet, cymbals, and a bell. It's a beautiful day, and the music draws workers on lunch break out to watch the passing spectacle. I see lots of people in the crowd smiling at the fun of the music and also at the dumpster-pirate-hippie array of clothing worn by young MJSers. Several marchers work the sidewalks, passing out literature about MTR.

At the convention center, songs are sung and speeches are made, including a rabble-rousing primer on MTR by Bo: "I come up here this morning from the coalfields of West Virginia, from the Coal River valley, where 3 million pounds of explosives are used each day to blow the tops of our mountains off and get down to thin seams of coal. There are 2 million pounds of explosives used each day in Kentucky, another million pounds in Tennessee and Virginia.

"Make no mistake about it—these coal thugs in this building are nothing but terrorists, pure and simple. They're the ones with the explosives. They're the ones killing us and running us out of our homes. We are here today to give notice to these evil people," he says, looking up at the convention hall, "that your reign of terror will soon be over. We're also here today to demand that the United States government uphold its sworn oath to protect *all* Americans, including Appalachian coalfield residents. We refuse to be their sacrifice zone." Looking up again, Bo says, "You can't hide anymore. Good people from all over this country have come together, continue to come together, every day. A movement has started. It's called Mountain Justice Summer. Get used to it." The crowd cheers.

The sun is hot today, the glare off concrete at the convention center oppressive. By the time Bo finishes his speech he's awfully red in the face. The rest of the crowd looks hot too. By the end of the rally, although there's a general sense that this was worth doing—a good start on taking the MJS message to a city outside the MTR zone, and directly to the coal industry—everyone looks wilted. The local organizers are exhausted, the out-of-town MJSers out of sorts.

Meanwhile, in Knoxville, an MJS demonstration is ending in three unintended arrests. I hear about this the next evening, June 8, at the camp being set up in Louisa, Kentucky, as MJSers are arriving there from Pittsburgh, Knoxville, and elsewhere. All three arrestees are still in jail in Knoxville, as far as we know.

"The basic plan was to invade the National Coal Corporation's very first shareholder meeting," one of those who was at the action tells me. Although NCC is a Florida corporation, its main offices are in Knoxville, where its CEO and other executives live, within an hour's drive of the company's extensive and expanding coalfield holdings up near the Kentucky border.

After john johnson and other KEFers blockaded the Zeb Mountain mine's entrance in 2003, the company that owned the mineral rights then apparently decided the site was more trouble than it was worth. They sold it to NCC, which indicated its intent to mine aggressively there and elsewhere in Tennessee. In the fall of 2004, NCC's office in Knoxville was deluged with faxes and emails demanding an end to the company's MTR activities. No one person or group was responsible for this protest, but Katuah Earth First! was known to oppose MTR and thus was a visible target for NCC retaliation, which came in the form of a SLAPP suit (Strategic Lawsuit Against Public Participation) filed against john johnson, Amanda Womac, Chris Irwin, and another KEF! activist. The pretext for it, Chris has told me, was a demonstration they'd held at NCC's office in Knoxville that fall. As demonstrations go, this one was pretty lame. "We [first] went to the wrong office—they had moved out. Only three of us showed up. We brought the wrong signs—I had to make signs there. We were in this parking lot in front of the building, and it was a Sunday, no one was there at all. We didn't give out a single piece of information. We sat on the lawn for an hour, bored out of our skulls. Amanda started reading. I sat there drawing for a while. It was depressing. I was a little embarrassed. I didn't even put it out on the listserv."

And then police came to Chris's and john's doors with warrants. "I'm in law school, and I was insulted," Chris continues. "They say that we showed up with bludgeons, chasing people around in the parking lot, blockaded it, terrified employees, harassed people going in. It was a complete lie. What they thought, because they're top-heavy with attorneys, was that they were going to be able to threaten us and we'd freak out and maybe just disappear." KEF!'s consolation in this is that NCC has had to pay expensive attorneys to dig them out of the mess the suit has become for them, while the KEFers are being represented by volunteers. "It's costing them a frigging arm and a leg," Chris says, cheerfully.

Yesterday, at the NCC shareholder meeting, according to the fellow telling me about it now at camp, "we were going to invade them, and make our demands known, educate the shareholders a little bit. We feel they've been lying about us, have spread various rumors about us that have no basis in fact," including that bombs have been put in mailboxes by members of KEF!

When he says "invade," he means "just that: Walk right in, raise as much Cain as we can without being violent, but definitely not walk out unless the cops tell us to," and just as definitely to leave on police orders. There was no plan for anyone to break the law or get arrested that day. "We expected that the police would eventually show up, and they would order us to disperse, whereupon we would, and go outside and hold our signs until they told us to disperse there. We just wanted to stretch it out as long as possible."

The Holiday Inn where the meeting was held is a conference center with several meeting rooms. "We sent a scout in earlier to ascertain exactly where they were at. It turned out they were in a very small little conference room.

"When we got the word that they were actually starting the meeting [at around 10 AM], we were all assembled at the shopping center across the street." The plan was for a couple of dozen protesters to go into the building. Two more would keep an eye out for the police and radio the people inside when they arrived, and still more people on the outside would be available to talk with hotel management and police, and generally keep an eye on things. "We walked in, went in the back door, and just as we went around the corner we saw some guy in a white shirt and he said, 'They're here.' And he walked in the door. We wondered, 'Huh. What's that all about?' It was just a white polo shirt [with a logo on its chest] and he was wearing normal slacks, dark slacks. We thought maybe he worked for the hotel. We didn't see any police around. We didn't have any reason to believe that they had been tipped off."

Although the protesters didn't know it at the time, the man in the polo shirt was Deputy Sheriff Thomas W. Walker, with the Knox County sheriff's department. (That logo was actually a sheriff's office insignia.) Walker was there because NCC had called a contact in the department to hire an off-duty officer to provide security that day, as they had done in the past. The sheriff's office decided instead to send two *on-duty* officers responsible for Homeland Security operations, which, in Knoxville at least, have persistently dogged Earth First! Neither NCC nor the protesters that day clearly understood that Walker was on duty rather than hired by NCC.

"The idea was to be quiet until we actually got" to the conference room. "We got there, and the door was locked. I started banging on the door and yelled 'Surprise!' We had lots of homemade drums, somebody had brought a trombone, there was somebody with a saxophone, various noisemakers." john johnson, with a bullhorn, kept up a loud stream of anti-MTR rhetoric.

"We [also] had four of these high-decibel battery-powered personal alarms that look kind of like beepers. (I've heard them called rape alarms. If you're attacked, you pull the little pin and it starts screaming. It makes an ungodly noise.) The idea was that after a while, when we found out the cops were coming," they'd set off the screamers.

The protesters banged on the door and made a racket. "We didn't think we'd ever get in, because they'd closed the door on us. But a couple of minutes later the door opened and that same guy in the white polo shirt came out and told us to go away. And we tried to charge past him, tried to barrel on right past the guy. But he was pretty big, and he was shoving people around."

As Chris Dodson, also at the action, later tells me, "Somebody from the meeting stood in front of the door. I thought it was the meeting's security—and it *was* the meeting's security." The unobtrusive insignia on Walker's shirt "didn't register with me for a long time," Chris says. "So we're chanting and drumming in the hall, and I sort of moved up front somehow. And I was right across from him. I saw [him] grab somebody by the throat, sort of choking him a little. That's the most out-of-hand thing I saw." While Chris was facing Walker, he noticed he was wearing a bracelet marked WWJD—What Would Jesus Do? Chris was appalled by this and asked him if he thought Jesus would be blowing the tops off mountains, and what would Jesus do about that. The guy got angry and told him that "Jesus would arrest you" and "Jesus would get a job."

Meanwhile, another demonstrator was egging the man-in-the-polo-shirt on, making goofy faces and gestures up close and in his face, escalating rather than defusing the man's aggression.

The eyewitness who began this story continues: "So we're trying to hold the door so people can get in, this guy [Walker] is trying to shove people out, I'm backed up in the door[way] facing the outside, with my hands up in the door frame, he's trying to move my hands, and there's other people trying to get in. There's small people trying to crawl between our legs. All kinds of stuff going on." Videotape taken by the protesters shows Walker briefly wrapping his arm around the neck of the guy holding the door, who simply stands his ground, still and apparently calm, refraining from fighting back or struggling to get away. Walker then shifts his attention to one of the other protesters at the door. The eyewitness in the doorway, like Chris, sees Walker grab that protester's throat. The fellow in the choke hold flails around, and at that point another protester, a very short young woman, rakes a hand across Walker's face.

"So we're doing all of this," the witness in the doorway continues, "and all of a sudden a couple of the guys in suits [inside the room] come and try to help the guy trying to push us all out. People are yelling, people are screaming, I'm turning my face around yelling in, telling the shareholders what's going on, why [MTR] is such a horrible idea. Eventually they did succeed in forcing us out. The guy in the white shirt stayed outside.

"But just before they shoved us out, I managed to take the alarm that I had in my pocket, pull the pin on it, and toss the alarm inside the door. So that thing is sitting there screaming, they finally shut the door on us, but we could hear it on the inside: WEEEWEEEWEEEWEEE! It was pretty funny. Another one got thrown in there too, and there were two that got tossed [above the hallway's] dropped-ceiling panels. So there's all this racket going on, it's crazy. People are still drumming. That guy [in the white shirt] is still shoving people around." (There was some confusion after the action about whether consensus had been reached prior to the action that it was OK to throw the screamers into the room. Several people said afterward that they felt doing so was aggressive, too much like throwing something *at* the people in the room.)

After the door closed, the eyewitness continues, "I was kind of looking around, wondering what to do, and then I noticed that around the corner there was an entrance to a courtyard. 'Oh! maybe there's a window!'" he thought. "I got a friend of mine, and we went around the corner and sure enough, there's a window. So, like little schoolkids, we jammed our faces up [against the glass], and we started banging on the window and making funny faces. You should have seen their faces: '*What* is going on? Oh my god this is craziness.'"

After a while "we went back [to the door to the conference room] and I look down and there's a watch on the floor. I reach down, I pick it up, and [show it to] the guy at the door, the guy in the white shirt: Is this yours? And he looks at it, looks really disgusted, and sticks it in his pocket. After a minute, I look close at his shirt, and what I thought to be a little corporate logo said: 'Knox County Sheriff's Department.' And I thought: 'Uhhh, oops. I wonder if this is a cop.' I start telling people: 'This guy may be a cop.' Several of us decided that that might be a good time to leave. So we did." They went to a restaurant pre-arranged as a rendezvous point.

Hotel staff came and addressed the remaining protesters in the hallway, pleading with them to leave out of consideration for other hotel guests. As they spoke, Walker smiled, did not identify himself as police, and gave no order to disperse. While the hotel staffers were still addressing the group, another officer arrived, identified himself as being with the sheriff's department, and ordered the protesters to leave the building, which they then did immediately. When some of the protesters continued drumming in the hotel parking lot, the officer who had ordered them to leave the building asked that the drumming stop. He told the protesters it would be OK for them to stand quietly in the parking lot, which they then did.

Then, unprovoked, the arrests began. Walker, john johnson remembers, "came outside and was obviously fixin' to point people out. And so I got pointed out, presumably because of my possession of the bullhorn. I would also imagine that the National Coal people [with their SLAPP suit in mind], said: 'You need to nail him.'" It was Walker and an officer in uniform, not the policeman who came inside and asked them to disperse, who actually arrested john. He was charged with inciting a riot and assaulting an officer with the bullhorn. (Videotape of the event shows no such thing.) Chris Dodson (accused of poking the polo-shirted cop in the eye with a drumstick—also contrary to the video) and one other protester, a young man named Sequoia, were arrested as well. (Sequoia "was way in the back of the crowd during the whole thing" at the door, Chris recalls.) All drew multiple felony charges with steep bails. "At our initial book," john says, "it was just assault and disorderly conduct. Then later on it turned into burglary, incitement to riot, aggravated riot, aggravated assault, and disrupting a public meeting.

"Initially when I got arrested, it was like: whatever. I've been arrested so many times. And I know there's a crackdown. All it takes is a cursory search of the internet to find out that there's all these people—just people holding signs in front of the presidential caravan, standing on the side of the road—have been arrested." (Larry Gibson has told me he went to a photo-op rally George W. Bush held in Beckley a while back, where President Bush endorsed MTR while folks bused in to attend the rally cheered. Larry snuck in and held up a sign that said "Stop Mountaintop Removal." He was arrested. "They told me I wasn't allowed to hold a political sign," he says. At a taxpayer-subsidized political rally.) "There definitely was an increase in penalties on nonviolent direct action protest" after Bush became president, john says—even before 9/11.

"So I know that's gonna happen, and that's part of the risk that you take when you do this kind of work, and stand up for the Earth and what you believe in," john continues. "So that whole part of it was not that big of a deal: Alright I'm going to jail, one more time, it's probably going to be disorderly conduct, criminal trespass, whatever.

"And then I found out it was assault—well, I didn't assault the guy. I would never assault a cop. You'd have to be a dumb-ass to assault a cop, unless the cop's like trying to kill you." john affirms that Walker must know that the people arrested didn't do what they're charged with. "And the affidavit says: These people are known Earth Firsters, who are known ecoterrorists, whose protests often end in violence. And that's never happened before. Our protests don't end in violence, unless it's the cops kicking *our* ass—and then it's not usually an Earth First! thing but some big street mobilization thing. And so he [Walker] got primed. I'm sure he was primed by National Coal and by other people in law enforcement: This is who it is, and this is what they're gonna do, blah, blah,

blah." (The uniformed cop who arrested john and drove them downtown asked on the way there where Chris Irwin was, said he's usually at these protests, and wondered how's he doing in law school.)

Chris Dodson finishes his part of the story: When "we were asked to leave, we went outside and reassembled. And some cop [in uniform] took me aside, I don't remember why—I wasn't being out of line or anything—and gave me this lecture about how I want the coal companies to follow the environmental laws, so I have to follow the laws as well. And I said 'yes I do want them to obey the law and yes, OK, I understand that.' I finished conversing with him and walked back, ten feet away or something, where we were just standing with our signs.

"And then we were asked to leave, and so we started leaving. The next thing I know I'm being grabbed really forcefully by my arm, by the guy [Walker] who was guarding the door. And the exact exchange there was: I said, 'What is this?' And he said, 'This is an arrest.' I said, 'Why are you arresting me?' And he said, 'Because I want to.'

"And so then I was cuffed, and they took my cymbal thing and the drumstick, and put me in the car with johnjohn. And I was in there for like an hour or so." Sequoia wasn't with them: "I didn't realize that Sequoia had been arrested until sometime after."

The police took them to be processed, "and I was thinking: OK, this is bull, but this is how things happen and I'm going to be charged with disorderly conduct or something, and that's going to be that. And bummer, I promised my mom I wouldn't get arrested until my grandparents had died. I'm thinking about my mom and how stressed she'd be.

"So I'm processed, and through the grapevine I hear the word 'assault' is associated with us somehow. I called Chris [Irwin], still thinking I'll be out of here in a couple of hours. And Chris said, 'We don't know what's going on, we heard the word assault, the warrant wasn't signed. You guys might have to sit tight for a few days.' And I thought: 'Oh bummer.'

"I was put in maximum security and thought: 'This is bizarre.' Things were beginning to set in on how much it sucked, but I was still on top of myself. That's one thing about this whole thing that was really empowering to me. I was just praying and stretching and singing—and every few hours would have this Omigod! [moment]—but it was fine." And he'd go back to praying and stretching and singing.

"So then like 10:00 or so, or 9:30 maybe the first night in there, Tuesday night, they put us before the magistrate (or as Chris likes to say the angry judge in a box). I was the first of the three of us to be read the charges, so my jaw was just on the floor when he was reading the arrest report. The report said that twenty-five people pushed into the room, that I hit him in the head with the drumstick. And it said that john hit him with the bullhorn. Obviously none of that is true. I was being charged with aggravated assault, aggravated riot, burglary, and disrupting a public meeting. My bond was like $13,000 or something.

"I went back to my cell and was spun out about it, but still trusted that people were going to get me out, and that this is how things happen with activists and it'll be pleaded down."

The next day, they were moved to a maximum security facility downtown, where Chris got a cellmate. "That was kind of intimidating right at first, but he was friendly to me, and the guy next door was friendly to me. I told them about why I was in there, and they recognized what an injustice it was. They were really a blessing to me, to have two people to talk to. Did my same routine in there except I wasn't singing because I was embarrassed I guess. I was stretching and praying and stuff, trying to read these horrible Louis Lamour books," which were all the reading material available, "until I found my roommate's New Testament. I started reading that, and that was so comforting. 'Blessed are the persecuted' was one of the things I read, and the story of Jesus is born and Herod is like: 'Kill him!'" He'd been reading the Bible for about an hour when he was bailed out by MJSers who were collecting funds for him and the others.

Overall, Chris says, "I feel OK, because I think I'm not gonna go to jail, and even if I do go to jail I think that will be OK too, in the grand scheme of everything. Even though I don't want to go to jail."

The Knoxville demonstration has a disturbing, unsettling effect on MJS overall. Hillary later tells me that, in West Virginia, after the actions in Knoxville and Pittsburgh a lot of people "rolled back into the house very late, sometime after 1:00 in the morning, and we had a discussion that went till 3:00 or so about nonviolence. And it was really, really interesting. At one point I asked everyone in the room: 'Wait a minute, this is why we had nonviolence trainings at camp. Who went to the nonviolence trainings at camp?' And a surprising number of people raised their hands. And I thought: Goodness, how can that be? Do people really understand what nonviolence is? Because in this conversation people were thinking: Well, we're being *less* violent than the police. By pushing, we're not *hurting* anybody—no one's being hurt so therefore it's nonviolent. By running away, we're hurting nobody, so this is nonviolence. The power [in nonviolence as a tactic] comes from accepting the oppression onto yourself by resisting it. In order to truly resist oppression, you cannot run from it. That's somehow submitting to it. Even if people say: 'Oh, I got my lick in and got out of there,' it's saying: 'I wasn't willing to face the consequences.' And they *are* unjust. That's what makes oppression oppressive."

After the Knoxville action, many MJSers seem to feel a need for reassurance that the nonviolence consensus won't be breached in future actions. Unless and until this is settled, quite a few people will be uneasy about planning actions with people they don't already know well. The organizers of MJS have acknowledged from the beginning that any lapse in practicing nonviolence, or simply undisciplined behavior, or lack of clarity about what behavior is expected, can put everyone in the group at risk, not only for serious legal charges but also for becoming targets of physical violence, the likelihood of which depends on circumstances that aren't fully predictable. It also can make MJS look bad and undo a lot of good work in coalition building and in community, media, and police relations.

Watching videotape of the action, a couple of weeks later, I realize that I too have been uneasy about whether and to what extent and by whom MJS's nonviolence consensus might have been breached. I'm relieved that the video shows just two people making physical contact with the then-unidentified cop, in panic, apparently unintentionally, flailing around in reaction to his aggression, and just one person escalating that aggression by egging him on. (Apparently all three were among those who left the scene before arrests were made. Some MJSers not at the demo have expressed dismay, concern, or disgust about those who left, viewing their early exit as running away or failing to take responsibility for and accept the consequences of their actions.) I'm also relieved to see several examples of individuals choosing *not* to be aggressive, instead becoming still and apparently calm when physically challenged. The most serious problem shown on the video was that no one at the demo made much effort—and no effective effort—to calm the people who were out of line, de-escalate their behavior, and get them out of the way of trouble.

"I'm disappointed in myself for not helping with our own kind of crowd control more aggressively," john says, looking back on the action. "It really shouldn't have happened like that. I thought we were all on the same page about having a pretty solid, strict nonviolence code. And obviously we weren't, for whatever reason. We're gonna have to address that as a group.

"I'm glad we did the action. I totally would stand behind what I think is our human right to disrupt a meeting of a corporation. I just don't think that corporations have the same rights as we do, and when it's a corporation that's destroying the mountains, all bets are off. I'll totally defend that."

For the past few years, KEF! in coalition with other groups in the region has set up an Eastern Forest Defense Camp each summer featuring training in such things as how to do a tree sit, how to set up blockades, how to design direct actions, how to talk to the media. The MJS camp in Louisa is to be of this nature, offering training for people who want to do backwoods actions. When I arrive at camp on the evening of June 8, I find twenty or so people, with more expected overnight.

Camp is a cluster of building lots on a mountain with young, patchy, mixed-hardwood forest. The camp's gathering place is at two adjacent cabins and their surrounding yards, owned by Patsy Carter and her sister Judy Maynard. Patsy, a middle-aged woman with curly light-brown hair and a shaky voice, allows the MJSers to take over her kitchen, and she and Judy prepare some of the food for them.

Patsy and Judy became involved with MJS as part of their efforts to stop damage being done by coal trucks. I'm told that coal trucks in Kentucky are allowed to haul up to 126,000 pounds—far more than the normal federal limit of 80,000 pounds. Apparently even that's not enough. Kentucky officials have acknowledged that coal trucks along Rt. 23 near Louisa commonly haul more than 200,000 pounds. All that pounding takes a toll: Kentucky spent more than $110 million on repairs to Rt. 23 between 1996 and 2003. Overweight and recklessly driven coal trucks also take a toll in human life throughout the coalfields. Dozens of people have died and hundreds have been injured in collisions with coal trucks in the past few years.

One of those killed was Patsy's daughter. "It's hard to comprehend how dirty these coal companies are," Patsy tells me. "My daughter was twenty-one years old. She was my life. She had mountains in her, our heritage. I taught her to pick greens, I taught her to can, taught her how to wring a chicken's neck. You know, survival. She was eleven days [from] graduating from Southern West Virginia Community College. She was working and going to school, and she called me every night when she got off work. I knew what time she was coming home, and if she was five minutes late, I knew something was wrong—I was afraid she'd have a flat or something.

"We were living in Mingo County, West Virginia [close to the Kentucky border], and this truck came out of Pike County, Kentucky, and went into West Virginia. And this man driving this truck, he was on a prison work-release program. He had an ankle bracelet on him, and he was supposed to be monitored. They allowed him to go to work, and home.

"He had driven this truck for eighteen hours." Coal is hauled twenty-four hours a day, seven days a week. "Nobody checked on him.

"She called me, and told me she was on her way home, 12:33 at night. I knew it took her twenty minutes to get home." When she didn't arrive home, Patsy remembers, "my husband was in bed. He had to get up and go to work [the next morning] and I debated whether to get him up or not. So I went by myself.

"It was bad. That truck was hauling 158,000 pounds of coal. They had tried to tamper with the evidence, and tried to move the truck, and another driver that was supposedly in front of him gave a statement at the scene that my daughter was on their side of the road. They tried to say she fell asleep, and I knew better. She was a night owl.

"They almost had me to worrying it was her fault, and then the deputy sheriff's office in Mingo County lost the blood work. It was supposed to have been sent to Charleston [for analysis]. We had some real good friends that worked in places, and got a blood report on him." He had taken thirty Xanax pills, tranquilizers, before the accident. "I don't know how he drove."

Patsy's daughter was killed in 2000. After that, Patsy suffered a long nervous breakdown. "For a year, I didn't know hot water from cold water in my own house. I didn't know a slice of bread from an egg. I completely lost my mind. But I was totally normal before this. We were an average family. It destroyed us. It devastated us. I couldn't put into words what it has done to us."

Meanwhile, the overweight coal trucks continued to roar past Patsy's house at all hours of the day and night, on a narrow, winding road where schoolchildren walk. She and her family have been fighting to fix this, and to fix the wider problem of coal trucks killing and terrorizing people driving or walking along the roads throughout the coalfields. (Recently, one man was killed at his roadside mailbox.) It's an uphill battle; one result of it is that Patsy's had twenty-some flat tires since she started it, presumably in retaliation for her work.

At one point, "we were raising enough hell over in West Virginia that they did a bust," stopping coal trucks and writing fifty-three tickets for various safety offenses. Every truck they stopped was overloaded, except for three that were on their way to pick up coal. "We were so proud," Judy says, that the state police "had stepped in to help us. And then the tickets went to Mingo County courthouse and they were tore up." A magistrate bragged about it on local talk radio afterward. "It was a joke, and he was laughing, saying 'I tore up every one of them tickets.'"

While mourning her daughter, Patsy also mourns the mountains. When she sees a coal truck go by she thinks: "That's our mountains being shipped out, that's our mountains leaving."

Patsy thinks of the MJS campers as "my kids. Before they even got here I was going to Goodwills and thrift stores and pulling stuff together that they can use," from camping gear to kitchen utensils. "I just got in the habit: Oh, my kids might need this."

My sense on arriving at camp is that people have lost focus and are a bit off stride. After a morning of setting up camp—digging latrines, rigging tarps for sun shelter, marking trails, checking gear, scheduling shifts at the registration desk down by the road—the campers seem in a much better humor, more themselves. (There was concern that the surveillance encountered at Pipestem would recur or escalate here, but blessedly there's no discernable surveillance whatsoever, other than by the camp's own security volunteers.) Focus still seems lacking, though, and there seems to be little sense of urgency about finding it. Roughly fifty or so people gather in Patsy's yard after lunch. Chris Irwin, who arrived during the night from Knoxville, reports that Chris Dodson and Sequoia are out of jail and that john is expected to be out tonight or early tomorrow.

Many of the campers spend much of the afternoon in tree-climbing training. Chris notes that they're going at this very carefully and thoroughly, with the intention that trainees should actually use the knots, climbing, and other skills learned here in actions later in the summer.

One of the trainers, a young woman called Amerika, talks with me for a while about tree sitting as an activist tool here compared to out West, where the trees are a lot taller. Activists seeking to save western old-growth forests have prevented or delayed logging by simply climbing trees in patches of forest slated for logging and refusing to come down. Trees here in the Cumberland Plateau, most of which is in relatively young, mixed-hardwood forest, without the tall, tall conifers of the west coast, typically can't be climbed and sat in higher than where a cherry-picker can be brought in to remove you. For this reason, Amerika and others in the campaign have been thinking that setting traverse lines to allow movement between trees and making a sort of tree village, where the "sitters" are moving rather than stationary, might be a sensible adaptation of western techniques to eastern landscape. "It's important to see exactly where you are, and what you're trying to do," she says. "If your goal is to stop them from entering an area, a tree sit isn't going to be all that effective. Maybe [more effective would be] a tripod in the middle of the road, with plenty of different support lines coming off, and with support people being able to talk [to whoever comes to dismantle the tripod] about how each of these lines is important to the integrity of the structure," to explain how efforts to dismantle the tripod could endanger the person sitting on top of it. "We're the small fish fighting the big shark. Tree sits and tripods are very photogenic. It really sets us up well for being publicized, particularly in this area, where it's not happened before."

The afternoon becomes hot. Rain threatens but never quite comes, and then the temperature drops. Campers who'd earlier thought of going swimming at a nearby lake instead hang around on Patsy's porch and lawns. The mood is relaxed and good-humored, especially after word comes from Knoxville that everyone is now out of jail. (Patsy and her family put up a property bond for john, along with $1,500 cash they know they won't get back. The joke around camp is that among "her kids" Patsy's already bailing out a problem child.) Anyone lucky enough to snag one of the half-dozen rocking chairs on the porch doesn't want to move. Roadkill venison is being prepared for supper, and there's talk about "ninjas" and "pirates," labels some of the campers apply to themselves and use in making good-humored fun of their friends. Campers who favor ninja style claim vast superiority over those who favor a pirate style, and vice versa. Ninjas tend to enjoy scouting and sneaking through the woods; pirates are more likely to do canvassing and door-to-door work. Ninjas wear black and camouflage; pirates favor more flamboyant dress. Ninjas think they're more competent; pirates are sure they have more fun. Ninjas are (mostly) indifferent cooks; pirates know the power of the kitchen.

Campers spend the next day in workshops on plant identification, woods skills, climbing, and stealth (avoiding detection when you're out in the woods). In the evening, the whole camp gathers in Patsy's yard to talk about what happened at the demonstration in Knoxville.

The major part of this meeting is a Chris Irwin rant—not the soapbox, public-event kind of rant he's admired for, but a long, angry scolding, directed primarily at people who were at the Knoxville demo. Paloma, who arrived at camp today, joins in from time to time. Most of the KEFers present are offended by the scolding; it opens old wounds from past and ongoing conflicts about leadership and group dynamics. But no one confronts Chris.

Chris, obviously angry, says that the problem with the action was that people diverged from nonviolence and tried to push past the cop and the people attending the meeting to get inside. This would have been a disaster in West Virginia or Kentucky, he says, where such action would have cost support for MJS from locals and local organizations. But this wouldn't have happened in West Virginia or Kentucky, Chris says. He's particularly angry that "tourists" felt free to come to Tennessee and make such a mess. KEFers from North Carolina take it that by "tourists" Chris means them, as there weren't many traveling activists from farther afield involved in the hotel action. They find this especially offensive, as KEFers from Asheville and Knoxville have worked together in Tennessee for years.

We need to have our own peacekeepers at actions, Chris continues. We need to make sure that groups involved in actions don't break consensus. We need to avoid peer pressure when seeking consensus—it's important to really listen to people's concerns about what should and shouldn't be done at actions.

"If we're going to continue" having MJS people and actions in Knoxville, Chris says, "we need assurances" that what happened at the hotel won't recur. People in Kentucky and West Virginia also want these assurances, he asserts. (Later, Chris tells me the challenge is to have 100 percent compliance with nonviolence, every time—even one or two people failing to adhere to this once invites disaster for all.) Chris still feels that MJS is the best tool at hand for what they want to accomplish. "We've worked our asses off for this campaign. [It's] our best shot" at ending MTR.

In response, one of those at the Knoxville action says he didn't see "peer pressure" in the planning for it. Without giving a specific example, Chris tells him that a couple of people he talked to did feel pressured, to which the response is: Let's affirm that there should be no such pressure—and that if anyone *does* feel pressured, they should say so. Squirrel, a young woman from North Carolina, adds: "It's OK to stand aside," to refrain from either supporting or blocking a consensus decision, but agree to abide by it out of respect for the group. "Nobody's going to hate you." (This begs the question of what happens to anyone who feels strongly enough to want to *block* all or part of what the group is planning, rather than just stand aside from the decision, but no one pursues this.) Abigail says we need better consensus-in-a-crisis communications and contingency planning.

Dave Cooper wants to talk about damage control. Concerning what to tell mainstream, moderate groups such as KFTC and Sierra Club about the action, Chris suggests noting that the three arrestees were targeted because they were perceived as leaders (or simply annoyed the man in the white shirt), the charges against them are baseless, and we have video to prove it. And concerning press, the group (which yesterday decided not to allow reporters, other than myself, to come to this camp) agrees not to volunteer more information about this demo to the media, to let it drop. Knoxville's daily newspaper, with which KEF! has had good relations, didn't mention MJS in its coverage of the incident, so letting it drop seems feasible as well as desirable.

There's general agreement that peacekeepers at actions are very much needed, that MJSers need de-escalation training, and that de-escalation, a focused effort to calm the situation rather than aggravate it, could have saved the Knoxville action from such a bad end. But Amerika demurs, pointing out a contradiction: When we plan actions like this one, invading someone else's meeting, we're aiming to *escalate*, to have more effect. How, exactly, does de-escalation fit?

The next morning's workshops focus on blockades, with most of the camp in attendance. Much of the training is about creating "soft" block-ades, using just the bodies of groups of people—different ways of linking yourselves together with handholds and other grips that avoid an aggres-sive appearance and make it difficult for police to pry you apart or tip you over or reach sensitive parts of your body to cause enough pain to compel you to give up. (The Orwellian law-enforcement term for this is "pain compliance.") Blockades using human bodies are based on the assumption of human decency—that no one will actually run you over with a truck, say, or bludgeon you while you're immobilized. They're safest when employed at a time and place when media or other observers are present, as police and workers inconvenienced by the blockade are less likely to behave brutally if they know they're being watched.

After practice with soft blockades, the discussion shifts to hard blockades, where protesters lock themselves to something that makes it more difficult to move them. Hard blockades can involve attaching people to something stationary on site (a heavy piece of equipment, a gate) or to something heavy brought in for the purpose (a junked car, a bin filled with concrete). To lock down to such objects, or to each other, protesters often use lockboxes, typically heavy metal pipe into which hands are inserted and invisibly locked together. After some practice with cardboard mockups of straight-line and 45-degree lockboxes, the workshop concludes with a brief discussion of tripods. These large, quickly assembled blockades are typically used to block a road, with a protester locked to the apex of a sort of teepee made with long poles so that moving the poles endangers the protester at the apex. The tripod training today is by no means enough that anyone who's never done it before could go out and do such an action safely, just enough to sketch an overview of how it's done.

The afternoon's workshops focus on tree sitting again, both climbing and ground support for tree sitters. Unfocused as this camp was at first, by today—the last day of training—the campers are fully engaged with learning new skills and working out how to move forward. Less training has been accomplished than was intended, but there will be opportunities for more at another backwoods camp later this month.

The group's focus and efficiency carries over to the next morning, which begins with a brisk meeting about how to avoid further missteps like what happened at the Knoxville demo as the campaign moves ahead. The group consenses on a protocol for planning actions in the future: 1) all participants in any action should gather right before the action, both to make sure everybody's on the same page and to explicitly affirm a commitment to nonviolence at that action; 2) after each action, participants should gather to go over what worked well and what didn't, from logistics to nonviolence to media and community liaison; 3) peacekeepers or nonviolence observers should be present at each action, although the group remains a bit hazy about whether it's enough that everyone is expected to be a peacekeeper or whether specific individuals should be responsible for this; 4) group communication-in-a-crisis procedures or signals should be agreed upon before the action, especially some way to communicate when adherence to nonviolence is slipping; and 5) everything at an action should be videotaped. More discussion will follow, and details remain to be worked out, but the group now seems ready and willing to move forward together.

Today, June 12, is the first day of a week of post-camp activities in Kentucky. To introduce MJSers (most of whom are from out of state) to the impact MTR is having there, KFTC has arranged a tour.

The first stop is at Mickey and Nina McCoy's house in Inez, a pleasant little town by the West Virginia border surrounded by an appalling concentration of MTR sites. The agenda here is informal conversation among about fifty MJS and KFTC people, and a barbecue lunch.

The food today is good—hot dogs and hamburgers from the grill, veggie dogs and lots of salads for vegan and health-minded visitors, and red-velvet cupcakes supplied by Mickey's good Republican aunt who lives next door. Mickey grew up here. His family and neighbors apparently accept his activism and hillbilly-hippie attitude, in part because he's his late, well-respected mother's son but also because he's not just a troublemaker. He and Nina have taught at the local public school for many years, long enough that he says they've given up trying to get rid of him. Mickey's well-liked enough locally to have once been elected mayor, on a write-in ballot in the late 1980s. "We're the token environmentalists for the county," Nina says.

With everyone fed, Mickey and Nina stand side by side in their yard and tell MJS and KFTC their story. "Welcome to Inez," Mickey begins. "It's so good having you here. I'm glad to see so many people give a damn about the problems that we have here. [Most] people that live here are either unable or will not speak out about it.

"See, this area has always been run by the mines. In 1970 the mines came back into this county in full force with Massey, and in 1974 the coal boom hit. Now in 1974 some of y'all probably weren't even born. I graduated from high school in 1974. Many people in my class immediately got a job in the mines, and in '74 they were making $16, $17 an hour. And so they thought they had it made.

"One of the things Massey made sure of was that it would never go union. Because with a union, people get to feeling good about each other. If you can keep people separated and in their own little worlds, then it's divide and conquer.

"So in '74 a high school graduate coulda got a job in the coal mines and bought himself a four-wheel drive, bought himself a trailer, bought himself either a wife or a boat, whichever one he cared for. Now, I don't mean that to be a sexist thing. A lot of ladies also looked for—'Oh, I gotta get me a coal miner.' And they got married and that was the end of it for a long time."

Having set the scene, Mickey talks next about sludge: "Once they clean the coal they have to have somewhere to put this waste, so they put in what they call a pond. I have a problem with the wording of that because if you've seen these things—the pond that broke here in Martin County back in 2000 was seventy-two acres. Ladies and gentlemen, I think that constitutes a lake. So a lot of times when you hear 'slurry pond' or 'sludge pond,' if you investigate, these ponds are gigantic."

They're also unnecessary. There are other ways to process coal that don't generate such vast amounts of liquid waste—using slurry ponds is just a bit cheaper, as long as you don't have to count all the environmental and human costs. Coal companies have not been held to account for most of those costs, nor for the plain stupidity of what they're doing. One woman I've talked with points out how dumb it is to pump all this liquid *uphill* to where it threatens everything below. Now she's just one of those ignorant hillbillies, she says, but even she knows how gravity works. And she can see that it's dumber still to do this in a place where coal companies are in effect creating earthquakes all the time by setting off enormous quantities of explosives.

"There was no life lost" in the 2000 flood, Mickey says. ("Except in the creek," Nina notes.) But "there were hundreds of lives affected, and we don't know if there will be life lost later. Because we get our [municipal] water supply from a reservoir that comes from the Tug River. Wolf Creek flows into the Tug River. Our water supply was downstream of the sludge spill. So it was being pumped into our reservoir." Mickey and Nina still don't drink the water that comes out of their tap, and all food prepared at their house is cooked with bottled water. "One of the biggest sales in the two supermarkets here is bottled water," Mickey notes.

The sludge that spilled down Wolf and Coldwater creeks "is like a black lava. When it came down the creek, you could throw a can in the creek"—Mickey's holding a mostly full soda can—"and this can would have just floated right on top. It was so thick, and slow-moving, it smothered any kind of aquatic life.

"But of course we have agencies that protect us. My wife will tell you something about those agencies and how they work to protect us under the present administration."

Nina continues the story: "We got a real education from this. This was, according to the EPA, the worst environmental disaster that ever hit the eastern part of the United States." The investigation Jack Spadaro pursued found that the sludge pond had already broken in 1994, and that MSHA ordered them to fix it. "Well, they didn't fix it. They knew from the records that it was gonna break again, and that it was releasing into our water supply. It's almost hard to believe that people would let this continue on.

"But you have to look at what the people here see it as, and how they're dealing with it. First of all, you have a lot of people who make their money in mining. They're good people, they're hard-working people. They actually are the people who think they can control their destiny here, because they're working. Those are the people who we would really need to have on our side, as activists, because working people are the people who realize that what they do makes a difference. But those people are usually working for the mines. And you know you can't hardly work for something every day, go to work every day and think that you are doing evil. So it would be very hard on them to come out and speak against mining—even though they were *so* mad about this sludge spill. They were fightin' mad about this. But it's very difficult to go against the company that feeds you.

"So you have that. And you also have the environmental agencies that we assumed would just come in and [fix things]. We know that we can't depend on them a lot of times, but we thought that something on this scale—there's just no way you can get around this. But in fact they did."

"You know," Mickey adds, "we don't hate coal truck drivers. We don't hate coal miners. Really, I'm not against deep mining. But mountaintop removal is the work of the devil.

"Bill Caylor, the president of the [Kentucky] Coal Association, said in one meeting we were at that he would eat sludge." There's a lot of chuckling from the crowd in the yard at this, as MJS is scheduled to march right past his office in Lexington later in the week. One voice from the audience asks: "Who wants to bring him some?"

Mickey used to have a jar of Inez sludge but gave it away to a KFTC fundraiser. "But we may get some more of it today," he says, "because it's still around. It didn't disappear. We'll go up into Coldwater, and I'll bet my house against a donut that I can get in the creek, and get a shovel, and turn that shovel over and you'll see sludge."

Mickey leads the caravan of MJS and KFTC cars from his house up Coldwater Creek, just outside of Inez, past the few dozen houses dotted along the road that runs along the creek. The hollow is narrow enough that there's only one road, which dead-ends just before reaching the mine site at the head of the hollow. (Massey takes its own traffic out of the mine onto public roads elsewhere.) There's little obvious evidence of the 2000 spill now, other than some erosion along the banks of the creek, likely a result of trees having been removed from along the creek to enable access by equipment used to remove the sludge.

As Mickey predicted, much of that sludge is still here. Although the creek looks normal now, every time it rains hard it still runs black, as the rushing runoff finds and leaches away more sludge. Mickey takes a shovel down to the creek and plunges it into the creek bed. Up from beneath the thin layer of sand below the water comes a shovelful of dense, black, sticky-like-clay, oily-smelling sludge. He puts some of it in a container and hands it to MJS people from Lexington, who promise to put it to good use.

The caravan bids Mickey goodbye and moves on to a federal prison built on a "reclaimed" MTR site nearby. It's the damnedest looking thing. We turn off the highway, there's a valley fill in front of us, its wide, steep slope thinly covered with grass and streaked with erosion lines—and up on the dead-level top of the valley fill is a guard tower, floodlights, and a fence. Yes, someone thought it reasonable to build a multimillion-dollar prison on top of millions of cubic yards of irregularly sized, unstable mining debris. Predictably, the prison has settled unevenly, costing tax-payers tens of millions of dollars to repair it. Locals now call the prison "Sink Sink." I've heard it's the most expensive federal prison ever built.

Just uphill and beyond the entrance to the prison a grandiose sign marks the entrance to the "Honey Branch Regional Business Park," part of the "Big Sandy Regional Industrial Authority, Inc." We turn in at the sign and find a vast and very flat area adjacent to the prison grounds, with a nicely paved and curbed road cutting across many, many empty acres of lifeless rubble. It looks like whoever prepared this site for construction just ran a bulldozer over the top and hoped for the best. Obviously, businesses are reluctant to build up here because of the Sink Sink experience—even though, according to Dave Cooper, developers who build here get big tax breaks for doing so. The only development we see consists of two medium-sized warehouses, (one unoccupied) and a storage depot and parking lot associated with the occupied warehouse.

Basically, what a prudent developer would have to do here is put up a building that's disposable, so that when the site settles the owner can afford to walk away from it. Dave says the whole "reclamation" claim for the prison and the industrial park is essentially a scam. "There's hun-dreds of thousands of acres of this," he says, kicking at the raw surface of the rubble. "They continue to justify blowing up mountains by say-ing: Oh, we're creating badly needed flat land for development. There's already hundreds of thousands of acres of this!" And no one's building on it. "You see that Wal-Mart there?" Nope, nothing but rubble.

MJS's main event in Kentucky this week is a rally and march in down-town Lexington on Friday, June 17. About twenty speakers from all over the coalfield region address the crowd in a busy park in the downtown business district: Chris Irwin and john johnson deliver rousing rants;

Patsy Carter tells the story of her daughter's death; and Ali, a student at the University of Kentucky, describes how, shortly before the rally, all dolled up in a dressy gown, she held a silver platter and offered sludge from Inez served on china to the Kentucky Coal Association's Bill Caylor outside his office up the street. (He dipped in a finger and tasted it.) After the rally, MJSers march through downtown past Caylor's office to the Kentucky Utilities building, where they post three demands on the front door: that KU use no more coal mined by MTR, that it adopt the best available pollution controls, and that by 2020 at least 20 percent of its electricity come from renewable sources.

That evening, where the marchers have gathered for dinner, I talk with Kentucky organizers about how MJS's week in Kentucky has been. All seem pleased, particularly by the rally, which, with scores of people participating, was an unusually large event by Lexington standards.

One MJS action in Kentucky turned out, unintentionally, to be very funny. The evening before the rally, MJSers visited what a little research told them was the home address of a Massey executive, to flyer the neighborhood and protest at his house. Turns out the executive had sold the house and moved on. According to Jamie, who was there, the new owner came out and told them: "He doesn't live here anymore! He doesn't live here anymore! He moved out last November. I don't like him [either]. He screwed me over with my house. I've got a few choice words for him." So everybody had a laugh, the MJSers apologized, and that was that.

Compared to West Virginia and Tennessee, anti-MTR activism in Kentucky is much lower in intensity and less focused. It might just be that Kentucky isn't quite ripe for coming to grips with MTR and its bigger context the way folks in the Coal River valley and Tennessee are, for different reasons. (Coal River has Marsh Fork's second silo as the last straw; Tennessee is seeing MTR just getting started and coming at them right now.) Kentucky suffers, perhaps, from too much of the same old thing, which breeds burnout in activists and can't-make-a-difference apathy in everyone else. MJSers in Kentucky hope that the growing energy in other states will ignite their state as well as the campaign continues.

From Kentucky I head back down to Tennessee, to tag along on a tour of the public roads through the Eagan Mountain mine site with MJS organizers from Knoxville. After meeting at the cemetery high on the mountain there, the group splits up. Some go to scout parts of the site with protest in mind, looking for patches of healthy forest and evaluating the terrain for possible civil disobedience action. I join a convoy of several other cars driving along the public roads, stopping from time to time to get out and look.

Our longest stop is at a part of the site for which a hearing is to be held tomorrow in a nearby school, in connection with TDEC's consideration of whether Mountainside Coal may alter one of the streams that feed into Tackett Creek.

Right by the road here, beavers have dammed up a pond. Its waters are murky now with runoff from clear-cutting just uphill, where bare ground has been left to erode in sheets. A bridge, presumably built for the convenience of loggers and miners, crosses the pond. Across the bridge, I make my way up the steep hillside on a rough roadway of exposed, eroded, yellowish subsoil. It's hot today, and with no tree cover here now, the sun is vicious. At the side of the roadway, where the trees are gone but scraps of soil remain, the tender green leaves of may apples that must have emerged under their accustomed forest canopy this spring tell me this slope was clear-cut within just the last few weeks. At the top of the hill, I can see hundreds of acres of clear-cuts beyond the ridgeline. To the right, along the ridge, is a glimpse of what's just been lost here: The logging has closed in around a remnant patch of young mixed-hardwood forest, a little drier here on the ridgeline than it would have been on the slope I just walked up, which must have been a lovely young hardwood cove a few weeks ago.

A short walk on the logging road near the ridgeline leads to a small ditch that runs across the road. The ditch itself is apparently devoid of life—just bare dirt and bare rocks. But to the side of the road, uphill just a few yards—well, there's some moss there, in the small channel that flows into the ditch. Looking a little closer, I see wet mud, then water. Picking up a wet rock, I find a caddis fly; a stream biologist here with us today finds a crayfish. It's pretty dry here now, late on a hot afternoon in mid-June, but this is obviously the headwaters of a stream—a perennial stream, the caddis fly and crayfish tell us, a living thing full of other living things that feeds bigger streams and rivers and their communities of life downhill from here. In fact, this stream, along with hundreds, perhaps thousands like it—many of them threatened by MTR—ultimately feeds the Big South Fork of the Cumberland River, one of the jewels of the U.S. national park system. This is the stream that Mountainside Coal proposes to "alter." Of course, the logging road and the ditch and the trees knocked over into the stream by loggers here mean that it's already been altered. But the mining operation slated for after the logging is done would obliterate hundreds of yards of stream entirely and replace them with a lifeless "wet-weather conveyance," as the industry calls them. (Chris Irwin calls them "industrial drainage ditches.") These impermeable chutes, fed by rapid runoff from the clear-cut mine site, move water faster than natural streams do, in unnatural pulses that cause stream-bank erosion and episodes of flash flooding all the way down the watershed, degraded surface water quality, and reduced refilling of aquifers used for drinking water.

If the loggers and the miners stopped right now, the stream, the hardwood cove, and in time probably another healthy beaver pond would all come back, healed and regenerated by the extraordinary resilience and abundance of life in this bioregion, much as the patch of young forest remaining on the ridgeline has come back from previous logging. What's happened here so far this year, though sad, is largely reversible. What's proposed simply isn't. Once this hillside is blown up, moved around, rearranged into terraces and a drainage ditch, the community of life that is natural to this place, that evolved here over millions of years to a rare profusion of diversity, life-giving in its production of plant life and clean water and oxygen, will be gone and will never live here again.

All this is especially sad because it's a fait accompli. The mining permit for this site has already been granted by the Office of Surface Mining (OSM). All that's up for approval at tomorrow's TDEC hearing is the alteration of the stream. TDEC is a state agency, and because it's OSM, a federal agency, that regulates coal mining in Tennessee under SMCRA, the state's authority is pretty much limited to regulating the effects of mining on waterways. As the effects of MTR (or "cross-ridge" mining) on all waterways downstream are catastrophic, the state could effectively ban it entirely. To date, however, TDEC has generally enabled rather than impeded strip mining.

The TDEC hearing is held on a Monday evening, June 20, at the elementary school in Clairfield, near the Eagan Mountain mine site. At the school, about seventy people assemble for the hearing, maybe forty of them supporters of Mountainside Coal, all but three of them men, most wearing shirts or hats with company logos. They're likely most or all of the company's local employees. More than a dozen MJSers are in attendance, plus Jim Massengill (the fellow I met in the woods near Caryville, who's since got to know some of the Knoxville-based MJSers), a local woman who's been allowing MJSers to camp on her land, and the stream biologist who toured the site with us yesterday. TDEC has sent four people to run the hearing.

Chris Irwin has told me that he used to think that asking for hearings and attending them and testifying was "lame." Then, he says, "we heard the companies start screaming in their [reports to stockholders] that it's costing them a frigging arm and a leg because of delays in permits." And he and his fellow Tennessee activists learned that by doing their own scouting and water testing, they're able to introduce information at hearings that contradicts what's being presented (no, the pH of that stream isn't x, it was y when we tested it last week) or provides missing context (hey, there are five landslides that you have no record of on the land we're discussing). "There's a war of attrition aspect to what we're doing," Chris says. "If we can see that we can cost these companies money, we'll do it. Death of a thousand nicks."

As unsatisfactory as the hearing at Marsh Fork Elementary School was, with state officials apparently just going through the motions of recording speakers' testimony, this hearing is worse. The TDEC official in charge announces that people who want to testify will be led, one by one, to a separate room to speak into a tape recorder for up to five minutes. When an MJSer complains that, at a *public* hearing, the *public* should be able to hear the testimony, the official answers that this meeting will be run by his rules. One by one, opponents of the stream alteration are taken out to testify. Not one of the coal company supporters testifies. If their bosses asked them to attend this meeting, they apparently didn't ask them to speak.

This is the first hearing or meeting about nearby strip mining to be held in this area—despite the fact that thousands of acres are already being actively mined within a few miles of here. It's hard for people who live nearby to understand fully what's going on up there overall, not just the fragments they might know from neighbors who work for a coal company or from roaming around on their ATVs. What's happening now is so much bigger than the mining and logging that's happened here before. People remember smaller-scale strip mining from decades ago and think, "Oh, they're mining up there again"—but what's going on now is vastly more destructive. And it's very difficult to figure out exactly what *is* going on up there. People who live in this community don't have access to airplanes to fly over and take aerial photographs. How can they know to go down to Knoxville and find exactly the right government offices to ask exactly the right questions to get bits of information about what's going on in their neighborhood? Nor do most people have the skills and persistence required to piece that information together to make sense of the overall situation. (They only reason MJS knows about it is that Chris, Paloma, Gena, and john have been almost insanely persistent about tracking what OSM and TDEC are permitting. The only reason even this belated hearing is happening is because they demanded it.) At no point in the process of allowing all this mining to happen—the process of government agencies granting coal companies the right to destroy entire mountain ranges—at no point is anyone required to present to nearby communities an overall accounting of the disaster that's about to befall them, let alone seek their consent. This evening, one of the TDEC officials here acknowledges to me that this is so—but adds that all is being done according to the rules.

While testimony is being taken, MJSers question the two TDEC officials remaining in the meeting room. Many of the coal company supporters leave the room and stand outside, chatting. Then something interesting and unexpected happens: One MJSer starts up a conversation with a miner, then another conversation begins, then another.

For close to an hour, MJSers listen to miners talk about what they do at work, and why they think Mountainside Coal isn't a bad company, as coal companies go. And the miners listen to MJSers talk about the long-term ill effects of mining, both on nature and on the local community, which at the rate MTR is going here will be surrounded by an economically useless wasteland by the time today's schoolchildren are grown up and looking for work. Whatever's going on back in the room with the tape recorder, a real public meeting is now taking place here.

"I didn't feel like these people were villains," Paloma tells me the next day, at home in Knoxville. "They're trying to feed their family, and this is the only job in the area that's paying anything. The reality is it's that or pretty much nothing." The conversations kept coming back to this, and getting stuck there.

After the Eagan Mountain tour and hearing, MJSers begin to voice doubts about whether Eagan is really a good focus for MJS in Tennessee. One problem is the site itself; it's awfully big, with few patches of healthy forest left to make a case for saving, and none of those in good locations for tree sitting or blockading or other such direct action. Another problem is that most locals know so little about what's going on up there, and what's slated for their area overall. A lot of education would be needed before they could reasonably be asked to support any civil disobedience at the site. In addition, several incidents of arson have taken place in the community recently, apparently related to private disputes. Arson for any reason, Paloma notes, conveys that "there's real repercussions for stepping out of line." Furthermore, according to Paloma, one of the pro-coal locals at the hearing told MJSers that "'if you people go up there [on the mountain] and try to do anything, you need to know that we have shotguns.' The [MJS] person responded: 'Are you threatening me?' And he said: 'Well, no. I'm just saying you need to know people have shotguns and use them.'"

The only immediate plans agreed upon right now for Eagan are to do another round of Listening Project interviews there. "We need to establish credibility within the local community," Paloma tells me. To help with that, she says, "I'd like to see the people that are going door-to-door meet certain criteria that I have. They're all going to be showered, shampooed, and shined. They're going to be not looking like they're coming from the urban punk scene, dressed in a way that's not going to be offensive or disconcerting to the local population.

"Part of being a good grassroots organizer is to make as little ripples [as possible] in the areas that you don't need to be making ripples, because what you're there for is going to be a pretty big ripple in and of itself, so don't add anything extra to that. I think a lot of times that's real difficult to grasp for people who are like: 'No! This is a statement of my individuality. These are my beliefs. It's totally fine to skinny-dip.'" And now, in this campaign, Paloma's thinking: "No, not really. Not without offending a lot of people. It's fine in your own culture. But now you're in this different culture." On the whole, Paloma's impressed with how well MJSers are managing cultural sensitivity. "But you keep on seeing little things, little blips, little accidents that they just didn't think about. You didn't tell them about that part."

After the Eagan hearing, MJSers gather at a camp in Jefferson National Forest, near MTR sites in southwestern Virginia. A key reason for choosing this location is the ongoing relationship between KEF! and local forest activists.

"For about four years we've been fighting a timber sale there," Chris Irwin has told me. They've been working with members of the Clinch Coalition, a mainstream local group that includes former miners, some of whom took part in mine strikes in the 1970s. "A lot of the Clinch Coalition people are really comfortable with civil disobedience, because they did it against the mining companies in the '70s. But the president of the Clinch Coalition, her son is in mining to some degree, and they're not quite on board all the way with the anti-MTR stuff."

Last summer KEF! "hosted our action camp there, where we put [tree sitting] platforms up, we put banners up, we did demonstrations with them." Then, after camp was over "someone went and glued some locks" at the office of the mining company responsible for Jeremy Davidson's death. They left behind a cardboard sign attributing the action to Katuah Earth First! "And everybody thought we did it," Chris says, even though leaving a calling card for doing something illegal you don't intend to get caught for seems pretty stupid. The perpetrators were never caught.

The first day of MJS camp here is a day off, designated as a "retox" camp—a party that departs from the campaign's usual sobriety and focus on work. Some people party well into the night. The working part of the camp begins in earnest on June 23 with about two dozen people gathered around the camp's cooking fire at 11:30 AM. Paloma, who's keen to get to work, goes to get others up out of their tents.

Erin, from Blacksburg, announces that tomorrow afternoon Larry Bush, a former mine inspector now retired on disability, and perhaps other local people will come to camp to talk about doing a Listening Project in nearby coalfield neighborhoods later in the week. She says Larry's sense is that locals are now, for the first time since Jeremy Davidson's death, ready for a new wave of anti-MTR engagement.

Following announcements around the campfire, Chris and another trainer, Deb, offer tree-climbing training to whoever wants it. Meanwhile, for much of the rest of the day, the greater number of those

at camp meet to discuss potential actions to be taken in Tennessee later
this summer. The group consenses on allowing me to sit in on this and
future planning meetings; I tell them I'll take no notes and bring no
tape recorder to any meetings where civil disobedience is being planned,
nor will I identify anyone at such meetings who doesn't explicitly give
me permission to do so. (Several members of the group are uncomfortable with me or anyone else who's purely an observer, not a participant,
being present when arrestable activities are being planned, but they
stand aside from the group's decision, agreeing to abide by it rather
than block it.)

From the beginning of this meeting, it's clear that the focus of attention for direct action and protest in Tennessee has decisively shifted from
Eagan to Zeb Mountain. Beyond that element of clarity, decision making
today is slow, group cohesion hesitant. This is partly due to tension
between folks primarily or exclusively interested in direct action and
folks more excited by the power of building a grassroots movement with
a direct-action *component* linking locals in Tennessee with like-minded
anti-MTR activists in other states.

Paloma finds this meeting "really frustrating," she later tells me.
In other states, "when we're planning an action with Mountain Justice
Summer there has been a deference to the local organizing group that's
from that state. Meaning that your plan has to fit into what's being
planned [by] the organizers, so that it harmonizes with it. And [the local
organizers are] also giving you their information and their feedback.
But—and this is a reason why I'm leaving Earth First!—that [isn't happening with MJS in Tennessee] because we're also Earth Firsters."

Paloma, Chris, and Gena have decided to form a separate Tennessee
organization, United Mountain Defense. "As Earth Firsters we don't
get a lot of respect from other nonprofits," Paloma says. "Even if you're
working your butt off and you're getting tons and tons of really good
grassroots organizing done—you're that wacko fringe. And then, within
our own community, I didn't feel like we got that respect either, as a local
organizing group.

"People [at the meeting here] treated me as if I was just like some-body who was just joining the scene, and that we were all on equal foot-ing about how much knowledge we had, instead of me being a Tennessee organizer." At today's meeting, "they wanted me only to talk as much and give as much information as everybody else was giving, which was weird. Because I'm the only one [at the meeting] with some of the infor-mation," including a lot that's been tediously gathered from TDEC and OSM. "And I didn't know how to deal with that. I was looking around and saying [to myself]: Who else [here] can start talking about this? And I'm realizing: Crap. It's me.

"I was actually told: Oh, you should let somebody else give some of that information. Am I supposed to write notes: 'Can you say this?'" In truth, when she'd done just that before, sent information up from Tennessee to the Louisa camp with two young women (California col-lege students who'd joined MJS at Pipestem and chose to follow the campaign to Knoxville) to a meeting she couldn't attend, people didn't take it well. The emissaries' reception at Louisa was so bruising, and they felt so isolated from most of MJS beyond Paloma and Chris, that the two soon left the campaign.

At today's meeting, Paloma continues, "I started noticing per-sonality stuff, people saying things like: 'Well you can't tell us no.' So instead of [accepting that] this is what the organizers here [want], this is how it's going to feed into their campaign, it turned into these power struggles: Why can't we have it on [this date]? Why do we have to have it in Tennessee? Why don't we have it in West Virginia?" These were the voices of people whose primary interest in the campaign wasn't in Tennessee specifically but in doing one or more big direct actions on mine sites anywhere in the region—they want to see MTR ended every-where, and direct action rather than community organizing is what they personally are best prepared and prefer to do. But contrary to Paloma's sense that MJS is failing to respect KEF! as the lead local organizing group in Tennessee, it was primarily KEF! members who've worked in Tennessee with Paloma and Chris before who clashed with her at the meeting. The conflict is at least in large part a factional dispute within KEF! The other key Tennessee organizer at this camp, john johnson, didn't participate in this or subsequent action planning meetings because of his multiple legal troubles; if he had been there, he would not have completely sided with Paloma about how much deference should be given to Tennessee's local organizers, himself included.

Paloma was also frustrated that decision making at the meeting took as long as it did, but acknowledges that people there were not only not on the same page, they weren't even in the same book as far as immediate goals and tactics are concerned, and that consensus in that situation can take a lot of time and effort. And she's not real patient with this. "I'm not. I'm just not. Different people are better; they can be really, really patient. They can sit there for hours and hours discussing something that should take five minutes. And they're totally good with that."

Process aside, Paloma's reaction to where the meeting ended up is: "Good. People took on roles and got some dates set, and people signed up for different tasks. And I feel good about the location [the shift from Eagan to Zeb] and the action plan."

In general, she thinks MJS is "going great." She's particularly happy to see people getting Listening Project experience, and experience with other kinds of work that she expects the campaign to undertake in Tennessee, "so they'll already have these skills, and we won't have to keep on starting from scratch with everybody."

Midday today I stop to talk with Beth, who tells me that she and her boyfriend, Jamie, are leaving camp to spend a few days in Boone, North Carolina (Jamie's home base). Beth tells me she's not sure about whether she wants to continue with MJS. She's uncomfortable with the sort of secrecy/security/paranoia culture that she feels has come to the fore here at camp, where so much of the group's energy is focused on planning for direct action, and that planning excludes people who don't meet need-to-know criteria. (Neither she nor Jamie participated in the Zeb action-planning meeting.) Beth was much more comfortable with

MJS in Lexington, she says, where there were things for her to do. Here she feels shut out of what's going on, and at loose ends. I suggest that she talk with Matt Noerpel, who's just arrived today from the Naoma house, about what's going on in West Virginia. Lots of things to do are being planned for anyone who wants to go there, whatever their talents, affinities, and preferences.

Beth's not the only person here feeling excluded. She's more likely to, though, because she's a young woman. Young women are mostly on the sidelines with MJS—more men than women are involved in the campaign, the men have louder voices, and the group tends to pay more attention to male voices. Some people—primarily, or at least most vocally, a few men—seem more bothered by this than others. Although some individuals do make special efforts to include young women and encourage them to speak up, those efforts are individual rather than a group priority.

During a walk in the woods at camp, john johnson and I get to talking about "some of the failings of more radical politics, and perhaps age. If you're a super-militant, you just want to jump right in and do militant stuff. On the ultra-left scene, on the anarchist scene, it's really a minority body of thought that says: Put some time into organizing. [Instead] it's like: direct action, direct action, direct action. The radical wing of the movement has suffered from [this since the 1960s], in my opinion. It's [also] kind of symptomatic of just growing up. When I was twenty or twenty-one I just wanted to raise hell.

"I totally believe in direct action as a legitimate tool for social change, but I also see the necessity of more long-term organizing and educational work. And so I try to do both."

Our conversation comes round to the "open revolution" goal of bringing in more people and support from the mainstream to team up with the radical fringe. How do you keep it from falling apart, I ask, when people with different values and worldviews try working together and inevitably disagree about personal style, ideology, or tactical choices?

The larger and more diverse the group of people working together, the more likely conflicts are, and the more likely they will be serious.

"I don't know," how to manage this, john says. "I have no idea. We have to wait and see what happens. I think that most people are smart enough to try to keep [offensive] comments to themselves." john notes that he chooses what he talks about based on who he's talking with. He's not lying or misrepresenting himself, just seeking common ground. He hopes that everyone involved with MJS will make that effort. In cases where that effort fails, how it can be healed will depend on the individuals involved and the nature of their differences.

The camp in Virginia turns out to be a great place for walking and talking in the woods. One day out walking, I ask the fellow who's notorious for sneaking up on people in the woods what he thinks of the idea that people who devote themselves to a campaign like MJS are in some fundamental way misfits—that if we were fully comfortable with the world as it is, we wouldn't be doing this. "True," he says. "Definitely. Speaking from my own experience when I was a kid, not being popular gave me exactly that perspective, the outsider looking in. That definitely started very early for me a process of questioning the commonly accepted actions and beliefs of my peers."

I note that he seems very self-maintaining, and he agrees that this has been for him a strategy for dealing with being an outsider—"almost like a survival mechanism." How do you make that work with being part of a movement, I ask, and he laughs. "Oh, it gets very frustrating at times, because I work a lot better in small groups or by myself. My preferred working group size would not exceed five members." But there's a limit to how much five people by themselves can do. "That's true. And at the same time, there's a limit to how much an entire group of twenty or thirty people trying to make decisions together can do. There are pros and cons to each.

"One of the greatest advantages to having larger numbers is you can have different task groups who can focus on different parts of it. The group as a whole [can empower] smaller groups of individuals ['affinity groups' as activist jargon calls them] to bottom-line tasks. If those smaller groups need the help of the bigger group, they can ask for that help.

"I think that one of the key principles of sound leadership is to be able to recognize [individual capabilities] in the people you're working with—and I'm not talking about leadership in terms of being in charge. I think that everybody should be encouraged to take that leadership mentality into themselves, to recognize your own strengths, your own weaknesses, and also those of your peers, and figure out for yourself how to plug in. Especially when new people are coming in."

MJS has had a core group of people working together for months now, and they have developed a sort of shorthand for understanding each other and working together. And now so many new people are joining. How does this change things? "It's definitely tricky," he says. "I think it is functioning. Things are getting done. But there is definitely a lot of tension. Those of us who have been organizing this since before it became a big thing, we have more rapport with each other. And since we've been working on it all along, we're accustomed to seeking out certain individuals to bounce ideas off of when we're trying to come up with a project or a plan," and not so accustomed to reaching out to newcomers.

"There are some people [in this campaign] who have more of a tendency to act on an executive level, giving orders, stepping forward [with]: 'OK this is the plan that we came up with for all of you, now here's what you're gonna do.' In some cases, I think that that can actually be beneficial, especially when you have some people who do have a better feel for what's going on, and you have a lot of new people coming in who don't necessarily. I think that a lot of the newer folks who don't have the experience to have their own vision on where to go with things, a lot of those folks don't really have a problem with a handful of people stepping forward and just laying out the plan and saying 'this is what we're gonna do, plug into this.'"

Of course, this isn't the way MJS has sought to do things, by consensus. You run the risk of losing MJS's painstakingly built coalition of diverse individuals and organizations if instead of the campaign making space for different people to do things differently, autonomously but with mutual respect, you have a handful of people who've been around for a while giving orders. "Right. And I feel like that's happening right now. There are a lot of folks, a lot of the original organizers, who feel like *some* of the original organizers are calling the shots more than they should be."

He's talking here about "Chris and Paloma. Those of us who know them, who've worked with them both—they're notorious for it. For as long as I've known anything about who they are, that is who they are. They are the ones who come in and take charge of everything. The language that they use sounds very empowering to everybody, but the effect is still that they have their agenda."

Intentionally or not, Chris and Paloma are apt to dominate simply because they're so hardworking and know so much essential information, much of it obtained through such mind-boggling tedium (keeping track of TDEC and OSM, for example) that no one else wants to do it. But in addition, while they're amassing all that information, they're also setting their minds on what should be done with it. "I think it's very understandable and natural that they do that," my walking companion says. "But seeing the disempowering effect that it has on other people—there's a group of us that have been asked by others to approach them, off to the side, not calling them out in front of everybody, and not in an attacking way, but approaching them and talking to them about it. And to be honest, we are very hesitant to do so, because in the past when they've been confronted about that exact same thing, it has not gone very well. They get really defensive—at least that's been my experience. And so we're very hesitant to say anything about it, and that's really unfortunate." Particularly unfortunate as he genuinely likes and respects Chris.

Our conversation shifts to the challenges of organizing covert actions—actions that need to remain hidden from public view until they're unfurled—in the context of a bigger, broader campaign coalition. The people directly involved with these actions need to maintain security.

However, if people are thinking and working separately without being open to the wider group's full range of ideas and resources, they'll likely miss things that would make for a better plan, and might not coordinate their work well with others outside of their affinity group.

"This is something that's not exactly a new experience [for us], but it's one of our weak points. Definitely we don't want to withhold anything that the [larger] group [needs]. It's definitely detrimental to group process to be withholding information, yet at the same time, sometimes it's good to have a backup contingency or a couple of other ideas under your sleeve you can pull out in another way. Sometimes there's an activity that if it got out too far before it happened, it might get blown, that maybe it only takes a small group to do. And so that small group can keep it amongst themselves that they're doing that."

People in this campaign but not part of "that small group" can sense that this is going on. How do you avoid giving them a general feeling of being excluded, rather than that their exclusion is limited to just those plans? Those being left out don't know, obviously, exactly what they're being left out of. "A big part of pre-empting [this sense of exclusion] would be for those of us who [are making secret plans] to be much more discreet. Like when we were having the meeting [for Tennessee action planning] and very blatantly, in front of everybody [at camp they announced]: 'OK, we're supposed to have a meeting now that not everybody's gonna be a part of. If you're not supposed to be a part of it, can you go somewhere else right now?' I think that was very tactless and a little inconsiderate.

"I know of at least three individuals who have quit this campaign because a meeting about [an] action was happening, and as they were approaching the group [they were told]: 'We're having a meeting about something that I don't think you're a part of yet.' And they were just like: 'OK, fuck you guys.' And they're not coming back to the campaign, just because of being hurt emotionally by that."

He says that another way to counter the exclusion problem is "making sure there are things that they can be part of, making a point of directly connecting everybody. I think that that's one of our weak points at this point. I think a lot of people are feeling disempowered."

Encouraging affinity groups within the campaign is intended to allow people to choose both who they want to work with and what kind of work they want to do. But when members of a growing campaign organize themselves into subgroups focused on their internal affinities, how do new people get welcomed in? How do the affinity groups collectively avoid shrugging people off who may be valuable precisely because they don't match the likes and dislikes of the groups as they currently exist, but instead bring different talents to the table? Affinity isn't the same as community, and enjoying affinity seems to trump building community for many of the people involved in this campaign, especially many of those most inclined toward direct action and secrecy.

At the camp's cooking fire, I catch up with two ninjas, members of the League of Shadows, Jake and Squirrel. (The League of Shadows is part joke, part clique, part affinity group of folks who enjoy wearing camouflage, sneaking through woods, and comparing gear. They often volunteer for security duty.) Seeing them reminds me that this camp is very ninja, with few pirates. "The pirates don't have the self-discipline that the ninjas have," Jake says, "so they can only handle a certain amount of such a stressful situation, then they have to run home and hide in their cities."

I ask if they miss the pirates. "I do," Squirrel says. "I miss the pirates." (Jake misses their food.) "Pirates definitely liven things up. What do you think?" she asks another League of Shadow member who's joined us. "Do you miss the pirates?"

"Uh-huh," he says. "It's sad that I don't have as convenient a target for my mischief and my pranks, being that pirates are generally so unaware and oblivious that they make an easy target. The other night, I was trying to creep on the campfire [and got spotted]. People here are a little more alert. You don't get that from pirates. So in a sense I've missed them, but that doesn't mean I wish they were here."

"Pirates," Squirrel says, "the pirate cliques, hang out more in cities, and the ninjas hang out in the woods more."

"There are city clans [of ninjas], though," Jake points out.

"Most of us dwell in cities part-time," Squirrel allows.

There's strength in affinity, I suggest, but also strength in difference.

"Well, we love each other," Squirrel says, citing the grappling hook, used to forcibly link two boats so people from one can board the other.

The third ninja explains: "The grappling hook is the love child of a pirate-ninja affair. From what I've been told, its origins date back [centuries ago] to coastal regions of Japan, where there was much pirate activity and there were also ninja clans who would act as pirates. And the grappling hook is a very effective tool that evolved from that relationship. There are definitely positive things to be gained by working in alliance with pirates."

Cliques and factions notwithstanding, community-building and inclusiveness and even love does go on here, much of it around camp food. Pots, utensils, and food are shared and tasks divvied up—fire building, food tending, vegetable chopping. The menu might be grits in morning, vegetable stew in the evening, with whoever wants to cook making enough to share, with the help of whoever's around and wants to help. I've learned that if I show up with beer, an empty bowl, and maybe a tomato or garlic or melon, I can count on eating supper, sometimes very well, even though I'm traveling without cooking equipment. One day we pass around a pan of foraged wild mushrooms sautéed with onions scavenged from a supermarket dumpster and a bit of butter. Everyone eats from the case of tortillas john scavenged at a festival where he did MJS fundraising before coming here. Nettle leaves are carefully picked in the woods and stewed over the campfire to make cooked greens and tea passed around with salt and pepper. Sometimes there's raw biscuit dough popped from a supermarket canister and wrapped around a stick to be cooked over the fire like toasted marshmallows. john notes that when a can of biscuits is opened everyone *coos* and looks for a stick, then all gather in a circle with their sticks over the fire, like a religious ritual: the church of biscuit-on-a-stick.

One afternoon about a dozen of us go for a hike in nearby woods. It's a long hike, with several long lazy pauses along the way, very pleasant, relaxed. Boulder jumbles and cliff sides are explored for possible caves by people who like that sort of thing. john johnson is tickled to see dozens of American chestnut shoots sprouting from the roots of trees felled long ago by blight. Each new sprout will itself die back from the blight in a year or two. john marvels at the roots' persistence. He and I often lag behind the rest of the hikers, most of whom aren't so interested in pausing to consider every single chestnut, or trying to read the logging and fire history of each patch of woods in what's growing there now, or identifying wildflowers.

Early on in our walking, we pass scattered clumps of bear corn, a sort of parasite that grows on tree roots and sticks up out of the ground in clumps of fat fingers that look rather like small cobs of corn. Bears, I'm told, eat it as a laxative when they come out of hibernation in the spring. Sassafras reminds me that these woods are filled with plants that are useful for humans too, not just for bears. The relatively dry slope where I notice these plants has no rhododendrons, but is all deciduous trees and shrubs, including some umbrella-leafed magnolias and quite a few chestnut sproutlings. In the past, before they were felled by blight, chestnuts would have dominated this patch of forest. No one tree species dominates the canopy now, but some, like the many tall, straight tulip poplars, are growing in greater numbers than the chestnuts would have allowed.

At the top of this slope, up at ridgeline, moisture-loving ferns drop out of the mix of greenery on the forest floor, and it's crackly dry underfoot. Where there's just a little less rainfall than here, just slightly to the east on the Blue Ridge, for example, most of the trees on such a ridgeline would be oaks, but here, even at the ridge, it's moist enough that maples and other hardwoods grow as well. Blueberries here are showing green fruit. A significant amount of deadfall left to rot, no noticeable stumps, and a scattering of trees well over half a century old tell me this place hasn't been logged in recent decades. The line of the ridge bends a bit, so as we walk along it we soon find the slope off one side facing northeast, where shadier conditions have called forth a sprinkling of rhododendrons and hemlocks.

The biodiversity of any single patch of the forest we're walking through today is extraordinary. Yet each patch is only part of a bigger patchwork, each part of which has its own extraordinarily diverse assemblage of species different from neighboring patches with slightly different slopes, exposures, moisture. The Clinch River watershed, which includes this forest, has been called the most biodiverse watershed in North America. It's at the junction of the Blue Ridge, Ridge-and-Valley, and Cumberland Plateau geophysical provinces. All three provinces are fairly similar in the mix of species they support but each has some different species and here, uniquely, their ranges overlap.

Still walking along and near ridgeline, we pick up an old logging road. On one side of the ridge here is a mixed-age stand that hasn't been logged for maybe fifty to seventy years and is now about to be cut, although more conservative, long-range management would leave it alone. On the other side of the ridge is a very young, maybe fifteen- to thirty-year-old forest, all trees the same age, obviously recovering from a clear-cut.

After a long rest under a sassafras tree, still on the logging road but now beyond the old/young forest boundary, we travel off-trail through a series of different habitats each in a subtly different patch of forest—jumbles of rock overgrown with moss, tangles of vines, sweeps of nettle in soft, rich soil under a high canopy, piles of deadfall, dry creek bed. Seeing one particular habitat doesn't begin to do justice to the diversity of this region's forests. But because each patch of habitat is itself so rich and diverse, a kaleidoscope of different observations can be made about any one place you care to look.

The coalfields in Virginia are a relatively small part of the state—just a slice of the state's southwestern corner, along the Kentucky border. But MTR has been as intensive and devastating here as anywhere in Appalachia. Each year, for the past decade or more, 13 to 15 million tons of coal have been hauled out of the northern tier of Wise County alone, near where Jeremy Davidson lived; still more coal has been extracted in neighboring counties. More than 100,000 acres of this small slice of Virginia now look like a moonscape because of mountaintop removal. And well beyond the MTR sites themselves, people and their home places suffer the typical ill effects of forest and watershed destruction, dust, homes cracked by blasting, unemployment, and depopulation.

On June 24, about fifteen people from MJS camp prepare to go on a Listening Project up several hollows near the town of Appalachia, formerly a thriving boomtown built by coal a century to half a century ago, now withered to a remnant. Erin talks with the volunteers beforehand about what they'll do: Go up and knock on each door, in pairs, preferably including a woman in each pair so as to seem less intimidating. Identify yourself, saying that you're there as part of a Listening Project because you've heard about mining in the area and want to hear what they have to say about it. If they're willing, ask the list of questions Erin hands out—questions intended to get people talking, to find out what their concerns are, and to identify whether they might want to work with MJS or be kept informed.

During this brief training, john tells the group: "I'm not afraid of getting arrested. I'm not afraid of getting beat up by police. But I am afraid of going door to door." He asks to be paired with someone who's done this sort of work before, and he is, with a young woman named Julia. The pairs of volunteers do some role-play practice before going out. They also clean up as best they can down at the creek and put on clean, relatively conservative clothes.

That evening, they gather around the campfire, and Erin asks: "How many houses did everybody hit up?" The teams respond: five, eight, five, four, three, five, seven—and one.

"Julia and I, embarrassingly, sort of, went to one," john says. After knocking on several doors that nobody answered, they came to a house where a woman answered the door. "Julia did a great intro rap. And as soon as the word 'mining' got out of her mouth, the woman's face totally lit up and she said: 'Hey, have a seat here on the porch.' And she sat down and totally opened up to us, which was awesome. And the reason we only went to one is her husband came home and pulled out a shotgun and tied us up for a few hours." There's a pause here, then everyone laughs.

"No, he was really into talking to us as well." Eventually the man asked them: "So, y'all want to go up there and take a look around?" john and Julia said yes, "and then his neighbor came over, an elderly gentleman who we also spoke with. He used to live up in—some of the hollows used to be heavily populated and now there's no habitation at all. This guy was [from] one of those.

"After chatting for a really long time," the husband of the woman who'd invited them to sit on the porch said: "'Let's go, I'll take y'all up there.' And so we spent the rest of the time up on top of Black Mountain [the big ridge just north of Appalachia, along the Virginia/Kentucky border], looking at atrocious, absolutely atrocious logging, really bad strip mining, and then a couple of mountaintop removals. We actually drove over a valley fill. It was really intense. Because we weren't trying to proselytize, I actually had to kind of shut down internally, because usually when I'm faced with that sort of destruction"—john is getting teary remembering this. "I just had to shut down to deal with it. And deal with him. But it was a really cool experience."

Julia adds: "He hunts. He goes four-wheeling out there. He and his grandson go out there and look for arrowheads. He was taking us to places where a month ago there were trees there, this was forest. And he talked about how hard it is for him to take us to places that just got cut.

"You know, people laugh. I don't think they think it's funny, but they laugh. We were talking to [his wife], and he came in, and she [said]: They want to know about the mining. And they had a laugh about it. Like that's all you can do about it."

(During this debriefing, vehicles belonging to the Forest Service and the local sheriff's office patrol down the road that dead-ends at camp. Just after the meeting, as I'm carrying a pot down the road to the creek to be scoured with sand, a car with two men from the sheriff's office stops and asks if I'm alright. When I say yes, just fine, they say: "Just checking on you.")

Other people interviewed in today's Listening Project complained about dust, about mudslides landing big rocks on roads, about cracks in foundations from blasting, about the paint on their cars being chipped by rocks off coal trucks, about trucks going too fast and damaging roads, about wondering whether the town water is safe to drink, about once lively creeks now smothered in silt, about clusters of cancer and other disease, about flyrock. People seemed more apt to focus their anger on specific problems like coal trucks, rather than on the overall effect of losing the mountains.

Answers given to questions about local employment varied a lot. Some people said most or all of the people they know are employed in the nearby strip mines; others said the MTR workers all come in from Kentucky, that the only local jobs in mining are in deep mining. The teams also heard from people whose work depended on MTR and were troubled by it. One man who didn't want to attach his name to what he was saying, certain that to do so would cost him his job, said: "Do anything you can. Just make it stop."

Erin talked to a woman who was born and grew up here—but the house and the hollow she grew up in are no longer there, both obliterated by MTR. She notes that older people especially seem proud of the community's "rough and rowdy" history of confronting coal companies in earlier times in support of the miners' union and against past strip mining. People with that experience "recognized it was the union that gave people the courage to stand up to the coal trucks, to the mine owners and operators." The union brought people together, meeting regularly, developing camaraderie and a sense of common purpose.

Several people said that the coal companies want them out, would rather there be no community here at all so they can do whatever they want with no one left to complain about it.

Some people expressed concern about a recent U.S. Supreme Court decision allowing a town in Connecticut to force people in a certain neighborhood to sell their homes to a private developer, not for any public use but because the developer had an economically more valuable use for the land. The concern here is that coal companies owning the mineral rights under their homes might, with the connivance of government, force them out to clear the way for MTR.

"They're just gonna drive people to us, doing that," john says, speaking of the court decision. "Everybody who thinks we're anti-private property and then all of a sudden they find out that these elected Republican and Democrat local, state, and federal governments who supposedly are ideologically for private property, and then they destroy private property for capitalism—they're totally going to drive people into our arms. They're idiots.

"Even if we can't do it this summer, we need to figure out how to spend more time here."

A rattlesnake maybe four feet long has been seen moving through camp. Skunks have been regular visitors at night, nosing around the tents. One saunters through camp during the Listening Project debriefing. So far, no one has been sprayed.

At the campfire that evening, just before a planning meeting for an upcoming MJS action targeting Massey's headquarters in Richmond, Virginia—linked to G-8 protests elsewhere around the world on July 8—I hear a conversation among several young MJSers, most of them fairly new to the campaign. Pooh-poohing the MJS nonviolence commitment, they'd rather go to Richmond feeling free to jump in on whatever action they see happening, and to break loose and run away if police grab them, rather than accept arrest as a consequence of their actions.

During the meeting that follows I'm disturbed to hear quite a few people asking: 'Well, what counts as violence? Does resisting arrest, tussling with a cop to get away from him?' Being mindful of CRMW folks who aren't here to speak for themselves and who'll bear the brunt of any fallout from the action in Richmond, I say that according to MJS's previous consensus, yeah it does. A key reason for that consensus, I recall, is that any introduction of violence into this campaign puts coalfield activists at risk for an unleashing of violence against them, as has happened in the past. Breaking with that consensus now risks losing the moral high ground as well, as a time when holding it is crucial to the campaign's political and public-relations efforts to compel Massey to do the right thing in West Virginia.

That we're having this discussion now shows both that MJS training for newcomers is lacking and that consensus can't be maintained without it. At the meeting this evening, lip service is paid to the idea of a tactical commitment to nonviolence and to avoiding property damage, but some of the newer young people at this meeting—a large proportion of those in attendance—seem to resent and have little patience with this. They'd clearly much rather roll trash cans into the street and tangle with cops. Further, it's not at all clear that if that happens others will step in to de-escalate, no more than anyone did at the hotel action in Knoxville. It's still not considered cool to tell other people that they shouldn't be doing whatever it is they're doing.

Ultimately everyone at the meeting tonight agrees that several announcements will be made in Richmond, at the concert the night before and at the rally immediately before the march and action, asking all participants to respect the wishes and protect the safety of coalfield activists by honoring MJS's nonviolence commitment. I'm still uneasy about this, in particular worried that some individuals who say they're unwilling to wear anything identifying their MJS affiliation at the action will decide they're free to disassociate themselves from MJS on the spot and act on whatever temptations to make mischief that arise. Whatever anyone at today's meeting does that day will inevitably be attached to MJS, for all of these people will be eating and sleeping in MJS-arranged housing and using MJS-arranged jail support. They *are* MJS. Furthermore, MJSers engaging in genuinely nonviolent civil disobedience at Massey headquarters would be vulnerable to retaliation afterward if other demonstrators have pointlessly provoked the police. Enough people in MJS are aware of these potential pitfalls that it's reasonable to hope that they'll persuade the newcomers to avoid them. The planning for this action illustrates that avoiding them in the future will require ongoing vigilance.

West Virginia

A few days later, more than a dozen people travel from West Virginia to Richmond for a different sort of action—to deliver to Massey management the same set of demands presented in May at the Goals Coal facility, and to ask Massey for a commitment to meet those demands. On Wednesday morning, June 29, two of those people—Hannah Thurman, one of the Naoma house interns, and Herb Elkins, whose son attends Marsh Fork Elementary—enter the vestibule at Massey's headquarters in downtown Richmond, ring a buzzer, and ask to be let in to speak with Massey management. When they are refused entry, they remain in the vestibule, showing photographs of the school to passersby inside the building and repeatedly renewing their request to come in for a meeting. "I thought a lot about my tone," Hannah later tells me, "and how I wanted to come across. I wanted it to be almost pleading with people. I wanted people to feel like I really could not leave until I got some sort of response."

Hannah, a college student who grew up in Putnam County, West Virginia, between Huntington and Charleston, a little north of the MTR zone, thought she'd find the experience of being in the vestibule, standing her ground, empowering, "but I ended up feeling very, very small. The workers—some of them were going by laughing, pointing. One woman held up her hand and did a peace sign. I felt like they were really trivializing what we were doing. They could just stay behind that glass wall and not have to confront anything that was happening." Inside the vestibule, Hannah can't see that behind her—beyond the smoky glass doors to the outside of the building—the people she came with are clustered with several reporters and passersby who *are* very interested in what's happening.

Massey calls the police, who join Hannah and Herb inside the vestibule for well over half an hour. From the outside, it looks like they're doing a sort of MTR 101 workshop in there. "We were," Hannah later tells me. "I had the pictures of the elementary school and the dam and we were just showing them. One of them was saying: I've got a son, and I feel for you.

"Herb was telling them about his son. When it rains, they cover up the water fountains because they don't want the kids to drink the water. Obviously wrong things are happening. I think they were feeling it a little bit.

"Somehow we got to talking about crime in Richmond, and [one of the police] got to talking about child molesters, and how she thinks that they should be put away for life, no matter what. It was really interesting. One person, one child molester—that's such a bad thing, a horrible thing for someone to do, and it is. But then I just said: So is poisoning children. That's a form of abuse as well."

In the end, Hannah and Herb are arrested and charged with trespassing. They are released later the same day, and ultimately settle the matter by paying fines.

Among those in Richmond that day is Sage, who's been staying at the house in Naoma. He tells me that MJSers in West Virginia are pulling together nicely and looking forward to the influx of people expected at the end of the month and in early July. Much of what they've been doing is Listening Project work, mostly coordinated by Hannah. "That's been very successful," Hillary Hosta tells me, back in Naoma, "almost too successful, because it's really hard for [the MJSers] to get out of people's homes. People are coming back with these stories: Well, I was sitting with them for two hours. Four pairs of listeners have been going out," and when they come back at the end of the day Hillary will ask: "How many did you guys talk to? Five families. All of you? Yeah.

"And then of course we've had a *few* incidents of horn honking," people driving past the house, on busy Rt. 3, and blaring their disapproval. ("Few" is quite an understatement.) The front of the house has been splattered with eggs and paintballs. And last week, at about 4:30 AM, someone smashed in the back window of the cap on Sage's pickup truck, parked in front of the house next to the road. "It was so sad," Hillary says. "I stood there with tears in my eyes, looking in the back of his truck and seeing all this glass that's shattered all over his Bible.

"You really got the wrong truck, man. My goodness."

Bo Webb, too, has experienced some low-level intimidation recently. Two guys in two pickup trucks, wearing Massey uniform shirts, blocked his way on a narrow gravel road he was following down off the side of a mountain near his home where he gathers firewood and hunts. When he got out of his own truck carrying a gun, they left in a hurry. But "the very next morning, on Saturday morning, about 6:15, the phone rang and I said hello." The voice on the other end of the line asked: 'What are you doing?' I thought it was Ed Wiley, because he calls me a lot of times early in the morning. I go: 'I'm making a pot of coffee—who is this?' He said: 'It's not important who this is—what size shoes do you wear?' I say: 'Who am I talking to?' He says: 'I wear size 11, and I'm gonna stick it up your—.'" Bo hung up the phone.

The week before Hannah and Herb's Richmond demonstration, Bo, Judy, Ed and Debbie, Jackie Browning and his wife, Sister O'Connell (a nun who lives and works in Whitesville), and Herb Elkins all traveled to Charleston to meet with Gov. Joe Manchin about Marsh Fork Elementary. "He told us that he was going to put together a few people that he trusted to look into this matter," Bo says, "and that he would call me. He took my phone number and said he should call me within the next five to seven working days. And he said that [they] would test the soil, the grass, inside the school, the air quality. He was quite surprised that the West Virginia Department of Health and Human Resources hadn't cooperated with us." When I express skepticism about the governor being surprised, Bo responds: "Well, he pretended to be." Bo's still willing to give Manchin the benefit of the doubt. "I don't know if he was pretending to be naive, or uninformed, or he actually was. He said he thought that coal was cleaned by water and a screening process. And I said: 'Well Governor, things have changed. It's chemicals.' He goes: 'Chemicals?' I gave him a list of chemicals that we know that they use. I gave him [flyover] photos of the school. I also gave him some of the Listening Project forms, probably twenty-five of them, of families that we found with sick children. And I gave him a videotape of interviews with parents of sick children. I didn't want to overwhelm him with too much, but I wanted to open his eyes up. Hopefully, he's reviewed it. We'll see."

The day after the Richmond action, someone from the DEP calls CRMW and tells Sarah Haltom that the underling on whose desk the permit for the second silo next to the school had been sitting for a month (these things are usually rubber-stamped in less than a week) had been unwilling to sign it and instead passed it up the hierarchy to a bureaucrat one level below Stephanie Timmermeyer, head of the agency. They're stuck with a hard choice: If they approve the silo, they appear careless about the health of schoolkids; if they turn it down, it begs the question of why is it OK to have even the first silo in operation.

Bo's been thinking about July 8, and the risks of association with G-8 protesters in Richmond who might be inclined to clash with police. "My big fear is that if we are there and there's something going on— someone eggs Massey's building, or someone throws a rag on fire in the street—and there's a reporter there and he takes a photo of john johnson or Bo Webb: 'That's Mountain Justice Summer. Look what they're doing.' That's my fear. At the same time, it's America and we have a right to be there. We have our right to protest. What we need to do Saturday [at the next MJS organizing meeting, to be held in Whitesville] is, I think, to hash out what benefit are we gonna get out of going there. Let's think about that. Let's think about it real deep.

"We have really brought media attention to the issue. We could call a TV station right now, and they're gonna come running. They didn't do this before. We've seized the high moral ground. We could blow it all in one stupid day by being in the wrong place at the wrong time."

Bo's keenly aware that there's no time to waste and the stakes are high. "How long do you think this is gonna go on? Steve Walker, the owner of CAT Walker [a supplier of mining equipment], told me to my face: 'I don't know what you're so in an uproar about—we'll be done and out of here in twenty years, and you can have it.'" Bo would like to tell every local person whose work depends on strip mining: "Twenty years from now, if you're thirty years old [today] you're gonna be fifty. Think about your future. You're gonna be fifty. Who's gonna hire you? What are you gonna do? What are your kids gonna do? You need to think about what you're doing." Not only will you be fifty and out of work, the entire region you've been working in will be "nothing but a toxic wasteland," he says, its future potential trashed for the sake of a few decades of coal production.

After talking with Bo, I drive to CRMW's office in Whitesville, where a brand-new mural of green mountains and blue sky has been painted by MJS volunteers on the outside of the building. Inside the building, Judy Bonds, Patty Sebok, and Sarah and Vern Haltom have just learned that the permit for the second coal silo has been approved. Vern says they're already at work at the site—which implies Massey knew about the approval before it was made public. Everyone in the office is hopping mad. If Massey learned about the approval when CRMW did, today, Judy asks, "how in the world did they get an order in to the cement company for that much cement? I don't think any cement company can produce that overnight"—let alone on the same morning it's ordered—"and get their truck drivers together and get everything together. So they had to have known this ahead of time. Had to have. There's no other explanation for it." Judy thinks the permit approval was a done deal even back before the public hearing was held in the school gym. In any case, it obviously was a done deal at some point before CRMW and the public heard about it—during which time Bo and everyone else at CRMW were patiently and hopefully waiting to hear from the governor. "At our meeting with the governor a few days ago," Judy says, "the governor could have picked up the phone and said: 'Look, hold off on that permit until we investigate the citizens' concerns.' He didn't do that."

"It's just the same old, same old," Patty says. "We're gonna have a meeting with you and pretend like we're gonna do something, while at the same time we're saying [to the coal company]: 'Go for it, go for it, go for it.'"

"And the governor's gonna have a *post*-meeting," Judy says. "That's been the problem in the coalfields all along. Everything happens *post*. Go ahead and give the coal industry what they want, and if there's deaths to deal with, we'll deal with it afterwards. We'll have an investigation *after- wards*. That's what happened with Buffalo Creek." People there raised safety concerns well before the dam failed. "One lady asked for a meeting with the governor, and the governor never granted her a meeting until after—and the only reason that woman survived is because it was raining and on nights that it rained she chose to go stay with someone else." The flood washed through her own home. "It's the same thing happening over and over and over."

Later that day, back at the Naoma house, Bo and Ed Wiley and Sage arrive in Bo's truck shortly before dinnertime. (Ed, I later hear, had been calming Bo down—the reverse of their usual roles with each other.) After hearing the news about the coal silo permit, Bo took a cooler, filled it with beer, and went off with Ed and Sage. Their first stop was at Goals Coal, where they saw clearly that the foundation for the new silo was being poured. Bo says he's making "contingency plans" that he's too tipsy to talk with me about tonight. He also says they got snookered by the governor. He invites me to join him for more beer by the river, at his house.

There, sitting on rocks and watching the water, he tells me that when he was eighteen he joined the Marines and volunteered to go to Vietnam because somebody he'd known growing up here in the valley had died over there and Bo wanted to go "kill the bastards" who did it. When he got to Vietnam, he got disillusioned pretty quick. While he was there he saw evidence of lots of what he now calls "human rights violations" committed by troops on both sides. When he came back to the United States, he lost two years of his life, drinking a lot and drifting. Life didn't seem to be something he could engage with or make sense of—believing that you could have a good life, let alone make a difference in the world, was beyond his reach. This began to change when he met Joanne, who became his wife, and he began becoming a person he liked being. Years later when he moved back home to the Coal River valley, he found what he by then was ready to see as human rights violations, not manifested in the same way as in Vietnam but rooted in the same kind of power relationship. The coal companies, with their overwhelming economic and political clout, are like a powerful army able to do pretty much whatever they want to do to people who don't have that power. This made Bo angry—still makes him angry. And today he got real angry, seeing that power-with-impunity manifested in the permit approval, with government officials who are supposed to be responsible to the public treating the people of Coal River as though their lives don't matter. What does matter, of course, is what Massey wants.

We agree that being angry about this isn't wrong; there'd be something wrong with him if he *wasn't* angry about it. The question is, what do you do with that anger? Self-destruct, as he nearly did when he returned from Vietnam? Or use it somehow to make change? Right now we're at a unique historical moment: Within our likely lifetimes (Bo's in his fifties), great change is coming whether we want it or not. The way things are done today literally cannot continue—in the Coal River valley or elsewhere. America's use-it-up-and-move-on way of life is in its endgame. MTR is a particularly obvious example of this—whole mountains and watersheds destroyed for a few decades of increasingly expensive coal that will ultimately run out and leave an entire region utterly trashed. But it's a pattern we can see everywhere our economy touches, in the depletion of topsoil and groundwater by industrial agriculture, in the ever-accumulating proliferation of toxic byproducts poisoning ever-more depleted landscapes and oceans, in the relentless extinction of species and diminishment of biological diversity. So right now, Bo and everyone else who's angry at the destruction wrought by all this can look at it and *know* it's not going to go on forever. Seeing that change is inevitable frees us of the temptation to despair of change ever happening, frees us to use the energy of our anger and the energy of the great change itself to direct that change toward better ways of life. Or at least try to. (Neither Bo nor I is a blind optimist, especially not this evening.) Whether we succeed or not, we've been dealt a much more plausibly hopeful moment than most people in human history have had. Bo aims to make the best of it.

Ed's anger over the approval of the second silo permit is slower to develop than Bo's. Eventually though, later that evening, as we talk at the Naoma house about how the DEP surely wouldn't have approved this, given the media attention, and attention from the governor's office, without first clearing that approval with the governor, he all of a sudden looks like he's been punched in the stomach. He gets teary. *Then* he gets angry—that people would do such a thing, putting schoolchildren at such risk—and starts thinking about what to do about it.

This month's MJS organizing meeting is held in a meeting hall just down the street from CRMW's office. On Saturday morning, July 2, during regional report-backs, after Hillary sums up what's been going on in the valley, Bo adds that Hillary and the interns and other folks at the Naoma house have done a great job bonding with the local community. (They must look hungry. Local people have been bringing them food—cakes and garden produce, and the freezer keeps filling up with meat that people bring over for them. In truth, the urban-punk kids who dominate among the traveling MJSers do tend to be skinny. The local people here tend to be beefier, and they're apparently looking at the incomers and worrying about whether they're eating enough. They also see that these kids don't have much money and maybe worry that they're just too poor to eat. So they bring pork chops.) But Bo also has had some negative feedback from local people about culturally inappropriate behavior and the sometimes immodest dress of some of the recent transients out in front of the house, right on Rt. 3. He asks that everyone at the house please be on their best behavior and especially keep the lower level of the house presentable to receive visitors. "The neighbors are watching us," he says. "They're watching every move. Go out in the woods and get as crazy as you want," but be thoughtful about what you do at the house, and how it looks.

Most of the day's meeting is devoted to discussion about the upcoming Richmond event—only a few days away now—beginning with an update from several people who've been preparing for it: housing in Richmond is more or less arranged, young people from Richmond with radios will accompany the march on bikes, more legal observers and video cameras are needed to document whatever happens so that can be presented in court if need be, nonviolence training can happen the day before the event, on the day itself speakers will address a rally at Monroe Park at noon, followed by a march ten blocks to Massey headquarters, with actions there yet to be determined.

Hillary expresses concern about the nonviolence training, that people with past confrontational relationships with police may hear a five-minute nonviolence riff, say "that sounds good," then, without any real alternative in mind, react in accustomed ways to police. The young woman who reported on plans for the bike escort says that the bike riders will act as peacekeepers; Hillary notes this is 9 people for a group of perhaps 500. Sage says he hopes that MJS organizers will feel empowered to act as peacekeepers that day as part of watching each other's backs, which should be our normal way of life. Someone else points out that MJS in the past has consensed that *everyone* is supposed to be a peacekeeper at MJS actions.

Bo weighs in: "I'm hearing things that make me uncomfortable. I think you're asking for a lot of arrests"—given that there's still been no permit requested for the march and the police have told us we'll be arrested if we block streets without a permit. "We're going to make mistakes as we go along, but I don't want us to make a mistake that blows the whole campaign." He thinks Massey will have people there aiming to make trouble. And he's uncomfortable with what he sees as inadequate planning for this event. "We don't have enough money to get fifteen people out of jail," he adds. The money and other resources taken up by a lot of arrests could incapacitate MJS in West Virginia right now, at just the moment when the coal silo permit and other pressing issues need timely response.

Sidestepping the issue of rights to assemble and be in public places without government permission (about which several people at this meeting feel strongly), another young woman says: "We need to think about our tactic here, and how it affects MJS. Way more thought needs to be put into this." There are legitimate concerns being raised here, she adds—much as concerns were raised before the Knoxville action, and not addressed then.

"This is a really important discussion," Abigail says. She doesn't feel comfortable going ahead without Bo and the other Coal River people being comfortable with this event—even though she feels strongly that it's real important to connect what's going on in the coalfields with wider issues of climate change, the theme of this year's G-8 protests.

"I really hate to operate under fear," john says, because it's not conducive to direct action. He doesn't want to assume that anyone who acts out is a coal company operative. He's heartened that he's hearing people here today truly listen to and address concerns. A lot of people are putting a lot of good work into this, he says, and he's willing to trust everyone in this room who'll be going to Richmond to do right. "I want to have trust," he says. "I think there's a place for nonviolent defiance [in MJS]"—and Richmond on July 8 can be such a place.

Vern suggests putting first things first: We need to decide whether we're going to march, and only then can we address the parameters of direct action that day. "If we don't get past that bottleneck, we're going to be here all afternoon."

Sage points out that if MJS doesn't march, there'll be no guidance for anyone after the rally, which will end with a large group of people all pumped up about mountaintop removal standing just a few blocks from Massey headquarters. "If we do march, we have more control over the situation." MJS's other choice, he thinks, is just to cancel "the whole damn event." Is this action happening just because it's July 8, a G-8 day of action, or because it contributes to MJS? Is it a good use of our resources?

The group decides to try to agree on what would be needed to make Richmond a success and commit to meeting those needs. If they can't do this, the event should be canceled. (Bo, stretching his legs in the kitchen next to the meeting room, is angry that the planners for Richmond haven't done this already, at this late date.) Bit by bit, the group assembles a list of what's needed: At least five full-time peacekeepers for every hundred demonstrators, with *everyone* connected with MJS to be ready to de-escalate conflict if needed. Nonviolence training both the morning of the rally and the day before. Two or three clearly identified police liaisons. At least five legal observers. At least three people not at the rally to be on call for jail support. More video cameras, five to ten total. As many still cameras as possible, at least four of them digital. A permit for the march to be applied for, and Bo to talk with police in Richmond about it.

There's general agreement that all this is doable, and various individuals agree to make sure that specific items do, in fact, get done. Trust wins the day; MJS will go ahead with getting ready for Richmond, but cautiously. Chris Irwin urges people to keep in mind the limits of MJS's resources, and "don't get forty people popped." One of those who'd been at the Knoxville hotel demo asserts the need for a "Plan B": If we can't or don't march, is it OK for small groups of citizens to walk up and down the sidewalks in front of Massey HQ? We've got into trouble before by not having a Plan B. (The group strongly agrees with this.) john responds that Plan B is an excellent idea, that small groups will come up with better Plan Bs than this large group will, and that we should trust them to do so. And so they do.

Every year on the July 4th weekend, Larry Gibson invites family and friends to a big gathering up at Kayford. This year, MJS is invited, so I drive up there on Sunday morning from Naoma with Judy and Hannah, stopping on the way at a gas station in Whitesville for coffee and to pick up bottles of water to bring along. (The mining around Kayford has destroyed Larry's water supply.) Judy starts a conversation with several young men hanging out outside the gas station, one of whom had moved south from here to find work—this is the first she's seen him since he's back. She encourages them to come to the house in Naoma, to come to movie nights there, and to stop in at CRMW's office. Inside the store we see a newspaper headline about the Patriot Act allowing military recruitment in high schools, and Judy starts a conversation with folks standing near the checkout counter, about what kind of a country we are living in that the government recruits schoolchildren as cannon fodder.

By the time we arrive at Kayford, at midday that Sunday, July 3, a few dozen people are there, with more and more arriving. Musicians are setting up a PA system.

During the afternoon, I take a walk with john johnson from the open park-like area where the gathering is centered, down the road past Larry's relatives' cabins, and off his property onto the edge of the mine site there, as we each want to see what's changed since we were last here. It's only gotten worse, of course. "It's atrocious," john says.

Walking back, we pass through a spread-out crowd of several dozen people near the cabins, kinfolk of Larry's and their friends having their own holiday celebrations. While alcohol is forbidden at Larry's gathering, there's obviously quite a bit being consumed here. As we walk back, john gets to talking with a big burly guy, red faced, with graying hair, somewhat drunk, who wants to know "what are you people doing here." We say that we're visiting Larry, and I let john do the talking both because the guy's being drunkenly flirtatious (he asks john twice if I'm his girlfriend) and because john's doing real well talking with him. The guy tells us he's a truck driver for Arch Coal, and that he's just doing this for a living, he needs to feed his family. He doesn't like what's happening to the mountains. john says that MJS has no quarrel with working guys trying to feed their families; the quarrel is with the big economic players, the guys in suits who own the draglines and make the decisions about mining coal this way.

They get to talking about the recent Supreme Court decision allowing a Connecticut town to seize people's homes to give them to a private developer for a private economic project. The truck driver brings this up as an example of: Look what our government is coming to, with no protection for little people, for people who aren't big economic players. For a few delicious minutes, I enjoy listening to anti-capitalist john defend private property rights, agreeing with the driver that, yeah, it's outrageous that the government can come and take your home. As we walk away, heading back to Larry's gathering, I tease john about this. Teasing aside, we agree that there's a difference between large spreads of land used by distant corporations solely for extracting resources and racking up profits elsewhere, and a homestead owned and occupied by someone who lives with the consequences of what's done to the land. What's needed in either case, though, especially in the case of distant corporate ownership, is a legal system (and an ethical system, john adds) that obliges and enables people who own land to meet responsibilities to that land's human and natural communities.

john and I aren't the only people from Larry's gathering who walk past the cabins to see the mine site. After we return, a series of confrontations occurs between MJSers and some of the men who've been drinking over by the cabins. Hillary and Matt Noerpel get drawn into a verbal confrontation and narrowly avoid Matt getting hit. Erin from Blacksburg, her partner Ali, and Keith (a young man from near Detroit who's recently arrived with Amerika)—all three quite young and slender—find themselves being bullied and taunted. Ali, whose heritage is Middle Eastern, becomes the object of racial slurs, but it's Keith who gets hit, punched in the face three times. It's really hard—especially for a young man—not to fight back when attacked, but Keith does the right thing. Avoiding escalation, the three of them walk away, back to Larry's gathering. Keith goes to sit in Amerika's car. He's crying, more humiliated and rattled than physically hurt, and wants to be left alone.

Meanwhile, the rest of the gathering is abuzz about what to do. Larry says: "They're my people, and I'm gonna go down there and talk to them." He says he wants to go alone, and so he does. He's gone for quite a while—long enough that we worry about him. (Everyone knows that Larry carries a gun, and people down there have guns, too.) When he comes back, he apologizes to the crowd for what happened. Several voices respond that he has nothing to apologize for. Larry reminds us that we have a plan we have to stick with, and part of that plan is nonviolence. It would be easy for him to pull his gun out, he says, because that's how he used to settle things, but that's not the way to accomplish what needs to happen. Larry adds that his relatives down at the cabins, most of whom do not at all approve of what happened to Keith, are going to be wondering if MJSers will stick with Larry. Larry wants us to know that we can count on him.

The threat of violence here is real, not imagined. It's not historical, it's present.

Late that day, I sit with Judy and several other people in the upstairs living room of the house in Naoma, talking over the events of the day. Judy tells us she found out from talking with Larry exactly who it was that hit Keith. She knows the guy—and knows his history of beating up the women in his life. Judy hates bullies, and she's angry about this—nobody picked on big, bearlike john johnson, she notes. But she's not surprised. The community as a whole has a battered-wife relationship with the coal companies, and that dynamic pervades personal relationships here as well. It's not surprising that MJS volunteers—particularly a slender, gentle twenty-year-old—should experience such bullying as well.

It's 9:30 in the morning on July 5, Tuesday, outside the state capitol building in Charleston, near the stone steps going up to one of the building's main entrances. The steps are very wide, leading up to eight stone columns across the front of the entrance. A dome tops the building, a big grand public building, meant to be impressive. It's already quite warm today—pleasant sitting in the shade, but getting to be uncomfortable out in the sun.

And here comes Ed Wiley, walking through the park, wearing a blue T-shirt and dark jeans, camo-patterned cap, and heavy boots. He's heading for the capitol steps, carrying a signboard with photographs of Marsh Fork Elementary School.

Ed, who's in his late forties, hasn't always been an activist. "I worked on these Massey coal sites," he's told me. "I worked for a contractor and we did reclamation work. We moved their equipment. We built roads. We helped build these big [slurry] ponds.

"Some of the older guys that were working for the company I'd worked for, they would get assigned to go up there to these cemeteries [surrounded by mining] and do a job, and they didn't want to do it. And I couldn't figure out why.

"They'd done a mountaintop removal all the way around [the cemeteries, and then] they went in with a highwall miner and undermined the cemeteries. There wasn't no [mining] activity up there [at the time], it was all real quiet. They sent me up there to do this job and I went up there, and it was to fill in the graves that sunk. You know, you could walk over to a grave (and these are old graves and new graves) and you could throw a rock down there and never hear it hit.

"What we had to do is take one of the bales of straw and stick it down in there first, kind of a plug. Then whatever you could find, what little dirt was left back on this mountain, go ahead and fill that in and seal the straw. And it wasn't that bad of a job." Unless you think about what you're doing.

"All of these old cemeteries back on these mountains—they had a little place over the hill that they kinda throw plastic flowers in the garbage, and [there was] some white picket fence that you see for yards, the little tiny white picket fence. I always took my string off the straw, and I'd take [the string] and break these little picket fences and make crosses, and try to put them back [on the graves that had fallen through]. There was baby graves in there and a couple of fresh ones—this baby got killed in a car wreck and I knew these people. It was really hard." He knew the people buried there had dropped out of their graves and been sent out with the coal. "No telling where they was at. I cried up there at the end of the day. That's why the old timers didn't want to go there. It wasn't the job itself that was hard labor. It was emotional to deal with at the end of it."

That by itself didn't turn Ed into an activist, although it bothered him. The last straw for Ed was when his granddaughter Kayla kept coming home sick from her school, Marsh Fork Elementary School, about a year and a half ago. When he figured out that what was making her sick was being in school, next to that coal processing facility, he had to try to fix that.

"I never thought it would go this far," Ed says. "You know, I thought maybe I'd get the school board's attention and maybe the health department's, and boom, bang, take care of this. I never thought it would be a political issue.

"I've made thousands of phone calls from [my] house, all day long, every day for a lot of weeks, calling everybody I knowed to call. You know, *everybody*. All of your organizations. People that should be helping these children or have any concerns about it at all. And nobody wants to touch these issues. I learnt quickly, you know, after a lot of phone calls, that the school board, the health department, the DEP, the EPA, anybody that I could contact, seemed like it was all one big happy family. Somebody had ties to another, all the way around the circle."

Ed's here today to try to break that circle. He approaches the steps alone; his support people are a ways behind him—Bo, Sage, and Abe Mwaura's brother Jesse, another of the interns at the Naoma house. Ed walks up the capitol steps, stops about two-thirds of the way up, takes out a cellphone, and calls the governor's office inside the capitol. Then he changes out of his blue T-shirt into a white one that, on its front, addresses the governor: "Joe: Kids First." (The back of the shirt has the universal "no" symbol—a circle with a slash through it—with "Timmermeyer" written inside the circle.) He unfolds the signboard to display photographs of the school, captioned "Where is your heart, Joe?" and "For the sake of the kids."

Ed tells me he's here today to talk to the governor about why he allowed that permit for a second coal silo next to the school. The woman who answered the phone at the governor's office just now told him the governor isn't in the office today. "And I politely told the lady that I'm here for the children of Marsh Fork Elementary, that I'm here to stay, and I'll wait him out until he comes back."

Shortly after 10 AM, Jay Smithers, head of security for the capitol, comes out to see Ed. They shake hands. Ed tells him why he's there. "The people in this capitol should be ashamed of themselves for allowing this to happen. They are putting a price on our children's heads, and it's wrong. My granddaughter goes to that school, and I'm not about to stand for this. I'm prepared to stay here as long as it takes. I'm not here to cause no trouble. I want an answer. I expect an answer out of the governor. Enough is enough. I really think that he's a good man. But I'm sorry to say: Joe, you're dragging your leg."

Ed asks Smithers why wouldn't the governor, after meeting with the group from Coal River, "have picked up the phone and called Timmermeyer [at the DEP] and said: 'Just hold off on that [new silo permit] for a few days until I see what's going on here.'"

"Well, I don't know," Smithers responds. "I'm sure he'll tell ya."

"If I get the opportunity to talk to him."

All the while they've been talking, Ed's had the feeling he knows this guy, so he asks: "Don't I know you from someplace?" It turns out that he and Ed have hunted deer in the same place. The guy whose land they've hunted on used to set Smithers to pulling pranks on Ed. Since Smithers was an undercover cop at the time, he kept changing his look, so every time Ed saw him he thought he was a stranger. (That's also why he wasn't sure he knew the guy today.) Smithers knows Bo, too, who later tells me he was one of Janice Nease's students in grade school. They're both relieved that the fellow in charge of security comes to this knowing Ed as a human being. It takes some of the worry out of what they're doing today.

Just as Smithers walks off, a cameraperson from Channel 3 arrives. Soon another comes out from inside the capitol, then another. A woman doing a photo essay on MTR for *Orion* magazine arrives. Jesse goes off with the photographs he's taken so far today to upload them to his computer so they can be sent out to still more media by folks at the house in Naoma. A woman from West Virginia public radio arrives to interview Ed, then the AP reporter who covers the capitol, and yet another TV cameraperson. Jesse returns and reports that MJSers in Naoma are sending out his pictures, with press releases, far and wide. Ken Ward, the excellent environmental reporter for the Charleston *Gazette*, arrives and talks with Bo and then Ed. It's now about 12:30. There's still no word from the governor's office.

It's hot, really hot out here, and relentlessly sunny.

Shortly before 2 PM, Bo, on his way to put more quarters in his parking meter, tells me that Ken Ward's just called him on his cellphone to say he's had a long chat with a spokeswoman for the governor, who tells him that the governor intends to come back to the capitol today and invite Ed up to his office. Ed and Bo think that's not good enough, that the governor must come down here and say publicly that he'll put the silo permit on hold, and get Stephanie Timmermeyer on the phone and tell her to do so.

Ed says he'll stay here as long as it takes, and plans have been made to back him up. There was a good bit of discussion among the dozen or so people at the July 4th picnic at Ed's house yesterday about having people from the Naoma house come to the capitol, to bring him food maybe. Ed's talking about a hunger strike, but others are discouraging that because he hasn't really prepared for a fast, and a fast is something that would be good to hold in reserve for escalating the protest further down the line, if need be. Folks at the house are prepared to bring Ed food and keep him company tonight with a candlelight vigil. This would tell the governor that Ed's not going to go away, that the governor will have to deal with him sooner or later, and so why not sooner?

Around 2:30 a fellow from the governor's office comes out to invite Ed inside to meet with the governor. Ed tells him: "No, right here. I was in there three weeks ago. The governor promised he would call us back, and he didn't. He also allowed the second permit to go on at the silo, and I would like an explanation of that, and I would also like to have an answer for what he is going to do for our children. And I'll be sitting right here."

The governor's representative goes back inside, and soon Carte Goodwin, the governor's general counsel, comes out to tell Ed that the governor "just said he is extending you the courtesy of coming into his office and sitting down and chatting. Then he'll come back out here and talk to as many persons as you want him to talk to, but he just wants to chat with you in private first."

"I'll do that," Ed says, "but I will not leave this capitol until he has gotten on TV today and stated that he is gonna help these little kids." Ed goes inside, and we wait.

While we wait, Bo talks on his phone, with a police lieutenant responsible for Homeland Security in Richmond, about July 8. "He wanted to know more about what we're planning on doing," Bo says. "He knows we have a permit for [a rally at] Monroe Park and he knows also that on a lot of websites out there are people talking about doing violence and civil disobedience and any number of things that day. He saw on [an] anarchist site where it says that they are urging everyone to be peaceful. He thought [that] was really good. I think basically he was looking for some assurances from me that we're not coming down there to cause a lot of problems. I told him that we're not coming to cause any problems. He wanted to know if maybe any of us wanted to be arrested, as [knowing] that would be helpful to them and helpful to us, but I said no, as far as I know, there are no plans for anything like that. We want to protest, we want to rally, and we want to march by Massey, and then I want to leave, is what I told him. And I told him we would all wear red handkerchiefs to identify ourselves. He liked that; he thought that was a great idea. And he said that he agrees with us on this issue [MTR]. He says, 'You do have a right to protest and peacefully march. As long as it's done that way, it's fine. But if you step over that line, of course we got to do our job.' I said, 'We understand that.'

"I told him [that] tonight I would contact people that I know who are down there and try to find out the numbers. He wanted to know roughly how many would be from our group. He says, 'Yeah, I understand that you can't control other groups. I totally understand that.'"

Shortly before 4 PM, Ed comes out and says that "the governor will be out here. He is gonna make a public statement that he is going to do something for the children. He basically said I got to give him a chance. And I told him that I couldn't leave this property until he come out here and made a public statement on TV that he was going to do everything in his power" to remedy the situation at the school. "He didn't want to come out here and do this on TV, but I told him that I could not go back to Coal River" unless he did. In addition, Ed says, the governor has agreed to convene a meeting in his office the day after tomorrow with people from the Coal River valley and state DEP and health officials. While Ed's explaining all this, media begin to arrive, having been called either by the governor's office or by folks at the house in Naoma—three television stations, West Virginia public radio, Ken Ward.

I don't know whether Joe Manchin always looks like this, but when he joins Ed at the top of the capitol steps his eyes look scared, defensive. Still, what comes out of his mouth is smooth and conciliatory and covers all the bases for him: "What we have talked about today is still the safety of the kids. How do we bring people together? While we were talking in my office, we called the Raleigh County board of education, we called the state board of education—we're having all those groups look at alternative sites, to put children in a much more safe environment.

We're hoping to bring all sides together. We even invite Massey and their representatives to be involved in this process, as far as taking the kids into consideration and moving them into the safest environment we possibly can.

"There's a meeting Thursday, here at the capitol, with all of the representatives of the agencies to make sure that they have done everything that they're supposed to. There are federal and state laws that they're required to abide by. I want to make sure that they've done that.

"I want to make no mistake: The most important thing we have is our children, and the safety of the children, and all the children that go to that school. So we're looking into everything we possibly can. With that, [Ed] knows that my commitment's the same as his as a grandfather. I'm a grandfather. We're trying to make sure that our children are in a safe environment. We're doing everything humanly possible, and the state will continue to do everything it possibly can." Tomorrow officials will look at alternative school sites; Thursday, at the meeting in his office, the permit process will be reviewed: "Did the professionals do the job they were supposed to do? Did they go through all the procedures? Were the federal and state guidelines and all the laws and regulations met, and everyone treated the same?" The governor is careful to make that latter point several times today, about everyone being treated the same, apparently to fend off complaints from Massey that it's being unfairly singled out and picked on.

At no point, though, does the governor suggest considering whether the permit process, even if followed to the letter, is inherently inadequate to ensure the safety and welfare of the public—including the safety of those schoolchildren he professes such concern about. When asked about this directly, he says: "Well I guess it depends on what you and I are calling unsafe."

The governor does, however, tell a lie about the meeting coming up on Thursday, presumably to save face with the reporters clustered around him and Ed. Making the point that Ed's sit-in hasn't changed anything, that the governor has been doing the right thing all along, he says more than once that Thursday's meeting was scheduled last week—which of course doesn't make any sense, as the meeting concerns the fairness of the process leading to a permit that wasn't issued until just last Thursday. If the governor had agreed on Thursday or Friday to schedule such a meeting, or during the three-day holiday weekend that followed, Ed wouldn't have arrived on the capitol steps this morning to demand that something be done. (In fact, the governor's office called CRMW to schedule Thursday's meeting shortly before Manchin went out to stand on the steps with Ed and talk to reporters.) Still, Ed says he's satisfied that the governor is publicly promising to do the right thing by the children of Marsh Fork Elementary.

The next morning, Ed, Bo, and other locals meet in the valley with staff from the governor's office, other state officials, local school board officials, and county officials. They tour both Marsh Fork Elementary and a possible alternative school site upriver a ways, and talk about possibly relocating the school. (Debbie Jarrell later talks with a teacher whose own kid attends the school and has to use an inhaler for breathing problems, "so he knows what problems are down there at the school. And he said, 'Let me guess who [from the school] was down there [at today's meeting]—all the teachers that didn't have kids, am I right?' I said yeah, and that have spouses that work for Massey.")

Later that day, Hillary tells me she's "disturbed" that the government officials are focusing on whether the school technically meets state environmental and public health regulations. "As far as we can tell," Hillary says, "the DEP is telling us that it meets those regulations. What I have to say is: then the regulations just simply aren't good enough. If children go to school, and walk around in the playground, and their shoes become black with coal dust, then the regulations just are not good enough. It's not acceptable for children to be breathing air that's filled with enough coal dust particulates that they settle into the grass and make their shoes and socks dirty. I don't care what else they found or didn't find at the school when they took a tour. That one simple fact is enough to tell us that the kids need to be moved and the processing plant needs to be closed.

"If you [the politicians and the coal companies] were any smarter than you are, you'd give us that [new] school right away. You'd move those kids immediately, because you'd realize we'd be scrambling for a new [anti-MTR] campaign platform." Of course, "if they gave us the school, what we would say is: Well then, you're admitting there is a problem and has been a problem. How long has that problem been going on? Why, when you have apparently a whole agency, the Department of Environmental Protection, with supposedly qualified staff who are there to assess environmental and public safety and health issues, and charged with protecting the public, and have the supposed education and know-how to do so, and the mandate to do so—why did it take a small handful of dedicated citizens to bring it to your attention and push the governor's office into shutting it down? Who are you truly working for? Is there a problem that goes much deeper than just this school? Is there an issue with the entire permitting process and the underlying founda- tions of the relationship that coal companies and energy companies have with the DEP?"

Bo goes to the county courthouse this afternoon and determines that in fact there has been some sort of coal facility at that location, by the school, since before SMCRA took effect in 1977. The DEP has been saying that they didn't really know about that, since the DEP didn't exist prior to 1982. They've just sort of assumed that the facility is grandfa- thered in and not subject to SMCRA regulation. But should any and all additions to the facility, such as the proposed second silo, be considered "grandfathered" and thus not subject to regulation, no matter how much larger in scale than the pre-SMCRA facility? The law may in fact allow that, but is that just? Is that the way it should be?

(Bo's busy today. After talking with folks more involved with the planning for the Richmond event than he is, he also follows up with the Richmond Homeland Security officer to say that several people may choose to be arrested for civil disobedience similar in tone to what

Hannah and Herb did at the Massey building and similarly nonviolent. The officer had asked to be given a heads up, and so Bo is giving him that.)

The meeting at the governor's office on Thursday isn't encouraging. The delegation from Coal River includes Ed, dressed as he was on the capitol steps, in jeans and what he calls his "hollow boy" boots—he's a West Virginia hollow boy and doesn't want to dress up to pretend to be anything else. Hillary, though also not pretending to be anything but herself, is dressed conservatively today, in black non-hippie clothes, her hair freshly washed and brushed and loose around her shoulders. They're joined by Bo, Vern, and Jackie Browning, and met in the hallway just before the meeting by Jack Spadaro. The governor's not here today. The meeting is run by his chief of staff, Larry Puccio. Other government officials present include Carte Goodwin, the governor's legislative director, a mine safety official, the state epidemiologist, the secretary of the Department of Health and Human Services, and several DEP representatives including Stephanie Timmermeyer herself, sitting directly across the big conference table from Bo, face impassive but looking uncomfortable, her fingers fidgety.

The Coal River representatives present a barrage of safety and health concerns and issues connected with the school. The state officials say they'll look into the matter. Bo and Ed and Hillary all press for a commitment to move the kids to a safer location. Larry Puccio says input from experts is needed before any decisions can be made. Carte Goodwin agrees to be available by phone to provide updates on how the "looking into" is going. At the end of the meeting, nobody seems happy, but no doors have been closed.

The Richmond action is to be big and urban, with lots of non-MJSers participating. Concern remains that, as this action is intended to connect with worldwide G-8 protests, which in other places have entailed property destruction and clashes with police, non-MJSers may diverge from MJS's nonviolence commitment. Richmond is a high-stakes test of MJS's ability to avoid the pitfalls of the Knoxville action—and a whole new set of pitfalls as well.

The rally starts at noon on July 8 in a park downtown. Speakers speak, songs are sung, and the crowd of perhaps 250 is asked to respect MJS's commitment to no violence and no property damage. It's hot, sunny, and windy. When the rally ends, the crowd marches down the middle of a street closed by police, heading for Massey headquarters. The march is colorful and good-natured, with banners, flags, signs, drums, an oversized puppet of King Coal, papier-mâché mountains on a wheeled cart, a cardboard-clad "school bus" wagon carrying two small children, bullhorn rants, chants, and dancing in the street. The police presence is minimal—two cars leading the parade, two more following behind, officers on bicycles blocking the cross streets. Judy Bonds (who spoke at the rally) and several others walk alongside the parade, on the sidewalk, handing out leaflets to people who have come out to see what's happening, drawn by the sound of the drums. Now and then they pause to talk about mountaintop removal with people stopped in cars at the cross streets, waiting for the parade to go by.

Turning the corner onto Fourth Street, with Massey's building just a block away, the marchers find traffic control sawhorses running down the length of the block, cordoning off the sidewalk. Police have hung a "Do Not Cross" tape at the sidewalk in front of Massey headquarters. Behind the police barrier are four officers on horses. Two guys in suits are standing in Massey's doorway, two police cars are parked at the far end of the block.

When the parade reaches the street in front of Massey's building, Larry Gibson is leading a chant: "Down with Massey, down with Massey." The big banner that's been at the head of the parade pauses in front of Massey's front door, and the three people holding it maneuver it to mask and shelter the papier-mâché mountains. The crowd chants "Shame, shame" and "Hands off our mountains." Five people—Amerika and Keith among them—holding bamboo poles with small banners on which are written the Marsh Fork demands, line up at the police tape at the edge of the sidewalk, facing the street. They then back up, forming a protective cordon allowing room for the papier-mâché mountains to be set just inside the police line, on the sidewalk. Three people quickly lock their arms into the mountains. The bullhorn, addressing Massey management now, urges them to do the right thing: "It would be much easier than putting up with us at your doorstep every few weeks."

A dozen or so people, including Larry, sit down together in a line in front of the people who are locked into the mountains. Other than Larry, I recognize only three of these as Mountain Justice Summer regulars.

The police refrain from any effort to move the sitters off the sidewalk—and in fact offer no response at all for a minute, then half an hour, then more. The crowd continues to chant, the bullhorn rants: "These mountains are our mountains." From inside the building, a woman leans out of an open third-floor window and says, "Y'all are crazy." The bullhorn responds: "We want to talk to you. We want to help you clean up your mess. We want to help you make reparations for the messes you're responsible for. We're tired of this, too."

Shortly before 2:30, Patty Sebok and three others ask the police whether a delegation of marchers might be permitted to knock on Massey's door to deliver their demands. The police officer Patty's talking with nods as though he thinks that's reasonable, and within moments Larry slides under the police barrier to do so. He gets no further than the outer vestibule door, and is refused entry. The officer accompanying Larry looks at him as if to say, "That's the best I can do," then shakes Larry's hand. Larry walks back to the crowd, tells them through the bullhorn that "They ain't gonna come out and talk to you today. They're cowards." The crowd cheers, a long, sustained yell.

Soon thereafter, police tell one of the protesters who's acting as a police liaison that the march permit has expired and it's time to leave. But they make no move to force the issue.

At 3 PM, the crowd gets a mixed message from the police. A lieutenant asks the sitting-down protesters if they need water, saying he doesn't want anybody to get sunstroke. Meanwhile, police at the upper end of the block are putting on riot gear. "I been looking around at what's

going on around us here, and I got some really good news," the bullhorn
announces. "It looks like a couple of riot squads are forming to arrest all
of the terrorists inside this building."

By 3:30, the drums are still drumming, and the bullhorn still going,
but a lot of people are sitting down in the street. They're tired. Larry
and Judy and Patty are talking to the three people locked into the papier-
mâché mountains, saying: We've won today. We don't need the arrests.
We can just take the victory and go home. The three people locked down
say they'll defer to the folks from Coal River and unlock themselves.

Shortly before 4 PM, the march has resumed, heading back toward
the park where it began, Larry leading the parade, bullhorn in hand. The
marchers look hot and tired, but not sorry to be here. There is a little
dancing on the way back, but not much.

Later, I talk with one of the anarchists who'd helped organize the
event, a young man with a lot of experience with urban street demonstrations. He was impressed by "one of the things one of the cops said to
Patty from CRMW when she was saying: 'Thank you for not rushing
us up today.' One of the cops said: 'Well, you know, I wish you luck in
your struggle. A lot of us on the force are with you.' I have never heard
a cop say anything like that to anything I'm involved in, because they're
usually not with you."

Altogether, the Richmond action, the meeting in the governor's office
the day before, and the media coverage of the situation at the elementary
school, apparently rattle Massey. On July 12, Massey sends CRMW a
letter, oddly neither addressed to anyone specific at CRMW nor signed
by anyone at Massey but cc'd to Jack Spadaro, stating: "Your organization has suggested that the [Goals Coal] facility is not safe. You have
made allegations that the impoundment is unsafe and that children are
being harmed. Given our confidence in the safety of the facility, we
are highly skeptical of your allegations… We ask that you immediately
provide us with any information you have to support the claims you have
made regarding the safety of the facility…. To aid you in your efforts,

we have also attached [newspaper] articles...detailing many of the allegations you have made to date.... We also ask Jack Spadaro to disclose
information and detail the basis, if any, for his comments." The letter
seems pointless except as either an implicit threat of or groundwork for
a SLAPP suit. A lawyer who advises CRMW tells them no response is
necessary, and none is made.

Also shortly after the rally in Richmond, Chris Irwin sends to the
MJS email list a digest of national news coverage of Mountain Justice
Summer, including many items published over the last few days. Articles
are being published in Florida, California, Mississippi, Minnesota. The
breakthrough in national coverage doesn't seem to have been triggered
by any single event—Richmond may be remembered as the turning point,
but these articles aren't all about Richmond. The Richmond story is just
the most recent in an accumulation of MTR-related news events that
have dribbled in to people in newsrooms across the country for months
now. They're now beginning to see this as a story they should be covering, which means that MTR is, in fact, becoming a national story.

An influx of about thirty new people arrive in Naoma after Richmond.
Some will stay for only a week or two, others longer. The organizers here
send them out to work on community service projects and the Listening
Project. The Naoma house is full to overflowing.

On the evening of July 14, Judy and Bo come to the Naoma house
to fill the newcomers in on the history of the campaign against strip
mining here, and to talk about plans for the weeks ahead. "You know, it's
not just the school," Bo says. "The school is an example of what's wrong.
But it's all up and down the river here is what's wrong. What we want to
do is continue the momentum we got going with the school. We want
to take that momentum and highlight what is wrong in the Coal River
valley, and all of West Virginia and all of Appalachia."

The next step, Bo continues, is to be a three-day march down the
valley, from Marsh Fork Elementary all the way to the processing plant
that's covering Sylvester with dust. "We want to do this march next

week," he says. "We want to go from Massey site to Massey site, and then the next day to another Massey site, rally, give 'em hell. Voice our opinions. Hopefully what will happen is that we'll pick up locals each day. We'll pick up more on Wednesday than we had on Tuesday, and hopefully when we go to Sylvester we'll pick up a whole ton of people."

Months ago, in early spring, the MJS campaign committed to making sure that people joining the campaign understood the potential risks. So this evening Judy tells the group about her experience a few years back on a weeklong anti-MTR march to Blair Mountain, the site of an early-twentieth-century struggle against coal company greed and violence. Judy was there with her grandson, along with Larry Gibson, Janice Nease, Ken Hechler, and a host of others. "We was marching along," Judy says, "and there stood men that could have played for the Packers. Each and every one of them weighed about 350 pounds. And they was coal people. We just had won a lawsuit [in which] the judge stopped a mountaintop removal site. So I watched them push around eighty-nine-year-old Ken Hechler like a schoolyard bully. There was one woman down there and she had some eggs, and she just swung her bag of eggs and knocked this woman that was dressed like Mother Jones to the ground. And there was a man and a woman there from New York that was filming a documentary, and excuse my language, but they told her to 'Put the fucking camera down and go back to where you came from.' She got scared and put the camera down. That's the last thing you wanna do. You *don't* put your camera down. I saw a grown man belly bumped. I saw them belly bump women. One of them told me that he oughta smack the piss out of me.

"So after that we had to have a police escort every day. We walked the gauntlet every day because some of the locals and the coal hoes would stand beside the road and throw eggs at us, throw rotten tomatoes at us. We got attacked every day. The worst thing was somebody spit on me, and I really wanted to go after that woman. You don't know how bad I wanted to go after that woman. We got harassed every day. And Ken Hechler—I'll never forget—Ken Hechler said, 'Walk, don't talk. Walk, don't talk. Don't talk back to 'em. Look at 'em and smile. Don't talk back to 'em.' Ken Hechler marched to Selma—he was one of the few people from West Virginia that went all the way down there and marched. So he's been through a lot.

"I just wanted to warn you [about] what happened. They even cussed my little grandson. These kids wanted to walk to remember the Battle of Blair Mountain because that was a historic time, and he wanted to be a part of that. And they cussed him. We walked by these people's houses that was miners, and that man walked along the fence with us and cussed us up one side and down the other."

Both Judy and Bo say they don't think the reaction to next week's march will be so violent. But they do want anyone who marches to understand and be prepared for that possibility—and definitely be prepared to control their own tempers when provoked.

Over the weekend before the march, MJSers disperse from the overcrowded Naoma house to several locations: camping in the woods by the home of a local sympathizer, sleeping bags on the floor of an old school building now used as a private home, even sleeping bags on the floor and sofa at CRMW's office. Even so, folks are still sleeping in every room at the Naoma house, which remains the central meeting place.

Also during that weekend, quite a few people disappear for a few days on a brief mystery exodus to Tennessee, for planning an action slated for Zeb Mountain next month. Many of those same people were involved, earlier this month, in planning a big covert action in West Virginia. Those plans were laid aside when it became known that the very large piece of mining equipment being targeted was going to be dismantled and moved to another site before the action would take place. Before the plug was pulled on the West Virginia action, many of those involved in both it and the plans for a Tennessee "mountain takeover" were leaning toward pulling out of the Tennessee action, mostly because of conflict with Chris and Paloma, specifically resentment of their perceived bossiness. After the plug was pulled in West Virginia, people wanting to do direct action saw that what was being planned for

Tennessee was the only big game of that sort going this summer, so their interest in it revived.

The three-day march is to begin at Marsh Fork Elementary at noon on Tuesday, July 19. By 10 AM, a dozen cars are parked along the road by the school, taking up all the roadside from the school's driveway down to where their cars block the entrance to a field used for parking. At that entrance, a big, professionally printed banner touts Massey as a good "partner in education." Along the road, more than a dozen women are holding up signs in opposition to the march and its goals: "If you don't support coal here, move out," one sign says.

Downriver at the CRMW office, and upriver at the house in Naoma, march organizers are adjusting plans in response to the counterprotest. Instead of parking at the school, they'll park along the road upriver just a little ways beyond Goals Coal. The marchers will all arrive at once, assemble away from the counterprotesters, then march right past them and on down the road. Plans are tweaked for both car security and personal security. When I stop at the house to figure out where I should leave my car, I explain that I'm heading down there ahead of everyone else so I can talk with the counterprotesters. A voice from the kitchen asks, "You going there alone?" When I say I'm safer going there alone than I am with any of them, the response is general laughter and agreement. Counterprotesters notwithstanding, the marchers are in good spirits.

At 11:30, as I walk past the entrance to Goals Coal, the sign says they're open for business today. Up ahead, about two dozen counterprotesters, nearly all of them women, stand by the road holding signs: "Massey supports *our* community!" "Coal River: Taking a stand. Leave our jobs and schools alone." "If they are against mountaintop mining, why are they only against Massey?" "We support Massey Energy and Massey Energy supports us." "Outsiders go home. Let our community decide."

A woman named Kathy tells me, "We've been in this [school] building for years, and every year they've had air quality inspections and the sludge [dam] above us has been inspected weekly or biweekly, and every report we have ever seen has been safe. We do feel we're safe. You know, we wouldn't endanger our lives or the lives of our children." I ask her why she's here today. "I'm just sort of here to see what's going on. You know, because I work here [she's a teacher; school's out for the summer] and it affects my school and my community. All of us that are here are local people, you know, and most of those other people are out-of-state people, whatever. So we're just sort of seeing what's going on."

Another woman, standing next to Kathy, who also identifies herself as a teacher at the school adds: "I just feel like outsiders have interfered with our lives. If we have a problem as a community, we want to solve our problems, we don't want outside people to come in and cause controversy where there is none. And they are working very hard saying they don't have anything against Massey Energy. But all their demonstrations point at Massey, no other mountaintop removal company. Only at Massey. They have a vendetta against Massey in my opinion, and our school is caught in between. And if there are chemicals in the playground or all through the building, why is our grass so green and we have flowers?"

Farther down the line, another woman tells me, "My husband works for Massey, he works on the mountain up here, my daughter attends [this] school. She's getting an outstanding education. These are wonderful teachers that just absolutely love our kids. And regardless, we love our children as much as anybody else, and we wouldn't put them in harm's way. My husband drives up there every day and he sees how safe it is. But he would be the first to say, 'Take her out of school' if he thought it was not safe. So she attends every day. And that's why I'm here. I think that people need to know that this group does not speak for the rest of us."

A woman holding a sign that reads, "Prove you don't like coal. Turn off your electricity." says she's here today "just to support our school, our community, and our husbands that work for Massey." Her husband works for Massey, she says, and she has a child who attends this school. So does another woman nearby, who's holding a sign that says, "My husband works for Massey. My child goes to this school. We're OK with it!"

Another sign says, "Outsiders have a hidden agenda. Leave our schools out of it." The man holding it, Ray Casino, tells me, "Well, I've had a grandson just graduate from this school here last year. I've got another grandson going to this school this year. And I can't see what they're trying to prove, I mean, trying to get this school shut down. I can't see no danger in it. I've been in coal mining for thirty-six years. I lived on this Coal River ever since 1953. I can't see no point in what they're trying to do. And I ain't gonna call no names, but anyhow he's supposed to have a granddaughter, he ain't even got no granddaughter, especially the one I'm talking about." He's talking about Ed Wiley here; Kayla's his step-granddaughter, both Ed and Debbie having been married before. "I knowed him all his life. So that's the way the ball bounces and the cookie crumbles."

Another sign says, "This is our livelihood you're messing with, not just a summer project. We support Massey Energy." The woman holding it tells me she's here today because "the people that are here protesting against this and saying that they are residents of this area, 95 percent of them are not residents of this area. And what they're doing is they're coming in and trying to dictate what happens in this area. You're talking about people's jobs and people's lives, this school, the future of this school, not only the coal company. The coal company supports this school and, as you see on the sign right here, they're partners in education. They're partners in education with most all schools in the area. And they're not going to do anything that would be harmful to these children because the workers that work at that mine right next to the school are the people that have kids in the school. Not the people that's up there gathered [to march] today. The people that are standing right here beside me today in support of this company and this school, are the ones that have kids that go here.

"My child is too young to be in school yet, but I was born here, I went to school here, and yeah, all of my family works for Massey."

That's what I hear on tape—but most of the counterprotesters are unwilling to talk with the tape recorder on. They've come here today with their scripted signs, which they've decided ahead of time they're OK with, and they're not comfortable going beyond that, certainly not with a tape recorder running. What people say on tape feels like the party line—they may very well believe what they're saying, but nonetheless it has a canned quality. Over and over I hear that the people coming here to march today are outsiders who should just go away; another theme is that Massey is being singled out and picked on.

Off tape, what I hear from the counterprotesters is a bit different than the scripted message. When they show something of what they're feeling, a good bit of what shows is fear. One woman talks (off tape) for quite a while about how the valley's already lost two schools to consolidation, and they don't want to lose this one. Other people express concerns about jobs, fear about what happens if coal mining is made impossible here. I'm reminded of what Judy and Hillary and others have said about the community's relationship with coal companies being like a battered wife's. That's why, I think, the outsider rhetoric is so prominent here today—it's easier to demonize "outsiders" than to deal with your very own demons.

But fear isn't all that's going on here today. One reason, I later learn, why so many of the counterprotesters are unwilling to talk on tape is that most of them aren't actually from around here. Judy, Patty, and Bo later tell me that their sense—and they confirmed this by talking with other local people who drove by the school and saw the counterprotest—was that most of the women in front of the school have been brought in from other coalfield counties to swell the counterprotesters' numbers. The relatively few counterprotesters who do live around here have apparently selected themselves (or been selected by organizers) to talk to media; the out-of-towners are holding back, creating the illusion that all of them are local.

Judy, Bo, Vern, and others here have said time and again that local folks who actively oppose CRMW are consumed by greed. And—there's no other word for this—there's evil in the mean, ugly, nasty way some of the counterprotesters talk about "those outsiders," evil abetted by a sort of willful blindness and a "how dare they" attitude. Maybe what has opened the door for letting that evil in is greed, maybe it's fear, maybe it's anger at something else in their lives. Maybe there's a universal human need to set "us" against "them." This is a community that's been pushed and pushed, and exploited for generations. People here have so little left, that the temptation to feel superior to "outsiders"—to anyone—is strong indeed.

One of the counterprotesters tells me—off tape—that the MJSers can say their thing and the counterprotesters can say theirs, and that that's what makes America a great country. When I agree with her and ask if I may turn the tape recorder on to talk about that some more, she won't allow it. What she's just said to me apparently isn't what Massey wants them talking about there today. They're here to do what Massey wants. Even if saying anything else isn't explicitly forbidden, they're just not comfortable doing it, and certainly don't feel free to speak their minds in any way that can later be attributed to them. Which is pro-foundly un-American.

Just past noon I hear drums, and in a few moments I see marchers—more than fifty of them—coming down the road toward the school. About fifteen of the marchers are local; the rest have come here from other places to support MJS. Bo's in the lead, carrying a bullhorn, walking next to Patty who's carrying a sign saying, "Tear it down," meaning the coal silo. Ed's carrying his big photograph of the school and the site. TV cameras and news photographers are taking pictures of the march. Bo leads a chant: "Save the kids," he says into the megaphone, then every-one else responds, "Tear it down." Apparently state troopers have asked the marchers to move into the lane opposite the school to put some distance between themselves and the counterprotesters, and so they do. Judy's carrying a sign: "Coal hoes bow down to Massey." Amerika and Keith are carrying a small banner reading: "To save heaven, you gotta raise some hell." Sarah's sign says: "Outside coal companies have hidden agenda. Go home." Bringing up the rear are Ukiah and her parents. The marchers pass the school without incident, and continue on toward the Montcoal facility, another Massey subsidiary, sharing the road with passing cars now. People in a few of those cars give the marchers a thumb's up sign and a toot of the horn. Only one presents a "fuck you" finger.

The march continues on through Edwight, which, like all the little towns in the valley, isn't what it used to be. At Tina's Country Kitchen, long closed now, the "For Sale" sign in the window is so old and faded the phone number on it is illegible. A few doors down a woman stands in front of her house yelling, "You better stay on your side of the road. This side of the road is my property, and I'm totally against what you want to do. Y'all hate coal, but you like electricity, too." After the marchers have passed, she still stands there, fuming.

Ed's leading the march now, but Ed's a fast walker and the folks behind aren't keeping up. They send Sister O'Connell up to walk with Ed in the hope that this will slow him down—but it turns out she's a pretty fast walker, too. "I always have been very involved in justice issues," she tells me, when I ask how she comes to be here today. "I was a schoolteacher for many years. I am seventy-eight years old, and I have been a sister now for fifty-eight years. And during most of that time, I have worked with children. So I'm very concerned that children are not being cared for and protected. I'm also concerned about what they're doing to our world, as far as what's going to be here for future generations, these children as they grow up. It's a very unjust situation, and the local people have not been heard. It seems to me that when we have a government, the government should protect them rather than a coal company that takes the income out of the state." Sister O'Connell doesn't agree with what the counterprotesters say about local people all favoring the mining. "No. That's not true. That's not true."

The next town along the march route is Stickney. There's very little left of it. "If strangers drive by here," Judy has told me, "they see a lot of weeds grown up, and trees. And I see where houses used to set, where friends and classmates" used to live—ghosts now, like the ghost hollows and ridges up behind the elementary school. Judy can remember when

Stickney was a solid grid of houses three rows deep. Most are now gone. Most of the land here, as in many coalfield communities, is owned by a land company that is owned or controlled by one or more coal companies—in Stickney's case, it's the Rowland Land Company, which Massey controls. People own their own houses but the coal company controls the land, which of course gives the company a great deal of power over the people living there. "Sometimes you don't even pay rent for the land," Judy says. "It's just the threat that the coal company can move you off their land, and how are you going to move that house?" Deed restrictions typically prevent owners from selling their houses to anyone but the coal or land company. So, as local employment dwindles, and people need to move elsewhere to seek work, they either sell their homes to the company—if the company wants to buy, at whatever price it chooses—or abandon them. Since Judy grew up here in the 1960s, many of the houses on company-owned land have been torn down.

Farther down the road, the marchers stop for a rest at Marsh Fork High School. Judy went to school here—so did her brother and her daughter. Her grandson would have gone here as well, but the School Board closed it down. Judy tells me that there was a push in the late 1970s to consolidate Marsh Fork and Clear Fork, on the other side of Coal River Mountain, and send kids to the high school in Glen Daniel, a good half-hour's drive east of here. Clear Fork High School was closed then. School officials said the closing was dictated by depopulation, though locals believe the timing of the closing was due to the influence of mining companies, because "there was a mountaintop removal permit right behind Clear Fork High School two years after it was closed," Judy says. Local resistance kept Marsh Fork High School open until June 2003. Locals believe that the decisive factor in closing the school then was that Massey and the Rowland Land Company (which owns the land the school sits on) wanted it closed because Massey, expanding its operations nearby, wants the site. "There is a strip mine permit right behind the high school," Judy says. "They're moving toward the high school." Last year, prior to MJS and not in connection with CRMW, some local person or persons spray-painted the high school: "Massey Did This. Mountain-Raping Bastards."

The deed for this land says that if the school closes and the building isn't used as a school anymore, after two years the land reverts to Rowland. Rowland acknowledges that it has an interested potential tenant or buyer. It's not clear whether Rowland can compel the school district to tear down the school, or if the community can retain control of the school and turn it into a community center. "The people don't want the buildings torn down," Judy says. The school has a million-dollar gym built in the 1980s that people would like to use. The buildings are sound, exceptionally so for school buildings in the region.

"We'd like to make it a living community center, a focal point of the community again," Judy says. She would especially like to see the center enable older people to share with younger people traditional mountain skills (quilt making, canning, making of tools, herbal lore) and knowledge that have economic and cultural value. She envisions a place that fosters economic activities not based on coal, using sustainable resources "and the culture of the people that's being lost."

The idea of reclaiming public space from government or corporate control is near and dear to the heart of anarchists. Both the Coal River locals who want to reclaim the school for community use, and the anarchist MJSers who support them in this, recognize that they come to this from very different perspectives. Finding themselves converged to much the same position on this is pleasantly surprising and encouraging.

Leaving the high school behind, the marchers head for the Performance Coal facility just down the road, in Montcoal. There are no houses along the road here now; everyone was moved out in the 1980s and 1990s to make room for the prep plant and its big conveyor belt, which brings in coal from deep mines back in the hills across the road.

Performance Coal also processes coal from strip mines and longwall mines back in the hills on the other side of the river, including the mine where Ed Wiley filled in the tops of graves from which the bottom fell out. Formerly, Judy remembers, "up on that mountain, Armco [which used to own the Montcoal plant] had picnics up there, and there's some of the biggest blackberries you ever seen in your life up there and they're good." Rather, they *were* good—the mountain they grew on is now gone.

In the 1940s, '50s, and '60s most of the mining here was still deep mining, underground. A wave of strip mining, relatively small in scale, began in the '50s and continued through the mid-'60s. Then the long coal boom that began in the 1940s went bust. That bust continued through the 1970s. MTR began in the 1980s, during the economic upturn that has continued (for coal at least) into the twenty-first century. Unlike previous coal booms, though, this one hasn't brought much in the way of jobs. Employment here has decreased even as production has increased, since the early 1960s, due early on to mechanization and more recently, dramatically, to MTR. "All machines, no people," Judy says. "That machine doesn't pay taxes, it doesn't live in our community, it doesn't buy in our local stores."

Three police cars and five state troopers wait by Performance Coal's front gate; so does a truck that's come from the Naoma house with lunch for the marchers. One of the state troopers asked Patty a bit earlier, "Now, do y'all have water? Are you getting hydrated?" So one of the guys who brought the food walks over to offer the state troopers something to eat. Their response is a shrug, noncommittal.

It's now 2:15, and really, really hot. The marchers, tired and sweaty, gather by the entrance to the facility and chant: "What do we want? Justice. When do we want it? Now." Bo takes the megaphone, points to the mountain back behind where coal is being processed and tells the crowd: "Many families grew up on that mountain. Back up on that mountain is cemeteries. They're surrounded by mountaintop removal all around them. We went to Asbury Cemetery last year. [There] was a 200-foot drop off the edge of the cemetery." Bo tells them about how the mining company sends workers "up there to clean up graves that had sunk because they highwall mined the bodies out of there." (The crowd shouts "Shame.") "I don't call that a good neighbor when you take our dead and you grind 'em all and ship 'em all to China. So we want to let them know that we're aware of that. That once we take care of [the elementary school] we got some issues with this mine site down here also. So we'll be coming back."

That evening, the marchers gather at the Naoma house for debriefing. Most of the talk is about how they can present themselves better tomorrow and what worked and didn't work today. Generally, people are pleased with how it went. One fellow—big and tall, with multiple tattoos, strange body piercings, dreadlocks, anarchist-punk black clothes, shirtless—suggests that maybe we look kinda scary to children. He means not just himself but also the other young people who've come to the campaign from the urban-punk scene, bringing with them styles of dress and hair and body decoration never before seen in such profusion here. There's some talk about how they might try to defuse that. Talking with him afterward, I suggest, teasing him a little, that he wear a big button with a smiley face on it that says: "Hi, my name is Puppy," as Puppy is the name he's going by. He tells me, rather earnestly, that that's one reason why he chose to call himself Puppy, to counteract his appearance.

Although the three-day march goes from Marsh Fork Elementary down the valley to Sylvester, its route isn't continuous. On the second day of the march, the marchers go upstream instead of down, from Whitesville to Marfork, where Judy Bonds used to live.

By 10 AM, half a dozen cars are parked on either side of Rt. 3 at the intersection with the road up into Marfork. Counterprotesters are setting up folding chairs and an open tent for shade. A sign says, "Support Massey or leave." I recognize some of the women who held signs outside the elementary school yesterday. Earlier this morning, Bo told me he's heard that yesterday evening at least some of the women who'd been in front of the school were calling everybody they knew in the valley to ask them to come swell their numbers today. Bo supposes that Massey orchestrates turnout by asking a supervisor's wife to start making the phone calls.

Marfork used to be a substantial community. Judy Bonds and both of her parents were born here. Her grandparents lived here. Judy's daughter and grandson lived here with her.

Massey now owns or controls the whole hollow, but you can still usually drive up the road off Rt. 3 a short distance. If you drive this with Judy, she'll point out the empty places where certain neighbors and relatives and she herself used to have homes. Today only a very few houses remain. Those that remain habitable are apparently used by Massey employees, likely as temporary housing. (Nothing Massey does here is permanent except the damage to the mountains and forest and streams.) You'll see open lots where trucks are parked or stored, sheds, metal industrial buildings, and an office building, headquarters for Massey's Marfork subsidiary.

The office building is at the right-hand side of a fork in the road, where the main hollow, Marfork, continues on up to the left and a tributary hollow, Birch Hollow, branches up to the right. Judy was born up Birch Hollow. You can't get up there now, she tells me. Massey has a warehouse there, and beyond that Judy has heard that it's now "a virtual wilderness."

It's still possible to drive a short distance farther up the main Marfork hollow, passing the empty place where Judy's grandparents lived, the empty place where a general store and post office used to sit, more empty lots and abandoned houses. There's a cemetery farther up the hollow where some of Judy's ancestors are buried. Between here and there is a guard shack and gate where you'll be turned away from the mining operations beyond. In early winter, Judy and others will go through an hour-long runaround with security at the guard shack here so they can go visit the cemetery. "You get to drive right through the preparation plant," she tells me. "But I ain't going up there this time of year [in warm weather]. The snakes are *bad*."

The mining here has displaced wildlife as well as the human community. "When I was a little girl growing up," Judy says, even still when her daughter was growing up, "we always knew there was wildlife up in the head of this hollow, but you didn't see the snakes, you didn't see bears, you didn't see squirrels, you didn't see any kind of wildlife whatsoever unless you went into their habitat. Until Massey moved in. When Massey moved in, the wildlife started pouring out of the mountains and come down on the people, on us. You wouldn't believe the poisonous snakes." Later, I learn that Massey has been having a hard time keeping security guards on staff because bears have come after them, looking for food in the guard shacks.

Other than occasional visits to the cemetery, "you can't get up Marfork any more, and this was a favorite for people to go up. People would go up there and go hunting arrowheads, and just go hunting and climb up to the mountains. Marfork was a very special hollow to people. Still is, particularly to me. [The creeks here] sustained a lot of life. I wouldn't drink it now, though. I wouldn't touch it.

"I played in these creeks when I was a little girl. My mother did, my father did, and my daughter." When her grandson was old enough to be playing in the creek, in the mid-1990s, that was when "we first started finding the fish kills and blackwater spills." Judy remembers her grandson one day standing in a creek surrounded by dead fish and asking her what was wrong.

There's been mining up these hollows since before Judy was born. "We thought it was mined out in the '60s and '70s. And then Massey came in and just pushed everything and everybody out [in the early 1990s]. All my neighbors moved out, and the dust it just got worse and worse. There's a preparation plant up at the upper end up here. They call it the super plant." The super plant pumps its sludge up behind the Brushy Fork dam, the biggest coal sludge dam in the state, much, much bigger than the one up above Marsh Fork Elementary. Like the one behind the school, the Brushy Fork dam has been built with strip-mine waste by bulldozers from the ground up, with the same weaknesses from gobs of uncompacted mud in it. You can't see any of this from the road, or from anyplace else open to the public. But although it's out of public sight, if this dam ever fails and even a fraction of the sludge behind it breaks through, the town of Whitesville will be obliterated.

Shortly before noon I find about a dozen people at CRMW's office on Whitesville's main street. They're all revved up and cheerful, ebullient today. More signs have been made, including one that says, "There are no outsiders in America" in red, white, and blue. Another asks: "Where is the livelihood in Marfork?" Judy has added a bunch of dollar signs to her "Coal hoes bow down to Massey" sign. MJSers are assembling just down the street.

A phone call comes in for Bo from Carte Goodwin at the governor's office. "I don't trust them, Carte. They've lied to us before," we hear Bo say. "I understand how expensive this is going to be for Massey," which is now faced with new evidence that even its first silo near the school is there illegally. (Reporter Ken Ward has discovered that, on maps submitted for various permits over the years, the plant's property boundary has shifted west, toward the school. Older maps show boundaries that place *both* the existing and proposed silo outside the facility's permitted boundaries, prompting the DEP to order that work on the second silo must stop until the boundary issue is sorted out.) The right thing for Massey to do, Bo continues, the good public-relations thing, would be to buy the school and provide the money to build another one nearby, someplace safe.

Just past noon we hear drums, and forty-some marchers come down the sidewalk, headed for Marfork. Everyone in the CRMW office joins them. Signs say: "Our kids' lives are more important than Massey's money." "Save the school. Tear down the silo." "Massey coal: Let our ancestors rest in peace." Ukiah's mom carries one reading: "When the mountaintops are gone and the miners unemployed, Massey will still be rich. This community will have nothing."

Whitesville has little enough even now. "Boy, has Whitesville changed," Judy tells me. "This was a boomtown [in the early 1960s]. It was a bigger boom, my mother told me, in the '40s and '50s." Passenger trains used to stop here, connecting Whitesville with Charleston and the world beyond. Now, "we got two funeral homes here, and they are the only two original businesses" doing well, as the dwindling population ages. Many more businesses used to do well here—a dry cleaner, more gas stations, a portrait studio, two drug stores with soda fountains and cooked food. Now there's just a chain pharmacy at the far end of town. Once there were four grocery stores in town, now there's only one—the only one from here to Glen Daniel, nearly an hour to the east. Two movie theaters have closed—there are none now. "We had a bowling alley," Judy recalls. "It's gone. There are empty, abandoned, dilapidated buildings all over Whitesville." Many stores look long vacant, and some are boarded up. "Whitesville is just sad. It's sad, sad, sad to look at what Whitesville is."

The march today is the most lively thing that's happened along Whitesville's main street in a long time. Drawn outdoors by the sound of drums, whistles, and cymbals, spectators point at the signs and the exotic appearance of the marchers with apparent amusement. Several spectators are wearing Massey stripes. A young woman laughs, more like she's laughing at the marchers than with them. A few more people have joined the back of the parade, so there are about fifty marchers again today. Once again, Ed's leading the march with a blown-up photo of the elementary school, wearing the T-shirt he wore at the state capitol: "Joe, kids first." A young MJSer walking alongside the march hands out leaflets. Puppy stops to talk with one spectator after another. Some people driving past the march honk horns in approval, others yell disapproval.

At the far end of town, beyond where the sidewalk ends, Bo stops to confer with a state trooper about the march route, explaining that no, they don't intend to march back through town, but at the end of the march will shuttle the marchers in cars now parked up beyond the road to Marfork. Moments later, a woman driving a sporty red car swerves as though to hit Bo, who gets out of the way. Bo later tells me that when he saw the car coming at him, he made eye contact with the driver and saw that she recognized him and wanted to hit him. Neither Bo nor anyone else thinks this was premeditated, just an ugly impulse. Immediately afterward, the driver pulls off the road, gets out of the car, and flips up her license plate so it can't be read. She looks as though she's surprised by what she's done, although flipping up the license plate like that suggests experience with this sort of concealment. (Days later, after the police track her down, she and Bo will meet at the police station. There she'll cry and cry, and Bo will tell her: "You know, you just weren't thinking. If you'd hit me, not only would you ruin my life and ruin my family's life but you'd ruin your own family's life." He doesn't press charges.)

The march continues. Up ahead, at the road to Marfork, about a dozen cars and sixteen or so counterprotesters are stationed on the Marfork side of the road. Massey has shut down the road to Marfork where it meets Rt. 3; wooden barriers and security staff block the way. A state trooper is talking with the counterprotesters.

It's hot again today, up in the 90s, and the marchers look sweaty and wilted. After a brief stop for water and a pep talk from Bo, the march-ers approach the counterprotesters, today as yesterday across the road from them. Vern, on the megaphone, starts up a chant: "King Coal has no soul."

Six police cars are parked nearby. The counterprotesters' signs say: "Massey supports *our* community," "We support Massey and Massey sup-ports our school," "Honk for our coalfields." Two signs simply say: "Go home." The back window of a pickup truck parked here has "Outsiders go home" soaped on it, and a sign propped on it: "Tree huggers leave."

The march halts across the road from the counterprotesters. The two sides face each other. The marchers chant: "Massey go home!" The counterprotesters answer: "We are home."

Judy, obviously angry, takes the megaphone, points up the road to Marfork, and says: "This is how Massey supports communities. There is nothing left of Marfork. That's how Massey supports communities."

The marchers chant: "Shame on you," then "Shame on Massey." The counterprotesters, some of whom are every bit as angry as Judy, shout: "Go home. Go home." Judy, still with the megaphone, says that the shame of it is that there are mothers who care more about money than they do about their own children. She's really angry, yelling at the women across the road, and they're yelling back at her. Pauline Canterbury takes the megaphone and tries to tell her story, about dust from Massey's plant in Sylvester. The counterprotesters shout her down, waving their "Go home" signs at her.

Eventually, the marchers continue up Rt. 3, leaving the counterprotest behind. A short ways up the road, the march ends for the day.

That evening, they gather at the Naoma house to talk over the day and make plans for tomorrow. People are depressed. What happened today, with the two groups yelling at each other, with neither side listening to the other, seems pointless. Negative outweighed positive. Certainly no progress was made in making it seem safe or attractive for more of this community to join CRMW in the fight against MTR.

Judy and Bo, we're told, feel bad about having got so angry today. (Both have gone home already, tired and needing rest.) What Judy did today, the across-the-road yelling, is not the kind of person she wants to be. Judy's also no longer happy with her "coal hoes" sign—it's name-calling, and though she's meant it to refer to anyone who prostitutes him or herself to Massey, it's been taken to mean that she's calling the women counterprotesters whores. She recognizes that she had an emotional reaction to being at Marfork and hearing them talk about "community" in a way that excludes her, and yelling "Go home" when her childhood home isn't there any more. She regrets that that reaction led her to start yelling in anger.

Not many local people have really got to know folks who've come here for Mountain Justice Summer, and there's some talk this evening that MJSers should be going to more community events. Hillary says there's no need to rush this. Some MJS folks will stay in the valley beyond the end of summer (she hopes to be one of them), and more should be back next summer. MJS intends to be here for the long run, as long as it takes.

The third and final day of the march begins midday, once again in Whitesville, at a community center on Rt. 3. Bo and Judy apologize to the crowd for losing their tempers and yelling yesterday. That's not constructive, they say, and add that there's a different script for today.

Shortly before the march resumes, Ed Wiley tells me a sad story. Yesterday his granddaughter, Kayla, who often stays with Ed and Debbie, mentioned that she'd seen tickets for Massey's big annual picnic at her parents' house. It turns out that Kayla's dad, who's married to Debbie's daughter, had been doing deep mining for another company but recently took a job with Massey, so they've been invited to the company picnic. Ed's not at all happy that they intend to take Kayla there, and he told them so yesterday. All the adults got angry, and Kayla's mom took Kayla away home. By the end of the day, everyone apologized to everyone else for having had words. But this is going to be an ongoing discomfort in the family—that Kayla's dad works for Massey, and Ed's fighting Massey.

The marchers have a few new signs today, in response to local gossip that they're a bunch of dirty hippies: "Soap won't wash away Massey's dirt," "There is not enough soap to clean up Massey's mess," "Massey: Your sludge stinks worse than we do." (The plumbing at the Naoma house isn't working well. But even when they're clean, the anarcho-punk style of dress and hair favored by most of the young MJSers *looks* dirty to most local people, who are much more conservative in appearance.) Sarah Haltom is carrying the sign that says "There are no outsiders in America."

As the march begins, I walk for a while along the other side of the road from the marchers. Wineberries grow wild there, and they're red, ripe, and delicious today. Benji Burrell, one of the Naoma house interns, yells across the road to ask me if they're good. They are indeed.

The whole march today seems life-affirming. No bullhorn today. No drums. People are singing, "Power, power, power to the people."

Bo, who's videotaping the march, is walking on the same side of the road as me, across from the marchers. "Hey, don't you be making yourself a target," I tell him, referring to yesterday's incident with the red sports car. He laughs and says, "Here, you walk on this side of me," between him and the road. The marchers are singing a variation on

"You Are My Sunshine," with the chorus ending "Please don't take my mountains away."

The marchers stop at Pauline Canterbury's house, right on Rt. 3 in Sylvester, for sodas and cookies and a little rest. It's awfully hot again. Abe Mwaura's come here from Huntington today, and brought with him Winnie Fox, the elderly woman who was arrested at Goals Coal earlier this summer. When the march moves on, she'll be given a ride to catch up with it at Massey's Elk Run coal processing facility, at the other end of Sylvester.

Sylvester, according to Pauline, is not a company town. People have built their own houses, on their own land, and a lot of retirees have chosen to live here. But from right in front of Pauline's house, you can see the ineffective dust-containment dome at Elk Run. Property values here have dropped to a fraction of what they once were. A great many of the homeowners here depend on Social Security for their income and have no other resources. So they're stuck, unable to sell their homes for a price that would allow them to move anywhere else, and inhaling coal dust all the time.

The marchers today walk through Sylvester with dust masks on, led by Pauline and Mary Miller. Following them is another Sylvester woman carrying a sign that says, "Stop destroying my home." More than fifty marchers follow them, soberly, single-file, in complete silence. The march passes by people on a porch who'd been shouting "Go Massey go!" as the march approached. They fall silent, too, looking a little cowed by the marchers' quiet purposefulness. Hillary hands them a leaflet as she passes, which they take without comment.

At the gate to the Elk Run plant, about fifty counterprotesters have assembled today, their numbers roughly double what they were yesterday and the day before. They're joined by perhaps twenty employees from the plant. Half a dozen state troopers stand by. Shortly before reaching the plant, several of the marchers confer with the police, saying they want to walk down the side of the road opposite the gate and the counterprotesters, and they'd like to have that space to themselves.

Keeping the two groups separate suits the police just fine.

In silence, the marchers walk single-file down the road and stop in a long line directly across from the gate. The counterprotesters are chanting, "We are Massey, here to stay." An older woman gleefully drums a tire iron against the metal guard rail by the side of the road. It makes an ungodly, violent racket. One man holds a sign saying, "Try soap." Another sign says, "Go home outsiders." A big sign, almost banner-sized and apparently professionally made (presumably with money from Massey) says: "If you're against mountaintop removal, why are you just against Massey?" A high-school-age kid holds a sign saying, "Tree huggers go home."

The marchers sit down facing the plant and display a series of signs that quote the Bible: "The earth is the Lord's and the fullness thereof. Psalms 24:1," "The Lord's foundation is in the holy mountains. Psalms 87:1," "Let them shout from the top of the mountains. Isaiah 42:11," "The mountains shall bring peace to the people. Psalms 72:3," "Thou should'st destroy them which destroy the earth. Revelations 11:18." Winnie, sitting in a lawn chair, holds a sign that says, "Our mountains. Our homes. Our children. Our heritage. Ourselves," illustrated with drawings of several faces, including one wearing a miner's helmet.

The counterprotesters continue to chant, "We are Massey, here to stay." A truck pulls out of the gate, and they cheer for that. An unusual amount of traffic is going by, apparently orchestrated by the counterprotesters, one of whom holds a sign saying, "Honk for our coalfields." Another says, "Show your Massey pride. Honk." And people do—some of them apparently going around the block to do so again and again, as after a while I begin to notice I've seen certain cars and pickup trucks go by more than once.

Shortly after 2:00, the marchers stand up and sing "Amazing Grace." Many of the MJSers need to use lyric sheets for this, but they're singing. The counterprotesters continue to yell, "We are Massey, here to stay." Cars continue to honk, with whistling and yelling in response. What the counterprotesters are doing seems very profane.

The marchers stand in silence for a moment at the end of the hymn, then still in silence walk back the way they came, holding their fists in the air. The counterprotesters wave goodbye and tell them to "go home, get out of here," laughing. One of the Massey employees says, "Go on back out of state where you belong." That makes Bo angry, and he starts to yell back in response. One of the marchers, a short, slender, gentle young man, puts his arm around Bo's shoulder—a reminder—and they turn and walk off together with the rest of the marchers.

Afterward, I hear Mary telling one of her neighbors, "People up and down the road here called these people dirty and I've never been so ashamed of my people in my life." Pauline and Mary both say they didn't recognize most of the counterprotesters. "What I saw was four people that I knew personally," Pauline says. "The rest [were] brought in here from other places and given the jobs that should have went to the people in this valley. I get so perturbed when Massey advertises that they've brought so much prosperity to this community. They have *not* brought prosperity to this community. Why do you think the rest of the world calls us 'poverty-stricken West Virginians?'"

"They shouldn't have hollered and screamed" when the marchers were singing "Amazing Grace," Mary adds. "I mean, that's a disgrace to God.

"Well, you know, this has been an ongoing thing. Massey tries to turn the people agin the people. That's one of their tactics, in every area that they go into, in order to get what they want from that area, is to get the people, you know, pitted against each other."

"I thought they made idiots out of themselves," Judy Bonds says. "We wanted to take back the high road, and I definitely felt better about today than I did about yesterday. I prayed and I thanked God all day long. And I think they just made fools out of themselves, God bless 'em. God bless 'em because they really need it."

Judy found it "very, very sweet" to see the "godless" anarchists singing a hymn with herself and Winnie and everyone else. "And that's what this movement is all about. It's about different types of people coming together and seeing different points of view. The elderly and the Christians and the anarchists, and you know, the *people*. I just think it's beautiful. That's what I think makes this summer beautiful, to have Christians stand with some anarchists and atheists—and respect each other."

In some cases, at least, that respect is a rather thin veneer. Two of the younger people from out of state got to talking today about how the march was "pretty lame," affirming the tendency among their peers to pooh-pooh protest that isn't rough and rowdy and hard-core confrontational. "Yeah," one said, referring to the sometimes-violent history of miner's union activism, "their ancestors must be rolling in their graves." Sarah Haltom overheard this, and was upset. Like Judy, she'd been feeling good about the day. She'd thought they were in this together.

Solidarity is hard. Sticking with your own kind and feeling superior to others is easier. But the young urban-punk-anarchist set aren't the only ones falling short of the campaign's ideal of finding strength in difference. It's a stretch for their West Virginia hosts, too.

Bo, for example, has been "pretty grouchy lately, and pretty anxious," he tells me after the march today. And in fact, he's been looking miserable. There's been concern all along within MJS that Massey—or law enforcement who might pass information on to Massey—shouldn't be allowed to infiltrate the campaign or know its plans. Over the last few days Bo has been possessed by that concern to the extent that he's excluded people he knows he can trust from discussions where their presence might have been helpful, or at least not harmful. It's as though he dropped down into a private abyss of paranoia. If some of the local Massey supporters have allowed greed to open the door to evil in themselves, Bo's been allowing paranoia to do the same in him. It's a measure of how basically good and decent Bo is that he's looked so uncomfortable with it. Today's march dispelled this, turning Bo around from isolating himself with a handful of trusted family and friends, heading him back in the direction of inclusiveness and community building. After the march, he looks much relieved, and apologizes to me, and I assume to other people as well, for shutting us out recently. "This is the best I've felt in a long time," he says.

Of course, just because you're paranoid doesn't mean people aren't out to get you. That evening Jake, one of the League of Shadows, addresses the very tired group at the Naoma house with a warning: Security at the house, and among MJS generally, needs to be heightened right now. Judy Bonds has had a phone call from a friend warning her that Massey men are angry that their wives have been called "hoes," and that they have guns. State police have been alerted, and a protocol worked out for people who volunteer for security duty. (Volunteers are now to be on security duty at the house round-the-clock.) They've also worked out a list of high-security house rules: Don't be drunk. Familiarize yourself with evacuation routes and fire extinguishers. Keep the phone line free. Keep keys and flashlights in their proper locations.

Squirrel adds: Don't be downstairs if you're not "centered." If trouble arrives when you're there, go upstairs if you're not on security duty. (The second floor of the house has a back exit, so it's not a trap.) Don't stand near windows. When you go to sleep, be dressed and ready to leave the house if necessary. Remember, though, that evacuation is a last resort, only to be undertaken if the house is on fire, because you're more vulnerable outside the house. Remember also that two days from now is Massey's big annual picnic, in a neighboring county, and people will be traveling past the house on their way to and from. "This is a serious campaign," she says. "When we are effective, people are going to be upset with us."

That night passes quietly. The next day, standing outside the Naoma house, I recognize a man sitting on a backhoe, here for some work on a neighbor's house, as Ray Casino, one of the counterprotesters I'd spoken with on the first day of the three-day march. He recognizes me, too, and asks if I've written the last chapter of my book yet. Puzzled, I say no, not yet. And he tells me, "Well, you better have." I'm not sure if this is a threat to me or to the MJSers living at the house, but the tone of his voice and the hostile expression on his face make it clear that he intends it as a threat, the implication being that time is running out for either me or MJS, that we or they are going to be run out of town. So I go inside to call Squirrel and Jake outside to get a good look at Ray so they'll be able to identify him if he makes trouble here in the future. Ed Wiley, who knows the guy, later tells me that this likely was just Ray shooting his mouth off, that he's not going to do anything violent to anyone himself, he just stirs up trouble. The worry is that the trouble he stirs up may lead other people to do bad things.

That same day, Judy Bonds talks with the school superintendent's secretary. There've been complaints, she says, that the MJS-organized "living community" fair scheduled for this coming Sunday afternoon on Marsh Fork Elementary school grounds isn't really a fair but just another protest. Ugly rumors about MJS have been building for weeks, the "poison gossip trail," Judy calls it at a meeting at the house in Naoma that evening. Judy notes that the same kind of poisonous gossip against "outsiders" was used to set locals against civil rights workers during Mississippi Freedom Summer. Now as then, it's primarily a few people stirring this up and intimidating their neighbors so they won't stand with the protesters.

CRMW and MJS had wanted the fair to be at the high school but couldn't get permission for that. Instead it's to be held at the elementary school. The group addresses whether or not, under the circumstances, the fair should be held at all. Amerika says it should go on as planned, because it's positive and not just anti-MTR. Keith adds that if anti-MJS protesters show up, we should just let them yell and ignore them, and hope that local people aren't scared off from coming to the fair. Someone else acknowledges that he's finding the anti-MJS demonstrations emotionally difficult. This is followed by some discussion, inconclusive, about maybe offering any anti-MJS protesters who show up food and inviting them to come to the fair, using this as an outreach opportunity. Jamie says let's go ahead with the fair so it doesn't look like we're backing down. A young woman who's been trying to line up local craftspeople and vendors for the event notes that only a very few have signed up; MJS will be doing this more or less alone. Judy weighs in, pointing out that we'll need to get there early, to make sure they don't block our access to the ball field and outbuilding where the fair is to be held; we need to bring a video camera, to document whatever happens; we have a permit from the school for this event and have every right to be there. "We can't back down on this one." The group consenses on going ahead with the fair. No one stands aside from that decision, but a lot of people are uneasy.

Looked at one way, the fair that Sunday is a bust. Massey supporters arrive early and stand along the road in front of the school, much as they did for the first day of the march. The fair organizers set things up in the ball field: tarps for shade, tables with crafts and food and swap meet items, displays of solar panels and a car powered by used cooking grease. Only a handful of local people actually come in to the fairgrounds. Others perhaps see the Massey supporters, assume that this will be another confrontation between Massey and CRMW/MJS, and decide to pass it by.

But in another way, the fair is an unexpected success. Early on, about half a dozen Massey supporters and half a dozen MJSers get to talking with each other by the grease-powered car. This goes on for quite a while, until a Massey security truck comes by, and then all the Massey supporters walk away. (Massey security doesn't do anything explicit to break up the conversation, but its presence there accomplishes this.) One of the MJSers involved in the conversation by the car, a fellow who was out of state during the three-day march and so didn't personally experience the rancor between marchers and counterprotesters, suggests to Judy that she go out to the Massey supporters standing along the road and talk to them herself. They're still upset with you and your "coal hoes" sign, he says.

So Judy walks over to talk with them. I recognize several of them as having been among the counterprotesters during the march, and they recognize me, too. One of them, a man in his thirties named Russell, offers me an ending for my book: "And the outsiders went home. The end." Ray Casino is there as well.

Then Judy gets to talking with them, and they talk for a long, long time—well over an hour. Eventually, Bo joins her, and so do Debbie Jarrell, Judy's daughter, and another local woman, a friend of Judy's. Debbie comes with a stack of pictures showing mining above the school and hands one to Ray Casino, who rips it in half and pushes it into her face. When several people say, "I saw what you did," he backs off and walks away from the group. Debbie, who'd been to church that morning, just reminds herself she's a Christian and lets it go. "A brick in the head wouldn't change some of these people's minds," she later tells me.

Toward the end, several of the MJS "outsiders" join in the conversation, but primarily this is about neighbors talking with neighbors. Most of the dozen or so Massey supporters here today live nearby, unlike most of the counterprotesters during the march. The talk today has the give-and-take of real conversation. The talk gets quite heated at times, but real communication is happening, not just opposite sides yelling at each other. Russell, for example, talks for quite a long while with Judy. One of the things he says—and here his tone of voice is pleading, not angry—is that if the MJS campaign continues here, people are going to get hurt. He doesn't want to see that. He certainly disagrees, fiercely, with Judy and his other neighbors who support CRMW, but he doesn't want to see them get hurt. I think that this is at the root of his wish that the "outsiders" would leave. But I also think that by the end of this conversation he knows that even if that happens, it won't be "the end" of this controversy here in the valley.

Immediately after the fair, I leave West Virginia for a few days. Driving back, heading for Naoma with an MJSer riding along with me, on Rt. 3 a little ways west of Beckley, Sage passes us in his truck going the opposite way, toward Beckley—and then makes a sudden, wild U-turn. Just as we're trying to figure out what that was all about, we pass a freshly killed deer by the side of the road. So we pull over in my car, and Sage pulls up, and he and Jake get out of his truck.

Both Sage and the fellow who's riding with me are affiliated with the Asheville faction of Katuah Earth First! They call themselves the

Roadkill faction because, well, they eat roadkill. It seems to them more respectful of life to eat a dead animal that's in good condition than to leave the meat there to rot. And they've learned that roadkill can make pretty good eating. They've eaten rabbit, possum, raccoon, and more. Sage is especially fond of squirrel meat. And venison, of course, is delicious whether it's been shot by a hunter or hit by a car. It's an amazingly unlikely coincidence that a car and a truck heading in opposite directions should pass each other on the road right by a newly dead deer—with the two vehicles carrying three people armed with sharp pocket knives and the knowledge, skill, and desire to dismantle the deer and take it home to eat. When I tell Ed Wiley about this later, he imagines the three of them each grabbing a deer leg and doing a little "roadkill dance." While they don't actually dance, they are almost giddy with delight at their good fortune.

I ask them if it's dinner, or just dead. They check the deer over and decide that it's in fine condition for eating. The send me down the road to the grocery store in Glen Daniel to pick up some large plastic bags. When I get back, they've got it roughly butchered, the parts they intend to use cut off from the rest of the carcass. We bag them and put them in the back of my car, stop at a convenience store for a couple of bags of ice to chill the meat down, and take it to where a dozen or so MJSers are camping, not far from the house in Naoma. A message is sent to the house asking anyone who'd like to eat venison grilled on the campfire to come on over.

Adding to the day's set of extraordinary coincidences, in the middle of the roadkill feast an MJSer who knows nothing about the deer comes in carrying a dead rattlesnake. He and a couple of other folks out walking had come across someone who'd just killed it, and they said: "Hey, we'll take that." He thought he'd bring it along to camp just to show people, and when he gets here he finds that camp has become a roadkill café. So, after the snake is properly admired, it too is skinned, butchered, and cooked. (The venison is excellent, the snake sort of stringy.)

About a dozen of us participate in this feast, which has something of a communion quality to it. There are only two forks among the lot of us. Chunks of meat are taken off the grill, placed in a communal bowl, and handed around. Early on, as the first few pieces come off the grill, individuals take a piece, take a bite of it, and put the other half of the chunk of meat in someone else's mouth, one person holding a fork and someone else eating off the end of it, reveling in how good it tastes. There are tomatoes and squash from Ed Wiley's garden. Bottles and cans of beer are passed and sipped from, not in a circle, but one individual deciding to give to another individual at just that moment.

People at the roadkill feast talk about how good it feels to be there, and not to be hashing stuff out at the house. For the moment at least, people have just had enough of meetings. And they've had more than enough of hashing stuff out, interpersonal stuff particularly. Unresolved "stuff" has been building and festering here all month, even earlier. The problems with people feeling excluded haven't improved—if anything, they've gotten worse as established cliques have welcomed, selectively, only a subset of the many people who joined MJS here after the Richmond action. Orientation for newcomers has been lacking—many know rather little about MTR itself, let alone the culture of the campaign or of coalfield Appalachia. Even the ground rules for living at the house have been less than clear. So a great many strangers, not fully in synch with campaign activities, have been living in intensely over-crowded conditions at a house where the plumbing hasn't been working very well and temperatures even at night have rarely dipped much below 90 degrees. On top of all this came the stresses of the three-day march, especially the emotional effects of all the ugliness, hate, and anger directed at the marchers. (Hillary tells me she went to bed and cried each night of those three days.)

All of this and more have come to a head during the few days I've been away. People have vented their anger and discomfort in a series of meetings at the Naoma house. During this time, one MJSer has been asked to leave the house and the campaign for what is later described to me as "unacceptable sexual behavior." (To the campaign's credit, it's been clear and unequivocal MJS policy all along that pressuring anyone for sex is forbidden.) Little has actually been resolved at these meetings, and they seem to have set off a set of exoduses from the Naoma house. Some MJSers have gone to Charleston for a week or so, to do "urban outreach" and to prepare for a big rally there at the end of the month. Some people have moved on to Tennessee. Others have taken time off to go to an anarchist festival in a nearby state. Quite a few have left the campaign entirely. Altogether, this has left the house much less crowded.

"I've never seen tension as high as it is now," Judy tells me, the day after the roadkill feast. "Even during the Blair march, with all the threats, the actual physical harm that happened, I've never seen tension as high as it is now. Never. And I'm not just talking about tension between opposing sides. I'm talking about tension among the people that's involved in the movement. Because we know what's at stake, and we're so afraid of making a mistake. We are so tired. We are spread so thin." However, she adds, "I think we're learning that people are gonna snip at you, but we're learning to let it roll off our backs because we understand. They're venting, and they're just in this god-awful mood. It's not about you, it's not about 'I can't stand you,' it's about, 'I'm in a bad mood and I'm gonna lash out right now, and you're in the way, get out of the way! But you know, tomorrow I'll be better.'"

And in fact the emotional tide does seem to be turning here. When I drive up to the house in Naoma I see a new sign facing the road: "Honk If You Love Mountains," in enormous block letters. For weeks now, Massey partisans driving by the house have been blaring their horns and shouting insults as they pass. Last night, with the new sign up, folks in the house heard drivers laying on their horns as usual as they approached the house—then suddenly stopping when they got close enough to read the sign. Now, from time to time someone drives by and gives a friendly beep, and everyone smiles and waves.

Over the next few days, the reduced number of people at the house, and those in Charleston preparing for the rally as well, are much better focused, more productive, happier. In addition to preparations for the rally, much of this week is devoted to delivering anti-MTR *Mountain Defender* newspapers (published by MJS for distribution this summer) here in Coal River valley and south of here, in Mingo County, with a special insert sheet added to counter Massey propaganda against MJS.

On Wednesday evening, July 27, Ed Wiley comes to the Naoma house to announce that he and Debbie have had a phone call this evening from a reliable friend who doesn't publicly support MJS and thus hears news from the pro-Massey side. This friend says that Massey employees and supporters have been told to shut MJS and CRMW up, no matter how. Both Ed and Debbie view this as a serious threat. Ed feels "a little group" is being put together. He says it's not unknown for coal company operatives, probably from another county, to drive by at night and shoot at a building. Ed asks that the Naoma house once again be under heightened security, that people keep away from the front of the house at night, and that no one walk along Rt. 3 alone—or walk there at night at all. Later that evening, I talk with Ed and Debbie about the pros and cons of all this for Massey. Firing a gun at the house in Naoma (or at Ed and Debbie's house, or Judy's, or Bo's) might result in bad press for Massey—if whoever would do such a thing were caught (not likely) and somehow connected with Massey. However, even the rumor that MJS supporters might get shot at certainly aids the goal of deterring locals from speaking out against MTR.

A couple of days later, as I'm driving from Ed's house through Dry Creek to Naoma, a paintball thwacks the passenger side of my car. When I reach Naoma I find that the campaign house too has been paintballed, the night before, the same shade of pink. The paint on my car is just a little splot, no harm done. But it's a reminder that there are people here who know who we are, and they aren't our friends. Ed's sense is that local kids did this. Still, the incident highlights how easy it would be for hostile people here to do real damage. It would have been just as easy to fire a real gun at my car or at the house.

For weeks now, off and on, furtive conversations have taken place at the house in Naoma about "Operation Vegan Cookies," aka the "March on Ed," a march by MJSers to Ed's house to show how much they love him and appreciate everything he and Debbie have done for them.

Finally, with MJS's main time in West Virginia running out, the March on Ed is set for Thursday evening. When the time comes, typically, Ed isn't where he's expected to be—he's supposed to be home, scheduled to meet Benji there at 8:00. Debbie guesses Ed's over at Bo's house. Benji catches up with him there, and eventually brings him home.

By the time this is accomplished, it's already dark outside, well past 9:00. Sitting in his living room, with Debbie and Benji and me, Ed hears a convoy of cars pull into his driveway. Ed, not knowing otherwise, thinks this must be an attack by Massey supporters. He goes into full combat mode—tells Debbie to get his shotgun, "call the law," and turn out the lights. Pulling his boots on, he looks puzzled at the three of us, as if he's thinking: "We're under attack, and what the hell good are you all?" Ed turns out the lights himself and goes out to his truck to get his "whup stick," a big heavy stick well-chosen to be effective in whupping someone, if need be. When he comes back inside the house, he's ready for anything. At this point, Debbie and I are pretty fully occupied with keeping straight faces.

The marchers start coming toward the house, carrying lighted sparklers and chanting: "What do we want? Ed! When do we want him? Now!" And then Ed realizes: "Wait a minute, that's Sage's voice." As we follow Ed out of the house, Debbie and I start laughing. Ed turns around, says: "You two knew, didn't you?" and calls us a name I don't think I've ever heard him say before.

By this time, we can see the signs the MJSers are carrying: "I'm an Ed head", "Ed—Much love." In imitation of the Earth First! motto and logo, there's "Ed First!" with a raised fist inside a circle and the motto "No compromise in defense of what's right." Another, "Friends of Ed," imitates the Friends of Coal signs commonly seen on people's lawns around here. Others read "Environmental Defender," "We (heart) kids," "We (heart) mountains," "We (heart) Debbie and Ed," "Debbie for President," "Ed Wiley—You *can* see your dreams come true."

Everyone hugs Ed and Debbie, then we all come into the house and drink beer and watch video footage of mountaintop removal sites. Once again, we're struck by how little coal is being taken out of these sites, for all the mountain they move. There can't be much of a profit margin in this—they're making what money they are on sheer volume. If mountain defenders can increase their expenses, through lawsuits, legal monkeywrenching in the permit process, security expenses in response to acts of civil disobedience, higher standards for reclamation—through *all* of these approaches—might that profit margin vanish? How many mountains, and mountain communities, might be saved by making mining more expensive?

One of the first people I see when I arrive at the rally in Charleston that Sunday is OVEC's Vivian Stockman. She's playing the role of King Coal today, dressed in a baggy men's suit and top hat, pockets bulging with "coal cash," and carrying a puppet with a photo of DEP head Stephanie Timmermeyer on its face. "Are you one of them media people? Well, you take this money," she says, handing me a phony bill, "and you shut up, honey. OK? You just shut up."

Vivian's having fun today, and so is pretty much everyone else I see. There's country music on the PA system, and it feels like a party—a people's party, here at the state capitol, taking over the plaza right by the steps where Ed Wiley staged his sit-in a few weeks ago. King Coal owns this place most days, but today it belongs to people who love mountains.

Most of the people here today are from West Virginia, a good number from Kentucky, and smaller numbers from other states in the region. Among the crowd are many of the folks who've been organizing MJS since early this year: Bo, Judy, Patty, Vern, Sarah, Larry, Ed, Debbie, Kayla, interns from the house in Naoma and more from Coal River valley, Abe Mwaura and others as well as Vivian from OVEC, Dave Cooper from Kentucky, several KEFers. And of course the traveling MJS crew is here in force. For most of them, this is the end of their time in West Virginia. Many plan to move on with the campaign to Tennessee.

Bo and Sierra Club's Bill Price emcee the events on the rally's stage today—an opening prayer, several musical performances, rousing speeches, even a squad of cheerleaders. A highlight of the rally is a beauty contest, judged by King Coal, featuring Ms. Blind Greed, Ms. Mountain Reaper, Ms. Overweight Coal Truck, and more, many of them young men in drag. One of them, Donna Sinkenship, carries a sign, "Don't make me sue you too. You know I will," in reference to Massey CEO Don Blankenship's well-known history of suing those who cross him.

Bo, introducing the beauty contest, says: "When the organizers were putting this rally together, we decided that, in all fairness, we couldn't just have one speaker after another come up and talk about how bad mountaintop removal coal mining was. We had to have a section of the program that, again, in all fairness, talked about the *beauty* of mountaintop removal coal mining. So we searched and we searched and we searched and we searched and we searched and we *searched* to find someone that would emcee this section of the program. And lo and behold, we found King Coal."

Vivian walks onstage, still in her King Coal costume. "You know," she says, "y'all are making me look bad because I keep saying, it's like twelve wackos that oppose mountaintop removal. And look at all you people!" The crowd numbers in the hundreds at this point. "You're making me look bad. So I've been circulating in the crowd, trying to buy off the press and I think we've had some success. We got King Coal cash, and it's been really good to shut up some members of the press. I actually tried to pay some outside agitators too, to come in and create a stir, so it would make y'all look like the wackos you are. But so far no good. But I'm gonna keep trying. And anybody that's speaking out against mountaintop removal—really, come over to see me, I got some really nice cash, and just, you know, *shut up* a little bit.

"OK, we have a lovely lineup of contestants, and we need you to help us decide who is the most beautiful of mountaintop removal. Number 1, ma'am, who are you?"

"I'm Miss Overweight Truck. I weigh more than 200,000 pounds, and I'm not gonna tell you how much more because ladies don't talk about their weight. Also it's a little bit illegal, but that doesn't matter anymore."

"Ooh, she's looking lovely to me," King Coal says. "What a sweetheart." The next contestant comes forward. "Ah, we have now one of my favorites here. Would you like to introduce yourself, ma'am?"

"I'm Ms. Blind Greed."

"Yes, Ms. Blind Greed. She's blind to the value of fresh water. She is blind to the value of clean air. She is blind to the value of forests. Ooh, but she's not blind to that lovely green stuff I've got here. Honey, I got more for you, come back and get your money. Ooh, I *like* her. I think, honey, you should come see me after this."

Looking at another contestant, King Coal is shocked. "Oh my God, what do we have? Oh, no, you're in the wrong place, yep, are you *ugly*! This is Ms. Renewable Energy. Ugh. Ugly! I don't like that chick, somebody get her off the stage."

After all the contestants have been introduced, King Coal says: "We had a reigning champion, that was Ms. Blasting. As you know, she is also a little overweight—we're talking 2, 3 million pounds a day that she is shooting off. But she couldn't make it here today. So we're gonna have to pick us a new winner, but, hmm, I don't know. What would the crowd want to be the winner? I guess we'll ask y'all."

To King Coal's disappointment, the winner is—Ms. Renewable Energy. When this is announced, Donna Sinkenship steps forward and says: "I would like you all to know that the organizers of this event can expect some litigation in the mail."

The last person to speak at the rally is CRMW's Janice Nease. "Mountain Justice Summer. They said it couldn't happen, right? Well, I feel a revolution coming on. And I'm very grateful to be standing here today and to be part of all of this. I thank everyone who's here today, and

I hope that you will not go away from here and forget what you've seen and heard. That you will remember what all kinds of people coming together can mean. I see a lot of love out there. I want to thank especially all the Mountain Justice people who've come in, all the young people who have worked their butts off helping us. They certainly don't deserve to be called names, and they deserve to be given credit for what they've done. I don't know how we're gonna do without them when they leave, but I want them to know that we love them and we love everything they've done for us, and we welcome them back anytime, and our love goes with you wherever you go."

Late that night, someone fires seven or eight shots at Larry Gibson's cabin up on Kayford Mountain. When I call him the next day, he says he's alright and doesn't think he needs any extra help with security at the moment. He tells me he spent much of the night walking around outdoors with a pistol, thinking how ironic it was that, just that day, speaking to the crowd at the rally, he'd been saying how important it is to keep the campaign's nonviolence pledge—and here he was walking around with a gun in his hand.

Larry also says a couple of things I've heard him say before. He says he doesn't think he's going to live much longer. I wonder if greed is going to spur enough anger for someone at long last to kill him. He adds that before he started standing up against MTR, nearly two decades ago, I wouldn't have liked him. He didn't like himself. By choosing to stand up for what's right, he's become a person who likes and respects himself, and who's earned the love and respect of many others. Although Kayford is now beyond saving, Larry hopes still to see other people's home places be saved, and to see MTR ended everywhere. But if he dies before that—if he dies today—he feels he'll die at peace.

Tennessee

As MJS moves on from West Virginia to Tennessee at the end of July, so do I, driving through southeastern Kentucky to the Tennessee border north of Knoxville. A short way south of that border, I detour west from I-75 to visit Elk Valley. The road winds through hills covered with young forest. Today, a hot sunny day, it feels good to look deep into the cool green darkness here. A little farther on, the road continues through Elk Valley, an unusually wide flattish place in this hilly part of the world. Much of the valley is in pasture or hay, vivid green in the summer sun. The view from the one main road that goes up through the valley is idyllic, a beautiful sweep of farmland dotted with houses and horses, cattle and churches and schools.

Just to the west is Zeb Mountain. You can't see the mine site from the road, and its owners don't trumpet what they're doing here. According to Chris Irwin, the three peaks on which mining is currently permitted at Zeb encompass about 2,400 acres, just under the limit that can be mined without an environmental impact statement. National Coal has recently requested a permit to mine an additional ninety acres. It looks to Chris as though they're aiming to take the whole mountain.

A few MJS volunteers have been doing Listening Project work here in Elk Valley, as well as around Eagan Mountain, east of here. Here as there they've found people who don't fully understand the extent of the strip mining now going on up in the mountains near their homes.

Other MJS volunteers have been scouting Zeb Mountain, off and on, evaluating its possibilities for a mountaintop takeover or other direct action. (The scouting has been more off than on. A great deal remains to be done.) From the air, up in a plane flying low, you can see that the Zeb mine site is surrounded by patchy forest. Down on the ground, the scouts have found that some of this is difficult terrain indeed. Much of it was strip-mined in the 1980s. (Yes, NCC is tearing up this entire mountain to get at leftover coal.) Although SMCRA, by then, demanded that strip mines be "reclaimed," much of the mining here was abandoned without restoring anything like "original contour." Enough time has passed, and the old mining was small enough in scale that it's well on its way to being engulfed by young forest. Ecologically, this is good. However, while the patchwork of forest and brush and meadow surrounding the active mining restores life to the mountain and provides cover for the scouts to hide in, it also obscures the bewilderingly irregular topography of the place. Wherever you walk there, you're apt to come across unnatural cliffs (old highwalls) and ponds and holes in the ground that make getting from point A to point B difficult and dangerous. Bit by bit, the scouts are working up a map of viable routes around the site.

In addition to being difficult and dangerous, Zeb Mountain is almost unbelievably buggy, especially now, in the latter part of a summer with a good amount of rain. Recently I talked with one fellow who several days earlier had been scouting up one of the branches that drain the site, following what looks from the air like a road but is really a sort of grassy path leading to a sediment pond. Knowing that other grassy places on Zeb are plagued with tiny, seed-like ticks, I asked him how many ticks he'd picked off himself. "I'm still picking them off," he said. Scouts have been amazed not only at the quantity but also the variety of biting insects—ticks, mosquitoes, chiggers, spiders, you name it. People come out of the woods with garish assortments of bite marks, sometimes unsure about what all has bitten them. There's little doubt, though, about the rashes scouts are developing: There's an awful lot of poison ivy there.

All this is pretty much what you'd expect from land that was torn up in a patchwork of strip mining two decades ago and left to recover on its own. Plant life has taken hold wherever the scattered remnants of forest on the site and surrounding it have re-seeded it. Assorted herbaceous weeds come first in this succession, then brushy plants like blackberry and poison ivy that are hell to walk through and harbor abundant insect life. Now a scruffy forest is beginning to take hold, beginning to knit the remnant patches of forest into a continuous fabric.

Or at least that fabric would be continuous, were it not for the re-mining NCC is doing in the middle of the site. What they're doing here today will make even the sort of recovery seen here since the 1980s impossible. The thousands of acres they're blowing up won't be left with remnants of forest sufficient to re-seed those vast disturbed areas. The streams will be not just interrupted by the mining activity as they were in the 1980s—they'll simply be gone. What will be left when NCC is done is a vast moonscape of crushed rock incapable of either retaining water or channeling it to streams that support life, with little or no soil or subsoil at the surface to enable a transition back to forest. What is at stake—here as elsewhere throughout coalfield Appalachia—is the very resiliency of this most naturally resilient landscape.

This is what MJS is trying to save—landscapes that can support life, human as well as wild. Scouts can see the land's homey quality even as they're hacking through brambles and poison ivy—they've been picking and eating ripe, tart blackberries by the handful. In a recent planning meeting for the mountain takeover action, someone asked how long they wanted to keep this takeover going. Others answered: "Days." "Weeks." "We're homesteading, aren't we?"

The patch of Tennessee woodland I've been visiting and re-visiting this year, up in the mountains just west of Caryville, is only a dozen or so miles south of Zeb Mountain. Much of the hilly land between these two

places, like Zeb, has been mined in decades past. The forest on this land
is still recovering. Also like Zeb, much of this land is slated for MTR-
scale re-mining.

Back in the woods along the trail today, it's hot, steamy. The fantastic profusion of foliage here is now so thick that breezes rarely reach
the trail. The trees are heavy with dark green leaves. On the forest floor
a wildly various jungle of herbaceous plant life swamps the path, hip
deep and sometimes higher. Here too is a fantastic profusion of bugs,
clouds of them, and a constant din of bug noise, sometimes the whine
of a mosquito, sometimes the buzzing of flies and bees, wasps, yellow
jackets, hornets, constantly the drone of locusts. I'm wearing bug spray
and I keep moving, so I'm not getting bit, but I think if I stood still
without benefit of DEET I'd be eaten alive. This is a place and season
of tremendous fertility and abundance.

A good ways along the trail, maybe a mile from the road, I flush
an elk that's been resting in a trampled bed of weeds right on the trail.
He jogs briefly up the trail then stops and looks back at me, maybe a
hundred feet away. He's beautiful, a bull elk with twelve points on his
rack, sleek, handsome, strong, big. For quite some distance, a good
quarter of a mile at least, we continue up the trail together, maintaining
a distance that the elk seems to find comfortable—close enough to get
a good look at me, far enough away to feel safe. We stop from time to
time just to look at each other. He seems unsure of what to make of
me. I don't look like another elk, don't look like a bear, don't look like
a deer or anything else about my size that he normally sees here. The
overgrown state of the trail here shows that it's not been used by humans
in weeks or months.

Though this is part of the elk's ancestral habitat, it's only within the
past few years that elk have been reintroduced here, after being locally
extinct for generations. So this elk is both a native and a newcomer here.
Watching him, it occurs to me that so am I. My family's lived in the hills
north of here for a very long time, but this summer is the first I've spent
much time in this part of Appalachia. Meeting the elk here feels rather

like meeting a distant, previously unknown cousin at a family reunion. It's sweet to think of him as family, as part of the same living community.

Eventually the elk decides to leave the trail. He stands and looks at me for a long while before melting into the woods. I walk farther up the trail. On my way back, half an hour or so later, I hear him again, ahead of me, moving parallel to the trail in the same direction as me, surprisingly quiet for such a large animal. Moving a little faster, I soon see him off the trail, once again about a hundred feet away. He turns, looks at me, and walks back a ways, still paralleling the trail but now moving in the opposite direction, back past me. And once again we stop and just look at each other for a very long time, five minutes or so, occasionally looking away and then looking back, neither of us moving on. In the end, he continues on in the opposite direction from where I am heading, and I head on my way as well.

Forty miles or so farther south, in Knoxville, I find john and Amanda cleaning house, as MJSers arriving in Knoxville will be staying at their home, and at Chris and Paloma's a few miles away. john seems distracted. He says he's having a hard time maintaining focus and feels like he's on the edge of burning out. He's worried about facing the month ahead with a great deal of work to do, without a whole lot of people he knows well and knows he can rely on. Chris and Paloma, on the other hand, tell me they're ready. They and their house look ready. They seem a little tired, but no more than usual for people who work so much.

A few days later, after dozens of MJSers arrive, john tells me he's really happy with the people who are here and how well they're doing. His near-burnout has evanesced, at least for the time being. Chris and Paloma are still looking tired, and increasingly harried.

Lots of things are getting done—distribution of *Mountain Defender* newspapers, preparation for upcoming public events, groundwork being laid for work in Nashville later in the month. Still, planning and preparation seem to be running late for the major mid-month action targeting Zeb. A lot of scouting is needed before they'll be able to nail down exactly what to do. They haven't managed to complete that yet. But they're making progress.

On Sunday, August 7, MJS has called for a midday rally at the gateway to the mine at Zeb Mountain. It's overcast and drizzly, not hot today. Parking is by the side of the road, a few hundred yards from NCC's driveway. john will stay there to keep an eye on the cars. (His terms for being out on bail after the protest action at the NCC shareholders' meeting include staying away from NCC property.)

While we're still at the parking area, an SUV pulls up with two people in it. One of the two, Josh, a tall and very big fellow, runs security operations for NCC. He takes pictures of the protesters and has a brief exchange with john, who tells him that the folks here are going to walk up the road to the gate and protest there. Then about three dozen protesters, mostly MJSers but also a few local people, walk on up the road, singing "Which Side Are You On?"

The road here runs along the outer edge of NCC's leasehold. Active mining is currently well inside this edge, so the forest along the road is unusually extensive for woodland at the edge of a mine site—at least for the time being. Not much logging is going on here right now, but that doesn't mean that more mining isn't imminent. The trees on this site are mostly so young that if logged now they're fit for nothing but pulp, and the price of pulp wood is currently so low that it wouldn't pay for NCC to haul it out. Scouts seeking trees big and high enough to hold a tree-sit platform have been having a really hard time of it. They have yet to find several big enough trees in a cluster close to each other, and close enough to active mining so that occupying the trees would prevent blasting.

Four pickup trucks and six SUVs block the entrance to the mine, including Josh's SUV. Half a dozen security men stand near their vehicles. No police are visible.

Paloma starts the rally off, speaking into a bullhorn: "We thank you for joining us. Why are we here? To shut National Coal down." Speeches alternate with music, and first up is Zach, a young woman relatively new to MJS who's a terrific fiddle player.

NCC's security people are clustered together behind the pickup truck nearest the road. Each person who takes a turn with the megaphone stands with his or her back to this truck, facing the crowd of protesters, who are facing up the driveway toward the mine site. The crowd has grown to about fifty people.

Eventually, a man and a woman step up to present MJS's demands to NCC: 1) Shut down the Zeb Mountain mine and stop all surface mining; 2) Employ local residents in real restoration of previously mined areas; 3) Give reparation to those who have been adversely affected by destructive strip mining.

The NCC security people don't want to accept the demands, so the two presenters lay the poster board on which the've been written down in the driveway. Josh, the big security guy, looms over one of the two and tells him to get it out of the driveway. Joe Schillinger, a stream biologist who teaches in the state university system, gets angry at this, points out that there are ten feet of public right of way off a public road, paces them off, and sets the demands down there. Josh, contemptuous, picks the poster board up off the ground, crumples it, and throws it in the back of a pickup truck. His colleagues laugh, nervously.

Shortly after this scene, I approach the security people and ask if they'd like to tell me their side of the story. Turns out they don't all actually work for National Coal; at least two are local people who came out to stand with their buddies who do. Soon two of the protesters join us, Brendan (who played banjo music for the crowd a few moments earlier) and his mother, Phyllis. The NCC supporters say there's no problem with the mining going on here. "Ain't nobody doing no damage or nothing," says one of them, who doesn't want to give his name. "Nobody hurting nothing. I worked in the coal mines all my life. I been here for forty-five years and we got more deer and stuff in these mountains than we've ever had. We even got elk now.

"How many people is there from Campbell County in this group? Nobody."

Phyllis disputes this: "I'm from this area."

"Where do you live?"

"My grandfather's from Elk Valley, and on my mother's side, Goodmans and Carrolls from Smokey Junction. What we're talking about is blowing the top off the mountain. You don't have to do that to get the coal. Nobody's telling you not to get the coal in a decent way."

"They don't know what they're talking about."

"Then why don't you tell me what I'm talking about? Why don't you tell me the good in it? If I don't know what I'm talking about, tell me what good you're doing. You can't, and that's why it's time to stop now. Because you can't tell me anything good. That's why he wants you to stop talking to me." (One of NCC's security people has been trying to discourage this conversation. Three NCC staff or supporters have already refused to talk with me on tape.)

The NCC supporter continues: "You know what? Forty years ago, there wasn't no deer, turkeys, nothing here. There's ten times [that] here now. And you talking about the stripping, getting rid of it, all right, that's a bunch of bull."

"Today we're talking about blowing the top off the mountain," Phyllis responds. "And you're trying to change the subject. I'm asking you to tell me the good of mountaintop removal."

"I'm fifty-one years old. Talking about the fish and all that stuff—ain't never have been fish in that creek. I's born and raised over yonder." (It's perhaps worth noting that he's not old enough to remember before strip mining started in Appalachia.) "There's never been no fish. The water up there [on the mountain where they're mining], water ain't that deep."

"But that water washes down to other water, see, so when it gets dirty up here, it gets dirty way down the road, too."

"Every time it rains, it changes the color of the water," the man acknowledges.

I ask him: "Have you been up and seen this mine site?" I haven't been there on foot, but I've flown over it, and it's so big, I find it hard to imagine putting it back together OK.

"Well, I ain't gonna say that [Zeb Mountain] is going to be as high as it was," he says. But he expects the forest to recover much as it has been recovering from previous strip mining, although "it'll be slow," he admits. "You get a better view of stuff if you looked at the mountain where it was tore up back in the '60s and the way they're growing back now."

Chris, who has the megaphone now, is bringing the rally to an end, waving up the driveway saying, "We'll be back, gentlemen."

Two days later, MJSers assemble at National Coal's Knoxville headquarters for yet another demonstration, to be followed by leafleting at some of the many strip malls in this part of town.

The protesters' numbers are much reduced from the fifty or so who showed up at the mine site rally. Plans for the large covert action at Zeb are taking the lion's share of the campaign's resources and energy right now. People who've been scouting and taking photos in recent days tell me that on part of the site, near the middle, it looks like they're pulling out the few trees that are useful as timber, with the rest of the young forest there being bulldozed to be buried or burned. There's a lot of active mining near where the trees are being cut, and NCC seems to be pushing into that area. Current plans are for that area to be targeted in the upcoming direct action. The scouts are also beginning to get a much clearer sense of the site overall—which areas are active and which currently aren't, and where major pieces of equipment are and how they might be targeted. One photo they've taken shows the inside of the cab of a big drilling rig in perfect detail, right down to the operator's empty coffee cup.

By 11:45 AM only two carloads of protesters have arrived for the demonstration, which is scheduled for noon. Two more carloads arrive soon thereafter, parking like the others down the road a bit, away from the NCC building. Chris Irwin is standing on the grassy edge of the road opposite the building's entrance. Across the road, three yellow plastic signs have been planted in the lawn: "Posted. No trespassing. Keep out." One car from the Knox County sheriff's department is parked in NCC's parking lot. (It's not a very big parking lot. Only eleven cars are there today, not counting the police car, with room for only about half a dozen more.) Chris, bullhorn in hand, yells across the street: "National Coal, come out and sue us," referring to the SLAPP suit NCC has filed against Chris, john, and Amanda. The police car moves into the driveway.

I walk across the street and sit down under a tree near the road, where I've got a good view of both the driveway and the protesters across the street. The policeman looks me over, and apparently decides not to bother with me. The MJSer acting as police liaison walks over to the officer to introduce herself, to explain that this is a peaceful protest, and to ask that if the police have any directions for the demonstrators would they please communicate with her.

Josh, NCC's security guy, comes out of the building and walks over to me. I remind him that I'm a writer, here to report. "I know," he says, "but I need you to get off our property."

I say there's a ten-foot public right of way by the road, and I'm standing well within it.

"On that side," he says, pointing across the road.

"On this side also. This is a public road."

"I think the right of way is on that side."

When I repeat that there is in fact a ten-foot right of way on both sides of a public road in Tennessee, he hollers "Five feet!" over his shoulder as he walks away. I sit back down. A second police car pulls into the driveway, but soon leaves. It's nearly noon. Half a dozen demonstrators have assembled, and another dozen or so are getting organized near their cars. The MJS police liaison crosses the road again, this time to talk with Josh.

People take turns with the bullhorn, making speeches and taunting NCC. A few folks are handing out *Mountain Defender* newspapers to people in passing cars. A few others are drumming away on five-gallon buckets.

I don't know if the timing of this is accidental or not, but a man on a very noisy lawnmower arrives to mow the grassy slope where the protesters are standing. He refuses the *Mountain Defender* that's offered to him, pauses while the protesters back up a little to get out of his way, then mows along the edge of the road, shooting cut grass over their feet and ankles. Back and forth he goes, him and the protesters keeping just out of each other's way. Eventually, I see he's going over places he's already mowed. He looks angry and flustered.

Another car from the sheriff's department pulls up, conveying a piece of paper to the policeman in the first car. Soon a third police car pulls up. The police wave the MJS liaison over, complain about MJSers obstructing traffic by leafleting nearby, and tell her that the owner of the property across the street has complained about not being able to mow his lawn. The police ask the protesters to move on. Chris argues with them about the ten-foot right of way. The discussion ends with an officer grabbing Chris by the arm, marching him down to where his car is parked, and giving him a shove in the back, pushing him toward his car.

The next morning, August 10, MJS assembles in Nashville, the state capitol, a few hours west of Knoxville, for several days of demonstrating and lobbying. A midday march to TDEC's headquarters is planned for noon. Far fewer people are here than Chris and Paloma had hoped. Most MJSers in Tennessee have remained behind in and near Knoxville, working on the upcoming Zeb action. Only eighteen or twenty are here now, including half a dozen local folks.

Today they pass out *Mountain Defender*s to state workers, particularly targeting TDEC for "education" about why MTR should be stopped in Tennessee. The next day, ten MJSers, half of them Nashville locals, go to Vanderbilt University with a letter for its chancellor, who sits on Massey's board of directors, asking him to end his association with Massey and stop supporting MTR. (While a vice chancellor accepts MJS's letter, outside, on the campus grounds, a furtive-looking fellow wearing an earpiece looks on, standing some distance from the protesters, in plain clothes with no law-enforcement insignia. I ask him: "Are you police?

What's your interest in this?" "I'm not going to discuss it, ma'am," he says, stepping away and pulling out a cellphone.)

The following morning, a few more people arrive from Knoxville, including Paloma, who'd stayed behind for a meeting with TDEC officials there. It's been indecently hot all week, and today the temperature is to be well up in the 90s again. I ask the lead local organizer, Joe Overton: "Gosh, couldn't you have arranged for a little more heat?" He tells me, deadpan, "Well, it would be too expensive. I didn't have the money for it."

We all head to the capitol for a demonstration under the governor's office window. Chris once again takes first turn with the bullhorn: "We're here today because the mountains of Tennessee are being ripped apart by coal companies. The governor is presiding over the greatest ecological destruction in our state's history." Once again, the protesters alternate music with speeches. We're standing on an unshaded porch that runs around the building. The sun on the pale stone is blinding, the heat nearly unbearable. Security officers come and look at the dozen protesters, then go away. Two state troopers arrive and say the bullhorn must be shut off: "You can talk and protest all you want. Just don't use the megaphone." The bullhorn is shut off, and the protest continues for a while. One MJSer gives a whole stack of *Mountain Defender*s to a woman who works inside, who says she'll pass them on to other people in there.

Later that day, back in Knoxville, john johnson tells me about the meeting with TDEC officials, which john attended along with Paloma, Gena, and a dozen or so other conservation advocates. Paloma and Gena and others presented various concerns about the effects on water quality (TDEC's bailiwick) due to mining (not TDEC's concern). And then, john relates, TDEC's deputy director, Paul Sloan, "really got straight to the point. [He said]: 'You want us to effectively ban surface mining in this state by denying permits.' And several of us were, like, 'Well, yes.'" Sloan "didn't think it was their place as a regulatory agency to do that.

"I think they're scared of doing something like that," john says. "I think they're scared of lawsuits. Even though [Sloan] said that he already told his people in the department that politics was not going to be a factor in their decision making, the fact that they refuse to interpret the law as clear cut as it appears to be spelled out really says something. He basically said that if we interpreted it that harsh, we would shut down commerce in the state of Tennessee.

"I think what it means is that we're gonna have to rethink our approach. Because it's gonna take resources that we don't have to try to get the department to see things our way."

At about 11 PM on Sunday night, August 14, ten MJS activists and myself disappear into the woods from the road that borders one side of the Zeb Mountain mine site. We're running late this evening, having had difficulty at the staging area for this action with assembling and packing all the needed gear. My companions tonight are carrying an awful lot— not just what's needed for themselves to be out in the woods overnight, but also an array of climbing gear and other hardware, two hollow-core doors for tree-sit platforms, and many, many gallons of water, including enough to supply two tree sitters for at least a couple of days.

Our route this evening takes us steeply uphill, in the dark, through brambles and poison ivy. I soon learn that several of those with me here are just not comfortable being in the woods at night. (Mostly this is due to lack of experience. It was not required during the preparation for this action that everyone intending to go out in the field tonight should have or should acquire at least a little nighttime woods experience.) Flashlights flash far too often for stealthiness, and far more than is needed under tonight's nearly full moon. People chatter like magpies, as though dark silence unnerves them. It's a good thing we're on a part of the mine site far away from current mining and thus not regularly patrolled by security guards. An experienced woodsman bringing up the rear tells me, gloomily, that he's just here to try to make sure no one gets hurt. He thinks this action's chances for success are slim.

At last night's action-planning meeting, the tree sitters (aka the monkeys) had said that they weren't ready to go yet, that not enough equipment and supplies had been cached in the woods near where they would set up the tree sits. (This was only partly due to lack of volunteers willing and available to sneak stuff back into the woods ahead of time. The primary problem was that the tree-sit location hadn't been selected until just a few days ago. With so much bulldozing and blasting going on at the site, previously selected trees had been felled already.) The monkeys asked that the action be put off for a week. Others responded that they couldn't stay around that long but still very much wanted to take part in the action. Feeling pressured, the monkeys agreed to go ahead on schedule. And here we are, heavily laden.

As luck would have it, our drop-off tonight put us into the woods not quite where the scout who's navigating for us expected. He's not been exactly here before, but he knows roughly where we must be and where we need to go. So we bull our way steeply uphill in that direction, through thickets and thorns. We fall still further behind schedule. Shortly after 3 AM, we stop and cache one platform and other supplies for one of the tree sits, figuring we'll travel quicker if we're carrying less. The crew still hopes to set up one of the two platforms on schedule. By 4 AM, we've traveled no more than a few hundred yards from where we were dropped off, five hours ago.

Time matters because we're not the only ones in the woods here tonight. There are the miners to consider—their next shift change is due to begin around 4:30, the changeover from a skeletal Sunday crew to the full working crew of Monday morning. And there are other teams of activists elsewhere on the mountain, several dozen people altogether, whose plans are timed to coordinate with ours, and vice versa.

Here's what I'd thought we'd be doing tonight: By midnight or so, the monkey crew and its gear was to have arrived at the site of one of the proposed tree sits. Leaving folks there to set up the platform, and then a second platform in a tree nearby, I and two others were to have continued on to another location to rendezvous with a different crew. That crew intended to lock down to one of the mine site's two big drilling rigs; one person was to lock herself inside the cab of the rig, another to the outside. I was to stay hidden in the woods near the rig, to watch and document whatever happened. With any luck, I'd also be able to watch the tree sits from my vantage point. (Since the trees to be occupied had been chosen so recently, the scouts weren't certain I'd be able to see them from there but thought it likely.) The two people I'd been traveling with would next go up to the other drilling rig, lock it up mechanically, then disappear into the woods. Meanwhile, other activists were to be deploying in various places around the mine site. Some were to be hidden watchers, either like myself keeping an eye on vulnerable activists in trees or locked to equipment, or keeping an eye out for security or police so as to alert others in the field via cellphone or radio. Two medics were to be in the field, in case anyone needed their help. In addition, another, very large crew was to set up a double block-ade at the mine's main entrance. After the various lockdowns, tree sits, and blockades were established, and both NCC and the police became aware that the action was under way, yet another crew (including the two who'd locked up the second drill) were to play cat-and-mouse. The cats, as they called themselves (although they'd be more like smart-ass mice) were to move around the site, from time to time using a whistle or a flag to alert security or police to their presence, then running like hell to another location and doing it again. Part of the intention of the cat-and-mouse game was to provide distraction that could help support people attempting to re-supply the tree sitters, if the tree sits could be continued that long. It was also thought that the blockades would be broken pretty quickly, the tree sits would last a while longer, and then the cat-and-mouse game would continue to prevent a resumption of mining, allowing the "mountaintop takeover" to continue longer.

Well, that was the plan. The reality for the monkeys is that by 4 AM it's obvious they'll not be able to set up either tree sit before dawn as planned. Nor are they the only crew running into trouble that night. Shortly before 4 AM, the monkey crew makes radio contact with an activist elsewhere who says that *someone* in the field has reported that the area around the drill to be occupied was "crawling with care bears."

Maddeningly, the person on the radio isn't quite clear about who that someone was, and more maddeningly still no one is quite sure what "care bears" meant—did it mean security guards or police? (The code names and phrases for this action, intended to enhance radio security, have proliferated beyond anyone's ability to reliably remember them.) Worse still, when we try to make radio contact with the drill-occupation crew, we get no response.

After some discussion, the monkey crew decides that they're too tired to make good decisions right now, that the tree sits aren't going up before dawn anyway, so they should catch a few hours of sleep and decide how to proceed in the morning, with clearer heads and perhaps better information. Several of those who had tried to convince the action-planning meeting to put it off for a week are pretty angry right now, as the night's events certainly attest to inadequate preparation. Mostly, though, we're all just exhausted, as well as disappointed and worried that the risks we're facing are higher than expected. By morning, NCC and the police will know that activists are on the site. We no longer have the advantage of surprise.

Meanwhile, crazy things are happening elsewhere on the mountain. One scout, who expected to be playing cat-and-mouse by morning, later tells me: "I was with the two medics. We got dropped off [at about 9 PM] on the west side of the playing field, a side which none of us had been in through before. We were already like an hour late. So we scurried up a steep hillside into the brush, and then we heard a car coming. We were hoping maybe it was another drop-off. [He laughs] It was very humorous, actually. The vehicle stopped almost exactly where we had got dropped off, and we heard car doors open, the engine still running. We hear things being removed from a truck, and we're like: Oh good, they're here already. And then we hear very loud conversation, and we're wondering: Why are they talking that loudly? After a while, finally, the vehicle leaves—and we hear a *horse*." Somebody was unloading a horse there, at night, moments after they'd left that spot in the road themselves. Weird coincidence, but coincidence nonetheless. "So we continued to make our way up that hillside. It was pretty rough terrain, especially in the darkness, and not wanting to use bright flashlights. It was very steep. There were lots of briars. We had to do a lot of crawling, carrying things in our hands at the same time. I thoroughly enjoyed it." (It is perhaps worth noting that they did this for only about two hours, and weren't carrying as much stuff as the monkey crew. It's also worth noting that this fellow is typically kind of crazy this way.)

"We'd been told that if you go straight up, you'll hit a trail that connects with the wet-weather conveyance, and from there you can find your way up to where everybody's going to be working. So we made our way up, we found a trail. I walked around the south end of that particular ridge just to verify our position, and see if I heard anything going on. I did hear a security truck driving through the middle of the [mine site]. It was about 11 o'clock. That was the last security vehicle we saw or heard for the entire evening up until 5 o'clock in the morning.

"From there, we continued to make our way up [trying to reach the drill that the occupation crew was targeting]. After a lot of back and forth, and coming to new plateaus, and following roads, we found a series of wet-weather conveyances and followed those for a while, because we knew that those would take us to the road [through the mine site]. It was kind of tricky and almost treacherous because on the one side there's this bright green toxic water, and on the other side there's a very steep descent, and there's only like a foot-and-a-half wide ledge to walk on, and we've got heavy packs. Again, I thoroughly enjoyed it.

"Finally, we connected with a road, figured out where we were, and continued to hike on the road, out in the wide open, because we had to make better time. It was getting pretty late.

"We had been told that the drill we were looking for had moved from where we had last seen it, to around the corner. So we were heading up that way, and as we were approaching we noticed a red light, a stationary red glow. Each of us had our own reaction. One person was like: Omigod it's a cop, it's security. Another person [reacted]: Well, no, what if it's the drill, and [they] are already inside, and it's the glow from somebody's red headlamp. And I was like: Well, we don't know what it is, so let's fall back to the edge of the tree line where we won't cast as much of a silhouette, and make our way slowly around the edge until we can see. And that's what we did. Eventually we decided: We don't have a good vantage point, let's approach it slowly and cautiously. And we come to find out it's a dump truck whose brake light was on."

Meanwhile, the crew intending to occupy the drill had got a reasonably early start and should have been doing well—but wasn't. As one of them later tells me, they got dropped off at the mine site at about 5 PM—five of them, three to do the blockade and two to hide with cameras to document it. "We had not been to that specific site before," she says. "It [the drill] moves, pretty much every day. So we began hiking up there on directions from a person who was not part of our group. We had full backpacks. I had at least a good sixty pounds on my back. [Among the stuff they were carrying was] a whole bunch of water, food, a 2x4, and bike [lock] cables. We got slightly lost a couple times, going through brambles, trying to be quiet. Night fell after we had crossed a very sketchy area where there's a pond on one side and pretty much nothing on the other except for a straight drop down. They're blasting right there, and one of the roads we were supposed to go up was no longer there. Things change very fast. It's like you're working with a disappearing map."

After nightfall "we proceeded up a very steep hill, and one of the members of our group freaked out and started crying, and did not want to continue any longer. At that same point, we saw roving security"— most likely the same security truck the fellow who was thoroughly enjoying himself heard at around 11 PM. "It was fairly far away from us, but we were on the top of a ridge, [so] there's a good chance they could see us even if they were pretty far. We were about to have to go up a wet-weather conveyance—fairly large rocks, very muddy in between, fairly dangerous, rocks slip very easily."

The crew member who was so upset refused to walk without a flashlight on. Where they were, this was obviously an unacceptable security risk. "So from that point on we had to go very slow, it was very stressful. Two of the members of our group did not have much experience with being in the woods. Only two of us knew how to read a map and compass. At the point where that person freaked out, in our heads I think several of us decided that that person should not lock herself down to anything," although that was a role she had been slated for in this action. "If [she was] behaving like this now, then who would know what would happen if violence occurred up there.

"We finally made it up to the active mine site. We were all tired as hell, beat up from falling, covered in mud, in very low spirits. You know, you hit that wall, when your body just does not want to go on any more, and you're just like: Turn back, this is stupid, this isn't gonna work. But after experience, you know to ignore that wall and keep going, and eventually it will go away. Which is, I feel, where the breakdown in our group was. Some people didn't have the experience to know to break through that wall, and when they hit the wall they thought that was the end and couldn't push themselves through it. And started crying."

Finally, they got close enough to see the drill. "Apparently I was the only one who knew what it looked like, who could figure out if that was it or not," despite the fact that photos of the drill had been taken by scouts weeks before the action. "We headed down. We were completely out in the open, because it was completely blasted away. Not really any place to hide. To the right of us was a sheer straight drop down, to the left was sheer straight up. No tree cover. We got about halfway [to the drill] and I saw a red light.

"At that point, what we perceived to happen and what happened become two different stories. What we perceived to happen was: I gave the order to drop down when I saw the light. It took way too long for everyone to jump off the side and get as much footing as they could and hold on. Fortunately we were at a spot where there was a little bit of a ledge, not much. We were basically holding on to, like, nothing, and trying to assess what this red light was. I looked and had a pretty good idea it was a reflector. Another member of my group said that it was a person, that they saw them sitting there and reading a book. [In reality, they later learned from another crew, what she saw was a hardhat sitting on a chair.] I never saw that, but you have to trust what your group sees, and we didn't have enough time to argue. If it was a person, we were in trouble. We needed to get out of there. I asked again if [she was] 100 percent sure, and [she said]: 'I can see them reading the book.' That was enough for us, and we made a quick decision to get into the tree line as fast and quietly as possible. Which wasn't very quiet. People were sliding down into beer cans and being very loud. I myself probably was being more loud than I should have been.

"We ducked into the trees and stopped. At that point, another team member was fairly sick—[feverish with a bad cold that my source was coming down with as well]. She was wearing camouflage, and every time we stopped she'd fall asleep and we couldn't find her. So we sent a scout up. I was gonna do it myself, but at that point I was frustrated with the group and wasn't feeling well, and also felt like it should be one of the people who's actually doing the action [rather than a support person]. So we sent one person up to see if it was a security guard, to double-check that. [That person] definitely saw people. There were people up there." What they see, in fact, is the medic crew. What the scout thinks they're seeing is security. Or police.

They spoke via radio to a person on the east side of the mountain, who "said that they had been through there an hour or two before and there was security—and gave the code word that there were cops in the area." Apparently the code word for "cop" was used when "security" was intended. "From the way they said it, they made it sound like multiples."

(The same erroneous report made the rounds of everyone involved in the action that night. One person who heard about it at the staging area later tells me: "Apparently it traces back to one person making a phone call real early, saying that they spotted police or that they spotted security guards. And didn't specify how many. And then, when they told someone else in the field, it was like the game of telephone—all of a sudden the number tripled. And then it gets to base camp and it, like, quadrupled.")

"At that point," my drill-crew source continues, "the one member of our group was still freaking out and basically wanted to leave. So [they decided]: Why don't we get further down [into the woods, toward the road where we'd be picked up] and chill out, and see if we can communicate with the other groups, see what's going on. [Then] we found out that the monkeys were not going up, at that moment anyways, and that they would be, possibly, later. So we decided that we would wait to hear what was going on. At that point, I didn't even know if the [blockade at the road] was going on. The cats were all over the place and no one [it seemed] was able to get in contact with them. So it seemed like: Why should we lock a person that's bugging out to a drill, when we don't even know if it's worth it? I was actually willing to lock myself to the drill before I'd let that person." She and her crew slept off and on until daylight.

At the very time the drill crew was mistaking the medic crew for security guards, the medic crew was trying to rendezvous with them, so the feverish member of the drill crew could get some medical attention. "We were trying to get them on the radio every fifteen or twenty minutes," the scout leading the medics recalls, "and there was never an answer." They later learned that the drill team "didn't have any ear buds, so they didn't turn [their radio] on because they didn't have a way of using it quietly—at least that's what I've been told." Ironically, during this same time and on into the night, the monkey crew called the cellphone that one of the medics was carrying, again and again, and again. The monkeys, having heard the same erroneous report that the area around both the drill and the tree targeted for one of the tree sits was crawling with security, were trying to make sure the medic crew was someplace safe, while also trying to avoid the security risk of using radio. They got no answer, because the medic's phone's silent-ring feature didn't vibrate, so no one knew it was ringing.

"From there we made our way up to the drill," the medics' scout continues. "Checked out the drill. They weren't in it yet, and we were like: don't know what's happened to them, we can't find them, they're not here."

Their original plan had been for one of the medics to stay with the drill crew, and the other medic and the scout were to move on to a cache at the other side of the mine site. "So [all three of us] did that, walking straight back through the playing field on the open roads, all the way back. We were trying to get to the finger," a narrow ridge that, on a topographic map, looks finger-like, "and through the labyrinthine switchbacks and this way and that way—we had a ridge that we had pin-pointed, we said: 'OK, by the shape of it and geographically, that looks like it's gotta be the finger.' So we're heading for the finger, and we're switchbacking and switchbacking, and we're like: 'this isn't it—wait! No, there's one more switchback, maybe this *is* it, but we just haven't found the part that we know yet.'

"No, it absolutely was not the finger. We were technically lost. Technically and actually." At about 5 AM they saw headlights from "the one security vehicle that we actually witnessed—crap! headlights! So we scramble up this hillside [and decide]: We're just going to sleep here. We know that we're just like one ridge away from the finger, we're going to find ourselves in the morning. Turns out, we were exactly where the cache was. We were so lost, we were accidentally found." (He insists he deserves some navigational credit for this: "My intuition was correct. It was just operating on a subconscious level.")

"Next thing I know, we wake up at 8 o'clock to the sound of machinery. The thought process through my mind was: machinery, wake up, day's starting, get up, be careful, there's machinery—oh, wait, what the hell? There's machinery! There's not supposed to be machinery!"

By then I too was awake and hearing machinery. If the mine entrance had been blockaded at all, surely it was over by then. Miners had got through and started their day's work.

In fact, setting up the blockade at the mine entrance had been just about the only part of the action that night that went pretty much as planned. After it was all over, several of those who were there told me how it went.

Zach, who'd never done anything like this before, was "really nervous" when her crew was getting ready to leave Knoxville. But "the minute we were out on the highway, I was OK. I was in the truck that we called the dinosaur, because it had the tripod in it, and one of the tripod's code names was triceratops. It was really funny barreling down the highway in the middle of the night with huge forty-foot poles sticking out on both ends."

They got to Camp Longpants (code name for the staging area near Zeb) and rendezvoused with other activists involved in the blockade. "Everyone was rushing around and seemed really excited, and also kind of fidgety and nervous. Finally, [we] got the call from one of the scouts who had gone out half an hour before us that it was all clear and we could come.

"So we drove the last four miles up to the site, and the whole time I was just thinking: 'Oh my god, we're taking over a mountain.'" It was about 3:30 AM.

"So we pulled in. The junker car that people were locking down to went first. They pulled in at a certain place in the road that was the narrowest and flattest place [along the driveway to the site, up close to the gate]. They pulled over and blocked the road, and the scouts came tearing down the road, and I was afraid that they were like police or something. I thought: 'What if one of the bad scenarios happen, and we're gonna be arrested right away, right after we'd actually trespassed but not actually accomplished anything.'

"But it was fine. They jumped right up on the truck and started untying ropes. We hauled the tripod off and carried it all the way around the car. They were taking a tire off [the car], jacking it up and putting [next to the car] this big, like 300-pound concrete barrel that they had made." (This time they made sure the concrete hardened before being installed.)

They set up the tripod, three forty-foot poles arranged in a barely stable teepee, "pretty fast," recalls Mere, the young man slated to sit atop the tripod. From when they arrived to when the tripod was up took maybe ten minutes. And then Mere climbed up immediately, to a sort of hammock-chair about twenty-five feet or so off the ground, and pulled the rope up after himself. After that, "for the next fifteen minutes I was just getting comfortable and getting things where I wanted them," including his lockbox.

"I hooked a carabiner to the hammock-chair and hooked that to the apex [of the tripod]. I had a piece of webbing wrapped around it, and I had other pieces of webbing girth-hitched to the poles so I could hang stuff—hang my backpack, my water, and my food." Mere was hoping to be up there for a while. "I figured I'd get taken down in the first day," but he wanted to be prepared to be up there as long as possible, so he had enough food and water for two or three days.

Once Mere started climbing up, Zach "went over to find out what my friends were doing who were locking down [to the junker car]. They had already locked in, and they were just trying to get themselves comfortable."

To set up the junker-car blockade, "they took off one of the wheels, and they had cut a hole into the wheel well. One of the lockboxes was going through the wheel well, so that one piece was sticking out and one piece was sticking into the car—they had taken out half of the dash. So one person [a fellow named Nable] was lying down inside the car with the door shut. They had tried to make it so the door could not be opened, and [Nable was] lying down, not able to see out, one arm stuck into the wheel well, and one arm stuck into this big concrete barrel that was right outside the front door—there was a hole cut through the door for the lockbox." Sarah was outside the car with her arm going through the wheel well from the other side. "That was arranged in a very delicate way—it had a counterweight with a 2x4 to hold it in place, and if anyone had moved it, it would have broken arms." The tire that had been removed was propping up the barrel. "If anyone had messed with that, or tried to flatten the tires, or move the car at all, it would have seriously hurt or possibly could kill [Sarah or Nable]. They were stuck in there.

"My job was to make sure that they had the nourishment they needed, and to stop people from doing anything that would seriously injure them. It was pretty scary. I didn't know what to expect. I didn't know what kind of behavior to expect from—our opponents, I suppose. I gave them some food [they had energy bars, carrot chunks, trail mix] and some water and tried to figure out the mechanics of caring for someone who can't move at all." The two who were locked down had hydration bags with hoses near their mouths, so that if their support people were forced to leave, they'd at least have access to water.

"At the beginning, we were in very high spirits. It seemed like a lot of fun. It was very adventurous. We felt like we were such bad-asses. We were doing what we said we would do. It was great."

In addition to the two blockades, they added a new lock to the front gate and, "a good distance [down the drive], we had set up signs that said: 'Road Closed.' We put a slash pile up to stop people from just running over the sign. We had flares for a while."

After the blockades were set up, Mere says, "we had a lot more time [than we expected]. We were preparing for the worst, for someone to come right away. But we had maybe like an hour until security came down, maybe forty-five minutes, something like that.

"When they got there, they were yelling: Oh, we're going to call the police; you're trespassing." Most of the set-up crew was still there, intending to stay until the police got there. The cars and truck that had brought them there were gone. Drivers were standing by to pick people up at the site (or at jail) when requested. "We had people who were there to observe," Mere says, "and specific support [people] that wanted to stay until the very last moment possible. So we were waiting around.

"And then we see a car—we had people down [at the public road] so we knew [it was] coming, they had radios." An SUV with a driver and one passenger came "screeching in, and the whole atmosphere changes: This is serious, this is a real situation now that, if not properly handled, could result in serious injury or death. Because that guy was prepared to hurt or kill somebody."

No one who was at the blockade thinks Mere is exaggerating. The driver of the SUV roared up the driveway, right over the slash pile and the "Road Closed" signs. He and his passenger got out of the car, and according to Zach, "they were angry, they were really angry, and violent. They started throwing around the rocks and slash that we had piled up."

Paloma, whose role at the blockade was to be a liaison with miners and police, says that the passenger in the SUV "was wearing a blue shirt that looked like a sheriff's shirt, with a big star. And that guy came out of the car acting as if he was a police officer: 'You're all going to get arrested.' And I tried talking to him because I thought, well maybe he *is* a police officer. And then, [after talking with him a bit, stating that the protesters had called the police and that this was a blockade] I realized this is not a police officer. Which was kind of weird. That's when I was hollering to Hillary [who'd come down from West Virginia to help]: Call the police again." Hillary's initial reaction was: "'Isn't he the police? I thought he was the police.' And then she realized, and she called again" and was told that the police were on their way.

Soon, Zach recalls, the driver "got back in his car and started going really fast up toward where the [junker] car was. He wasn't bluffing. He wanted to ram right into Sarah. And so all of us started screaming: stop! stop! you can't do this! this is murder! And [six or eight of us] ran in front of the car and got in front of Sarah so that he knew he'd have to hit all of us. And he stopped."

Paloma, one of those who got in front of the SUV, says, "He was *not* bluffing. He was absolutely not bluffing. He was somebody who came prepared to kick ass. I think what he wanted to do was to smash some heads and make it clear that you don't mess with the coal companies."

"So he stopped," Zach continues, "and Paloma started talking to him. She told him over and over that there would be legal consequences, and just because this was private property didn't give him license to murder. He was very aggressive and belligerent. He had a large tow chain with him, and he wanted to connect it from the junker to his car, to start hauling it. He didn't want to listen, but she kept on repeating herself and arguing until finally he stopped.

"It was really strange. These people showed up, the cops still weren't there, the sun was just starting to come up. We'd only been there for an hour and a half at most. And it was already so tense and so crazy that we didn't know what to expect at all. It was the first time in my life that I actually wanted the cops to show up.

"And finally two cop cars came, and I guess there were about six cops there. At first I was like: OK, now there's going to be at least some order to this. Now all I have to do is stop them from taking them out in unsafe ways. I'm not going to have to put my body in front of an SUV. But it turned out that the cops were not really there to make sure that the laws were obeyed. They were there basically to give the NCC staff license to do whatever they wanted, within very flexible boundaries.

"There were always more NCC people there than cops. That never changed. More cops arrived, but there were always more NCC people."

Paloma continues, "Those police officers were acting like hired thugs working for the coal company, allowing them to kick people and abuse them and be violent toward them *after* I had told them very specifically, and pointed to [the SUV driver], and said: This man tried to kill us. If they were doing their job, they would have kept him separate, realizing that he was a violent threat. You don't then let that person have full access to people who are locked down. And they did. *And* they stood back while he abused people and basically just laughed about it."

Mere, up on his tripod, watched the SUV driver charge at the junker car and considered his situation. He wasn't locked in to his lockbox at that point. As more NCC people arrived, "they got more confident. They'd come up [to the tripod] and smile and laugh and say: 'What are you doing up there?' And they kicked the pole. The tripod is not a very stable thing." In fact, it's supposed to be unstable, so that kicking it or taking it down can hurt the person up top. Activists on the ground explained this, "but this guy didn't really give a shit.

"So they were kicking it. They'd shake it every once in a while, to see how stable it was. I was [saying]: 'Don't do that unless you want to kill me!'" The man who'd driven the SUV told him: "Nothing would make me happier than to kill you."

One of Mere's support people, Daniel, was standing next to the tripod, talking to the SUV driver, telling him, "Don't do that, don't kick it, it's really unstable, you could hurt him, you could kill him," Mere recalls. "And he turned around and kicked Daniel in the stomach. At that point, the cops were there." The police reaction was: "This is their property. They can do what they want."

Shortly after the police arrived, at about 6 AM, they told all the activists that they'd be arrested if they didn't leave. (By then, Josh, the very large NCC security guy, had joined them, arriving around the same time as the first policemen.) About ten people did leave at that point, as planned. Some, including Zach, remained to continue to support Mere and the two people locked to the junker car.

At the foot of the driveway, those who were leaving found a crowd of miners waiting to get past the blockade and go to work. The MJSers stopped to talk with them. "The actual miners were not violent at all," Paloma recalls. "They were at first kind of accusatory. We gave them some *Mountain Defenders* and started dialoguing with them.

"They were saying 'Look, we've got to feed our families. What are you suggesting?'" MJSers replied that they weren't opposed to deep mining, just to the destruction caused by strip mining, and that "these companies will cut and run as soon as they're finished, and they'll leave the destruction behind, and they'll leave you with an area that's no longer sustainable for living in.

"It was not hostile. At first it was a little bristly," but when the protesters spoke to the miners politely, they responded politely. "They're not getting paid to come in here and fight. They don't want to come in here and fight. They just all stood there waiting" for the road to clear so they could get up to work.

Meanwhile, up at the blockade, Zach "thought that the [NCC] staff would be asked to stand aside while the cops took over, taking people out. But that didn't happen. It was basically a coordinated effort of the staff and the cops to extract the locked-down people and the tripod person, in a pretty painful and vicious manner."

Soon, over by the tripod, Daniel and another support person, a young woman called Summer, were arrested. Next, police approached Zach and another support person over by the junker car and "basically told us that if we didn't take our packs off and be arrested, they would beat us up. I guess we could have let ourselves be beat up, but we didn't see anything constructive [in that].

"There were two cop cars right in front of the junker, and we were taken to the rear one. Daniel and Summer were already there. We were all four handcuffed. We could see what was going on [with the blockade] to an extent. We could see Mere up in the tripod, and we could see the cops and the NCC people around the car. We couldn't actually see the faces of our friends" who were locked to the car.

Zach and the others in the police car watched as two NCC people carried a big yellow ladder over to the tripod.

Mere tried to kick it over since he was still in the hammock at this point and had enough mobility to do so. This went on for a couple of minutes. They couldn't climb the ladder because Mere kept kicking it, but since he could just barely reach the top of it with his foot, he couldn't completely kick it out of the way. "Eventually," Mere recalls, "Josh [says]: 'Don't worry about it. We'll get him later.' And so they move the ladder away from me, and they go back to their car. So that gives me the chance to [climb] up to the top [above the hammock]. I'd set up my lockbox up there. And so I locked in. I was locked in to two of the poles. I was not on top of [the apex]. I wish I had been. I was suspended from my harness, right next to the apex." The lockbox was made of tubes of sturdy metal, welded together at a 45-degree angle. Mere put his arms around two of the three poles then brought his hands together inside the lockbox and locked himself in.

While he was doing this, "they were all kind of like looking at me, wondering what I was doing." They'd apparently never seen anything like this before. Even if they understood what was going on, "they couldn't really have done anything because I could get up" to the apex and lock to it "quicker than they could get up."

Next, Zach recalls, the NCC people "started messing with the car, then all of a sudden everything stopped and they were looking off into the woods." Two activists had been hiding with video cameras there. One must have made a noise, and some of the NCC people "dashed off into the woods to find them. The next thing I knew Julia was down on the road with us." Some of Julia's film got away, though, handed off to the second person hiding in the woods, a young man so skinny he actually managed to hide from the security people by lying on the ground behind a fallen log. Around this time one last support person, Lulu, was arrested. She and Julia were put in the other police car. "At this point all the support was gone," Zach notes. "All we could do was listen and watch and worry about our friends and hope that they would be OK.

"We could see there was a [police]woman, the only one there, doing something to Sarah but we couldn't see what she was doing. They brought in a hacksaw, and that made me really happy because I helped to make those boxes, and we didn't have the right tools so we used a hacksaw to cut some of the pipes and it took *hours*.

"Apparently they got fed up with the hacksaw pretty quick.

"I found out later what this woman cop was doing. She had really skinny arms, and she stuck her arms into the pipe with Sarah's arms and pulled the chain off of her link by link, cutting into her arm with her hands. We had wrapped the boxes in duct tape and yarn and glue and all kinds of stuff, and the first thing they did was take all that off. And then they unlocked Sarah, and that really weakened the blockade. Neither Nable nor Sarah unlocked by choice—they were completely passive about it."

While Nable and Sarah were being detached from the junker car, NCC and the police "decide to capsize the tripod," Mere says, "which is really dangerous, 'cause I'm attached to it. If the two front [poles] had slipped and come apart, my arms could have been ripped from their sockets. I don't know how likely that is, to be ripped all the way off, but [even short of that] they could have done a lot of damage.

"So they got like six or seven guys, miners and cops." Mere explained to them the risks of what they were doing. "I feel like I had a pretty good dialogue" with the man who appeared to be the policeman in charge. "He's like: 'How old are you? You know better than to be up here. There's better ways, legal ways. You've got to talk to the governor.'"

Mere said: "Well, we have talked to the governor, and he's not enforcing the [laws] right now. I'm not gonna come down, because I have strong convictions. You can understand that.

"And he's like: 'Yeah, I can understand that. And I respect that. But I'm going to have to do my job and take this down.'

"When they took it down, they jerked it out, kind of, a couple feet at a time. I was screaming really loud, because it was really scary: *drop! drop!* a couple of feet at a time," and each time Mere didn't know whether the whole thing was going to collapse, with him still attached to it. "It wasn't like they were easing me down. And then I was like four or five feet [from the ground], and they dropped it on top of me. The poles are laying on top of me, and I'm like: Get it off of me. They cut the ropes that were holding it together and slid the poles out. So I was just laying there, without the poles and with the lockbox" still attached to his arms." And they said: "OK, now take the lockbox off." Mere said no. "One of the cops took out his Mace and said: 'I'm gonna spray you with this Mace if you don't take it off.' I'm like: 'OK, go ahead.' And the cop that I had the good dialogue with [said]: 'Don't. There's no need for that.'"

So they dragged Mere and his lockbox to the police car. "I was sitting in the cop car with [the lockbox] on, and I wasn't blocking the road any more. At that point, I was just making myself uncomfortable." So he unlocked himself and disengaged from the lockbox.

Like the others, Mere is charged with criminal trespass, and released when MJS jail support hands over bail money.

While all this is going on, the monkey crew sleeps. I wake up at 7:30 AM, hear mining equipment moving around, and call my neighbors' attention to this. Met with blank, sleepy faces, I too go back to sleep for a while.

Soon, though, we are all awake. After breakfast from our packs, the crew is in surprisingly good humor. We learn, via cellphone, that the blockade at the main entrance did in fact go up but has been broken. Efforts are made to contact others out in the field, to find out what has happened to them—are they still out here? what are their plans? The scout who led us here last night looks around and finds we're only fifty feet from the trail he'd been trying to locate. The general sense of the monkey crew is that they want to stay and see if they can do something after all. But they need more information to make a decision.

Gathering that information isn't a straightforward process. At this point, we're relying on cellphones and trying to avoid using radios. (Miners use them, too, and we'd rather not give them the opportunity to happen upon the frequency we're using and listen in.) We're assuming, for the time being at least, that neither the police nor mine security know we're here, that they think the blockade at the mine entrance was the entire planned action, so that at this point they're not looking for us. So far as we know, no one has been arrested anywhere but at the mine-entrance blockade. But we haven't accounted for everyone who'd planned to be out in the field, and our efforts to do so are hampered, not only by the muddled communication among different crews in the field, at base camp, and at Knoxville, but also by our decision to avoid using the radios. Not every team in the field went equipped with a cellphone, and not all of the field gets a reliable cellphone signal.

When we make contact with the drill-blockade crew, they report that two of them are now quite ill and they want to leave the field. Joining up with the monkey crew is the simplest way off the mountain for them, as at least some of us will be leaving today and we're not very far from where the drill crew is now hidden. The scout who led us up the mountain and another crew member agree to go fetch them. Their roundtrip will take more than an hour.

By this time, a tentative monkey plan is emerging: try to install and sustain at least one tree sit, together with some cat-and-mousing. The sense of the crew is that it would be a shame to have made this much effort and come this far just to turn around and leave. There's also a sense that even if what's done here turns out to be much less than what was planned, the learning experience should be pushed to the maximum. Part of what's being attempted here, primarily by the monkeys, is an adaptation of western forest defense techniques to an eastern forest setting. If they can learn from this year's experience, here, then next year they hope the campaign can unleash tripod, tree sit, tree sit, tree sit, cat-and-mouse, tripod, one right on top of another.

Several of the monkey crew go back to where we cached supplies for the second tree sit, to make sure the cache is well-hidden enough not to be spotted by any helicopters passing overhead. Another pair go off to scout the intended tree-sit site. When they come back, they report there's no sign that security or police have been there. We're still trying to sort out who else remains in the field, particularly prospective cat-and-mouse or support personnel. And we're still waiting for the drill-blockade crew and their scouts to reach us. But we've got plenty of food and water, enough for days. We can afford to take our time sorting out what comes next.

By 11 AM, through several cellphone conversations, we've heard more about how the mine-entrance blockade went. The monkey crew is disturbed to hear about the violent behavior of the SUV driver. Given the will to violence displayed at the mine-entrance blockade, it now doesn't seem so wise to put a sitter up in a tree to become a target for further violence. The monkey crew now leans toward coming down off the mountain today, but wants to wait until the whole crew reassembles here before making any final decision.

By now, though, those of us remaining on the mountain are getting a lot of pressure from Knoxville to make a decision immediately. Paloma, by now back home in Knoxville but being kept well informed about the activists still up at Zeb, has been wanting to call the Office of Surface Mining since their office opened at 9 AM, to let OSM know that activists are still up on the mountain so they should order NCC to refrain from blasting. Making that call would, of course, immediately alert police and NCC security to our presence here, trespassing. The monkey crew asks that she not make this call, at least not yet, because they don't want police and security guards trying to flush us out and arrest us while either setting up a tree sit or sneaking down off the mountain. They also send word that where we're now located is far enough from active mining that it should be safe from blasting. None of this convinces Paloma. She continues to insist that OSM be notified. People up on the mountain resent this keenly. Among direct-actionistas, it's taboo for off-site support personnel to second-guess operational decisions made by people at risk of arrest who are trying to adjust to conditions in the field. It rankles further that Paloma's insistence on calling OSM immediately seems, to at least some of the monkey crew, to be mainly about retaining UMD's and her own credibility with OSM. People in the field feel that they are better judges of their own safety than she is, dozens of miles away. And maintaining credibility with government bureaucrats is not a high priority for them today.

Eventually, by early afternoon, the whole crew reassembles here, joined by the drill crew. We sixteen are now the only activists left on the mountain. The four monkeys (two tree sitters and two backups) meet off to the side to figure out among themselves whether they still want to go through with tree sitting and, if so, what might their revised timeline be, and what resources would they need from the larger group. They report back to the rest of the crew that, yes, they still want to go up, but, no, they don't want to do that today. They propose that we instead come down off the mountain, regroup, check in with people in Knoxville, and seek a commitment from them to provide a more realistic set of resources to support a rescheduled tree sit and cat-and-mouse action. In particular, they say that many more person-trips are needed to haul in supplies—perhaps twice the capacity to carry things that we had last night, and preferably not done all at once. They further propose that we leave some supplies cached here now, with the rest to be brought in by smaller crews on several nights.

The whole group falls in readily with the proposed plan. We call folks in Knoxville to let them know we're coming down off the mountain, and where, so cars can be sent to pick us up. No one calls OSM, which is a blessing indeed as the pickup operation is so inept. The driver who picks up me and several others doesn't bother to turn his communications radio on to let us know to come out of hiding in the woods and quickly jump in the car. Instead, the car cruises ostentatiously up and down the road, stopping from time to time so the driver can peer into the woods looking for us. We have to break cover to verify that this is in fact our ride. The driver has also invited a passenger along, so it takes awfully long to pack us all in, sitting on each other. If NCC and the police had known to be looking for us, we easily could have been arrested for trespassing.

Most of the next two days, Tuesday and Wednesday, is consumed by long, long meetings about what went wrong and what to do next. Because of concerns about the potential for violence by NCC staff or supporters, and for a host of logistical reasons as well, a decision is made not to go forward with any tree sit or other blockade in which people would be sitting ducks for attack. Instead, planning begins to focus on locking up equipment or gates and then running, with the locking-up to be followed by cat-and-mousing, and both perhaps to be coordinated with banner drops in Knoxville.

The greater part of these meetings—and by far the most emotional part—concerns what went wrong. Much of that discussion focuses on failures very specific to the action: not enough scouting, people inadequately prepared, not enough supplies cached ahead of time, poor communications, and so on. But part of the discussion concerns broader issues of dysfunctional power dynamics within both KEF! and MJS, focusing particularly on Paloma and Chris. Paloma's persistence about calling OSM, contrary to the decision made by people in the field to delay doing so, still rankles. It especially rankles KEFers who see it as emblematic of a pattern established long before Mountain Justice Summer: Chris and Paloma say they want to work consensually, but consensus for them seems to mean everyone else toeing whatever line they decide upon.

While these meetings are going on, Chris and Paloma and a very few others, still trying to pull off more Listening Project work, a downtown rally, and an end-of-the-month concert for MJS, are becoming wildly frustrated. The OSM issue still rankles for them, too—and on top of that, most of the dwindling number of MJSers in Tennessee are *still* busy with Zeb Mountain instead of helping with other aspects of the campaign. They see both the OSM issue and the lack of people working on things other than direct action at Zeb as evidence that the direct-action component of the campaign is not supporting the overall strategy that they, as UMD, have devised. Supporting that strategy is what they believe MJS should be devoted to in Tennessee. They also believe that this strategy, focusing primarily on pressuring state government, is working, that they are close to seeing MTR outlawed in Tennessee, and that the direct-actionistas focused on Zeb are jeopardizing all this. They're concerned that direct action that's not well-coordinated with the overall campaign risks doing things—such as the failure to call OSM—that undermine, rather than support, the broader effort.

Nonetheless, MJS was, from the beginning, conceived to be a sustained campaign of civil disobedience and direct action. As the MJSers pursuing direct action in Tennessee see it, they're doing what they joined up for—what they were *invited* to join up for by MJS organizers including Chris and Paloma. Many, if not most of them, are stronger in the skills for direct action and more interested in it than in other aspects of the campaign. In addition, the more skilled among them are stretched so thin that they don't have time to do anything beyond what they're already doing. (Several experienced scouts have, for weeks on end, spent so many nights in the field, followed by days in meetings, that they're apt to fall asleep within seconds—literally—whenever the opportunity arises.) While these factors are obstacles to integrating direct action into the wider campaign, they are not inherently insurmountable. But many of those working on direct action here raise Chris and Paloma's hackles, and vice versa—an ongoing replay of past conflicts within KEF! In addition, for legal and professional reasons Chris has avoided direct involvement in planning any sort of civil disobedience this summer, and Paloma's involvement has been more or less at arm's length, her primary attention focused elsewhere. So their overall strategy for MJS in Tennessee has had little connection with the Zeb action planning.

Late Wednesday morning, Chris, Paloma, and Gena send word to the ongoing Zeb meeting that they've decided to block consensus on (in effect, to veto) any further direct action at Zeb. They cite concerns about direct action not supporting the overall campaign strategy for Tennessee, and add that the wishes of the local Tennessee organizing group, UMD, are not being respected by MJS here as CRMW's leadership was respected in West Virginia. (KEFers bristle at the assertion of UMD's primacy here; UMD has been in existence for only a couple of months, and KEF! has been involved in organizing MJS from its very beginning.)

Following an initial venting of outrage, and a good bit of unresolved discussion, the Zeb meeting kicks the problem to a conflict resolution committee. After meeting separately, the committee recommends that Chris and Paloma be invited to sit down with two representatives of the Zeb group, and two mediators, so that the group can present its current plans, Chris and Paloma can offer feedback, and the two sides can listen to each other's concerns.

Just as the committee is presenting this recommendation to the larger group, Chris walks into the meeting. He reiterates their concerns about direct action at Zeb and says that Paloma is home in bed crying, that she just doesn't want to have anything to do with this campaign any more. Chris says he'll talk over with Paloma the conflict-resolution recommendation; later that day, he sends word that they agree to the meeting. The Zeb group decides to attend tomorrow's downtown rally en masse, as a gesture of solidarity with the overall campaign in Tennessee.

Heading to the rally at midday on Thursday, I talk with one of the conflict-resolution mediators. He tells me that Chris, Paloma, and

Gena are no longer blocking further action at Zeb. His sense is that the next round of mediation, if it ever takes place, will be more difficult and complicated.

The rally takes place at Market Square in downtown Knoxville, right across the street from the headquarters of the Tennessee Valley Authority, a major purchaser of MTR coal. Bo Webb and Ed Wiley have come down from West Virginia for the event. About three dozen MJSers are here. As in Nashville, there are people here in plain clothes carrying communications devices—not MJSers, and rather obviously law enforcement of some sort. I notice at least four—three men and a woman.

A public-relations representative of TVA, Gil Francis, arrives, and Bo Webb tells him: "I'm here today because I live at ground zero of mountaintop removal. Our homes are being destroyed. And TVA is purchasing a lot of [MTR] coal. We're asking you to refuse to buy coal that is mined by mountaintop removal."

Ed Wiley introduces himself to the TVA rep, and tells him his granddaughter attends Marsh Fork Elementary School, which Bo's just been describing. "What people need to understand is once these mountains are gone, they're gone," Ed says. "This is wrong. You people need to help stop this." The TVA rep says he'll pass that information along.

After Paloma talks with the rep a while, detailing what TVA's purchase of strip-mined coal abets not just in West Virginia but throughout Appalachia, Ed resumes. "I see you're a married man," he says, looking at the rep's wedding ring. "Do you have children?"

The rep says he does.

"Well, I highly care about my granddaughter. Do you care about your kids?"

"Absolutely."

"Do you care about their future?"

"Yes."

"If you keep letting these people blow up the mountains, what's left for these kids? You know, when my granddaughter—I'd like when you get done for you to look at me." The rep's been taking notes, and Ed insists on his full attention.

"I'm sorry."

"I had to go down to that school three days in a row and get my granddaughter. The third day her face was purple. And I asked her: 'Kayla, what's the matter, baby?' And she looked at me—she had a tear coming down out of her eye. That tear did not lie.

"I didn't come all this way just to save a tree. I come here to save children's lives. I do love my mountains. I do love my streams. But I'm here to save lives. And if you care about your children, you need to think about this too. [This is about] your children's future. You need to keep that in mind. When you go home and lay down tonight, you think about my granddaughter's tear. That tear did not lie.

"And I hold everybody, everybody in the United States, I hold them highly responsible for every death that this has caused. And it has caused deaths. We've got kids that have died with asthma." Ed gets a bit tongue-tied at this point. "I'm getting tore up here," he says. john johnson sees this, walks over, and puts his arm around Ed's shoulder.

The rep continues to listen politely. "You have a responsibility," Bo tells him, "to lead the way to renewable energy. Coal, you only burn it one time—you're aware of that. The TVA's a huge organization. What are you guys going to do when the coal's gone? I know you are involved with some green energy, but it's very small scale. You really need to look at what's happening to real people—real people's lives are being destroyed because of so-called cheap energy. And it's not cheap. What value do you put on someone's life?

"It's just greed. It's just corporate greed. And you guys could really help out. You're a *big* organization. You could make a strong statement. You could say: Listen, we believe in the future of America. We believe in the future of Appalachia. We refuse to buy from a coal company that is destroying our very life-support system."

After the rally, I have a long, late lunch with two of the people making plans for Zeb. We've spoken earlier this week about good reasons for some sort of follow-up action there. One reason is that quite a few people simply don't want to give up on Zeb, having already invested so much effort and resources. That previous investment has left a good bit of infrastructure (drinking water, supplies, equipment) out in the field that is more or less ready to go. In addition, it would be very good simply to demonstrate that it's possible to take over—however briefly—a mountain controlled by a coal company. This could have a strong, positive psychological effect in coalfield communities through-out Appalachia. Another good reason to go forward at Zeb is to try to play out aspects of the first action that were aborted, to see how well they really work.

Today's conversation is more concerned with the negative side. Foremost are the safety concerns—not only the dangerous terrain, and the hazards of doing anything on a mine site, but also the risk of violence at the hands of angry NCC partisans. In that connection, the inexperi-ence of many of the people who went out last Sunday night is especially worrisome. Many lacked woods experience, and far too many seemed not to appreciate the seriousness of the situation, both the risks of get-ting hurt in the woods and the risks of getting caught. Stealth skills were obviously lacking as well, raising the risk of people getting caught unintentionally in a place where we now know bad things beyond just being arrested are apt to happen to activists caught trespassing. Being able to accomplish what you're there for, undetected until such time as you might *choose* to be discovered, is crucial if part of your goal is to demonstrate that it's possible for activists to take over all or part of a mountain. Having an action end in failure, with people getting uninten-tionally caught and possibly hurt, sends the opposite message: that this sort of thing can't be done, and that coal companies and law enforcement will hurt you if you try.

So, our discussion continues, given these concerns, what do you do? How, for example, can you tactfully but effectively deal with people who might want to return to the field but probably shouldn't? More generally, how do you redesign the action to be as safe as possible?

The pair I'm talking with come to no firm conclusions about any of this. However, one of them is leaning toward bailing out of the action now, with the intention of coming back later with a smaller crew that's more experienced and better able to do a smaller action well. The other of the two fervently hopes he won't bail out. The action currently being planned urgently needs people with his skills and experience.

Over the next few days, I talk at length with Chris and Paloma about how they see things. Paloma tells me she's been thinking "quite a bit" about "some big mistakes that were made" in connection with Zeb. Some mistakes are her own. "I wasn't able to go to the last few [planning] meetings because I had too much on my plate," she says. She also, to some extent, held back from action planning so "that UMD would not necessarily be associated" with anything that might jeopardize its nonprofit status.

Other mistakes, she says, came from action planners failing to prepare adequately and failing to heed safety warnings. Paloma herself has been on "mine site after mine site after mine site, because of work I was doing for UMD in which I was taking people on mine tours—but also I went back on my own, walking back into these areas and looking at these highwalls. And I stood underneath one highwall [up at Eagan Mountain] one time and watched a big chunk of it just collapse. [There was] this whole avalanche, [and] there was nothing that made it. There wasn't even anybody who made a loud noise. It's so unstable. The mountain is just cracked, and those cracks go pretty deep. It's broken. It's breaking not just in the area that they're shearing off to get to the coal. It's breaking deep into the mountain.

"From the beginning, when the idea for this action first emerged, I realized that if it wasn't done right, people could die."

When, during planning for the action, the subject of letting OSM know that activists were on the mine site had come up, Paloma "had just said: 'OK, we're calling them at 9 o'clock in the morning.' But [we] did not do a long discussion about it, and repeat it when we had" an influx of MJS newcomers shortly before the action took place. However, before the action began, Paloma and everyone else thought that everyone and everything would be in place by 9 AM—blockades and tree sits up, cat-and-mousers ready to go. Paloma now thinks that people in the field were thinking that OSM would be called when everything was in place, while she was thinking 9 AM, ready or not. "I was thinking if I could have called them at 7 o'clock that would have even been better. But they don't open until 9 o'clock. I was thinking safety. I was thinking that this was a really dangerous thing." Still, everyone *was* in agreement before the action started about calling OSM at 9 AM. Conflict arose only when things went differently than planned. In changed circumstances, people in the field wanted to alter this part of the plan, and Paloma didn't.

Paloma notes other mistakes made in the run-up to the action: "They had a massive long period to prepare" for this action, ever since the Zeb site was targeted in June. "I had been doing everything that I could, all my research, everything that I could deliver to prepare for it. But everybody else didn't even start working on it until [the beginning of August]."

Nor were preparations, even then, adequate. "Meetings are different than going out and walking it," Paloma notes, and only a minority of those who intended to be in the field taking part in the action participated in scouting. And scouting was an especially big job for this action, with so many people planning to spread out over such a large and difficult site. "That's why from the get-go there should have been people out there—like every single person [involved in the action] going up there, and hitting it all the time. And that didn't really happen. And because it didn't, people weren't prepared." Curiously, neither Paloma nor anyone else, so far as I can recall, has observed the discrepancy between the agreed-upon need to alert OSM to the presence of activists on site the day of the action, and the very obvious need in scouting to send people to the site repeatedly *without* notifying OSM (and thus NCC) that they're there.

When Paloma returned to Knoxville on the day of the action, "and I first discovered that OSM hadn't been called, it felt like such a kick in the stomach. It was not safe. It just was not."

Aside from the OSM issue, several people involved with the action pretty much agree with her about how dangerous the Zeb mine site is. After the action, I speak with the fellow who brought up the rear of the monkey crew. "OK, I'll let you have it" he says. "When I got to Knoxville [a week or so before the action], this was already under way, it was already decided this was happening. I was asked to help do the running fast through the woods thing [cat-and-mouse], and take the security on goose chases so we can get through to people. I raised many concerns as what was being done was revealed to me. And the consensus process answered me with: 'We've already discussed that, and we've moved on. You weren't at that meeting, so we're not gonna address your concerns.' Over and over again.

"People have done tree sits to stop logging operations before [out west]. But as far as mining operations—it's a totally different animal. We really didn't know what we were doing. We didn't know the blast range. We assumed that we did, just because somebody said 300 feet and we adapted that." A 300-foot buffer zone between active mining and human habitation is typical, but that has more to do with defining a limit beyond which mining companies are free to blast than with the reality of how far away mining like this can affect its neighbors. I personally have seen flyrock thrown from its blast site much, much farther than this.

"It became clear to me that if I kept complaining and criticizing," he continues, "I was gonna be shut out of the process entirely, and my friends and allies were gonna move on and do this without me. And I'm sure they could do this without me, but I have a certain conceit in me that thinks maybe I could be there at the right moment to help one of my friends not get hurt. So I figured I'd keep my mouth shut and go along.

"It seemed unlikely to me that we were gonna pull it off. After scouting how difficult it was for three of us to move through there, with just heavy packs," he didn't see how they'd move a couple of dozen people through the site, to and from different locations, carrying an enormous amount of supplies and equipment. "The third person on that scouting trip with us didn't even have a pack on, and busted his behind several times, where [the monkey crew was] going to have to carry all this equipment with a huge caravan of people." On that scouting trip, "in the daytime we did the hardest part." On the night of the action, when the monkey crew finally stopped, exhausted, the most dangerous part of their planned route was still ahead, up a boulder-filled wet-weather conveyance and along near highwalls—in the dark.

"Every time we went in to scout, we'd have to take a different route because the road we took last time had fallen away. It didn't fall away while we were walking on it—*that* time. You know? If you're [caught] in a mudslide, you're just *gone*. There was no other footprints where we were walking. The miners don't walk where we were walking. We were doing our best, figuring out as we went along from what we had to work with, which was hands-on experience, going in there and scouting. We're not experts on mines, how it's set up, how it falls apart, what's dangerous or not about it. We were learning by trial and error. And, fortunately, we didn't have to learn by a really big error.

"I think we're very lucky that we didn't get farther than we did that night. I was committed to getting us as far as we could go. I said I would help. I would never sabotage us, try to make us not get where we were going, but at the point when we lay on the ground and waited to die [from exhaustion], I was grateful."

On his last scouting trip before the action, a former mine worker joined them. "I felt really humiliated when I found out afterwards that his opinion was that we didn't know what we were doing, that it was totally too dangerous." Separately, the former mine worker tells me that he'd never been on such a dangerous site in his life, combining, as it does, the worst features of an unreclaimed strip mine with all the hazards of an active mine site. At one point, they walked along a narrow ledge and heard the cliff side crumbling below them. In the dark.

In connection with the Zeb action, Paloma says she "was kind of [wearing] two hats [UMD and EF!] and I'm not going to do that again. That was a learning for me: I have to stick with one or the other, I can't do both. I'm not going to do any kind of direct action stuff any more. I'm just going to be doing UMD. I don't think UMD can be associated with anything like this again."

I'm sad to hear Paloma say that one of the reasons for this need for separation is that some of the groups and people United Mountain Defense is trying to mobilize—such as hunters—would be put off by direct action. This directly contradicts the more hopeful and inclusive position Chris was taking earlier in the summer, that it's a myth that rural people in Appalachia are too conservative to approve of direct action. And Paloma does say she still feels strongly that direct action is valuable, and should be welcomed in this campaign even by nonprofits. But she's come to believe that for her to be involved with it herself, at this point, jeopardizes UMD's other work.

She and Chris have been organizing here for years, on various issues, but very intensively now on mining issues. "That we've had people who've just moved up into our community telling us that we're not a local organization is pretty offensive to us," she says, sidestepping the matter of whether UMD or Katuah Earth First! is the primary "local group" working with MJS in Tennessee. Of course both UMD and KEF! are based outside the coalfields, and that might be a factor in MJSers' reluctance to defer to Chris and Paloma's leadership as readily as they would to CRMW's in West Virginia. In any case, it definitely rubs Asheville KEFers the wrong way that Chris and Paloma, who've worked with them as colleagues for years on various issues, expect them too to defer to their "local" leadership of MJS in Tennessee. john johnson, who definitely sees KEF! as central to MJS in Tennessee, has very different relations with the MJSers who come from outside Tennessee. He tries *not* to be in charge, both because as an anarchist he seeks to avoid that, and because the pending felony charges against him make it unwise for him to take part in any further civil disobedience until they're resolved. And people like and respect john regardless of whether they perceive him as "local." He's not had the conflicts with MJSers that Paloma and Chris have.

That said, regardless of whether Chris and Paloma have been inappropriately authoritarian, some young MJSers of the traveling anarchist-punk set have been unconscionably rude to them here, violating the guest-host relationship in ways that have little to do with principle and much to do with Chris and Paloma being too "grown up" for the twenty-somethings to accept socially. Hillary got some of the same sort of treatment in West Virginia. john doesn't get treated that way, not just because he's less authoritarian—john's just very likeable. But you shouldn't have to be exceptionally likeable for people to be willing to work with you in this campaign. That the culture of MJS attaches no stigma to shunning or insulting people you don't find socially congenial is once again undermining solidarity and effectiveness.

In addition, Paloma says, "You have people coming in from urban activism, that have just joined the campaign, and didn't go through our cultural sensitivity trainings. Because they don't have a long-rooted connection, and they're just there for doing an action, and then they want to leave right afterward, they did create a very different culture."

One problem with that "culture" is that it disfavors making a decision to call things off or delay them. Another, Paloma notes, is that "there's a psychological pressure not to step out of the group idea of what's considered radical, or what's considered hard-core, or whatever." Group-think pressure has been rife in this campaign for several months now, exacerbated by successive waves of newcomers. "When you join a new group, and you're wanting to fit in and find your place within that group, you're a little bit more malleable, you're pushing your comfort zone a little bit more sometimes. You want to be accepted."

People who resist this pressure do so at the risk of being shunned. "And that was happening in this campaign," Paloma says. "And there were a lot of people who left the campaign because of it. And left teary-eyed. I'm not talking about people who are hippies [repelled by the urban punk style that has dominated among younger members of the campaign this summer] or people who are flaky—*good people*, really good people that were solid, dependable, hard-working, committed, had good skills to offer. And they left. Throughout the campaign this was happening. They couldn't find a fit-in place, and they felt really alienated, and they felt like if they didn't agree with everybody that they were getting shunned." She's also heard from people still in the campaign who feel they don't have a voice in it, that if they speak up in a meeting they'll be met with blank stares rather than be taken seriously, as though the group waits for them to shut up so that someone whose opinion is considered important can speak.

Most of the examples Paloma gives of this, of people who've talked with her about it, are young women. She might be hearing from women disproportionately because she's a woman herself, but what she says definitely fits with my own observations all summer long that people have been leaving MJS because they've felt shut out, and that women have been more likely to be shut out than men. There's a good bit of sexism in this campaign, primarily among young "radicals" who'd howl with outrage if you called them on it: "How *dare* you say I'm sexist?"

Much of the exodus from MJS has been nearly invisible, with individuals or pairs of people deciding to leave when they felt too uncomfortable. But many people left in two waves, last month in West Virginia and now here in Tennessee, after an intense time of interpersonal rancor. In each wave, some people felt that their input at meetings was being treated by the group as a waste of time, to be tolerated rather than considered seriously. When that's happening in a setting where decisions are made by consensus, differences tend not to be resolved and consensus isn't reached—meetings go on and on and on, with little accomplished. And in that situation people get testy, and personality clashes can take over the agenda.

Early on in the campaign, meetings went on for *two days* and didn't feel at all too long because so much was being accomplished, participation was welcomed, and participants felt obliged to be focused and useful in what they contributed. Paloma thinks the balance shifted, with meetings becoming increasingly unproductive, at the MJS camp in Virginia. She tells me she doesn't know why this happened then, but that she definitely observed it then, particularly in one painfully long and not very productive meeting to plan what eventually became the Zeb action in Tennessee. I'd guess that the timing of this had to do with a) an influx of young newcomers who lacked experience with MJS, needed training they didn't get, and often didn't even know much about MTR, and b) the fact that that meeting was about plans for Tennessee, Paloma's turf, where she expected a dominant role in calling the shots.

Long and unproductive meetings have, inevitably, also stolen time from work that needs doing. "People spent more time in meetings than actually scouting," Paloma notes. "They didn't get the time and the practice they needed doing really practical things.

"Direct action has a very useful role in campaigns and in trying to help elevate an issue to a public conscience," Paloma says. "It's hard to get media to give air time to certain issues"—and direct action *does* attract media coverage—"the drama of it, visual aspects, the danger element sometimes. Also sometimes direct actions are a way of slowing down destructive practices." Direct action can sometimes buy time, as tree sits in the Pacific Northwest have done by halting logging on certain sites while legal challenges to that logging work their way through the court and regulatory systems. "Direct action is most effective when it's doing something in a way that the general public can absorb, meaning that they can relate to the people somehow." When the civil rights movement used civil-disobedience tactics in the early 1960s, "people looked at their TV screens and saw these well-dressed people getting hosed down with pressure hoses, or getting attacked by dogs, or getting beaten by clubs. And they could look at these people and think: 'Whoa, that could be me.'"

It's not clear, though, whether Paloma thinks that the attention-getting function of civil disobedience has already been accomplished in this campaign, making further direct action unnecessary—direct action in the coalfields, at least. "We have to," she says, "let people have room to do creative direct action without having to be micromanaged" by nonprofits who, like UMD, need to distance themselves from civil disobedience. Paloma thinks there's good potential for direct action in urban areas outside the coalfields, targeting coal companies and their shareholders and customers and other businesses that support them. In this way, urban activists who like to do a lot of direct action can do so, in support of the effort against MTR but on their own turf "without jeopardizing the local coalfield residents, or jeopardizing the other types of work that are happening," like legal work and lobbying.

Compared to the mountain-takeover attempt, far fewer people are involved in preparing for the follow-up Zeb action—perhaps one-third as many. This is, in part, because many people are leaving the campaign this week. In addition, it's generally accepted now that plans for the first action were too big and complicated for its players to pull off, resulting in a gigantic "clusterfuck" of miscommunication and missed coordination. (First used the night of the action, the "clusterfuck" label has become definitive.) The follow-up action is intended to be smaller and more tightly organized, and will require fewer people. It's also now generally accepted that perhaps it's just as well the original action was mostly aborted, that having so many inexperienced people, far too heavily laden, continue to stumble in the dark over such bad terrain could easily have resulted in someone getting hurt, perhaps badly.

Planners are still concerned that they're short on people with woods experience, even for the smaller follow-up action. By Thursday evening they are evaluating whether maybe they don't have enough skilled people on hand to do this well and safely.

Eventually they decide to go ahead, on schedule, exactly one week after the initial Zeb action, on Sunday night and Monday. Instead of trying to take over the whole mountain, their goals are simply to demonstrate their ability to move around the mine site and lock up equipment undetected, to shut down work on the mine site for a day, and to raise NCC's cost of doing business a bit. If all goes well, no one will be arrested.

Press Release [sent anonymously by email at 9 AM on Monday, August 22, 2005]:

Early this morning, Appalachian activists inspired by the Mountain Justice campaign against mountaintop strip mining of coal used locks and cables to disable mining equipment, including a large drilling rig, at National Coal Corporation's Zeb Mountain mine site near Elk Valley in northern Tennessee.

Although care was taken not to damage any equipment or create any hazards for workers, it is assumed that NCC will carefully check equipment before allowing it to be used again.

The mining equipment temporarily disabled on Zeb Mountain is being used by NCC to cause permanent, irreparable damage to the mountain, its forest, its streams, its wildlife, and its nearby human communities. Large-scale mountaintop strip mining of coal—whether it's called mountaintop removal or cross-ridge mining—forever destroys living southern Appalachian mountains, among the richest and most productive biological communities on Earth, for the short-term profits of distant corporations and individuals heedless of the mountain communities whose future is also destroyed by this catastrophic form of mining.

The action this morning is intended to stop mining activities (however briefly), cost NCC money, and serve notice that activists can take such action at will, here and at other mine sites throughout Appalachia.

Activists remain on the site. The federal Office of Surface Mining's office in Knoxville (865-545-4103) has been informed of their presence in the expectation that it will forbid NCC (865-690-6900) from blasting at the site.

Attached to this press release are photos of a drilling rig, taken in daylight on an earlier visit to the site. One photo shows clearly what the whole rig looks like. The other, of the rig's interior, is taken at close enough range to demonstrate activists' access to the equipment.

Press Release [sent anonymously by email at midday]:

Appalachian activists supporting Mountain Justice's goals of ending mountaintop strip mining of coal have demonstrated their continued presence this morning at National Coal Corporation's Zeb Mountain mine site in Tennessee.

Midmorning today, activists assembled a signaling device consisting of several green-colored fireworks "smoke bombs" (sold legally in Tennessee) nestled in a child's inflatable flotation ring and rigged to a simple time-delay system (powered by lit cigarettes) for lighting their fuses. (Photo to come.) Once assembled, the signaling device was pushed afloat out onto one of the settlement ponds at the mine site. Care was taken, in setting off the device, in a body of water, to avoid the risk of setting a fire or harming anyone.

Earlier this morning, the federal Office of Surface Mining's office in Knoxville (865-545-4103) was informed of the presence of activists at unspecified locations on site at Zeb Mountain in the expectation that it would forbid NCC (865-690-6900) from blasting there. Given this morning's demonstration of the continued presence of activists on site, it is expected that blasting will continue to be forbidden until a thorough search can be made of the site.

Press Release [sent anonymously by email, late afternoon]:

Attached is a photograph of the smoke-producing signaling device used this morning to demonstrate the continued presence of Appalachian activists inspired by Mountain Justice at National Coal Corporation's Zeb Mountain mine site...

The actions taken today at Zeb Mountain were designed to damage no equipment and pose no threat to safety but nonetheless cost NCC time and money, directly interfering with its destruction of this mountain. Locking up mining equipment required NCC to take time to remove the locks and check equipment before putting it back to work. The continued presence of activists on the mountain, demonstrated by the signaling device, required that blasting be halted today.

NCC and other mining companies will take note that activists can and will take direct action to stop and call attention to the permanent, irreparable destruction caused by large-scale strip mining of coal, here and at other mine sites.

NCC and other mining companies *should* take note. But unfortunately they're not compelled to do so by this particular action, on this particular day. The plan for this action relies on secrecy—and that turns out to be something the activists don't have going for them this Sunday night. In the middle of the night, activists in the field, ready to launch this action, call their support people to say there are far too many security guards on duty (really—not a mistake this time), so it will have to be called off. The scouts come out of the woods, and those press releases don't get sent. Presumably the increased security that night is in reaction to the previous week's action. It's some consolation that MJS's Zeb Mountain "clusterfuck," after the fact, seems to be at least costing NCC security money they wouldn't otherwise be spending.

One of the activists involved in this, the fellow who'd been leaning toward bailing out, is more relieved than disappointed when the action is called off. He had ultimately decided not to bail out because he has a lot of woods experience, and people who *weren't* having such doubts convinced him that he was needed. When we'd talked between the first action and the follow-up about his leeriness, he'd said he couldn't quite articulate, even to himself, why he had such a bad feeling about it. I told him then that I thought much of what we call instinct is the result of things we've observed without noticing them consciously: It's our subconscious nudging us to pay attention. After the follow-up action is aborted, he tells me he'd figured out what was bothering him: that *not* doing it didn't seem to be an option, which of course it must be if you're to make an intelligent decision about whether to go ahead.

Although the MJS schedule of events in Tennessee continues right through to the end of August, MJS pretty much peters out after the aborted follow-up action at Zeb. Shortly after that night, I take part in a conversation, primarily with john and Amanda, at their house, with other people dropping in and out of the conversation as well.

We talk about the difficulties of the past couple of weeks here—the rancor, the long and unproductive meetings, the exodus of activists.

john sees MJS's current "demoralization" as related not just to the less-than-fully-successful actions but also to Chris and Paloma in effect imposing their leadership on what's supposed to be a leaderless campaign. "They're certainly not looking to be given orders the way they've been given orders here recently," john says. "I think there were people who were here in Tennessee who were feeling pretty empowered, and it was particularly damaging for them to get the kind of treatment they got."

During this conversation I suggest—and people respond with nods—that there's a connection between the leadership issue and the miscommunication that contributed to the "clusterfuck." Decision-making in MJS is supposed to work by consensus, but, as john puts it, there are people in this campaign for whom consensus means you have to agree with *me*. The group dynamic is thus set up so that communication is fundamentally not quite honest, and things end up being done in ways that aren't fully consented to. People aren't fully informed, things aren't fully explained because it's easier to paper things over than to deal with the fact that some people aren't seeking consensus in the same way that others are—that some people are playing the role of leaders who expect to be agreed with. That's not how Chris and Paloma describe themselves, but it is an effect of the way they behave in the group. And so in the planning for the first Zeb action differences were papered over, and because people weren't fully in tune with each other, because they held back rather than fully explored differences, there wasn't a good foundation for communication and improvisation when things went awry. The scale and complexity and multifacetedness of the action was perhaps too big for it to work well in any case. It certainly was too much to be managed by people who, in the course of planning, avoided getting to know each other very well. Furthermore, these problems were worsened by using a quasi-anarchist affinity group system for managing the action, with small groups working independently but needing to have their work coordinated with that of other groups. In this campaign, "affinity" has pretty consistently trumped solidarity and enforced social cliquishness. Thus the implementation of "security" and "need to know" have often meant that not everyone gets to know what they need.

Toward the end of that week, I talk with Chris Irwin about the state of the campaign in Tennessee. I tell him that Paloma has told me that she feels she has to choose between doing direct action and UMD. What's his view on this? "I'm still really down with direct action," he says. "I think it can be a really effective tactic. But you've got to use it like a rifle, not a shotgun." Chris doesn't feel he needs to choose, but he does feel a need to be careful about how he personally participates in direct action because he wants to become a lawyer soon. And he agrees with Paloma that "she can't be doing direct action with people who are going to do something stupid that'll bring it down on UMD. She wants to have a degree of separation." She's especially concerned about people getting hurt or killed. "All it would take would be something like that to go down, and us to be tied to it, and we would be ruined as an organization."

Chris doesn't see direct action as an effective way to cost coal companies money, at least not enough money to make a difference. He's skeptical about whether it's possible to come up with any combination of direct action, lawsuits, and whatever else can be devised, that would cost NCC so much that they'd shut down the Zeb mine site or any other site as unprofitable. "That [strategy] would make sense for a normal business model, in a normal business. But when you're dealing with a company whose objective has never been to make money—I mean, they are putting themselves hundreds of millions in debt, twice as much this year as the previous year, and they've never turned a profit. And I don't think they ever will. Their whole purpose was [to] double their stock, or triple it, and then everyone in their administration has doubled salaries and are multimillionaires. If the company goes bankrupt, who cares?" Other mining companies, the big, profitable ones, are even less likely to be affected this way. "You could take half of Massey's mines away from them, and they would still be a multimillion-dollar corporation. I think we can cost them money, and from every direction we should." But that's only part of what needs to be done.

"National Coal could go out of business tomorrow, and we'll have three other coal companies pop up, as long as the economic incentive is there." Which is why Chris and UMD are focused on "getting something in the general assembly" to end strip mining in Tennessee.

"Tennessee didn't really get anything from MJS," Chris says. "And it was a shame that it ate up so much of our resources and cash, that one action.

"It's easy for people to focus on the bad, and on one action. But even that—you know, I was really down initially because of how much it cost." And then he decided that he and Paloma had done the right thing. "Despite all the inconveniences that personally I experienced from saying there's safety issues here, and how it kind of turned into a popularity contest, I felt in my gut that what we did was the right thing."

Among the action planners, Chris says, there was a "macho attitude. Yeah, there was a lack of communication but it was coming from an attitude, a sort of group-think—we're gonna do it this way, and you get punished if you step out of bounds." Lack of communication wasn't the problem, Chris notes, when the scout concerned about safety tried to get the action-planning group to address that issue. He presented his concerns, people heard them, and they were dismissed apparently because they weren't what the group wanted to hear.

Chris thinks that the interpersonal conflict in MJS this summer was caused in part by "trying to recruit people from all over the country and then saying: OK, do a direct action together. So you've never done one before together; work together."

In addition, he says, "we didn't really get that diversity of people that we needed. The majority of our people were crusty punks, for lack of a better word. We got some teachers, and some terrific medics, but we didn't really get that much diversity in the people that we drew. And the crowd that we drew, crusty punks, by definition causes some problems. If we had perhaps recruited from a broader base and got people who had more diverse background and skills," then they could have done more door-to-door and lobbying work. "One of the premises for Mountain Justice Summer was to provide the locals with more [volunteers] for grassroots work." Instead of MJS taking work off Chris's hands and multiplying the number of people engaged in it, "I ended up doing ten times the work."

What Chris and UMD did get out of "the process" of MJS this year was that "it forced us to get our water testing together, it forced us to get our Listening Projects together, it forced us to get our [*Mountain Defender*] paper printed, it forced us to form links in Nashville." What they didn't get was several dozen volunteers willing to do specific kinds of work that Chris and Paloma had wanted done: Listening Projects up in coalfield communities, flyering in Knoxville to raise awareness, canvassing the Oak Ridge area to raise money.

During that last week of MJS in Tennessee, I also talk with john johnson about the state of the campaign. We talk first about Paloma's decision not to be involved with direct action anymore. john thinks that direct action and the sort of legal, lobbying, and coalition-building work that UMD does "very obviously can be coordinated. Her personal decision is her personal decision.

"I sat down and had what I felt was a really healthy and productive conversation with Gena the other day about a lot of this stuff. And she expressed to me these concerns that the kind of thing people seem to want to do with Mountain Justice Summer is potentially damaging to United Mountain Defense. She had three separate spheres of concern. One was [UMD's] relations with other nonprofits, two was their relationship with the government, and three was her ability to get on the bar and practice law. And I told her I felt that the third one was way legitimate.

"But I said I've been a very obvious and vocal proponent and practitioner of direct action, in east Tennessee since 1993 [when he was first arrested], and I've been an activist longer. And I always go to meetings and mouth off. And it has not discernibly impacted my relationship with other groups. Certainly there is some impact, but not to the point of people being like: You're crazy, we don't want to work with you. Some of the things I've engaged in have probably put some people in SOCM [Save Our Cumberland Mountains, a mainstream Tennessee nonprofit] on edge. But it's nothing that couldn't be fixed if they had a more open mind and I had more time to spend talking with them.

"Of course, I don't desire the same kind of relationships that they do. Overall, I view the government as very bad and only want to appeal to it and work with it on very short-term, specific, reform-minded goals."

Gena, Chris, and Paloma apparently believe they're close to persuading state government to ban strip mining in Tennessee, but john doesn't think that's a likely scenario. "When we [first] decided to target Bredesen, I actually spoke out against that, thinking that it was a waste of time. I'm really uncomfortable being a real blatant Earth Firster and radical and then asking people to beg the government. I think it's inconsistent with our core philosophies. So I spoke out against that, but everyone wanted to do it, so I was like: OK, I'll go along." Of course, if government *could* be persuaded to ban surface mining that would be a good thing. "Exactly. That's why I go along with that kind of thing."

john, like Chris, is doubtful that any combination of legal challenges and direct action could cost coal companies enough to compel them to shut down marginal mine sites. "The problem is that the price of coal is so high now that it's not going to be the same as when SMCRA was passed in the '70s, and all of a sudden the regulations get implemented and [mine operators say]: 'Fuck this, I can't afford to do this anymore.' And mines start closing. Personally, while I'm no economist, I don't think the price of coal is going anywhere but up.

"I'm pretty cynical at this point. *Maybe* it puts the squeeze on National Coal. But if Arch or Massey comes in, they're going to be able to afford it. A multinational corporation can absorb regulatory costs. They do it over and over and over again across the planet. They absorb the costs, the small guys go out of business, there's no competition. And they can afford to do it. If there's tighter regulations but you can still wreck a stream and you can still rip the top off a mountain, they're going to figure out how to do it and still make money.

"[That's] the doomsday trajectory of this economy and this society, and they're just not shifting away from it. It's gonna get to the point where they're just like: Fuck you, we're taking the coal, and we don't care about the environmental regulations. We need the coal, and we're gonna get it, and it doesn't matter what happens to people and the environment. Because the war machine has to keep running. The production machine has to keep running." If coal gets more expensive to produce, "they're just going to charge more for the coal. And the utility companies, not having set up an alternative form of energy production, are gonna pay it. And they're gonna charge the rest of us.

"My personal philosophy is we need it all: direct action, laws, whatever. It all needs to work. And I'll choose to work in whatever arena I'm comfortable in. Personally, I think if they're gonna choose to *really* distance themselves from direct action, and really not put any faith in it and not have it count as part of the equation then 1) they're underestimating the people who are here and how they care about the mountains, and 2) they're shooting themselves in the foot, for if and when the other paths don't work."

Beyond Mountain
Justice Summer

At the end of the summer of 2005, Mountain Justice Summer activists dispersed, returned to their homes, took time off, rested. But soon, through the fall and into winter, work resumed and plans were made, looking ahead to the following spring and summer. Activists also assessed the successes and shortcomings of the summer of 2005, and of the campaign against mountaintop removal in general. One decision made by MJS organizers that fall was to drop the "S" and become simply Mountain Justice (MJ).

Another decision was not to have another "traveling circus" of activists move from state to state the following summer. The sense was that this approach had done more to wear out than to energize and aid local groups fighting MTR. The activists who felt most strongly about this—particularly Hillary, Chris, and Paloma—had had the most conflict with younger self-styled radicals among the travelers, who were often dismissive and rude to them when they were acting as hosts during MJS's time in West Virginia and Tennessee.

Partly as a consequence of this, Mountain Justice in 2006 and 2007 lost most of its pan-regional character and became primarily a state-by-state affair. It also lost its emphasis on civil disobedience: At only a handful of actions during those two years did activists choose to use civil disobedience tactics, and only one of those events was publicized as an MJ action.

In November 2005, the federal 4th Circuit Court of Appeals struck down Judge Goodwin's 2004 ruling that the Army Corps of Engineers' Nationwide 21 permits violate the Clean Water Act, ruling instead that it's okay for the Corps to class MTR as a "category" eligible for blanket approval without site-by-site evaluation. Joe Lovett responded by going after the Corps' issuance of individual permits for MTR. (Since Judge Goodwin's decision, coal companies had been avoiding the Nationwide 21 process and applying for individual permits instead.) Lovett and his colleagues argued in federal court that the Corps should be required to complete a full environmental impact statement (EIS) demonstrating compliance with the National Environmental Policy Act (NEPA) for each and every individual permit for MTR. Since it's hard to imagine any MTR site passing muster with NEPA, the EIS requirement had the potential to prevent future MTR operations entirely.

Legal maneuvering concerning the permit processes continued through 2006, 2007, and 2008. And still the Corps continued to enable MTR to continue, however contrary to the laws that give the Corps its authority.

Meanwhile, in mid-2007, the Office of Surface Mining announced its intent to go ahead with gutting the stream-buffer-zone rule, saying that the EIS it had begun on the matter in 2005, now complete, supported the change. (At least the report's recommendations did so. The science in the body of the report, once again, differed.) Public comment on the proposed rule change was overwhelmingly against it.

In West Virginia, Marsh Fork High School was destroyed by fire months after summer's end in 2005. Hillary Hosta stayed on in the Coal River valley, renting a small house down the road from Ed Wiley and working with CRMW and OVEC. Sage Russo went to work for Christians for the Mountains in 2006, and eventually set up and helped run a pair of campaign houses for them in West Virginia while attending seminary. Bo Webb took a step back from MJ, while his daughter and son-in-law Sarah and Vern Haltom became increasingly active. Ed Wiley, still seeking a new school for the children of Marsh Fork Elementary, walked 455 miles from West Virginia to Washington in 2006, raising awareness and support all along the way. The second silo wasn't built. The first remained in operation, the school remained open, and children attending the school continued to be exposed to all the risks associated with the coal operations next door. Mountain Justice in West Virginia mostly focused on bringing in young people, mostly recruited on college campuses, for relatively brief visits. In 2007 and 2008, West Virginia hosted Mountain Justice Spring Break (MJSB) gatherings of college-age young people intended to educate and mobilize them to fight MTR.

Out of MJSB 2007 came the only civil-disobedience action owned by MJ in 2006 and 2007, a sit-in protest at the West Virginia governor's office that resulted in thirteen arrests. The thirteen were among fifty or so who had gathered there to demand that Gov. Joe Manchin sign a pledge to build a new school in a safe location for the students of Marsh Fork Elementary.

The protesters were primarily residents of West Virginia, although those present also included supporters from North Carolina, Kentucky, Tennessee, and Virginia, as well as college students who'd come to West Virginia for MJSB. Protesters ranged in age from young children to Winnie Fox from Coal River valley, who celebrated her eighty-seventh birthday that day by getting arrested.

The group occupied the reception area of the governor's office late in the morning, singing and chanting. Several protesters entered the vestibule between the reception room and the governor's office and refused to leave.

Joe Martin, deputy chief of staff for the governor, came out to talk with the protesters. At one point, Martin approached Ed Wiley, took his hand, and privately asked him to help him out with quieting things down and persuading the crowd to leave. Wiley shouted: "Enough of this whispering in my ear, telling me to settle this down. We'll raise the roof off the dang place." Other protesters in the room cheered and applauded.

Early in the afternoon, state troopers and capitol police asked the protesters to clear the vestibule and part of the reception room nearby. More than a dozen police approached and began arresting protesters who refused to move—including Ed Wiley and Bill Price, who'd taken the day off from his Sierra Club job.

Police used unnecessary force in arresting several people who obviously posed no threat of violence. Among those was Hillary. Police asked to her to move and she agreed to do so but was nonetheless pursued across the room and arrested there. Police pinned her to the floor, handcuffed her with her hands behind her back, then carried her out in a painful hog-tied position, facedown with officers carrying her by her handcuffs and ankles.

The thirteen who were arrested were charged with misdemeanor obstruction. All were released from jail later that day on personal recognizance bonds. Their bonds required that they not return to the capitol to protest.

At the time, the governor's office protest looked like the beginning of a new wave of MJ civil disobedience and direct action in the coalfields. Instead, the lull in such action since the end of the summer of 2005 resumed, and continued through the rest of the year and into 2008.

In Tennessee, the break between Chris-Paloma-Gena and Katuah Earth First! became complete and final when Chris established a Knoxville-based Three Rivers Earth First! faction. Chris remained very active in MJ, wearing his United Mountain Defense hat. UMD became MJ's exclusive presence in Tennessee, and it did a great deal of very good work, mostly on mustering political opposition to MTR in the state, challenging permits, and other legal work. (Both Gena and Chris became lawyers during this time.)

While john johnson remained supportive of MJ and friendly with the KEF! faction based in Asheville, most of his time was devoted to school, working toward a degree in forestry. He felt strongly that he had to be a top student for his degree to have credibility, given that he intended for it to be used in future activist work.

In April 2007, john finally went on trial for charges resulting from the MJS action at the National Coal shareholders' meeting in Knoxville in 2005. The prosecution argued that he should be held "criminally responsible" for any felonies committed by anyone at the protest that day, on the basis that he was "a leader" implementing a plan to commit assault and burglary. The judge refused to allow this. Nor was john compelled to identify others at the protest, who appeared in a videotape shown at the trial. Ultimately, the jury acquitted john of all felony charges, finding him guilty only of disorderly conduct and disrupting a meeting—both misdemeanors. After john's trial, the other two arrested that day plea-bargained to much the same result.

As MJ shifted toward state-by-state campaigns, MJ in West Virginia and Tennessee came to be run by small circles of insiders open to newcomers only if they were willing to follow instructions and carry out plans made and directed by those in charge. Overall, MJ came to be much more successful in recruiting short-term newbies than in retaining experienced campaigners.

This model was not a good fit for Kentucky, which lacked an MJ-friendly local group willing and able to assert this sort of leadership. (Kentuckians for the Commonweath continued its long-term efforts to organize and educate against MTR in Kentucky with minimal involvement with MJ, of which KFTC remained wary.) Kentucky very much needed to see pan-regional efforts, successes, and support linked to conditions in its own coalfield communities for the fight against MTR to gain local support. Although MJS began making such connections in 2005, follow-up was lacking.

Through 2006, 2007, and 2008, Dave Cooper continued his road-show, traveling and speaking to just about any group wanting to hear

about MTR. Dave also persistently worked to connect people fighting
MTR with others who might help them or they might help. His network
of contacts numbered in the thousands, and he habitually informed individuals within that network of new contacts or other opportunities they
might find useful. During this time, MJ's presence in Kentucky consisted
of the efforts of Dave, Patty Draus, and a handful of other activists, who
hosted MJ meetings occasionally and organized educational events and
a few local protests, none of which involved civil disobedience. (The
number of MJ activists in Kentucky dwindled by the latter part of 2007
to perhaps one-third of what it had been in 2005.)

If the new MJ wasn't a good fit for Kentucky, it didn't fit Virginia's
coalfields at all. At the end of 2005, locally based organizing in Virginia
was in its infancy and lacked resources to start up and run an effective
campaign entirely on its own. Nor did the new top-down leadership
model fit MJ's then-substantial base of anarchist/Earth First! support in
and around Asheville.

By then, I too was living in Asheville, a two-hour drive from the
coalfields of Virginia. It nagged at me that MJS had blown in and out
of Virginia in not much more than a week in the summer of 2005, then
abandoned the place. I knew that KEFers in North Carolina had had a
supportive relationship with mainstream forest activists in southwestern
Virginia long before the MJS campaign. Then I learned, in late 2005,
that two lifelong Wise County residents, Larry Bush and Pete Ramey,
with the help of Sierra Club's Bill McCabe, had started up a new local
group called Southern Appalachian Mountain Stewards (SAMS). Their
main focus was to recruit their neighbors to join them to fight MTR.
I knew from my travels and conversations the previous summer that
specific people throughout the MJS coalition cared very much about
Virginia's coalfields, so I organized a meeting in a church in Wise County
in January 2006 bringing together Larry, Pete, and other locals with
out-of-area folks offering their help.

From that meeting and subsequent contact with SAMS, it became clear that SAMS's requests for assistance with research about local effects of MTR and with getting the word out locally would be hard to meet as long as outside support came from people who lived two or more hours away and had no place to stay overnight. Around the same time, Earth First! in Asheville—which was slated to host EF!'s national Round River Rendezvous that year—was seeking a Rendezvous location in or near Appalachia's coalfields, preferably in Virginia. Furnishing and running a campaign house, both to enable MJ volunteers to come help SAMS and to enable Rendezvous organizers to connect with local efforts, seemed a useful thing that I could do, so I undertook it. With a good bit of financial and practical support from Asheville EF!, I rented a house in Virginia and moved there at the end of April 2006.

I wish I could report that this venture worked out better than it did. For a good couple of months, things went really well. A few MJ volunteers got to know SAMS members and helped with local work against MTR. A wider network, mostly derived from MJ's network, promised more help in the future.

Then came the Earth First! Rendezvous. Each year in early July, Earth First! holds a weeklong social-and-networking gathering of its activists from all over the United States. This year it was to be held at the same forest campsite MJS had used in Virginia the year before, with the stated intention of educating activists from all over the United States about MTR and generating support for local efforts to fight it.

That was the theory. In practice, neither the Rendezvous's Asheville-based organizers nor the Rendezvous itself ever really connected with anyone from SAMS. In large part, I think, this was due to a cultural gap between Earth Firsters and coalfield residents: In recent years, Asheville EF! in particular but also EF! nationally had come to be dominated by a young urban-punk set who, for the most part, seemed uncomfortable with rural people and settings. In addition, most coalfield activists are a good bit older than most current Earth Firsters.

Larry Bush led a coalfield tour to show interested Earth Firsters the effects of MTR in his community, and that was about the extent of

SAMS's involvement with the Rendezvous. Neither Larry nor any other local resident was included in the planning for the post-Rendezvous action; the planners quite clearly felt uncomfortable doing an action with people so unlike themselves. (Locals were amused by the action, a good-humored and peaceful blockade of a coal-fired power plant just outside Wise County, but didn't find it particularly relevant.)

The Earth Firsters did, however, feel comfortable with the young MJ volunteers who'd come to Virginia to help local anti-MTR efforts. Most of them attended some or all of the Rendezvous, and most left Virginia afterward, some of them moving on to other activist scenes. Some returned, but only briefly or intermittently, and to little effect. In short, the EF! Rendezvous sucked up outside support for local anti-MTR efforts, and blew it away.

I returned to Asheville that fall, but before I left, I helped Larry Bush arrange to set up an office for SAMS on the main street of Appalachia. A young MJ volunteer named Hannah Morgan, a terrific exception to the general rule in coalfield Virginia that young outside volunteers come, don't do much, then leave, stayed on and did much of the work of keeping the office open and useful in 2007. As of early 2008, SAMS membership had grown to well over a hundred. By then, however, SAMS was quite aloof from MJ: Although, at Hannah's request, SAMS agreed to allow MJ to hold a pan-regional "revisioning" meeting at its office in November 2007, no local SAMS members attended.

By the latter part of 2007, several counterproductive trends were evident in MJ. One was the campaign's continuing inclusiveness problem. Early on, MJS was envisioned "as a movement that will bring in a broad spectrum of people from all walks of life," as Bo Webb put it. But since 2005, MJ's recruitment and activities had been primarily geared for urban-oriented college-aged people from outside the coalfields. This effectively excluded, or at best failed to encourage, others who didn't fit that profile to lend their talents and resources to MJ. It specifically excluded most coalfield residents, few of whom can be described as "young urban activists."

A related trend concerned Mountain Justice as an indigenous movement. By 2007, many of those most active in MJ seemed to perceive it as simply part of a wider struggle against climate change. That was not how MJS started out, nor was this shift in focus discussed and decided upon in the MJ consensus process. MJS began as an effort by people living in Appalachia's coalfields, aided by outside supporters, to end strip mining and enable coalfield Appalachians to begin building a better, sustainable, self-determined future for the region. MJ's shift away from that vision paralleled its shift from being driven by people living in the coalfields to being driven primarily by the desires and goals of activists based and working outside the coalfields, few of whom had any strong connection to any coalfield community. (It's perhaps worth noting that of the two dozen people attending MJ's "revisioning" meeting in late 2007, only one—Vern Haltom—was a long-time coalfield resident.)

It is, of course, an excellent thing that MJ has networked and linked itself so effectively with the national, indeed global, network of people seeking to mitigate human effects on climate change by reducing the burning of fossil fuels. Their efforts to stop the building of new coal-fired power plants, phase out the old ones, and in the meantime insist that coal mining not destroy Appalachia, are Appalachia's best hope for building a national constituency willing to demand an end to the many evils of strip mining. (It is also excellent, and critical to the development of that national constituency, that MTR is now covered by national media.) Their efforts overall to combat climate change are perhaps the world's best hope for a livable future.

But MJ's absorption into the global movement against climate change came at a cost: It sidelined, rather than supported, organizing within the coalfields. Nothing that outsiders can accomplish, however valuable and welcome, will suffice as a "solution" to Appalachia's "problems." Appalachia needs to find its own future, with Appalachians themselves envisioning and building that future, beyond the dysfunctional economy and culture of coal. Otherwise, the groups and individuals fighting MTR might win individual battles but are doomed to lose the war. A particularly bad mining operation might be stopped here and there, but others will continue, destroying more and more of Appalachia as the price of coal rises ever higher. Even if *all* strip mining were to end, Appalachia would still be a colonial economy and society ripe for exploitation by other big-money enterprises. A sustainable future for Appalachia requires a locally based, nationally supported network of communities capable of demanding and creating better ways of living and making a living there.

MJS was founded to bring nonviolent direct action and civil disobedience to Appalachia in aid of the fight against strip mining. But, after the summer of 2005, these tactics almost entirely vanished from MJ. To the extent that they were still used in 2006 through early 2008, it was outside the coalfields by activists who were based outside the coalfields. For example, Chris Dodson (now going by his middle name, Willie) beginning in late 2007 organized and inspired a wave of actions at banks that fund MTR, with small groups visiting bank branches in places outside the coalfields to sing and play old-timey Appalachian music, talk with customers, and hand out anti-MTR literature. Such actions taken outside the coalfields in support of the struggle against MTR are, of course, not a bad thing. To the contrary, they are very much needed for success in that struggle. But the key word there is "support." The home ground of this campaign is the coalfields. In 2006 and 2007, MJ diverted the campaign's direct-action energy far from that home.

It was particularly worrisome that this narrowed the possibilities for coalfield residents to connect with the campaign against MTR. A local person in Virginia, for example, who's really, really angry about a strip mine near his house and wants to do something directly to stop it might not think that the sort of work on lobbying, lawsuits, hearings, and petitioning government that SAMS engages in is enough. And SAMS collectively isn't comfortable with participating in civil disobedience. The genius of the early MJS campaign was that it recognized that both sorts of work are needed if the fight against MTR is to succeed.

MJS was intended to be a big-tent framework within which lots of different people doing different sorts of work could amplify the effectiveness of each of their work. The MJS guidelines—no violence, no property damage, civil disobedience is okay, focus on strip mining in Appalachia—were intended to encourage individual or group projects aimed at ending MTR without everyone affiliated with the campaign needing to agree to participate. Sierra Club could participate in MJS in its own way, Earth First! in its way, SAMS in its way—and if through MJS that lone angry person in Virginia could connect with someone from elsewhere willing to help him blockade a mine entrance, that would be good too.

A key reason for MJS's original openness to direct action was a recognition that violence is very close to the surface in the coalfields. Support for autonomous, nonviolent direct action encourages and enables angry, frustrated people to do something radical in a focused and effective way, rather than, say, going to a mine site and trashing the equipment or shooting at someone. One of MJS's founding premises was that if we're violent, we lose. There was thus real danger in the campaign's unexamined shift to direct action only *outside* the coalfields.

For these and other reasons, in the latter part of 2007 some activists began to talk about a new wave of direct action in the coalfields. Both local people and individuals living outside the coalfields would be involved. The aim would be to annoy, inconvenience, and cost MTR operators money—as often and in as many places as possible.

One model for such actions might be the second, aborted Zeb Mountain action described in press releases above. Such an action would be cost-effective, with minimal resources and risk expended to maximum effect both on mining companies and on public awareness of MTR. It could be accomplished with simple, inexpensive equipment by six or seven activists, perhaps four on site plus two or three to drive, email the anonymous press releases, and sit by a phone in case something went wrong. If all went well, no one would go to jail.

Of course anyone undertaking such an action could decide to skip the press releases altogether, allowing the action to speak for itself. I believe, though, in the current political, legal, and media climate—in which any direct action in the name of environmental justice will likely be called ecoterrorism—that failing to broadcast the activists' own, truthful description of an action risks having the action do more harm than good. Truth is powerful, and the truth is on the activists' side here— especially since media are likely to find their story more appealing than the stories the coal company or hostile law enforcement are likely to tell. Imagine, for example, if the photo of the signaling device described in the press releases in the previous chapter shows something that's not only obviously harmless but hilarious, with perhaps a friendly seahorse head on the prow of the inflated plastic float, and a waving Barbie doll nestled inside it among the fireworks. Imagine if instead the activists provide no information at all, ceding the story to coal propagandists.

Perhaps the best reason to do such actions, though, is that they are replicable, adaptable, inspirational. People living in the coalfields with the many evils of MTR, faced with the enormous economic, political, and legal power of the coal companies, have had little reason to believe that anything can be done to change things and have many reasons to despair. Actions such as this can show clearly that individuals or small groups can indeed stand up to a coal company and make a difference, crippling at least one small part of the enormous death machine of MTR for at least a short time, and doing it in a way that encourages coalfield residents, calls attention to the terrible injustice going on in Appalachia, and supports broader efforts to stop MTR and right its wrongs.

As for reasons not to do such actions, many of them, at each and every egregiously destructive strip mine in America—well, I can't think of one.

By mid-2008, a good many MJ activists based outside the coalfields were shifting their focus back toward coalfield communities. One manifestation of this was the launch of an "intake" effort to better connect MJ volunteers with tasks that grassroots coalfield anti-MTR groups such as CRMW and SAMS needed help accomplishing.

At the same time, ongoing MJ efforts to prevent construction of a very large new coal-fired power plant in Wise County, Virginia, became better coordinated with the efforts of people living near the proposed plant. By mid-2008, new and deeper working relationships were developing between young, urban, climate-change-oriented "outsider" activists and local people who didn't want this plant—or any more MTR to fuel it—in their backyard.

MJ's involvement with this issue began in 2006, when a consortium of five power companies led by Dominion proposed building a large new power plant near St. Paul, Virginia. The plant was projected to begin construction in 2008 and start operating in 2012.

A wide range of local, regional, and national activists expressed concerns about the plant. MJ, SAMS, and other anti-MTR activists foresaw that the plant's voracious need for coal for decades to come would preclude chances for a transition to a healthy post-coal economy in southwestern Virginia. In recent years, more than 100,000 acres in Virginia's coalfields had been devastated by large-scale strip mining. In Wise County, more than 41,000 acres were permitted for surface mining at the time the new plant was proposed. If MTR accelerated to meet the demands of the new plant, there'd be little of the region's water and forest resources left with which to start anew after the coal ran out.

Social-justice activists in Wise County and elsewhere raised concerns about having a plant sited there, in the poorest part of the state, that would primarily benefit wealthier consumers to the east. (The company that supplies electricity locally in Wise County was not one of those building the plant.) The plant would generate 500–600 megawatts of electricity—enough to power as many as 360,000 homes. The people who live in Wise County and nearby coalfield communities already suffered from some of the worst air quality in the nation, largely due to emissions from other coal-fired power plants in the region.

Clean-air advocates were, on the one hand, cautiously encouraged by the proposed plant's relatively tight air-pollution controls, which were about as good as coal-fired power plants get at minimizing smokestack emissions of the main toxins associated with burning coal. However, on the other hand, the plant's "circulating fluidized bed" (CFB) technology would enable it to burn waste coal (a byproduct of coal processing that's mostly rock) and biomass (trees or construction waste) as well as regular coal. It wasn't at all clear how well pollution controls devised for regular coal would work with those alternative fuels, which create different combustion products.

Climate-change activists, generally opposed to building any new fossil-fuel burning facilities, were particularly opposed to the proposed plant's relatively inefficient CFB technology, which extracts only about half the energy from the same amount of coal consumption and greenhouse-gas production as "gasification," a more efficient kind of coal-burning technology. Worse still for global warming was the proposed burning of waste coal, which produces even more greenhouse gas (and more toxic wastes, too) per kilowatt of electricity.

Water-quality advocates (locally, primarily the Clinch Coalition) were concerned about the plant's effects on the Clinch River, as Dominion had struck a deal with the county's public utility authority to take 1 million gallons of the river's water per day, 20 percent of which would be discharged after use, according to a Dominion spokesman. An additional concern was the potential for rainwater leaching out toxins from the vast quantity of ash this plant would produce, polluting waterways and aquifers. If waste coal were burned, that concern would grow; for every 100 tons of waste coal the plant burned, about 85 tons of ash would remain. And if biomass were a significant part of the fuel mix, the economic incentive to cut even immature forests nearby would increase, threatening the river's watershed.

Dominion, on the other hand, described the proposed plant as a "clean coal power station," with state-of-the-art pollution controls. It emphasized its intention to buy coal mined in Virginia as a benefit to the area's economy. Together with local and regional political and business leaders, Dominion also claimed that the proposed plant would add many jobs to the local economy. Skeptics noted that most of those jobs would be temporary, for construction work at the plant, and that much or most of that work would likely be done by specialist contractors from outside the region, rather than by local contractors and workers.

In addition, the proposed plant would likely accelerate a *loss* of jobs at another plant nearby, the old and very dirty coal-fired power plant operated by AEP, one of Dominion's partners for the new plant, along the Clinch River in Carbo, just a few miles away. (The Carbo plant was the site of the protest following Earth First's Rendezvous in 2006.) Operating since the 1950s and lacking modern pollution controls, the smokestacks at Carbo emitted as much as a quarter of a million pounds of sulfuric acid and 2 million pounds of hydrochloric acid each year, along with mercury and other toxins. AEP had long avoided installing pollution controls at Carbo by cleaning up other, more modern plants it owns elsewhere, as allowed under federal cap-and-trade rules. It apparently had no intention of making such upgrades at Carbo, but surely expected that someday either the state or the federal government would no longer allow it to pump out so much pollution there. When that happened, it's a good guess that AEP would shut the Carbo plant down rather than upgrade it. AEP's stake in the new power plant, so close to its old one, made closure of the old plant in the near future look more likely. In that light, Dominion's claim that the proposed plant meant a gain in local jobs looked even more hollow.

Nor would the new plant's demand for coal likely create new jobs in mining. In the past half-century (roughly the time since the Carbo plant opened), as coal mining in Appalachia mechanized and shifted from underground toward large-scale surface mining, coal production in Virginia doubled while jobs for miners dwindled. Those trends had accelerated in recent years—as recently as 1990, more than 10,000 miners were employed in Virginia; in 2004, only 4,000 such jobs remained. There's no reason to believe that jobs in coal mining would increase in the decades ahead, new power plant or no.

The proposed Wise County power plant was thus a perfect example of everything that's wrong about coal, locally and globally, from its mining to its burning to its wastes. As such, it presented a perfect opportunity for people with diverse interests (MTR, climate change, clean air, and so on) and from diverse backgrounds (urban college students, retired coal miners, local and national environmental organizations) to work together to stop the plant. Aware of the possibility that Dominion and its allies might seek to divide and conquer by pitting these diverse elements against each other, folks who'd previously not worked with each other began early on to make efforts to meet and talk with each other about their opposition to the plant. No grand, unified coalition emerged from this effort. What did happen was perhaps more hopeful: an ongoing effort to consult one another, to work together when possible, and to avoid undermining one another's efforts against the plant and, more broadly, toward building a better future.

Not that this effort was perfect. Inevitably, with such very different people involved, it was often awkward. Other than Hannah Morgan and a very few others, MJ in 2006 and 2007 didn't take collaborating with local people in Wise County as seriously as it might have done. SAMS and the Clinch Coalition, the main local groups opposing the plant, collectively remained wary of MJ's use of civil disobedience. But individual members of SAMS and the Clinch Coalition saw civil disobedience tactics as legitimate, though not something either of their organizations would explicitly endorse. And eventually MJers working on this issue came to devote much more effort to coordinating their work with that of local activists.

In March 2007, SAMS held its first public meeting in opposition to the plant. Fifty or so local residents attended, asking Dominion representatives tough questions about the plant and finding their answers mostly unsatisfactory. Over the next year and longer, SAMS and other local activists focused their efforts on mobilizing local support, commenting at public hearings, allying with mainstream environmental organizations elsewhere to mobilize statewide opposition to the plant, and collaborating with those organizations on legal challenges. MJ activists sometimes joined SAMS in these efforts, but primarily focused on protests outside the coalfield region, at Dominion's offices in Richmond, for example. In August 2007, Blue Ridge Earth First! (BREF!), a new EF! entity based in central Virginia and closely affiliated with MJ, announced its existence with banners opposing various Dominion projects, including the proposed power plant, dropped off northern Virginia highway overpasses.

BREF!'s emergence was critical both to MJ and to efforts against the power plant, in two distinct but ultimately related ways. It gave impetus to a sharp escalation of civil disobedience directed at stopping the power plant: In protests in April and June 2008, activists blockaded Dominion headquarters in Richmond—at the latter protest, twelve were arrested. It also gave impetus to a refocusing of MJ attention toward coalfield communities, particularly Wise County. One result of this was the September 12–14, 2008, "Weekend in Wise," an event that included workshops about local and national coal issues, strategy sessions, hikes, mountaintop removal tours, power plant tours, and a coalfield activist panel. BREF! and MJ activists worked closely with SAMS members and other Wise County locals to plan and present this event, which took place shortly after Dominion began construction on the power plant nearby. And then some stayed on until Monday, when quite a different event was planned.

Shortly before 6 AM on Monday, September 15, a convoy of two pickup trucks, loaded with equipment, followed by two passenger vehicles pulled up to the office entrance of the construction site for Dominion's Wise County power plant. Within a few minutes, in the dark, a blockade was assembled. Eight protesters locked themselves to seven fifty-five-gallon drums pulled off the trucks and spaced across the main gateway. The line of drums and protesters was just long enough to allow the protester on either end of the line to lock to a gatepost. A ninth protester closed the gate and locked it by attaching himself with a lockbox to the gate's two swinging panels. A tenth closed and locked himself to a gate at a secondary entrance to the office. (The site's main entrance for construction vehicles remained open.) Several other protesters assumed support roles once the blockade was established: media liaison, police liaison, photographers, and watchers to see that those who were locked down came to no harm.

Police soon arrived, and set about assessing the situation. Relations between police and protesters began and remained courteous.

Shortly after 6:15 AM, more than a dozen additional protesters marched single-file along the edge of the busy highway fronting the site to join the protesters at the entrance. They carried signs and banners demanding clean energy, clean jobs, and a better future for this place than the power plant portended. Solar panels atop two of the fifty-five-gallon barrels reinforced this message. So did slogans printed on the T-shirts worn by the locked-down protesters: "Today's Destruction Is Not Tomorrow's Prosperity" and "Invest in Appalachia Don't Destroy It."

Most of the nearly three dozen protesters there that day didn't live nearby. A good many came from parts of Virginia east of the coalfields (and downwind from the power plant), where BREF! is based. Others, affiliated with Mountain Justice, came from states nearby. (Bo Webb, for example, came from West Virginia to stand with the protesters.) Still others, including several affiliated with Rainforest Action Network (RAN), which provided logistical and financial support for the action, came from as far away as California.

Only a few of those who marched along the road to show support for the protest were longtime local residents. Only one of those who locked down lived locally: Hannah Morgan, who by this time owned a small house in Appalachia. But other local residents had participated in the planning for the action, and many more had been consulted. In sharp contrast to the planning and execution of the nearby power-plant protest after the Earth First! Rendezvous in 2006, a persistent and extensive effort was made to include local people and address local concerns in this action. Some of those consulted couldn't attend the protest for personal or professional reasons but nonetheless supported it whole-heartedly. Others were uncomfortable with the law-breaking aspect of civil disobedience. They were assured that no violence and no property damage would be committed by the protesters. All of those consulted were asked: "How can this protest be done in ways that help rather than harm other local efforts to stop the power plant and end MTR?" Their input was decisive in shaping the protest, especially its serious tone and positive messaging.

The blockade held for more than four hours. That it lasted so long is something of a mystery. There wasn't anything extraordinarily sophisticated about the lockdown techniques used, and there certainly was no shortage of law-enforcement personnel. So many arrived at the scene that the lone protester at the secondary gate, locked to it with one very ordinary WalMart bicycle lock and a padlocked length of ordinary hardware-store chain, was for a time surrounded by ten policemen and a fireman in full fire-fighting regalia. During those four hours, traffic often slowed to a crawl as motorists first noticed the many police vehicles with flashing lights near the site, then paused to look at the blockade.

I spent most of that time holding a sign by the side of the road near the protest and waving at cars going by. About half the drivers waved back. These included school bus and ambulance drivers, construction workers, even a few coal-truck drivers. Drivers and passengers who gave clear signs of support such as thumbs up or friendly toots on the horn greatly outnumbered those who showed disapproval for the action. Protesters holding signs a little ways farther along the road from me who kept a tally of this say the "yeas" outnumbered the "nays" by about five to one. Only one driver-and-passenger yelled at us, telling us we should go home. Soon after that happened, a passerby on a motorcycle stopped to applaud the protest, telling us it's about time the "outsiders" responsible for the power plant—Dominion, he meant—be sent home.

Standing by the side of the road there, I got to thinking about the three-day march in West Virginia in 2005. Then, Bo Webb recalls, "we were told to go home and that we were a bunch of hippie troublemakers."

Now, three years later, Bo is heartened by what he sees here today. "I think the difference is that although we talked about jobs back then, we are now more specific about the types of jobs and have demonstrated how those jobs can become a reality for our community members. The positive reaction of folks passing by the action is further proof that we have come a long way in our struggle to expose coal industry lies and suppression of the truth."

Altogether, eleven protesters were arrested that day. Nine of the ten who were locked down were charged with misdemeanors related to trespass and unlawful assembly. A woman acting as police liaison was additionally charged with misdemeanors for allegedly inciting other protesters. So was Hannah, one of those locked to the barrels, apparently singled out for extra charges because she'd been such a vocal, local opponent of the plant for the past two years. (Local law enforcement officers responding to the blockade asked for her by name.) Both sets of incitement charges were preposterous. The role of police liaison at such a protest is not to lead but to mediate. As for Hannah, she had recently become a full-time student at Cornell University in upstate New York, a fourteen-hour drive from Wise County. The other arrestees had already committed to their roles before she returned to Virginia and joined them in preparations shortly before the action.

Along with SAMS, the Clinch Coalition, and a great many individuals from Wise County, elsewhere in Virginia, and beyond, Hannah had participated in the public hearing-and-comment process for the plant. But although lawsuits against the plant were still pending, opportunities for public input were now past. "We've gone through all the processes of comments, public hearings, challenging permits, demonstrations, and gathering 46,000 petition signatures of people demanding clean energy in Virginia instead of a new coal plant," Hannah says. "We've even resorted to acts of civil disobedience before, twice blockading the entrance to Dominion's corporate headquarters in Richmond. After years of fighting the blatant injustices of coal in Virginia, we felt it was time to take our actions to ground zero, the power plant site. We felt we have exhausted every other means of telling Dominion 'we won't stop until you do.' We have stood up to the injustices of the coal industry, but on September 15, it was time to sit down—and refuse to move."

The week after the September 15 blockade, former vice president and Nobel-Prize-winning climate-change activist Al Gore told an audience in New York: "If you're a young person looking at the future of this planet and looking at what is being done right now, and not done, I believe we have reached the stage where it is time for civil disobedience to prevent the construction of new coal plants that do not have carbon capture and sequestration."

The predominant reaction to this among MJ activists was: "Not just young people!" (One of the September 15 arrestees was forty-seven years old.) "You, too, Al! Come join us!"

Whether Al Gore would be willing to get arrested or not, that such a mainstream politician would say such a thing is evidence of how America's "mainstream" has shifted on this issue in the past few years. Maybe the lobbying and propaganda power of the coal industry isn't so all-powerful after all. Most Americans now accept that global climate change is real and potentially catastrophic, and that carbon emissions from human activities are contributing to it. Can the day be far off when most Americans also will accept that "no new coal-fired power plants" isn't some crazy radical idea but instead a commonsensical step to avert that potential catastrophe?

When a youngish state trooper walked up to one of those locked to a gate at the power plant in Wise County, he laughed and said: "Y'all are crazy!" From his point of view, what the protesters were doing *did* look crazy. But from a broader point of view, in this time of global climate change and wholesale destruction of Appalachia by MTR coal mining, surely the *really* crazy thing going on there that day was that a new coal-fired power plant was being built, not that its entrance was being blockaded.

"The saving of our world from pending doom will come," Martin Luther King tells us, "not through the complacent adjustment of the conforming majority, but through the creative maladjustment of a non-conforming minority." That "creative maladjustment" is too often dismissed as the craziness of people who just don't fit in this world. But as Judy Bonds has convinced me, and I hope by now convinced you as well: "Oh, *we're* not the misfits."

Climate Ground Zero

As the Bush administration approached its end, an interesting symmetry emerged. The history of anti-MTR activism in the several years prior to the launch of the MJ civil disobedience campaign had been an accelerating series of disappointments with legal maneuvers and with egregious failures to enforce regulations intended to protect the environment and people living near mining operations. This was what made many anti-MTR activists feel that going through legal channels wasn't working, and that resorting to civil disobedience was necessary or at least acceptable. Then, following the November 2008 election, activists saw an accelerating series of things to be hopeful about, including new opportunities in Washington, coal companies' stock prices falling, opposition to coal-fired power plants across the country, and more.

Still, MTR in Appalachia, and the ill effects of coal nationwide, continued unabated. On December 22, 2008, the containment wall around a huge pile of coal ash by a power plant in Tennessee broke, releasing perhaps 500 million gallons of toxic waste into tributaries of the Tennessee River. This was an even bigger disaster than the coal-slurry spill in Inez, Kentucky, in 2000. But unlike then, the spill in Tennessee was big news all over the United States, including the front page of the *New York Times*. Follow-up coverage highlighted the dangers of hundreds of piles of coal ash across the country. Senate hearings were called. Incoming

President Barack Obama's choice for EPA head, Lisa Jackson, promised to assess the safety of every coal-ash dump in the United States. Coal had clearly arrived as a national issue, one routinely covered in news reports everywhere.

The reaction to all this among anti-MTR activists—to both the hopeful signs and the continuing devastation—was to push even harder, on multiple fronts. Efforts would be made to influence the appointments and priorities of the incoming Obama administration and Democrat-dominated Congress. At the same time, activists would ramp up civil disobedience and direct action intended to hold coal and power companies accountable, to keep MTR in the public eye, and to make clear to politicians and others that greenwashing would not be accepted.

In coalfield Appalachia, the good news/bad news tug of war played out especially vividly in the Coal River valley. There, the fate of Coal River Mountain, the last mostly intact large mountain bordering the valley near Whitesville, hung in the balance.

Massey had long planned to strip-mine some 6,600 acres of the mountain, divided into four contiguous permit areas with a total of 18 proposed valley fills. For none of these sites, though, had Massey yet obtained a valley-fill permit. The mountain was thus slated for destruction, but still a ways off from where mining could begin in earnest.

In 2006 an engineering study had determined that Coal River Mountain had excellent potential for a large-scale wind farm—as many as 220 2-megawatt turbines, enough to provide electricity to 150,000 homes. To pursue that potential, to drum up support for a wind farm on the mountain, the Coal River Wind Project was launched by CRMW, OVEC, and others. They also commissioned a study of such a wind project's economic potential.

That study, released in December 2008, documented that "a wind farm would produce greater economic benefits to citizens of Raleigh County," more jobs and higher local earnings and tax revenues, than strip-mining the site would produce—even without taking into account the health and environmental costs that mining there would incur. In addition, a wind farm would leave nearly all of the mountain's forest intact, allowing its continued use as an economic and cultural commons, where local people could—as they had done for generations—hunt, pick berries, and forage for mushrooms, greens, nuts, and medicinal herbs. All those benefits would continue indefinitely, as long as the wind blows. MTR operations would end on the mountain in fifteen years or so, leaving a flattened, treeless landscape with much-reduced wind potential and insufficient stability for installing large turbines. However, the study noted:

> While wind provides greater economic benefits to the citizens of Raleigh County, a final decision about mountaintop removal rests with the landowners and leaseholders on Coal River Mountain, who are concerned with the value of their investments. This report computes the present value of revenues to landowners generated by a wind farm versus mountaintop removal. Wind farm revenues were found to be much lower than those realized through mountaintop removal. In addition, currently held coal leases on Coal River Mountain stay in existence until "all minable coal" is extracted, further inhibiting surface developments like wind farms. It is therefore no surprise that both landholding companies and leaseholders have pursued coal mining as opposed to wind farm development on Coal River Mountain. Without societal intervention, these companies will pursue mountaintop removal in order to provide the greatest private profits possible from the land and coal resources on Coal River Mountain.

Seeking that "societal intervention," CRMW's Chuck Nelson handed a copy of the study to Gov. Joe Manchin at a statewide "energy summit" on December 9, 2008. By then, the issue was becoming more urgent. In September, Massey had been given permission to dump overburden around the edge of the Brushy Fork slurry pond, adjacent to one of the Coal River Mountain permit areas. On November 20, they got permission to remove overburden from that permit area, the Bee Tree site. The way was now clear for Massey to start strip mining on the Bee Tree portion of Coal River Mountain, dumping the resulting rubble around the edge of the Brushy Fork pond instead of in a valley fill.

Such mining would require blasting quite close to the huge pond, first for building a haul road then for the mining itself. The Brushy Fork pond, much larger than the slurry pond up above Marsh Fork Elementary School, covers hundreds of acres, is held back by an earthen dam 900 feet high, is permitted to hold up to 9 billion gallons of sludge, and is located above a honeycomb of old underground mines. Blasting at Bee Tree not only would somewhat reduce the site's wind potential, but also ran the risk of causing a catastrophic flood by cracking the pond's floor, much like the big flood at Inez in 2000. But Brushy Fork is a much, much bigger impoundment, and its failure could result in a much, much bigger catastrophe. Massey's own disaster contingency plan, required of it after the Inez spill, supposes a wall of sludge forty feet high, moving down the Coal River valley, mile after mile after mile.

On January 6, 2009, Raleigh County commissioners, having been formally presented a copy of the wind study, refused to support or endorse the project. Nor, apparently, was support from Gov. Manchin forthcoming. The very next day, local activists discovered that Massey had started pre-mining clearing of trees, but not yet any blasting, at the Bee Tree site. Having run out of other options, and feeling urgency, they began to make plans for direct action.

For this, they had the support of Mike Roselle, a founding Earth Firster with decades of experience with nonviolent civil disobedience, and his Climate Ground Zero (CGZ) campaign. Back in 2007, Mike and others had started CGZ to apply civil disobedience to the problem of global climate change. In 2008, they held a camp in Montana, addressing coal strip mines out west. They intended to organize along a train route there, where coal was carried to power plants nearer the West Coast. "I guess the timing wasn't right," Mike says. "People were interested, we trained a bunch of people, but we couldn't get people to commit to the actions."

So in June 2008, after the camp, Mike came to Appalachia, to Larry Gibson's Fourth of July gathering. He'd known Larry and other people in Appalachia's coalfields since 2005, but hadn't spent a lot of time there. Mike suggested moving the CGZ campaign to the Coal River valley, and the local folks he was talking with encouraged that.

By this time, Hillary Hosta was spending much of her time in Canada, where she has family, and in fall of 2008, Mike took over the house where Hillary had been living since 2005, one of a row of four houses in Rock Creek across the Coal River from Rt. 3. Hillary's house was in roughly habitable condition, but the other three houses were in *very* rough shape. Mike and others he recruited set about renovating the houses to serve as headquarters and base camp for CGZ, a place for both long-term and short-term campaign volunteers to live and work. The volunteers would both launch civil-disobedience actions and help with other local efforts to end MTR and address local problems caused by mining.

"If you're gonna deal with climate change," Mike explains, "you have to deal with coal, the burning and mining of coal. And if you're gonna deal with coal, you're gonna have to deal with mountaintop removal because it's the least efficient, most carbon-intensive way of mining coal—also the most environmentally destructive way. The key part is that your opponents are these coal-state politicians—senators, legislators, governors—and they have put a roadblock up for any meaningful new laws or regulations to deal with climate change. Mountaintop removal is their sacred cow. They do not want to lose on this, they think that's just the first domino. And they're right. But if we can't stop mountaintop removal, we're kidding ourselves to think that we can do anything to address the climate crisis.

"So what [we're] trying to do here is to really put these guys under the spotlight, put some real pressure on them. Because once this logjam breaks, on mountaintop removal, then a whole set of other possibilities arise. But if we can't do anything here, if we get stopped here, then the whole climate reform is stuck in the mud. So here we're going after the biggest coal-mining state in the nation, with the most hard-core political support, going up against the biggest, meanest companies, and we're right in the middle of their territory. That's, to me, how you get pressure. Because without an indigenous revolt against these conditions, you can't build a national movement. It has to coalesce around what the local people are doing to fight it themselves, what kind of help they need. If they fall, if they fold, then it's very difficult to run a campaign.

"This is ground zero for climate in the U.S. right now. I can't think of a more important struggle. I can't think of a more urgent struggle."

Judy Bonds agrees. "This is more than just about mountaintop removal," she says. "This is about climate change and a transition to a clean, renewable future for our kids. I don't think they could manage any kind of legislation or movement in America without the ugly poster child of mountaintop removal. 'Climate Ground Zero' is indeed the correct name for this. Everything that's a change for the better, a transition [toward] a livable Earth for our kids, is all tied up in West Virginia and Kentucky and Tennessee and southwest Virginia."

By January 2009, three of the CGZ houses were at least approximately habitable, "and that's when [Massey] went after Coal River Mountain," Mike says. "That had been kind of the line in the sand."

It was Rory McIlmoil, who, since the summer before, had been working with CRMW to organize the wind project, "who really decided it was time for action," Mike recalls. "But he had never done one before. Boy, did he take to it, like a duck to water. So he was our action coordinator for that action. He [with the help of several others] planned deployment, did the scouting, and we [at CGZ] just played a support role."

Shortly before 7 AM on February 3, 2009, Rory, Mike, and three other activists locked themselves to a bulldozer and an excavator on the Bee Tree mine site, demanding a halt to all operations connected with strip mining on the mountain. Before locking themselves to the equipment, they had planned to raise up a model windmill on the site, a gesture inspired by that of the soldiers who raised the American flag at Iwo Jima during World War II. Unfortunately, the windmill, made of PVC pipe and other less-than-durable materials, broke. Two large banners were unfurled without a hitch, though. One read: "Save Coal River Mountain," the other "Windmills Not Toxic Spills."

By 8 AM, the lockdown had been discovered by a worker arriving to start up some of the equipment. According to Mike, the worker looked at the situation and said: "Well, you guys ain't gonna be here long." The protesters responded: "OK, it's cold, that's fine with us." (Sleet and freezing rain the day before had turned to snow and colder temperatures overnight. Several inches of snow covered the mine site that morning.) "It was a casual, friendly exchange," Mike recalls.

The protesters decided it was time to let the police know they were there, and sent word to supporters down in Coal River valley to do so. Other supporters hidden in the woods nearby watched and took photographs to document whatever happened. One photojournalist remained with the protesters.

Around 9 AM, a helicopter, rented to document the protest, flew over, with photographers inside taking pictures. Police were milling around. The protesters were still locked to the equipment. Workers stood nearby, looking on. Having the helicopter overhead "was really nice," Mike says, "because the miners knew that we were filming from the air at that point, so we knew that they weren't going to do anything bad for us. And they were all very friendly. The miner guys stood around and made crude remarks and violent threats—but nothing mean. They just said they would like to run over us with their machines and stuff—but they didn't say it in a real *bad* way."

The police stated their intention to cut the locks, arrest the protesters for trespassing, and take them to the state police station at the southern end of Whitesville. Six people were arrested, including the photojournalist who'd remained at the site. In addition to the photographer and Mike and Rory, two of those arrested, Matt Noerpel and Glen Collins, were veterans of MJS 2005; Matt had stayed on and worked in Coal River valley ever since. The other arrestee was James "Guin"

McGuiness, an old friend and colleague of Mike's, who'd arrived in Rock Creek just the day before.

Shortly after 10 AM, several dozen local people and outside supporters gathering at CRMW's office in Whitesville learned that the six arrestees had been cited for trespassing and were about to be released. Cars were dispatched to the police station to pick them up and bring them to the office, where they were greeted with cheers, congratulations, and food. And then everyone got organized to carpool to the other end of town, to the front entrance of Marfork Coal, the Massey subsidiary responsible for the Brushy Fork impoundment as well as for Bee Tree and the other proposed strip sites on Coal River Mountain.

The police had so far been remarkably low-key: They didn't hand-cuff the arrestees when they escorted them off the mine site, and the six left the police station carrying not only their citations but also the banners they'd displayed at the back-country action. "They were gonna confiscate the banners," Mike said, "but they left them outside [the police station], and after we all got cited they were just lying in a pile, so we just grabbed them, figuring, well, if they want them, they can call us."

Still, by the time the arrestees were released, an unusual number of policemen had gathered at the station. They'd been told in advance that there'd be a protest at Marfork's front gate at 1 PM today, but nothing about this morning's action up on the mine site. Apparently they didn't know quite what to expect next, but wanted to be prepared.

By 12:45, close to fifty people had gathered where the road to Marfork's headquarters meets Rt. 3, right across from the police station. Five police cars drove up the road toward the guard shack at the entrance. After a morning of clear skies, snow flurries were starting up.

Rory McIlmoil, holding the big banners used earlier in the day, looked for a good place to display them. He eyed a line of railroad cars filled with coal, parked just across the tracks—a perfect (and perfectly illegal) place to hang them. Tempting as it was (and Rory certainly was tempted), it wasn't the action that people were there for this afternoon.

Rory settled instead for laying them out on the ground. Meanwhile, at the side of the road, protesters held signs and smaller banners so that passing cars could see them: "Clean Coal, Dirty Lie," "Save Coal River Mountain."

The reaction from passing cars was far different from what protesters had experienced there in the summer of 2005, when the entire valley seemed to radiate hostility. No one yelled at the protesters today, no one gave them the finger, no one tried to run Bo Webb or anyone else down. A few drivers gave friendly honks. Some slowed down to read the signs. The strongest negative reaction displayed was drivers looking stonily ahead as though the protest just wasn't there. The protesters themselves were cheerful, upbeat, happy, confident.

"The hostility is not there," Judy Bonds affirmed. "I think we're beginning to feel a change in things, a feeling about what's happening on this river. I think that with the Obama election and the national trend of renewable energy, maybe these people [in the valley] are beginning to realize that we do want sustainable communities, and this is the way to get it. It's a real future," not just some hippie fantasy. "I don't feel hatred coming from them."

Teasing a young woman nearby, Judy added: "And when you've got pretty young girls waving at you," as most of those holding signs and banners that day happened to be, "of course you're going to wave back. That's the key to it."

"So you saying that they're *bait*?" a bystander asked.

"No, I'm saying that these girls can change minds."

Shortly before 1 PM, several police cars drove back from the guard shack and parked near the railroad tracks. Several state troopers walked toward the tracks. Bo, acting as police liaison that day, approached the tracks from the other side.

The trooper in charge, Sgt. Michael Smith, recognized Bo and said: "We're supposed to have six inches of snow by six o'clock! You know that?"

Bo responded: "We want to be quick." Everyone laughed.

Down to business, the trooper asked Bo: "What do y'all want to do?"

"Are you guys establishing the property line right here?" Bo asked, pointing to the railroad tracks. "We weren't sure. We thought it started up there [at the guard shack]."

"Well to be honest with you, I did too," the trooper said, "but I was informed of my wrong."

"We need to know where the line is—"

"From what I understand, the tracks."

That settled, the troopers wanted to know if many people were intending to be arrested there that day. Bo said: "I don't think there'll be that many, but there'll be a few."

"We can go across the road," the trooper said, to the police substation. "However you want to do it."

Speaking of Lorelei (pronounced "Lorella") Scarbro, a local woman who lives up a hollow by Coal River Mountain, who has been very actively involved with the wind project, and who intended to lead the protest, Bo said: "I think she wants to read a statement, and then she wants to attempt to deliver it."

"We have somebody here prepared to accept one, for the company," one of the troopers said, pointing toward a civilian car parked off to the side of the road on the Massey side of the railroad tracks. "But I don't think it's going to be who she wants."

Bo suggested that the protesters would "kind of mass over here," on the legal side of the tracks, "and step up here" to the tracks.

"I got no problem," Sgt. Smith responded. "Y'all need something, let us know."

The protesters circled up to hear a few words and a prayer offered by Allen Johnson, director of Christians for the Mountains. He told the crowd that the Biblical verse: "The earth is the Lord's" means that we're called to use the land "in a way that's supportive of God's purpose, [with] a respect for all Creation—the land, the water, the animals, the people that live there, the people that are going to live there in the future. When the land and the people are treated as holy, God is honored. When the land is treated as just something to make money at, for greed, then it is an abomination [against] God's purpose." He reminded them of the story of the moneychangers Jesus confronted at the Temple, business-men who had turned a place intended for the worship of God into a place to make money. Jesus overturned the moneychangers' tables that day and drove them out of the Temple, putting them out of business temporarily. "That," Allen told the crowd, "was a direct action."

After prayer, the crowd approached the railroad tracks. Lorelei, a grandmother and widow of an underground coal miner, read out the letter to Massey. It asked that Massey stop work at the Bee Tree site, especially any blasting. "Directly in the path of a possible spill [from the Brushy Fork impoundment] is a Head Start center, our senior center, and the town of Whitesville, with the potential for loss of lives in the west end of Raleigh County and dozens of miles into Boone County," Lorelei read.

The letter also called upon the state Department of Environmental Protection "to suspend the surface mining permits on Coal River Mountain. The DEP has failed to properly regulate sludge dams, accord-ing to a recent federal report, and halting mountaintop removal on Coal River Mountain is in the best interest of our communities and the sur-vival of our future generations.

"We believe there is a higher and better use for [these areas] per-mitted for mountaintop removal…which does not include the dangers associated with blasting close to a toxic sludge dam. That project is the Coal River Wind Project."

As the state trooper had predicted, Lorelei wasn't satisfied with pre-senting the letter to the Massey underling who'd come to accept it, but instead wanted to walk on back to Marfork's corporate office and seek someone in authority there. The Massey representative wouldn't allow this, and the police were clear that if she insisted on crossing the line she'd be arrested. And so she was, along with seven others, including

Vern Haltom, Larry Gibson, Chuck Nelson, and Allen Johnson. All were treated much the same way as the morning's arrestees: no handcuffs, no formal booking, just a citation for trespassing.

The action up on Coal River Mountain that day marked the first time since the Mountain Justice campaign began more than four years earlier that nonviolent civil disobedience was successfully carried out up on an active mine site, not just at the front gate. It was unlikely to be the last. Nor was Coal River Mountain the only potential target for such action in and around the valley (an especially "target-rich environment," as CGZ volunteers were fond of saying) and elsewhere in Appalachia's coalfields.

Now more than ever, with the Bush administration ended and a new political era beginning, anti-MTR activists felt the time was right for civil disobedience to catalyze an end to mountaintop removal and other harmful mining practices. "If we are willing and brave enough to step up to the plate now and make our voices be heard, I think we have an opportunity here to do something to end this," Bo told me that week. Lorelei and others in the valley noted that they'd tried everything short of civil disobedience in their efforts to save Coal River Mountain, and needed to take this next step if they were to have any chance of success.

"Take it to the national level" was how Judy Bonds put it. "The only way to end steep-slope strip mining is to do it on a national level, with a federal law that is actually enforced." What's needed, she said, is to "force the [Obama] administration now to recognize the fact that this [opposition to MTR] is just not going to stop, it's going to keep getting bigger. There's more and more people who've heard about mountaintop removal and find it absolutely disgusting." The civil disobedience at Coal River Mountain was intended to aid this process and increase its momentum. Additional actions in the near future would keep that momentum going.

On March 2, Judy, Bo, Lorelei, Larry, Chuck, and others from Coal

River valley joined thousands of people aiming to "take it to the national level" in a mass gathering and march to the coal-fired power plant supplying the U.S. Capitol building, a few blocks away, in Washington, D.C. The march's broad focus on "climate justice" brought together a wide array of activists dealing with various aspects of climate "injustice"—from global-warming protesters to public-health advocates concerned about air pollution. On other occasions, I'd heard Mike Roselle talk about "building allies through the whole chain of custody" of coal, from mining to burning to dealing with its wastes and its effects on health and climate. The D.C. gathering offered both a glimpse of how very extensive that alliance has become, and reassurance that coalfield resistance to MTR not only wasn't being eclipsed by other concerns but was being kept front-and-center. Leading the march were representatives of communities directly affected by coal—from Navaho homesteaders, to people living near the D.C. and other power plants, to anti-MTR activists from all over Appalachia. When I called Larry Gibson's attention to the thousands of people marching behind him, he looked teary-eyed.

Although Larry undoubtedly found this moment emotionally moving, the tears were probably mostly from the cold weather that day, well below freezing, following an unusual late-winter storm the night before that had covered the city with half a foot of snow. It got colder as the day wore on.

When the march reached the power plant, hundreds of people blocked all of its gates, stamping their feet and shivering. March organizers passed out cups of hot chocolate. Dozens of police officers stood by and watched. Organizers of the event had been planning for "the largest mass civil disobedience for climate in U.S. history." But the police declined to arrest them. "It's a whole lot easier to get arrested where I live," Mike Roselle noted.

In fact, at that point, Mike had already been arrested three times that year in West Virginia, first on Coal River Mountain on February 3, then twice more on the Edwight MTR site up above Bo Webb's house in

Naoma later that month. According to Bo, "blasting above my home began to escalate right after the February 3 action." Later that month, at an unrelated public hearing, Bo "approached Mike Fury of the West Virginia DEP and his supervisor Keith Porterfield. I asked Mike Fury to come down and walk up Clay's Branch with me so I could show him the boulders, flyrock, and rubble that were coming off the mine site area. He refused, saying he had sore knees and 'I'm not going to walk beneath a blast area.' I thought that pretty arrogant, being that some of us citizens live beneath that blast area." On February 16 and then again on February 25, Mike and Guin McGuinness walked up onto the mine site above Clay's Branch, each time blocking a road and displaying a banner. On March 5, just a few days after the march in Washington, five more activists affiliated with Climate Ground Zero were arrested hanging a banner at the site. Bo himself, in Washington, "showed the blasting video [footage] I had been taking to staffers in [Senator Robert] Byrd's office, [Senator Jay] Rockefeller's office, and [Congressman Nick] Rahall's office. I then went to the federal OSM and filed a formal complaint. Late March I received a call from the OSM field office in Beckley. They said they would come down and walk up the mountain for a look. The results were four violations and suspension of operations in Clay's Branch until the debris was cleaned up and returned to the permitted property it came from. That was April 4. Massey immediately moved their blasting crew out of Clay's Branch and began blasting around the bend from Clay's Branch into Pettry Bottom," a hollow adjacent to another part of the huge mine site. "Whether the enforcement action had anything to do with the protest and c.d. [civil disobedience] I have no way of knowing for sure, but I strongly suspect it most certainly did."

On April 16, three more activists affiliated with CGZ, together with two photojournalists, were arrested on the same mine site, up at the head of Clay's Branch, hanging a banner reading: "EPA Stop MTR." Massey's move from one side of a mine site to another wasn't going to stop the protests.

Anti-MTR protesters had, from the very beginning of the Mountain Justice campaign, been keenly aware of the possibility of being met by violence—especially in West Virginia, and especially if they took their protests onto active mine sites and faced Massey workers there. Following the first CGZ back-country protest in February, up on Coal River Mountain, police warned Massey management that worker attacks on protesters would not be tolerated—would, in fact, be prosecuted. If protesters showed up on a mine site, they were told, the proper thing to do was to call the police, who'd come deal with the situation themselves. News of this warning lit up the valley's gossip circuits and soon reached Climate Ground Zero and its local supporters. All of a sudden, anti-MTR protests up on mine sites seemed a lot less unreasonably risky.

So Massey, warned off by the police from encouraging its employees to bully protesters on mine sites, went after the protesters in court. In late February, at Massey's request, a judge in Raleigh County issued a temporary restraining order (TRO) barring individuals arrested in actions on Massey mine sites earlier that month from any further trespassing or interference with Massey property or business operations. This TRO was written very broadly, with language suggesting that anyone who knew about the order, even if just by reading about it in a news report, would also be subject to it. Shortly thereafter, Massey announced its intention to sue protesters for damages as well. In the weeks and months ahead, additional arrestees at other protests would become named targets of this or similar TROs.

The lawsuits underscored certain advantages that CGZ offered to the local campaign against MTR. Specifically, CGZ provided a civil-disobedience component in ways intended to complement other groups' and individuals' efforts at lobbying, local organizing, lawsuits, or whatnot, and to protect those others from legal liability. For CRMW or any established institution—for any individual with assets to lose, for that matter—involvement in direct action carries the risk of "a lot of liability," Mike notes. "You're an entity that can be sued, that can really be harmed by these big companies. If you've got a business, if you own a home, it's going to be difficult. So we [at CGZ] work with a group of activists [who own little or no seizable assets] that we've been working with [all over the country] for twenty-five years," building up from that core with new, mostly younger people coming in to join them. "The young people are just as important, with their enthusiasm and their courage. But none of us are afraid of losing our livelihoods or homestead. We don't have one." Mike is speaking of the front persons for CGZ here. A good many others involved in this campaign do have assets that could be at risk, and choose not to take on arrestable roles. Since pulling off an action typically takes several times as many supporters as arrestees, that's just fine.

In practice, action planning and execution at CGZ generally worked like this: Out of the mix of older and younger activists living at the CGZ houses, augmented by short-term volunteers staying at the houses and a network of supporters from around the region and beyond, a group of people would coalesce around a common idea of doing a particular civil-disobedience action together. That "affinity group" would consist of people taking arrestable as well as non-arrestable roles, including scouts, media and police liaisons, and people responsible for communication, food, and transportation. "The affinity group gets to plan their own action," Mike says. "They're responsible for their own strategy. And as long as they're willing to abide by the guidelines [of no violence, no property damage, and a clear focus on ending MTR], then they have a great deal of autonomy in how they want to express themselves," and CGZ supports them in seeing their action through.

The wider network, local, regional, and national, supporting CGZ has been extraordinarily diverse. "We're working with a lot of retired miners," Mike notes. "Military veterans. Church-going people. And they mix well with our more alternative-lifestyle types. They understand how important each other is to the campaign. There's been a lot of harmony and a lot of bonding. And our group just keeps getting bigger and stronger. We haven't had a lot of the divisions and disagreements over strategy and tactics here that I've seen in other campaigns. I think a lot of that is because we're just so damn busy moving forward we don't have time for all that stuff. We know what we gotta do every morning when we get up. It's not something we have to have a meeting about."

Partly out of respect for that diversity, CGZ has intentionally supported both back-country and front-gate protest actions. Not everyone is able and willing to do a back-country action; front-gate actions offer a broader range of opportunity for even less-than-spry individuals to take a stand, with or without risking arrest. "One is not better than the other," Mike emphasizes. "They're both very powerful." However, the fact that actions were now actually been taking place on mine sites has "had such an effect in West Virginia. Even the local activists here, some of whom were ready to go up with guns blazing, never thought that they could go up and chain themselves to a piece of equipment. But then when we did it, they were going: 'Of course we can!' And without that local support, we couldn't do that. We couldn't just come in here from California and get on that site. We need eyes and ears, we need people to explain the hazards. And we've had that—even though it is increasing the pressure on [local people who speak out against MTR]. I've really been impressed that they have been willing to weather this, that they understand that it's necessary, and it's helpful. Without that, we wouldn't be able to do this."

Ironically, the back-country actions have apparently made one group of local people significantly safer—the miners. According to Judy Bonds, one of Massey's workers told her daughter, at a chance meeting in a convenience store on Rt. 3, that "ever since they've been protesting [back on the mine sites] we've been going by Ps and Qs. We've been having to do it by the book, whereas before we never did. I will say that your mom has made our workplace safer.

"But I don't look for him to say that in front of a bunch of his cohorts," Judy adds.

One other change worth noting is this: In years past, the civil-disobedience campaign against MTR, including but not limited to MJ, had been a loosely affiliated set of individuals and groups that tended to plan and execute one action, then another, sequentially. By early 2009, various subgroups of the anti-MTR movement were habitually working on multiple actions *simultaneously*. In West Virginia particularly, activists focusing on their own current action were typically aware, more or less vaguely, that others were working on other projects—and they were comfortable with this, trusting others to do good things without needing to know the details before extending that trust.

The news coming out of Washington in those early months of 2009 was mostly hopeful for anti-MTR activists:

- The Obama administration took an early step toward tougher controls on mercury emissions from coal-fired power plants;
- The EPA announced its intention to propose regulations for CO_2 emissions from such plants;
- The Clean Water Protection Act was re-introduced in Congress, along with a parallel measure in the Senate, and each steadily gained co-sponsors;
- The EPA announced plans to study and regulate coal ash storage at power plants;
- The EPA ruled that CO_2 and other greenhouse gases are a danger to public health and thus subject to regulation under the Clean Air Act.

The most encouraging news of all came on March 24, when the EPA set aside close to 200 pending MTR permits for stricter review of their likely effects on streams and wetlands. At the same time, the EPA put on hold two permits that the Army Corps of Engineers was about to issue for MTR projects in West Virginia and Kentucky. (It was *not* encouraging that, in response to howls of protest from the coal industry, the EPA, in a follow-up statement, said that it didn't expect that most of the permits under review would "raise environmental concerns.")

Some of the news from Washington, though, was downright disheartening. By May, for example, it was obvious that proposed legislation to address climate change had become bogged down (or captured) by large business interests, including the coal industry, determined to profit from rather than be reined in by it.

Worse still, half a year after Obama's election, none of the "hopeful" news about coal had done anything beyond excite hope. Strip mining in Appalachia was still going full throttle. In early May, extensive flooding in Mingo County, just south and west of the Coal River valley, evidenced MTR's continuing devastation of the region's land and people. Jack Spadaro, flying over the area hit by floods, estimated that about 60 percent of the landscape there had previously been damaged and left vulnerable by MTR activities, including road building, open mine sites, valley fills, and slurry ponds. God may have sent the rain, but it was MTR that had destroyed the land's ability to absorb it.

Then, on Thursday, May 14, the EPA sent a letter to a West Virginia congressman stating that it had approved forty-two of forty-eight MTR permits they'd so far "reviewed" since March 24. Activists familiar with the permitting process noted that not nearly enough time had elapsed since then for anyone to go through all the paperwork for these permits, let alone conduct any real investigation. The sense that this was a rubber stamp, rather than a genuine review, was furthered by the EPA's public statement that it had decided not to comment on or explain its decisions to approve the forty-two permits "after consideration of the nature and extent of project impacts. Twenty-eight of the projects have two or fewer valley fills.… None have more than six."

MJ activists assembling for their annual summer camp the following weekend, once again in Pipestem, West Virginia, were outraged. "So much for hope," wrote the activist who posted the EPA's statement on the MJ organizers' listserv. In addition to venting their outrage that week at camp, they got to work.

On Saturday, May 23, several dozen activists, including MJ newcomers and old-timers as well as CGZ volunteers, deployed an ambitious three-part action in and around Coal River valley. (A fourth part— unfurling a banner from the coal silo next to Marsh Fork Elementary School—had been dropped from the lineup when the logistics proved more difficult than expected, and the available pool of back-country activists found themselves stretched too thin.)

Shortly before dawn, eight activists staged a lockdown around a giant dump truck on one of the mine sites overlooked by Kayford Mountain. Meanwhile, two young women in hazmat suits launched an inflatable rowboat onto the Brushy Fork impoundment to float a sixty-foot banner reading "No more toxic sludge!" (They were charged with littering as well as trespass.) Several hours later, at Marfork's front entrance, seven more protesters were arrested for trespassing when they crossed over the railroad tracks and approached the guard shack.

The dispatcher called by supporters of the protesters to let police know about two of the backwoods actions obviously wasn't accustomed to hearing from callers asking police to go arrest their friends. "Do your friends *want* to get in trouble?" she asked, incredulous. "Well, not exactly," the caller explained—but they are expecting the police to come arrest them.

Although none of the seventeen arrestees that day was charged with any sort of jailable offense (simple trespass and littering incur only fines), the Brushy Fork paddlers and front-gate arrestees were held in jail on $2,000 cash-only bonds. Since the magistrate who set the bond refused to allow use of a bailbondsman, and the arrests happened on Memorial Day weekend when judges weren't available and getting that much cash in hand was cumbersome, several remained in jail for days. The last of them were freed on Tuesday, when they could finally see a judge, who released them without bail money being paid.

All of those arrests took place in Raleigh County. The Kayford Mountain protesters, arrested and processed in neighboring Boone County, were released without bail. However, instead of an escalation in bond money and jail time, their cases marked a penalty escalation of another sort: The total fines and fees imposed for the Kayford Eight would ultimately exceed $15,000.

As bail, jail, and fine penalties for arrestees escalated in West Virginia's criminal courts, the Massey lawsuits continued to move forward in civil courts. In early May, Massey lawyers asked Raleigh County Judge Robert

Burnside to find Mike Roselle, photojournalist Antrim Caskey, the five arrested at the Edwight action on March 5, and those arrested at the Edwight action on March 16 all in contempt of the previously imposed TRO. Judge Burnside ruled that Mike and the March 5 arrestees were not in contempt—but that the March 16 arrestees were, since Antrim was with them, she was a named party on the TRO following her previous arrest at Edwight with Mike and Guin, and the others were "acting in concert" with her. Burnside made it clear that simply encouraging people to do actions did not constitute a violation of the TRO. (Even in West Virginia coal country, the rights of free speech and free association noted in the U.S. Constitution sometimes prevail.) Those found in contempt were assessed $500 in civil fines plus damages, which had the potential to be huge. Specification of dollar amounts for damages was deferred to a later date, but Massey lawyers indicated they'd at least be asking for $18,000 in attorneys' fees. Those targeted by the suit immediately sought to appeal the ruling.

At the beginning of June, when the appeal process had barely begun, Judge Burnside granted an injunction based on the TRO. The injunction applied only in Raleigh County, only to the Massey subsidiaries where protest actions had occurred, and only to parties named in the lawsuit and those acting "in concert" with them (i.e., on an action involving trespassing together). The penalties for violating this injunction would be up to a $1,000 fine plus damages. Other lawsuits against protesters acting in other counties and at the sites of other Massey subsidiaries remained pending and would be added to as other protests unfolded.

The lawsuits made it potentially very costly for protesters specified in the injunctions to participate in further actions. However, neither the lawsuits nor the escalating bail, jail, and fine penalties discouraged at least some of the named individuals from seeking other targets. Nor did they discourage others from taking action, on and off Massey property. "We haven't seen [any of] that put a damper on our recruiting yet," Mike Roselle told me in June. "When we sit down and try to explain what the risks are, people understand it. And they have come to the conclusion that it's a bigger risk to do nothing, that they have to do something. It's a personal thing."

On June 19, four such protesters climbed onto an enormous dragline at Massey's Twilight strip mine, a few miles west of Coal River valley, on the other side of Cherry Pond Mountain—or rather, on what's left of that mountain after years of MTR there. The protesters had intended to unfurl a large banner there and occupy the machine for the day, while a "B team" of activists on the ground beside the dragline engaged and distracted mine workers, and photographers took pictures. What actually happened was rather less than the plans called for.

Already with this action, other things had not gone as planned. The protest had originally been conceived as a splashy media stunt with actor Woody Harrelson up on the dragline with the climb team, all resting in a giant hammock suspended above the dragline's even more gigantic boom, chatting away on phones with reporters alerted to the story by the action's media team. The action had to be delayed several times to fit Harrelson's schedule, eventually pushing it so late that his training time with the other climbers had to be shorter than intended so that the action could take place before others involved had to fly back home. (The action was run mostly by former and present RAN and Greenpeace organizers based outside coalfield Appalachia. About a dozen of the action's arrestees and support personnel were flown in from afar for it.) And then the action was delayed yet again when lightning and rain were forecast for the rescheduled day of deployment—although as it turned out, the weather that day was fine. By that time, there was a good bit of uneasiness about Harrelson's shortened training time and his readiness to go up with the climb team. Harrelson decided to leave, and another climber left as well, to deal with a family emergency. It became apparent that getting that big and very heavy hammock up there was no longer a practical option, if it ever had been. And so the action went forward with scaled-back personnel and plans.

On the day of the action, several hours before dawn, four climb-ers, the B team of ground support personnel, and two photographers were dropped off at a deserted spot on a road in the vicinity of the dragline. After a hike through woods, up a steep slope, to the edge of the active mining area, everyone paused. The climbers put on their har-nesses. They couldn't see the dragline yet, and would have to approach it across an open mining area with little cover. After a bit of a rest, they all "headed on out into the war zone, a moonscape of destruction," Charles Suggs, one of the climbers, later recalled.

As they approached the dragline, "the B team pulled out their huge banner, and [the climbers] moved away from them to go toward the dragline itself. There were a bunch of workers up there—maybe twenty, thirty. [The dragline] was down for maintenance, and I guess it was about shift-change time. We didn't engage, didn't make eye contact, just walked right past a lot of them and got to the dragline. We were leaving it to the B team to really try and get their attention.

"We got to the ladder and started climbing up it, and workers were trying to pull us down off of it. I know when I was climbing up onto it a worker grabbed my arm and tried to yank me down off of the dragline." Charles wriggled that "arm out of his hands, and got up on it," all four of them in a line, heading for the dragline's boom.

At that moment, "a worker [came] out of the door on the side, and he stood right there in the walkway, where we couldn't get past. Someone on the ground said: 'Just let 'em go.' And, like he was leading the way, he just walked along the path toward where we needed to go." The worker opened and entered another door into the side of the machine, around the corner, "and we just kept on going.

"We started walking up the boom," heading for its upper end, where they'd climb out onto the cables that allow operators to control the boom and its enormous bucket. "The idea was to get on those lines, between the tip of the boom and the top of the tower, hang out up there, put up a banner, stay there for a while." The banner said "Stop Mountaintop Removal" and had the RAN logo on it.

"At this point, there was still nobody following us. So we [got] out to the tip, and the lines were very easy to access from the walkway." Charles pulled out his gear to test it on actual lines, "to see if my safety line would grab on those cables," which of course they'd only been able to guess at during training. The lines sloped away down from the tip of the boom, and he wanted to be sure they could stop themselves from zipping away forty feet down the line to the first spacer between that line and its neighbor. "It grabbed really well, and that was good."

"Melissa [one of the other climbers] came over, and we started getting up on the cables," Charles and Melissa on one cable, Chelsea and Lynn on another, parallel cable. "We started going out," down the length of their cable. "We threw our lines across [to Chelsea and Lynn] and were waiting a while for the banner to come across." Bit by bit, they moved down, securing the unfurling banner to the dragline's cables.

While the climbers were unfurling and attaching the banner, a police officer came up on a ladder that led to a connection between the boom and the cables. He told them he was afraid of heights and didn't want to be up there, and asked them to come down. They told him they would, but not yet, it would be a little while. "I told him I owed him a beer," Charles says, "and Lynn said, 'If you don't drink, I'll buy you ice cream.' He went on down."

A little while later, when the banner was maybe two-thirds of the way unfurled, another police officer came up and yelled at them, "telling us to get down right now. Some workers came up too, with harnesses on and safety gear, to climb." The workers headed along the boom to a part of the banner that was drooping a good bit between the cables, cut the banner with something like a razor blade, "and threw [the part that they'd cut] down on the ground. And they pulled on the line that was attached to the cable right next to my safety gear, so when they yanked on it, they yanked on me." Charles said: " 'What are you doing, pulling on me?' They calmed down a little after that, and we chatted some."

Charles started working his way toward other members of his team, who, by this time, had stopped trying to unfurl the severed banner. They instead had cut the word "Stop" out of what was left of the banner and were holding that up. "At that point, Massey had sent a worker out on the line after us. And the police allowed that." The climbers decided they "should go down, rather than risk more people coming up after us." And so they were all arrested.

As with the May 23 actions, the magistrate demanded a cash-only bond, adding up to about $10,000 for all the arrestees. The four climbers sat in jail for about twenty-four hours; everyone else was bonded out that same day. A key difference this time was that, although all of the charges were misdemeanors, some carried the possibility of jail time.

Among the fourteen arrestees that day, eight ground-support personnel and two photographers were charged with trespass and conspiracy. The four climbers were charged with trespass, conspiracy, fleeing on foot, littering, and battery. The battery charge—a misdemeanor for "unwanted touching" when the line of climbers encountered the worker on the walkway on their way up the rig—was particularly worrisome for a campaign committed to nonviolence.

Charles didn't know whether the climber at the front of the line might have touched this worker, but he knows that he didn't do so himself and that they certainly didn't push him out of the way. "There was definitely no shoving out of the way. He definitely went under his own power." (The Climate Ground Zero website later listed this as one of their Top 10 events of 2009: "Two young women bump into some strip miners as they make their way up and out onto the 300-foot boom.... Then they get charged with battery. Isn't this a crazy town?")

Ultimately, the dragline protesters agreed to a plea deal with no jail time, but thousands of dollars in fines and court fees. This was a very expensive action indeed, what with plane tickets, motel bills, a lot of gear, food and supplies for several dozen people, and then those fines and fees. The dragline was shut down for only four hours that day.

"In a lot of ways," Mike Roselle told me a few days after the action, "these campaigns are more about the symbolism [than about direct effects]. We may have shut the dragline down for four hours, but that was just four hours. It took us three months [of planning and preparation] to get to that point. It was a tactical victory—we sent a very strong message all the way up to Don Blankenship that we're comin' after him. But in the end it was the symbolism of the action that gave it its most power. So now those kids that are lobbying Congress, those people that are going door to door—they have a lot more hope that this campaign is building momentum, it's getting attention, and we're aggressively fighting back."

A few days later, on Tuesday, June 23, anti-MTR demonstrators returned, once again, to Marsh Fork Elementary School and the Goals Coal facility. The rally and mass arrest planned for that day was, like the dragline action, conceived as a splashy media stunt. (RAN and Greenpeace were much involved in the planning of this event as well.) And indeed, actress Darryl Hannah and climate scientist James Hansen were among those arrested that day. But a less-noticed, arguably more important story that day was this: Compared to the Goals Coal protest four years ago after the first Mountain Justice camp, far more people showed up to protest today—more local people, more people from around the region, more people from all over the country, celebrities included. Close to twice as many people offered themselves up for arrest. The movement against MTR had grown a great deal in strength, reach, influence, and numbers.

That morning, Judy Bonds and a few others arrived at the school hours before the rally was scheduled to start, to make sure Massey supporters didn't block access to the gathering and parking spaces. Police arrived at 10 AM or so, which was when Massey supporters arrived as well. From their arrival, Judy recalls, the Massey supporters were "very belligerent. Very rude. Very violent."

Early in the day, the Massey supporters outnumbered the folks trying to set up for the rally. They chanted at the rally organizers: "This is our state!" and simply "Massey! Massey! Massey!" They approached musicians setting up to play, blasted air horns in the musicians' ears, pulled the plug on equipment, and fiddled with the knobs on the sound system. "We complained to the police," Judy says, "to no avail. The police were badly outnumbered," maybe twelve or fourteen of them compared to a hundred or more Massey folks. "I don't think they had enough people there to control the crowd." In addition to blaring air horns, Massey supporters on motorcycles went round and round just outside the field where the rally was being held, revving their engines.

Judy and Bill Price, who also was helping to organize the event (once again, taking the day off from his official Sierra Club job), herded folks assembling for the rally to the back side of the musicians' platform, then asked the musicians to turn around to face them. "That seemed to really anger the Massey folks even more," Judy says. "It just enraged them."

By then, about even numbers of anti-MTR folks and Massey folks were present, 150 to 175 of each. "Some of them [the Massey folks, maybe twenty of them] were local people," Judy says, "some of them I had never seen in my life. They must have called for Massey workers from Beckley, from Logan, from other areas. Massey hardly ever gives a day off." ("If your car doesn't start and you're two hours late one morning, you're fired," another rally organizer, Mat Louis-Rosenberg observes.) But they obviously gave workers time off for this.

"When the speakers got up," Judy recalls, "it became even worse. They said some very vulgar things to Ken Hechler. It was awful. Just so embarrassing. What they said to Darryl Hannah was very rude and vulgar as well—wouldn't even let her talk. Same thing for every speaker that got up there, even the clergymen. It was very hard on our people to maintain a nonviolent stature. The police were very worried. They had received notice [and told us] that if we went up there, to Massey property, that there would be bloodshed." Judy had already heard this, from her daughter: A woman she'd talked with in a convenience store "told her that they were told, by Massey, that if we come across that bridge [to the Goals Coal plant] to beat the shit out of us."

Judy and the rally's other organizers had no intention of backing away from that threat. "We had a permit to be there," she says. "We had a right to be there." The rally was located and organized where and how it was because people who might be unable to participate in a back-country sort of action—Hansen, Hannah, the elderly Ken Hechler and Winnie Fox, and many others—"wanted to take a stand, wanted to be arrested at a site. And we were told by Massey lawyers there was no need for people to go up on their work sites, we could get arrested on the street." And that's exactly what many of those at the rally intended to do that day.

After the speakers spoke, the anti-MTR protesters gathered themselves up and marched two by two from the field by the school on up Rt. 3 toward the front gate of Goals Coal. As they approached, Judy saw that there were "more Massey workers than was at our rally, so I would say some had come across the bridge" from inside the coal prep facility to join Massey folks who'd been at the rally and were now massed between the gate and the road, filling that space.

The Massey workers and supporters were "six, seven, eight deep—just a wall, blocking the entrance" to the prep plant, Mat recalls. "Which I thought was kind of amusing, like they blockaded it for us."

"The police had dogs there," Judy continues. "As we were walking up, I turned my head away from the Massey crowd—didn't want to engage, didn't want to look at them. So I'm looking at the dogs, looking at the scene [across the road], the coolness, the shade, wishing I was in that shade," since it was hot and sunny that day. Then, just as Judy was turning around, a woman came out of the crowd of Massey supporters, heading toward Judy. "I didn't even see her until a moment before she hit me, full force, all her weight, slapped me off to the side." This aggravated an old whiplash injury Judy'd had in a car accident a while back, and "it hurt. I was very angry. I wanted to hit her back. But I grabbed hold of Sarah [Haltom] to get my balance, and that kept me from immediately retaliating back. She rared back to hit me again, and the police grabbed her, and while the police was handcuffing her, she lunged at Lorelei Scarbro. She was screaming something at Lorelei, and at me, but I couldn't hear it 'cause I was so stunned, and my ear was ringing at the time. I couldn't hear a word she said." But she could hear and see that "the Massey wives and security guards cheered her on.

"So I just continued with the march. The adrenalin was flowing, and I just let go of the pain until later that evening, and then my jaw started to really hurt."

By the time Judy was attacked, the marchers could go no further—the Massey folks had left them no room to get off the road. "There was no [way] that we could get on the property in order to do a nonviolent trespass sit-down," Judy says. "Dr. Hansen was going to present a letter to Massey Energy," but couldn't reach the gate to do so. The police said that "if we sat down [in the road] we'd be arrested for blocking the flow of traffic. So we did."

Among the thirty or so arrested with Judy and Hannah and Hansen that day were three protesters well over eighty years old: Winnie Fox, Ken Hechler, and Roland Micklem, who'd come to West Virginia to support the Climate Ground Zero campaign a few months earlier. Bo Webb, Lorelei Scarbro, Larry Gibson, Sarah Haltom, and several other local anti-MTR activists, along with a host of supporters from around the region and across the country sat down and were arrested as well. All were ticketed and released. By the end of the day, the total number of arrests at anti-MTR demonstrations in West Virginia since February, when Climate Ground Zero uncorked the action up on Coal River Mountain, was over ninety.

It had so far been a very busy year in West Virginia. In July, CGZ launched no civil-disobedience actions. Instead, the campaign stepped up its ongoing efforts to make its camp a better home for the dozen or more full-time activists living there, as well as the scores of volunteers coming in and out, staying temporarily or occasionally, part-time. Housing and feeding so many people, and finding weatherproof space for gear and food supplies, was a challenge. A great deal of work went into making the fourth of the four tiny CGZ houses marginally habitable. (In the course of renovations, it got new roofing, extensive interior repairs, a woodstove—but still had no back door.) A wooded area behind the houses was cleared of underbrush to make more room for visitors' tents. (Much of that underbrush turned out to be poison ivy. CGZ borrowed a goat to help get rid of it, but the goat preferred to eat nearly everything else it could reach.) An outdoor cooking area was set up under tarps. For much of the year, two successive buses fitted out with kitchens for mobile feeding of activist gatherings settled in and provided daily meals for the camp. Vegetable gardens were planted and tended. Funds were raised to allow the campaign to continue to squeak by financially. And, as always, activists continued to scout and prepare for future actions.

At 9 AM on August 11, four protesters locked themselves to the entrance of the West Virginia Department of Environmental Protection's main office in Charleston. CRMW, OVEC, and several other groups had previously petitioned the federal government to take over from the state DEP enforcement of federal laws related to mining and water quality. The four protesters locked to the entrance and dozens of supporters who joined them there demanded that the DEP be "Closed Due to Incompetence" (as one of their signs read) and also that DEP Secretary Randy Huffman resign.

Then, on Tuesday morning, August 25, activists once again targeted the Edwight strip mine site. Since moving away from Clay's Branch, up above Bo Webb's house, earlier in the year, mining operations had not returned there. Instead, blasting was having the same kinds of ill effects on another small community down below another part of the mine site, Pettry Bottom.

Before dawn, two climbers, Laura Steepleton and Nick Stocks, set themselves up on platforms in two 80-foot tulip poplar trees on a very steep slope near the edge of the Edwight MTR site's permit boundary, within 300 feet of where blasting had been taking place. Their aim was to stop that blasting for as long as they could remain in the trees.

The climbers' supporters, including the media team working out of the Climate Ground Zero houses nearby, were hoping to break the four-hour mark: to keep the tree sit going for more than four hours, which was as long as any previous action against MTR had managed to hold on before being dismantled by police.

But instead of dismantling the tree sit, the state police decided "to wait them out as long as we can wait them out," Sgt. Michael Smith told reporters. "If I put somebody up in the tree to take them out, it's going to be a danger."

The climbers stayed up all that day—and then the next day, and the next, and the next.

Two ground-support activists keeping an eye on the sitters near the base of their trees were arrested on the first day, ticketed for trespassing, then released by police and allowed to return to the tree sit site to serve as liaisons with the tree sitters. On Friday, the same two were arrested again after allegedly helping to re-supply the sitters, jailed this time, and released on $1,000 bond. The two tree sitters remained on their platforms through a mostly rainy weekend.

During that weekend, a good bit of discussion went on among sitters and their supporters about how to proceed in the days to come. Although the tree sit had already gone on longer than expected, the sitters still had enough food and water for several more days. They'd managed to stay warm and dry and were in good spirits. Batteries on their cellphones and radios were running low, though. And re-supply would be difficult. Early in the action, Massey workers had left the tree sit unattended for at least brief periods of time. By the weekend, workers were present 24-7, even during shift changes, blaring noise and flashing lights at the tree sitters through the night.

"They were banging on a metal chair, they were taking a hammer up against the tree, they were beating on their helmets," Laura later tells me. "By the fifth day they had brought out a real drum." Laura and Nick treated this as an invitation to a drum circle, and brought out their own buckets to play along. "Machines were honking. The lights started day one—and that wasn't really a problem, we just pulled our tarps over us, that didn't keep us up." They were able to sleep on and off. "What was

the worst for me was when they were hollering a bunch of gibberish."
She found it hard to sleep through that. (Some of the security guards
Massey hired to deal with the tree sit had formerly been in the military
and used sleep-deprivation tricks they'd learned there.) "During the daytime they would get quieter, so we would sleep during the day, knowing
at night you would be constantly awake."

"Their intent was totally to keep us awake and keep us disoriented,"
Laura says. Which is, of course, a dangerous thing to do to anyone high
up in a tree, dependent on maintaining safety protocols with harnesses
and lines to keep from falling. At one point, "when I was getting from
my line onto the traverse, to go up and talk to Nick about things," and
the noise and distractions were intense, one of the security guards told
the ones making noise: "You know, it's not like these people are terrorists,
you need to stop this."

Beyond the workers at the Edwight mine, local reaction to the tree
sit was "very positive," Judy Bonds says. "They love the idea of people
sitting in the trees. They also understand that it takes a lot of courage
and a lot of skill." And "it's not [just] symbolic. It actually stopped the
mining."

Ed Wiley tells me that after the tree sit was up for several days,
over the weekend, a local person came by CGZ to say that his family
had property back near where the tree sit was going on and wanted to
allow ground support to use the property so they'd have a legal place to
be close by the tree sitters. "He said, 'I could see them up there at night,
flashing the lights and harassing them.' He doesn't want to speak out
directly, and this is his way of trying to help."

Bo Webb "talked to a person in Pettry Bottom on Friday, asked
them what they thought of the tree sit, right above their home. And this
man told me, 'I think they're really courageous.'" From where he lives,
he could see the lights and hear the noise Massey workers were making.
Bo sees Massey and its supporters as "a cult. And they're in a frenzy.
Their jobs are being threatened and they don't care about the people living below them as long as they get their paycheck. They don't care that

they blast rocks and boulders on communities below them. They don't care that they're putting the silica dust in the air that we're all breathing. They only care about the dollar bills. They don't care about their kids' future. It's really obvious these people are sick."

By Sunday, the sixth day of the tree sit, a partial, tentative plan emerged among Nick and Laura and their supporters: Nick, who was due to fly to Montana on Tuesday, would come down on Monday morning, leaving his supplies with Laura, thus increasing the length of time she'd be able to stay up even without further re-supply. This would buy some time—but to what end? Laura, who, at this point, was comfortable with staying up there indefinitely, couldn't be expected to stay up there forever.

Several possibilities were considered that day: Scouts would go out in the woods to try to locate other trees suitable for sitting and located in places where sitters would continue to block blasting above Pettry Bottom. Massey's new office building south of Charleston was scouted for a possible blockade. And, from out of the blue, a supporter called to explore the possibility of using a friend's helicopter to re-supply Laura from the air. (As news of this last suggestion made the rounds at the CGZ houses, giddy laughter burst out again and again as supporters heard about it, one by one.)

Although, by this time, the tree sit supporters were stretched awfully thin, they decided to try to go for all three options at once. Preparations began for an action at Massey's office building. Scouts went out into the woods before dawn on Monday to look for other tree sit possibilities. Re-supply by helicopter remained a reassuring possibility.

Late on Monday morning, Nick came down from his tree and was taken to Beckley for processing. Also that morning, Bo Webb paid a visit to Sgt. Smith. He offered to stand at the base of Laura's tree that night to protect her, but Smith said he'd have to arrest him if he did that. "I told him he's arresting the wrong people," Bo says. By then, the Laura's supporters were uneasy about an apparent escalation in danger: Watchers hiding in the woods nearby had heard security guards or mine workers threaten Laura with gang rape, and chainsaws had been heard on Sunday night. But since communication from the field had deteriorated badly as batteries in the tree sitters' communications devices had faded, and as the watchers in the woods had had to pull back to avoid detection, it was impossible to know exactly what was going on up there.

Shortly after 2 PM, supporters at Climate Ground Zero received word from the field that Nick's tree was being cut down. They called state police to say that the two trees were tied together, that cutting one down would endanger the sitter in the other tree and must stop; police responded that it wasn't them doing the cutting and that they'd get on it. About ten minutes later, CGZ received word that *both* trees were down, that "arrests have been made," and that communication with the tree sit site had been lost. It wasn't at all clear whether this was just rumor—it was unclear whether anyone reporting this had actually seen the trees or seen Laura down out of her tree. Police, called again, said they'd made no arrests other than Nick that day. But with cellphone coverage as spotty as it is in the valley, the police dispatcher might not yet have received word of very recent arrests.

Later, Laura explained what really had been going on up there: "The night before Nick left, they brought out chainsaws. We knew they weren't going to cut the tree down, [just try to] intimidate us. What they were doing was putting the motor [not the saw chain] against the tree. It still was scary.

"What I was concerned about was that the one guy that had the chainsaw really didn't like us, and they were talking about how he had been drinking earlier. So at that point I'm like: Great. Drunk, angry security that doesn't like me is the one with the chainsaw. I could hear security on the other end of the radio telling them: 'Do *not* cut the tree! Do *not* cut the tree!' So that lasted a little bit, then they stopped." They started the chainsaw up again later; she didn't respond; they stopped.

The next morning, when Nick came down, "Sgt. Smith kept asking me: 'Come down—will you *please* come down,' and I refused to come down. At that point, I had gotten all of Nick's water so I was set. I had over five gallons of water and enough food. I could have been up there another week and a half." But the batteries in her cellphone and communications radio were nearly dead, and she had no fresh ones to replace them with. "I had already planned that after a couple of days I'd probably be out of batteries and have no contact whatsoever—which would put [the watchers hidden in the woods] in a lot of risk. I knew that they were always going to be within earshot of me and I was really worried about them too." The watchers didn't have Laura's high vantage point and so couldn't see much of what was going on around them.

"After Nick went away, they started racking up the noise level. They brought out sirens. That was just constant. That had been going on about an hour, and I could deal with this. I knew it had to be getting to them too," and that they would eventually quit when it bothered them enough. (Earplugs and spare batteries were the only things Laura felt she was really lacking up in the tree.) When the sirens finally did stop, around noon, "that's when the loggers came in [and said] 'we're planning on cutting Nick's tree.'" They told Laura, who hadn't seen them before, that "they weren't Massey employees, but that Massey had ordered them to be there, and they came in through the back way so that no one would see them.

"I said: 'Where's the state trooper?' They responded: 'Oh, he's not around. And this is Massey property, and we're allowed to lay what trees down we want. And you better cut that traverse line or you're going to go for one hell of a ride.'"

At that time, she was thinking: "You guys aren't really going to cut this tree down. You're just bluffing with me, to scare me. And they came over, and one logger started climbing up [Nick's] tree." She decided at that point she'd best get out onto her traverse line, and started getting herself and her gear organized for that. One of the miners saw what she was doing and said: "'She's gonna get on that rope! You need to get up there before she does!'" And the logger climbing the tree said: " 'It doesn't matter if she's on it. If she's harnessed in, I'm going to cut it.'" This would have sent Laura swinging on the rope, detached from Nick's tree but not her own, with no way to control her path, which most likely would end with her slamming into the side of her tree. She decided that the folks planning to do this were either crazy or clueless about safety, or simply didn't care how badly they might hurt her. So she climbed down out of her tree and was escorted off the site by workers to be arrested by state police. The loggers later that day cut down both her tree and Nick's.

The day after the tree sit ends, Judy Bonds says she thinks that the way Nick and Laura were treated "really backfired on Massey." A large number of people living nearby "could hear the horns blaring, could see the lights flashing. They truly understood what was going on and was really upset at the treatment of Nick and Laura. So there's a feeling right now of solidarity. Every time that the coal industry uses violence and intimidation, and thug-like tactics, it backfires on them. We gain more support when they use those kind of tactics.

"I definitely think that more direct action [like the tree sit] right now is the thing to do. If we're ever going to get anything done, it has to be done now. This administration has basically—Obama has lost his balls, and we need to help him find his balls.

"There's very few mountains left. If we don't stop it now, there's not going to be any mountains left and it'll all be about documenting the destruction of the land and the people."

Bo adds: "I think that this *is* the battle for mountaintop removal, right here in the Coal River valley. It's ground zero. It's where the most resistance has been, for a number of years. It's been building up to this, and this is where it's exploded—not as much as it needs to, yet, but we've got nearly a hundred arrests since February 3. Thirteen actions, and there's gonna be more.

"I don't like to use the word 'war' because that's what Massey and them say, that they're in a war. But in those terms, we need to get all of our forces in place here because this is where it's gonna be won or lost. We've got it going, and we really need more and more people to come in now. We've done a lot with a little. I said the night before the first action, February 3, that we are small but we are mighty." Now, months of persistent action later, "we're getting really thin. We need people coming in—fresh troops and reinforcement troops. We've got it to this point, and we just need to drive it home. We're getting government's attention, we're getting the media's attention. We're exposing a truth, and that's really what it's all about. It's not a war. It's about exposing the truth.

"I'd like to say to everybody in Tennessee, and Virginia, and Kentucky: You want to end mountaintop removal? Get over here! Get over here as fast as you can, and get ready to go to work. Each day that the Obama administration delays on doing anything about mountaintop removal is another day that puts our lives in danger, [those of us who are] here fighting this."

Stretched thin as they were, activists in West Virginia didn't stop. The blockade of Massey's office building outside Charleston, preparations for which had started during the tree sit, took place on September 9. Four blockaders, chained together across the driveway, and one videojournalist were arrested.

The ages of the participants in this action spanned six decades. The eldest was Roland Micklem, in his eighties but still spry enough to regularly volunteer for firewood duty at the CGZ camp. In joining the blockade, Roland said, "I am exercising a spiritual obligation as a steward of Creation. It was not God's intent that these mountains be destroyed to enhance the wealth of a few individuals. This should not be solely a young person's campaign. Now that they have provided the example and inspiration, we seniors need to make a statement with our own actions and share the risks that are part of this ongoing effort to stop the obliteration of West Virginia's mountains."

By then, Roland was already planning a multi-day, twenty-five-mile senior citizens' march against MTR, affectionately nicknamed the Geezer March by CGZ activists, including the geezers themselves. During the march, on October 10, two much younger activists (eighteen and nineteen years old) were arrested for dropping a banner, in solidarity with the marching geezers, off the Walker CAT building in

Belle, West Virginia, along the route of the march. (The banner read: "Yes, Coal is Killing West Virginia's Communities," in direct response to the "Yes, Coal" billboard advertisements Walker CAT had been running that year.)

Meanwhile, the news from Washington continued to be ambiguous at best. In September, the EPA announced that seventy-nine pending MTR permits would "undergo additional evaluation" by the EPA and Army Corps of Engineers (ACOE). "After careful evaluation of these projects," the announcement said, "EPA determined that each of them, as currently proposed, is likely to result in significant harm to water quality and the environment and are therefore not consistent with requirements of the CWA," the federal Clean Water Act. However, as if seeking to deflect criticism from any possible quarter, the report added that "EPA looks forward to working with the ACOE, with the involvement of the mining companies, to achieve a resolution of EPA's concerns that avoids harmful environmental impacts and meets our energy and economic needs."

Was the Obama administration trying to appear to do something about the ills of MTR without actually doing anything? Was there a tug-of-war going on inside the administration between environmentalists who really wanted to end MTR and advocates for business and political interests arguing either that the U.S. couldn't afford this economically, or that Obama and other Democrats couldn't afford it politically? Whatever was going on, one thing clearly wasn't: More than half a year into the Obama administration, there had been no curbing of the actual practice of MTR across Appalachia. And among activists in Appalachia itself, one thing was very, very clear: Now was not the time to let up on the pressure. Either Obama needed to be convinced he wouldn't get away with pretending to do something about MTR without actually doing it, or members of Obama's team seeking an end to MTR needed to have their hand strengthened by activists shining a light on the problem and demanding action. Or both.

In October, Coal River Mountain once again became the focus of urgent attention. Not long after the February 3 protests, pre-mining activities at the Bee Tree site had ceased. CGZ activist Mat Louis-Rosenberg speculates "that they stopped working up there because the market demand was down. It didn't make any sense for them to open up a new site which requires significant investment of money for no immediate return when they were shutting down other sites that were already producing coal."

But in early October, pre-mining activity resumed on the mountain, once again with clear-cutting and now blasting as well for road building at the Bee Tree site. Because Massey still had no valley fill permits for the site (nor for any of the other sites on Coal River Mountain), "they can blast now," Mat wrote at the time, "but only create as much fill as can fit around the Brushy Fork impoundment. Which is significant, but not even enough to finish Bee Tree." Why mining activity resumed just then was unclear. "I can't really think of a good business reason for that," Mat said. "I think that they are just doing it as a big F*** YOU to us."

In response, CGZ activists reminded their network of supporters that Coal River Mountain was their "line in the sand." Come join us, they said. We need you here *now*.

CGZ wasn't alone in sounding the alarm. CRMW and OVEC and the Coal River Wind Project mobilized their supporters. Appalachian Voices' "I Love Mountains" project asked its extensive network to call the White House to demand that President Obama save Coal River Mountain, and thousands of people did so. Even farther afield, Google Earth prepared to include Coal River Mountain among a handful of places endangered by the burning of fossil fuels they'd show in a presentation to world leaders attending the upcoming international climate conference in Copenhagen in December. Coal River Mountain certainly had many friends. Would that be enough to save it?

On October 19, Coal River valley residents delivered yet another letter to Gov. Joe Manchin's office in Charleston, this time asking the governor to use his executive powers to halt mountaintop removal operations on Coal River Mountain. Seven young activists sat down and refused to leave the governor's office until he took action; they were arrested and removed from the scene at the end of office hours that day.

On October 22, eight people were arrested for blocking a haul road at a mine site near Charleston. In addition to protesting MTR, they particularly wanted to call attention to the decline in mining-related jobs in West Virginia (62,500 miners in 1979, only about 22,000 today, 30 years later), and the improvement in the local employment situation that the Coal River Wind Project would bring. By this, the seventeenth CGZ-affiliated civil-disobedience action that year, presumably all the police dispatchers in the area had gotten used to the idea of police being called by protesters' supporters to please go arrest their friends.

And on November 21, activists once again took the protest to ground zero, up on Coal River Mountain. Four people were arrested at a drill rig at the Bee Tree site, one locked inside the rig's cab, one locked to the drill itself, and two support persons. This action was almost identical to the aborted drill-rig part of the 2005 attempted mountain takeover at Zeb Mountain in Tennessee. (Some of the same personnel were even involved. In a sort of inside joke, CGZ's website coverage of this action included a photo, illustrating what a drill rig on an MTR site typically looks like, taken by scouts at Zeb in 2005.)

This time, the action went well, even though that morning the rig wasn't in one of the two places the activists had expected it to be so they had to improvise approaches—and, for their covert backwoods support-ers, exits as well—to and from an unfamiliar and awkward location. The key differences between this action and the one at Zeb in 2005 were that the team was better prepared, better coordinated, and better supported. By this time, in this very busy year, after more than 120 arrests at 18 actions, Climate Ground Zero's support infrastructure for direct-action teams had a depth of experience the activists in 2005 could hardly have imagined.

West Virginia's weather in December and January—cold and ferociously snowy—forced a lull in backwoods actions in and around Coal River valley. Then, during a break in the difficult weather, CGZ activists once again returned to the Bee Tree site. Blasting had recently begun for construction of a haul road for taking "overburden" from Bee Tree to be dumped at the edge of the Brushy Fork impoundment. CGZ intended to stop that.

Before dawn on Thursday, January 21, a dozen heavily laden activists headed for the edge of the site. The hikers approached three trees, oak and poplar, previously selected by scouts as suitable in several ways: They were not far apart, with about fifty or sixty feet between them; each was suitable for installing a person on a platform high enough up to make removal difficult; they were in rough terrain where it would be hard for mine workers to bring in heavy equipment; and they were close enough to mining activities so that occupying them would prevent blasting.

Working quickly, the three prospective tree sitters and their supporters hoisted plywood platforms, tarps, food, water, radios, batteries, and other essentials up into the trees. Lessons learned from CGZ's previous tree sit were applied: More food, water, and batteries were packed in. A system of traverse lines, which would enable the sitters to move themselves and their supplies from one tree to another, was planned. The sitters had planned to share certain supplies: They had only two cellphones and one battery-to-phone charger between them, for example. Unfortunately, the set-up crew that night found too many branches in the way for the traverse lines to be set between the trees, especially working in the dark. The sitters would not be able to share equipment, and if one came down early, he or she wouldn't be able to pass unused supplies to the others. Still, each of them at least had a communications radio, spare batteries, and enough food and water for a week or more. The sitters—Eric Blevins, Amber Nitchman, David Aaron Smith (also known as Planet)—settled on their platforms and pulled up their ropes. Eric, who had the cellphone charger, would be the primary contact with the outside world; Amber would minimize use of her cellphone; and the three of them would communicate, as needed, by radio. They would make do.

Two supporters remained on the ground by the trees. Several others would hide in the woods, too far away to see the sitters but close enough for radio contact. If the sitters said they were in danger, these off-site supporters would run to their aid. Others who helped set up the sit left and began their long hike out of the woods.

As long as the sitters remained in their trees near the road-construction site, further blasting would be halted. "Our trees were right near where they were blasting," Eric later recalled. "We could see blast holes from our trees, really close to us, and we could see the [Brushy Fork] impoundment just a few hundred feet away."

The morning of the first day of the tree sit, the two ground supporters beneath the trees were arrested and taken away. Massey workers felled several saplings near the sitters' trees, but Eric, in a phone call to base camp, confirmed that the sitters felt safe.

That afternoon, workers set up bright lights and an extremely loud array of noise-making machinery, including both airhorns and pulsing sirens similar to those on emergency vehicles. Fortunately, Eric and Planet had earplugs. Unfortunately, Amber's had mistakenly been left out of her pack. (She plugged her ears with toilet paper.) Even more unfortunately, the noise was so loud that earplugs were only partly effective: "[They] kind of knocked the bass out," Planet later recalled, "but the high-pitched sounds were coming through clear as a bell."

Friday morning, amid the continuing noise, workers began erecting a ten-foot chain-link fence around the trees, apparently to deter any attempt to re-supply the sitters. On Saturday, the chilly mist and rain, which had fallen since the tree sit began, stopped, allowing the sitters a welcome opportunity to dry out a bit.

Meanwhile, plans were being hatched by the tree-sitters' supporters: One person, who'd been hiding in the woods within radio range of the sitters, would creep up during the night to get a good look at the fence, the noisemakers, and the security set-up, then come out of the woods to brief supporters at base camp. One or two of those supporters would attempt to re-supply the sitters and would presumably be arrested, but others would remain in the woods nearby, listening to the sitters on radio. Whoever made the re-supply effort might also try to get a decibel-meter reading of the noise near the trees before passing the meter on to one of the sitters in a re-supply pack. Those packs would also include better ear protection, as well as items (such as batteries) intended to make up for the sitter's inability to pass supplies from one tree to another.

The reconnaissance mission went smoothly, and the person who did it briefed folks at base camp on Sunday. The chain-link fence around the trees was completed, except for a gap of maybe twenty feet along the side of it nearest to the haul road. Security guards had attached a tarp to the fence to give themselves some shelter from the rain. The fence was close enough to the trees that the planned re-supply scenario seemed plausible—though success was far from certain.

The most disturbing information brought out of the woods that day concerned the noisemakers. In addition to the sirens, there were three separate airhorn rigs, each with as many as four of the kind of very loud airhorns used on big trucks ganged together and hoisted up beneath each tree-sit platform, where they blasted away continuously.

"We were able to handle it OK," Eric later said, "but it was a really cruel and unusual way to attack somebody who's doing something non-violent. [It] was just uncalled for, when our actions were completely nonviolent and in defense of the community of people living below and the mountain and water supply being destroyed by the mining."

It was obvious that exposure to this kind of noise could cause permanent hearing damage. Supporters at base camp got busy with legal research, seeking grounds to compel Massey to stop the noise. That afternoon, they advised Eric to call the police to file a formal complaint. Shortly thereafter, the noise stopped—but only for a few hours.

The following morning, Monday, January 25, Planet came down from his tree. Rain had resumed, and at some point the wind had blown open his tarp so that his sleeping bag got soaked and he could no longer keep himself warm.

Workers turned off the noisemakers when police arrived to arrest him, but the noise resumed after they left. Eric and Amber remained in their trees, and CGZ stepped up its efforts to stop the noise. At CGZ's request, hundreds of people called the Marfork subsidiary's headquarters, Massey's headquarters, and Gov. Joe Manchin's office to demand that the noise be stopped.

On Tuesday morning, a CGZ activist was arrested while attempting to re-supply the sitters. On Wednesday, another person attempting re-supply was arrested. No re-supply packs reached either of the remaining sitters.

Still, Eric and Amber had enough supplies to last for a while, and remained in good spirits. Eric was amazed by "how much the trees were swaying, because it was so windy up there most of the time—which just goes to show it would make a lot more sense to put windmills on the mountain, rather than to destroy the mountain for the coal."

That Wednesday afternoon, Charleston *Gazette* reporter Ken Ward blogged that Gov. Manchin was planning to meet with a county prosecu-tor and state police about the noise. Around 5 PM, the noisemakers were turned off. The next morning, following a meeting with CGZ activists at his office, Manchin declared a "moratorium" on the noise, pending determination of its legality and health effects.

By this time, Eric and Amber had been up in their trees for eight days—longer than any previous CGZ or Mountain Justice action. The weather for much of that time had been unpleasant, but not nearly as bad as the noise. Now, with the noise turned off, the weather was poised to take a turn for the worse: Snow was forecast—half a foot or more—to be followed by single-digit temperatures over the weekend.

On Friday, January 29, Eric and Amber came down from their trees. They were immediately arrested, but neither was willing to call it quits. "It's not over until the blasting is stopped," Amber said shortly before leaving her tree— stopped not just for nine days, but permanently.

"This is a large movement that we're a part of," Eric later added. "People are trying to do legislative work, and provide economic alternatives, and do all kinds of stuff to get us away from the destruction that the economy of this area has become so dependent on. Hopefully with all our combined efforts we can put a stop to this as soon as possible."

A few weeks later, other members of that "large movement" mounted a fresh effort at the headquarters of the Massey subsidiary responsible for the Bee Tree site and other Massey operations on Coal River Mountain.

"Protesters Occupy Marfork Coal Co.'s Office in Response to Mounting Violations," said a press release from Climate Ground Zero on Thursday morning, February 18.

A news release from Massey told rather a different story:

> Environmental Terrorists Invade Marfork Coal Company Office.... Three criminals clad in fatigues and carrying chains invaded a company office and chained themselves to chairs in the lobby. A terrified receptionist went into shock and was transported by ambulance to a local hospital.... One of the criminals, Mike Roselle, was a founding member of Earth First!, which is considered by many to be a domestic terrorist group.... These domestic terrorists are part of an anti-coal group that wants to shut down mining in Appalachia and destroy West Virginia's economy.

Massey's "news release" didn't specify who the "many" are who consider Mike and his colleagues "domestic terrorists," but even right-wing activist Ron Arnold, who's written an entire book on "ecoterrorism," asserts that "Roselle may be a terrible pain in the ass, but he's no terrorist." Writing shortly after Mike's first trespassing arrest on Massey property, at the Bee Tree site a year ago, Arnold scolded those who would "dilute" the meaning of the word terrorism by applying it to nonviolent protest. "Face it," he wrote, "what he did was civil disobedience, not terrorism."

The claim that "a terrified receptionist went into shock" was equally curious. "She was definitely startled when we came in," says Joe Hamsher, one of the three protesters that day. But soon "she calmed down. She was even laughing.

"We were definitely not much of a threat to her. I mean, we were locked down."

Joe, the first of the three to enter the building that morning, announced "this is a protest," then immediately sat down and locked himself to a chair. (That's why they were carrying chains.) Meanwhile, Mike posted a sign reading "CLOSED: Stop the Blasting!" on the building's front door. A Marfork employee tore the sign down, while the third protester, Tom Smyth, took pictures. Then Mike and Tom entered the building and sat down near Joe. Tom chained himself to a chair.

The three protesters had brought with them a "citizen's arrest warrant" for Marfork's president. The warrant read:

> Since 1994, the Marfork Coal Company has committed over 100 documented permit violations.... Marfork's continued operations in such close proximity to both Marsh Fork Elementary and the Pettus Head Start Program are not only endangering, but also assaulting the children at these locations with coal dust and other particulates floating off of the mine sites owned by Marfork Coal.... Marfork is continuing its operations on the Bee Tree Strip Mine, placing nearby communities in imminent danger. As President of the Marfork Coal Company, you are responsible for the illegal practices of Marfork. Given the absence of any intervention from West Virginia or federal law enforcement, a citizen's warrant has been issued for your, Christopher L. Blanchard's, arrest.

Two hours after the protesters arrived, state police took them away to jail. (When they left, the allegedly terrified receptionist was still at work, showing no ill effects, Joe notes.) The three were charged with trespass, obstruction, and conspiracy—all misdemeanors. Bail was set for Joe and Tom at $5,000 each, for Mike at $7,500—cash only.

Quoted in the Massey "news release" cited above, Massey CEO Don Blankenship said: "These criminals have been allowed to become more and more aggressive with little repercussion."

In fact, the "repercussion" against anti-MTR protesters in West Virginia had escalated dramatically over the past year. Early on in the Mountain Justice and Climate Ground Zero campaigns, protesters arrested for trespassing were simply ticketed and released. By the latter part of 2009, they were being sent to jail and required to raise large sums of bail. Although even accused murderers and child molesters are typically permitted to use the services of a bailbondsman, to reduce the amount of cash they have to muster to get out of jail before trial, West Virginia magistrates were now specifying large cash-only bonds for civil-disobedience arrestees at anti-MTR protests. This resulted in protesters being kept in jail after their arrests, but before any trial, sometimes for many days—longer than even those convicted of such nonviolent offenses are normally jailed. And as protest cases came to trial, the fines assessed were increasing as well.

In addition to these escalating penalties in criminal court, Massey's lawyers had recently launched an escalation in their multiple civil suits against protesters arrested on Massey property. Lawsuits demanding injunctions and so-far unspecified money for "damages" had already been filed in several West Virginia counties against dozens of protesters in 2009. Following the January tree sit, Massey filed suit in U.S. *federal* court against the three sitters, requesting at least the minimum of $75,000 in damages that would make such a case eligible for that court.

At a hearing for the federal lawsuit on Tuesday, February 23, Massey attorney Sam Brock referred to Eric Blevins as a "serial trespasser" (he'd previously been arrested at a front-gate action at Marfork) and said that activists protesting against Massey "just have to live by the same rules as everybody else." Sitting in the courtroom that day, I remembered Massey's 2008 settlement with the federal EPA for thousands of permit violations related to the Clean Water Act: Massey agreed to pay $20 million, although given the number and nature of the violations, the EPA could properly have assessed $2 billion or more—100 times as much. (Massey's own estimate of this, prior to the settlement, was $1.5 to $7 billion.) Furthermore, just a few weeks before, in January, a coalition of environmental groups, announcing their intent to sue Massey, cited documentation that the company's permit violations had become even more frequent since the EPA settlement.

Would an even-handed application of "the same rules" allow protesters to commit, say, ninety-nine (or more) civil-disobedience actions with impunity before being arrested for one of them?

"While Massey's lawyers were in court today trying to enjoin anyone anywhere from trespassing on Massey operations," Vern Haltom said later that day, "Massey was spilling blackwater from their Martin County, Kentucky, operation. And Pioneer Fuels (*not* a Massey subsidiary) was spilling blackwater into Clear Fork," which empties into the Coal River near Marfork's headquarters, upstream from Whitesville's public water intake.

"Unfortunately," Vern says, "our regulators don't escalate the enforcement of Massey's repeating violations that are endangering the community with the same vigor that prosecutors and Massey attorneys are suppressing the voices of endangered people."

Judy Bonds puts it more bluntly: "The justice system in southern West Virginia is discriminatory in favor of the coal industry. I think keep screaming about it is all we can do."

On April 5, 2010, twenty-nine miners died in an explosion at the Upper Big Branch underground mine, operated by Massey subsidiary Performance Coal near Whitesville. The mine had an extensive history of safety violations, news reports noted. "Violations," Don Blankenship responded, "are unfortunately a normal part of the mining process." At least some of the families and friends of the dead miners apparently disagreed. When Blankenship, escorted by more than a dozen police officers, tried to address the crowd outside the mine during the night after the explosion, he was shouted down by accusations that he cared more about profits than about miners' lives. One person threw a chair at him. Federal officials appeared skeptical as well. MSHA launched an extensive investigation into the cause of the explosion, and the FBI began its own investigation of whether anyone should face criminal charges.

A few weeks later, news of a very different kind rocked the Coal River valley. On April 30, in a high-profile press conference at the state capitol, Gov. Manchin announced that sufficient funding had been secured to build a new school to replace Marsh Fork Elementary, in a safe location somewhere nearby. Efforts to find funding for this had previously stalled well short of the money needed. The key to making up the shortfall would be $2.5 million supplied by the Annenberg Foundation, a charitable organization. The state school fund had committed $2.6 million. Massey and the county school board would contribute $1.5 million each. Ed Wiley, CRMW, and the many, many people who'd worked so hard for so many years to reach this point were thrilled.

Taken together, might the shock of the mine explosion and the promise of a new school mark a turning point in how people living in the valley see mining and their future? "I really don't know yet," Judy Bonds said in early May. Shortly after the mine explosion, "people drove by [the CGZ houses] screaming 'F-you, tree-huggers.' And then some people tried to say: 'Oh, you tree-huggers, you want them to go underground and now they're gettin' blown up.'" Judy's seen the same reaction after other deaths at underground mines. "You have to fight the same old battles: Excuse me, I believe in a safe workplace for *everybody*. [And] there's no sense in externalizing the danger from the workplace to the community," as MTR does, much more so than underground mining.

Although "the dynamic is unpredictable, so far," Judy thinks that some local people who'd previously been "sitting on the fence" about Massey and MTR have been moved by the promise of the new school. Recently, she says, "a coal miner and his wife came up to [a local person, a friend of CRMW] and told him to tell the tree-huggers thanks, because they know they wouldn't have a school without them. They know that, they recognize that.

"But then again there are some diehard Massey wives that have been on Facebook saying the tree-huggers didn't have nothing to do with it. Which is completely false, because Charlie [Annenberg] wouldn't have known we needed a new school unless the tree-huggers told him that.

"Loyalty to Massey is eroding for those that were sitting on the fence. But [among] real Massey supporters, it is not eroding. Lorelei [Scarbro] saw people wearing Massey shirts at some of the memorial [services for miners who died]. And then there's a T-shirt that says: 'Performance Coal, remembering the 29 that have died.' That's the strangest T-shirt I've ever seen in my life, 'cause you have the company that killed those men that's honoring them.

"You still have people that have no concept of how to separate the two things."

The people whose minds have changed are "people that were already thinking. But there are those that are not gonna think, and not gonna see beyond that paycheck.

"It's all about greed, about whether you want that new truck and a new four-wheeler and a new SUV for your wife." Judy believes that many miners would be willing to speak out, were it not "for the wife they're supporting. Massey knows this. The way to control the men is to control their wives. You control the wives through their greed. Not all wives are like that, but there's a good deal like that.

"And more and more people's talking about it," she adds. One local woman told her: "It's all about trying to keep up with each other. It's about keeping up with the Joneses. And if the man ain't working in the mines, she can't keep up with the Joneses, with the next Massey wife."

Neither Judy nor I think these jobs pay enough to be worth ruining your health or risking your life, let alone blowing up mountains and destroying entire watersheds around your home place. In the wake of the recent disaster, some miners might themselves be questioning whether it's worth it, "but some of the wives think it is," Judy says.

Still, it's hard to imagine making yourself go to work every day if the danger of losing your life is real to you. There must be a lot of denial going on. "They've put all of that danger out of their head," Judy believes. "They've put everything out of their head besides going to work and getting the paycheck. And they've tried to justify it by: They have to feed their families. But it's more than feeding their families. People can survive off $20,000; 25,000; 30,000. It's hard. But people can do it—people *do* do it. But for these people it's about the lifestyle. It's about *style*. Not about *life*, it's about *style*.

"I'm very much afraid," Judy adds, "that some of the miners are not going to speak out" to investigators looking into the cause of the explosion. "I do *hope* these guys speak out, because more people are gonna die if they don't." In late May, Charleston *Gazette*'s Ken Ward reported that about half of the Massey workers MSHA investigators had asked for information had not showed up for scheduled interviews, even though MSHA had taken pains to ensure confidentiality.

In a sane and just world, miners wouldn't have to be afraid to tell the truth about their working conditions. And in that world, too, taxpayers and the Annenberg Foundation wouldn't be paying most of the bill for building a school to replace Marsh Fork Elementary. Instead, Massey would be compelled to pay *all* of that cost, since Massey created the conditions that make the existing school unsafe. "Absolutely! Absolutely, they should be," Judy exclaims. But as it is, Judy points out, not only is West Virginia not situated in a sane and just world, "it's West Virginia. West Virginia is not in the United States of America. It's King Coal's fiefdom, and they do what they want to here. You're no longer in the United States. Coal rules here. Completely."

Prime examples of this have been the escalating penalties for non-violent anti-MTR civil disobedience in West Virginia, which, by early 2010, included more and more jail time, as activists came to trial and were sentenced for earlier actions. Nick Martin was sentenced to a week in jail for locking himself to the drill rig at the Bee Tree site in November 2009. Several of those arrested at the multi-generational action blocking the entrance to Massey's office building in September were sentenced to three weeks in jail. Then, on April 22, 2010, Jacqueline "Annie" Quimby was sentenced to *two months* in jail for sitting down in a haul road in October.

"What we're seeing," Judy says, "is more and more and more cor-
ruption of the state of West Virginia. It needs to be brought out in the
light in the rest of America. They're sending a message: It's OK to kick
the shit out of tree-huggers, but you can't sit down in the middle of the
road, you can't participate in nonviolent civil disobedience. You can't use
the Constitution of America in West Virginia. Because we're no longer
in America. It comes right back to that.

"And they're gonna keep raising it up," increasing those penalties,
Judy predicted in early May. And she was right.

On Monday, May 17, two young activists affiliated with CGZ
were arrested on misdemeanor charges for blocking the entrance to the
same Massey office building near Charleston that other CGZ activists
had blockaded in September. This time, the protesters attached themselves to a tripod set up in the driveway and displayed a banner reading: "Massey: Profits Over People and Mountains. Fight Back!" Boone
County Magistrate C. Porter Snodgrass set their bail at a stunning
$100,000 each—cash only. (By comparison, Snodgrass had previously
set much lower bails for individuals accused of various violent crimes:
for example, a $2,000 bail, with $200 bond option, for a woman charged
with stabbing her husband in the head.)

At the end of the week, another judge reduced the two protesters'
bail to a still-extraordinary $25,000, with permission to satisfy that obli-
gation by paying a bondsman $2,500. At that time, the two, EmmaKate
Martin and Benjamin Bryant, were offered a plea deal of time served
plus fifty-five days community service and house arrest. Ben took the
deal and was released from jail, fully a week after his arrest. EmmaKate
remained in jail. At her pretrial hearing on June 3, both the defense and
the prosecutor agreed on a sentence of time served (she'd already been
in jail for eighteen days at this point), with a community service option
for the remaining three days of a twenty-one-day sentence. Magistrate
Snodgrass disagreed, and the case headed for trial.

Meanwhile, the mixed signals from Washington continued. In mid-
June, the Army Corps of Engineers announced that it was suspending

its Nationwide 21 permitting process and would henceforth require full examination of the specific effects of each proposed strip mine calling for one or more valley fills. Anti-MTR activists welcomed the move, but were cautious about its likely effects. "Since new valley fill permits are going to be difficult to get," Bo Webb predicted at the time, "the coal industry will move quickly to obtain revisions and extensions on their permitted sites. This will allow them to continue to blow up more mountains for coal, using already permitted valley fills."

However, it soon appeared that new valley fill permits might not be so difficult to get after all. Days after the ACOE announcement, the federal Environmental Protection Agency announced its first decision on an MTR permit under new, supposedly tougher guidelines the EPA had adopted in April. That decision approved valley fills that would fill in nearly three miles of streams at the 760-acre Pine Creek mining operation in Logan County, West Virginia, in an watershed already heavily burdened with strip mines.

Following the EPA's decision, on July 8 four activists affiliated with RAN locked themselves together in the lobby of the agency's Washington headquarters in protest.

On July 15, activists affiliated with Climate Ground Zero locked themselves to a highwall strip-mining machine at the Bee Tree mine site on Coal River Mountain.

This story isn't finished. Massey Energy and the other big coal companies engaging in large-scale strip mining won't give up easily. At the same time, those seeking to end MTR are determined, persistent, and prepared to continue their efforts.

Although this story isn't finished, we can see already that the story of King Coal's reign is ending. Even Sen. Robert Byrd, the longest-serving senator in U.S. history and a steadfast supporter of the coal industry throughout his career, knew by late 2009 that time was running out for business-as-usual in Appalachia's coalfields. "The practice of mountaintop removal mining has a diminishing constituency in Washington," he wrote. "Most members of Congress, like most Americans, oppose the practice." However, he added, "the greatest threats to the future of coal do not come from possible constraints on mountaintop removal mining or other environmental regulations, but rather from rigid mindsets, depleting coal reserves, and the declining demand for coal as more power plants begin shifting to biomass and natural gas as a way to reduce emissions. Change has been a constant throughout the history of our coal industry. West Virginians can choose to anticipate change and adapt to it, or resist and be overrun by it."

Appalachia's coal is running out. What's left, after more than a century of mining there, is increasingly difficult and expensive to mine. Even enforcement of existing laws will make MTR less profitable and more difficult, perhaps simply impossible at many or most sites. And any new laws passed pertaining to strip mining (any version of the Clean Water Protection Act, any sort of carbon regulation) will likely increase expenses and reduce profitability still further. Many, perhaps all, of the remaining possible sites for large-scale strip mining of Appalachian coal will likely become forbidden or unprofitable to mine. The reign of King Coal is ending.

What we don't know, yet, is what's next for Appalachia. Will King Coal's demise clear the way for yet another new wave of extractive, exploitative industry, much as coal barons followed timber barons here a century ago? (Perhaps when rising fuel costs make it too expensive to ship cheap manufactured goods halfway around the world, sweatshops run in China for the profit of faraway owners will be replaced by similar sweatshops in Appalachia?) Or, instead, will King Coal be succeeded by a new pattern of economic and political life in Appalachia, a pattern that both maximizes human freedom and fosters the paramount goal of sustainability for the region's natural and human communities?

This, at this moment in history, is the big question facing not only Appalachia but all of America. How might we move beyond our use-it-up-and-move-on way of life, into new ways of living that could plausibly leave a world where our great-grandchildren can decently live?

The ending of King Coal's reign puts Appalachia in the vanguard of this transition. Americans everywhere have a stake in how well that transition is made there. And Americans everywhere can help make it go well: Ask your senators, congressman, and president to end MTR now by enforcing existing laws, and to pass new legislation to prevent any resumption of mountaintop removal in the future. Insist that the federal government require coal companies to pay the full cost of repairing the damage they do to human health and home places, and to fund genuine ecological restoration of land and water habitats harmed by strip mining. When that falls short, insist that public funding be committed to furthering that repair and restoration, and to building infrastructure supportive of Appalachia's transition beyond coal. Support the Coal River Wind Project and similar sustainable-development initiatives as they arise across Appalachia.

And don't stop there. Use the knowledge gained from Appalachia's transition efforts to inform decision making closer to your own home. Find patterns of renewable energy and sustainable agriculture and industry that can support healthy ecological and human communities in your own home place. Find your own way.

One evening at the Climate Ground Zero campaign house where Mike Roselle was living, I asked Mike if those beers I'd seen in the refrigerator were his, and might I have one. "As leader of the free world," Mike proclaimed, "*all* the beer in that refrigerator belongs" to him, and I should feel free to help myself. The next day, Mike clarified. He is, in fact, "the leader of the free world. But it's a very small world. Only one person lives there." Himself.

Mike's a free person. So is Bo Webb, having avoided what he calls the "slave mentality." So are Judy Bonds, and dozens of other Appalachians engaged in the fight against MTR and for a better future for themselves, their families, and their communities.

But those who depend on King Coal are not free—not free to speak their minds, not free to feel good about raising their children in a home place they won't have to leave. If you allow yourself to be dependent on work that poisons your neighbors, human and wild, that poisons even your own home and family, how free are you even to call your soul your own?

Across America, millions upon millions of us are likewise unfree. We're not, most of us, bad people. Most of us don't like the bad things that result from the ways we make a living and live our lives. But we feel we have no choice.

The fight against MTR in Appalachia is also a fight for better choices for all of us. Free people are choosing to engage in that fight not just to defend their own freedom—which is, after all, as Mike says, "a very small world"—but also to make it possible for more and more of their fellow citizens to freely choose to live, in grace and comfort, in ways that are good for the land and its people everywhere. Their fight is our fight too.

Acknowledgments

It's been five and a half years since I started work on this book. During that time, hundreds of individuals have helped by providing information, advice, or permission to observe them, as well as meals, places to stay, loans of equipment, and more. Some of those individuals are named in this book. Of the others, many but not all requested that their names not be used, as one would expect in connection with a campaign that uses civil disobedience to try to compel powerful corporations and associated politicians to stop a profitable practice. (Although names have been withheld, none has been invented. All the names in this book, including nicknames, refer to specific individuals who answered to those names at the times depicted in the book.) Much of the most useful information and help I received came from individuals who did not want their names used. I owe them at least as much gratitude as I do those who were willing to be named. So I'm not going to name *any* of the individuals who deserve acknowledgment here. You know who you are, and I'm thankful for all you've done for me.

Organizations are another matter. If, after reading this book, you feel moved to help with coalfield-based efforts to end MTR, you can do no better than to get in touch with any of these organizations, all of which both have been helpful to me and urgently need support from people outside Appalachia to continue their good work there:

— Climate Ground Zero (www.climategroundzero.net), anti-MTR civil disobedience campaign based in Rock Creek, West Virginia.

— Coal River Mountain Watch (www.crmw.net), community-organizing and anti-MTR advocacy nonprofit based in Whitesville, West Virginia.

— RRENEW Collective (www.rrenewcollective.wordpress.com), anti-MTR and community-organizing campaign that works closely with both MJ and SAMS, based in Wise County, Virginia.

— Southern Appalachian Mountain Stewards (www.samsva.org), community-organizing and anti-MTR advocacy nonprofit based in Wise County, Virginia.

I've put these four at the top of this list because I know their current work best, and believe that what they're doing is critical not only for ending MTR but also for building a better future in Appalachia. Other organizations (all but one of which also could use your help) that have been helpful in the writing of this book include, in alphabetical order: Appalachian Voices, Christians for the Mountains, Katuah Earth First! (now defunct, alas), Kentuckians for the Commonwealth (which allowed me to join a weekend-long Mountain Witness tour for Kentucky writers in 2005), the Mountain Justice campaign (which since 2005 has granted me embedded-reporter access), Ohio Valley Environmental Coalition, Sierra Club's Environmental Justice Program, Southwings (which arranges look-and-see flights for media, environmental groups, and politicians and has allowed me to join several flyovers of MTR sites), and United Mountain Defense.

Finally, I owe a different sort of thanks to AK Press, for seeing enough value and potential in this book and its subject to publish and publicize it.

Glossary of Acronyms

CGZ: Climate Ground Zero, West Virginia-based campaign to end MTR

CRMW: Coal River Mountain Watch, nonprofit anti-MTR advocacy group in West Virginia

DEP: West Virginia Department of Environmental Protection

EF!: Earth First!, national environmental movement

EIS: environmental impact statement

EPA: federal Environmental Protection Agency

FOC: Friends of Coal, pro-coal advocacy group in West Virginia

KEF!: Katuah Earth First!, southern Appalachian chapter of EF!

KFTC: Kentuckians for the Commonwealth, nonprofit anti-MTR advocacy group in Kentucky

MJS, MJ: the Mountain Justice Summer (2005) and Mountain Justice (2006 to present) campaign to end MTR

MJSB: Mountain Justice Spring Break, annual gathering of college students, affiliated with the MJ campaign

MSHA: federal Mine Safety and Health Administration

MTR: mountaintop removal strip mining for coal

NCC: National Coal Corporation

OSM: federal Office of Surface Mining

OVEC: Ohio Valley Environmental Coalition, nonprofit anti-MTR advocacy group in West Virginia

RAN: Rainforest Action Network, national environmental organization

SAMS: Southern Appalachian Mountain Stewards, nonprofit anti-MTR advocacy group in Virginia

SLAPP: strategic lawsuit against public participation

SMCRA: federal Surface Mining Control and Reclamation Act

TDEC: Tennessee Department of Environment and Conservation

TVA: Tennessee Valley Authority, quasi-federal entity with headquarters in Knoxville, Tennessee; a major purchaser of MTR coal

UMD: United Mountain Defense, nonprofit anti-MTR advocacy group in Tennessee

Index

Support AK Press!

AK Press is one of the world's largest and most productive

anarchist publishing houses. We're entirely worker-run and democratically managed. We operate without a corporate structure—no boss, no managers, no bullshit. We publish close to twenty books every year, and distribute thousands of other titles published by other like-minded independent presses from around the globe.

The Friends of AK program is a way that you can directly contribute to the continued existence of AK Press, and ensure that we're able to keep publishing great books just like this one! Friends pay a minimum of $25 per month, for a minimum three month period, into our publishing account. In return, Friends automatically receive (for the duration of their membership), as they appear, one free copy of every new AK Press title. They're also entitled to a 20% discount on everything featured in the AK Press Distribution catalog and on the website, on any and every order. You or your organization can even sponsor an entire book if you should so choose!

There's great stuff in the works—so sign up now to become a Friend of AK Press, and let the presses roll!

Won't you be our friend? Email friendsofak@akpress.org for more info, or visit the Friends of AK Press website: http://www.akpress.org/programs/friendsofak